An Introduction to Empirical Legal Research

An Introduction to Empirical Legal Research

Lee Epstein
Washington University in St. Louis

Andrew D. Martin
University of Michigan

OXFORD
UNIVERSITY PRESS

OXFORD
UNIVERSITY PRESS

Great Clarendon Street, Oxford, OX2 6DP,
United Kingdom

Oxford University Press is a department of the University of Oxford.
It furthers the University's objective of excellence in research, scholarship,
and education by publishing worldwide. Oxford is a registered trade mark of
Oxford University Press in the UK and in certain other countries

Published in the United States of America by Oxford University Press
198 Madison Avenue, New York, NY 10016, United States of America

British Library Cataloguing in Publication Data

Data available

Library of Congress Control Number: 2013937764

ISBN 978–0–19–966906–6

To an empirical scholar extraordinaire (and one of my favorite people in the whole wide world), Jeffrey A. Segal.—L.E.

To Stephanie and Olive, the two most important people in my life. —A.D.M.

Preface

To claim that research based on data—that is, empirical work—has infiltrated the legal community borders on the boring.[1] Social scientists and historians have long brought data to bear on the study of law and legal institutions.[2] In ever-increasing numbers, legal academics throughout the world are following suit.[3]

But it's not only academics who are making greater use of data-based evidence in their research. Arguments following from empirical studies have become such a regular part of legal practice that lawyers (and law students!) neglect learning about methods for collecting and analyzing

---

[1] In Chapter 1, we flesh out the meaning of "empirical work." Suffice it to note here that data in empirical studies come in two flavors: quantitative (numerical) and qualitative (non-numerical). Neither is any more "empirical" than the other (see Epstein and King, 2002).

[2] Though certainly not as long as in the sciences. Stigler (1986, 2) puzzles over why "it is only in the twentieth century that [statistical methods made] substantial inroads into the social sciences. Were nineteenth-century social scientists unable to read?"

[3] For documentation of the increasing use of data in law reviews and journals, see George (2005). She contends that "Empirical legal scholarship is arguably that next big thing in legal intellectual thought" (p. 141). But she also notes that "empirical research in law is not new" (see also Kritzer, 2009; Schlegel, 1995).

This is certainly true in the United States where several early empirical studies have attained landmark status, including Clark and Shulman (1937); Frankfurter and Landis (1928); Kalven and Zeisel (1966); Landes and Posner (1976). Though data work was slower to catch on in other corners of the world, no longer is "a lively interest in empirical legal research . . . confined to the United States and the UK;" there are "active communities of empirical legal researchers" in Australia, Canada, the Netherlands, Belgium, Spain, Germany, Israel, and Japan (Cane and Kritzer, 2010, 2). The World Bank notably supports empirical work in many new democracies with the goal of increasing their economic prosperity by improving their legal systems.

data at their own peril. We could say the same of judges who are all too often confronted with data or the results of empirical studies in cases ranging from bankruptcy to criminal law to environmental infringement to taxation.[4] As Oliver Wendell Holmes famously wrote, "For the rational study of the law the black letter man may be the man of the present, but *the man of the future is the man of statistics* and the master of economics."[5] That future is here.[6]

And yet there is no book designed to provide members of the legal community with a sufficient introduction to empirical legal work so that they can evaluate existing studies, become conversant in basic statistical methods, begin to undertake investigations of their own, or all of the above.[7] Hence *An Introduction to Empirical Legal Research—*

---

[4] For well-known examples, see Erickson and Simon (1998); Loh (1984); Monahan and Walker (2010).

[5] Holmes (1897, 469). Our emphasis.

[6] Justice Stephen G. Breyer of the U.S. Supreme Court (2000, 2) put it this way (our emphasis):

> The legal disputes before us increasingly involve the principles and tools of science. Proper resolution of those disputes matters not just to the litigants, but also to the general public—those who live in our technologically complex society and whom the law must serve. Our decisions should reflect a proper scientific and technical understanding so that the law can respond to the needs of the public. ... *[W]e judges [are] not asked to become expert statisticians, but we [are] expected to understand how the statistical analyses worked.*

[7] To be sure, there are scores of excellent texts aimed at training budding social scientists in research methods and statistics. On research design/methods, see Babbie (2009); Johnson et al. (2007a); King et al. (1994). General statistics texts include Agresti and Finlay (2009); DeGroot and Schervish (2012); Freedman et al. (2007).

It is also true that the principles are the same from book to book—a linear regression is a linear regression regardless of whether it appears in a text written for economists, sociologists, political scientists, or legal academics. It is the way the principles are conveyed and the examples invoked that can differ markedly. Within the law world, there tend to be two types of books on empirical research. The first focuses exclusively (or nearly so) on probability and statistics (e.g., Finkelstein, 2009; Finkelstein and Levin, 2001; Good, 2001; Jackson et al., 2011). They do an excellent job covering the basics (e.g., descriptive statistics) and even more advanced topics (e.g., the assumptions of regression models). But most do not mention, much less detail, topics central to understanding and evaluating empirical legal research, including research design, measurement, and data presentation. We could say the same of several reference guides prepared specifically for lawyers and judges, including Kaye and Freedman (2000).

The second type explores how courts use social science evidence. Prominent examples include Erickson and Simon (1998); Loh (1984); Monahan and Walker (2010). These too are excellent books but they are not meant to teach members of the legal community how to conduct empirical research (though they are valuable guides to how U.S. courts treat statistical studies). This leaves Lawless, Robbennolt, and Ulen's *Empirical Methods in Law* (2010), which is primarily a text for law students.

a book explicitly for law students, lawyers, judges, and scholars interested in law and legal institutions.

In producing *An Introduction to Empirical Legal Research* we drew heavily on materials we developed for an annual empirical workshop for law professors, courses we offer to law students, and a day-long educational program for judges. We also made liberal use of the handful of articles we have written on designing, executing, and presenting the results of statistical studies.[8]

Throughout our courses and articles we bring in many practical examples. Some are of our own devising, others come from existing empirical studies, and still others from court cases. No matter the source, we go beyond mere description; we make use of data so that our students and readers can experience the research process for themselves. This is extremely important here too. Regardless of whether you are reading *An Introduction to Empirical Legal Research* to consume or produce empirical studies, only by understanding the process will you be able to decipher its products—including scholarly articles, consultants' reports, and expert testimony.[9]

For readers hoping to learn enough about these products so that they can follow and evaluate them, working through the examples in the book may be sufficient. For those desiring to execute empirical studies, the book's website houses the tools necessary to replicate and expand the examples in the book.[10] In particular, you'll find:

Datasets. For each dataset we use in the book, we've created a comprehensive codebook and a downloadable data file in various formats (comma delimited text, Stata, SPSS Portable, R Data Format, SAS Transport, and Microsoft Excel).

Introduction to Statistical Software. We provide introductions to two different packages: Stata[11] and R.[12] The introductions include step-by-step written documentation and video demonstrations of both packages.

---

[8] See, e.g., Epstein and King (2002); Epstein and Martin (2005, 2010); Epstein et al. (2007, 2006); Martin (2008).

[9] If we were teaching this book at a workshop, we might say that only by entering the sausage factory will you understand how sausages are made—though we hope to make the process of learning about how experts produce their studies more pleasant than observing the production of sausages.

[10] <http://empiricallegalresearch.org>.

[11] <http://www.stata.com/>.

[12] <http://www.r-project.org/>.

Chapter-by-Chapter Command Files. Along with the datasets, the command files enable the reader to replicate (in Stata or R) every analysis in the book.

"Best Practices" Guide. This guide should help ensure that research employing R or Stata not only makes effective use of the software but also conforms to standard operating procedures in the field.

References. The website provides a list of some of our favorite books on research design, data collection methods, and statistics. It also includes links to datasets that you might find useful for law-related projects.

One final note. It's important to keep in mind the first two words of the book's title. We do indeed conceptualize *An Introduction to Empirical Legal Research* as a primer. Mastering all the topics we cover requires far more than we can possibly convey here; it requires training. That's why Ph.D. programs in the social sciences not only offer basic introductions to research design and statistics but also courses devoted to particular types of methods—maximum likelihood estimation, time series analysis, and structural equation models, to name just a few. Our goal is to provide readers with a sufficient foundation to read and evaluate empirical work and, if they so desire, to begin to design studies of their own. After attending our workshops, many participants (students and faculty alike) delved further into the subjects we covered and, ultimately, went on to produce high-quality empirical studies. We hope *An Introduction to Empirical Legal Research* encourages a similar investment of time with equally good results.

Let's get started.

L.E.
St. Louis, Missouri, USA
A.D.M.
Ann Arbor, Michigan, USA

Acknowledgements

Of all the many debts we owe, the largest is to Alex Flach, our editor at Oxford University Press. Alex conceived of the project and was with us every step of the way as it developed. Without him, this book would continue to reside on our hard drives in the form of scattered notes from the courses we've taught over the years. We are also grateful to Catherine Cragg, our production editor, who made the process as smooth as possible—no easy task for a book full of numbers.

Michael Nelson, a Ph.D. student at Washington University, also deserves a big shout out. On a near daily basis, we emailed Michael with long and odd to-do lists: remove the tick marks on a graph, validate the results of the (many!) analyses, fix miscellaneous typesetting issues, and track down esoteric statistics. He ticked off each and every assignment with diligence and even good cheer. Rachael Hinkle, another Ph.D. student at Washington University (who is now a full-fledged faculty member herself at the University of Maryland, Baltimore County), played an important role in the project by tracking down and processing most of the datasets we use in the pages to come and developing the resources on the book's website. Post-doc Elizabeth Coggins was instrumental in getting the project over the finish line.

Over the years, we have benefited, separately and together, from conversations with many fellow travelers in the world of empirical legal studies. They include: Christina L. Boyd, Barry Friedman, Tracey George, Micheal Giles, Mitu Gulati, Dan Ho, Pauline Kim, Gary King, Dan Klerman, Jack Knight, William M. Landes, Stefanie A. Lindquist, Adam Liptak, Richard A. Posner, Kevin M. Quinn, Margo Schlanger, Jeffrey A. Segal, Dan Simon, Harold J. Spaeth, Thomas G.

Walker, and Chad Westerland. We would also like to thank the students we've taught over the years—law students, undergraduates, and Ph.D. students alike—for asking difficult and probing questions about the research process. Also thanks to the hundreds of attendees of our annual Conducting Empirical Legal Studies workshop who have kept us on our toes and helped us to update our thinking about these issues.

Lee expresses her sincere thanks to the John Simon Guggenheim Foundation, and we are both grateful to the National Science Foundation for supporting our work on the U.S. Supreme Court, some of which is on display in the pages to come. We also thank our former and current institutions, the University of Michigan, the University of Southern California, and Washington University in St. Louis, for supporting and encouraging our interest in empirical legal studies.

Andrew's dedication acknowledges the most important people in his life. Thank you, Stephanie and Olive, for your patience and support through the duration of this and many other projects. Lee wants to convey her special gratitude to Nancy Staudt, the most important person in her life. Nancy, you'll see traces of our conversations scattered through pp. 1–294. For this and so many other reasons, I couldn't have done it without you.

Contents

1

Some Preliminaries

We start with some important preliminaries. First, by way of several examples, we provide a definition of empirical research and identify its unique features. Second, we ask you to perform a thought experiment with us—one designed to illuminate the problems with all empirical studies, as well as the solutions social scientists have devised. We end with a discussion of the various goals of empirical research.

1.1 Defining Empirical Research

In the not-so-distant past, women couldn't practice law in many societies much less become a judge.[1] Today, at least one female judge serves on many if not most high courts throughout the world.[2] Even more stunning, of the nearly 51,000 judges sitting on courts of first instance in Europe, 56% are women.[3]

---

[1] Not until the turn of the twentieth century were there female lawyers in Europe; even by the start of World War I women couldn't practice law in many countries, including the United Kingdom, Austria-Hungary, Russia, Italy, and Spain (see Clark, 2008). In the United States, women first entered "the legal profession in the 1860s, several decades ahead of women in other countries" (Kay and Gorman, 2008, 300). But even there, women, when they were finally admitted to law school, faced substantial obstacles gaining employment (see, e.g., Epstein, 1981; Kay and Gorman, 2008; Latourette, 2005).

[2] As of January 2013, one or more female judge (justice) serves on over 85% of the eighty-nine high courts listed on the Council of Europe's website.

[3] 28,196 of the 50,743. The data are from a 2012 report by the European Commission for the Efficiency of Justice and are based on 39 European states. Data are at: <http://www.coe.int/t/dghl/cooperation/cepej/evaluation/2012/Rapport_en.pdf>, p. 277 (Table 11.29).

These are facts no one debates, but there is considerable controversy over their significance for the law. To some scholars, judges, and lawyers, an increasingly diverse federal bench may have symbolic value but it is irrelevant to the task of judging. On this account, judges reach decisions by reference to legal materials. If a case is novel, the judges' ideology may come into play[4] but not their gender or other personal-identity characteristics. To other commentators, gender is far from irrelevant; it can have a profound influence on the development of the law because, they argue, female judges decide cases differently than male judges.[5] To provide one example, perhaps female judges are more sympathetic than their male colleagues to claims of sex discrimination in the workplace.[6]

How might we resolve this debate or, more pointedly, answer the question of whether the judges' gender influences their decisions? Certainly, we could talk with judges, interview lawyers, or closely read court decisions. In a recent study, we took a different approach.[7] We collected data on 8,895 disputes resolved in federal circuit courts in the United States (called U.S. Courts of Appeals). Our goal was to deter-mine whether male and female judges reach different decisions—were the women more likely to vote for the party bringing a claim of sex discrimination? Were they less likely to hold for the government in criminal cases? And so on.

La Porta and his colleagues deployed a similar strategy in their famous study of whether independent judiciaries promote economic freedom.[8] In theory, there are good reasons to believe that judges

---

[4] That's because "ideology is a worldview that gives one an initial take on a new problem" (Epstein et al., 2013, 45).

[5] Emblematic of this debate are the views of Sandra Day O'Connor (the first woman appointed to the Supreme Court of the United States) versus those of Bertha Wilson (the first woman appointed to the Canadian Supreme Court). Justice O'Connor has often said that "A wise old woman and a wise old man will reach the same conclusion" (e.g., O'Connor, 1991, 1558). Justice Wilson (1990, 522) believed (or, at the least, hoped) that "women judges through their differing perspectives on life [would] bring a new humanity to bear on the decision-making process [and so] perhaps they will make a difference. Perhaps they will succeed in infusing the law with an understanding of what it means to be fully human." For a review of this debate from a less anecdotal perspective, see Boyd et al. (2010).

[6] Some scholars even suggest that female judges can induce their male colleagues to decide cases differently than they otherwise would (e.g., Boyd et al., 2010; Peresie, 2005; Sullivan, 2002). This may be especially true in cases of sex discrimination because male judges might perceive their female colleagues as possessing information more credible than their own.

[7] Boyd et al. (2010).

[8] La Porta et al. (2004).

endowed with some level of independence from the government can act as a check on the government's efforts to interfere with contracts and property rights.[9] La Porta et al. wanted to know whether this idea holds in practice. To find out, they collected a lot of data on the degree of judicial independence and the level of economic freedom in seventy-one countries. This was not the only possible approach. They could have closely analyzed judicial decisions or talked with policy makers, citizens, judges, lawyers, corporate leaders, and financiers, to name just a few alternatives.

The La Porta et al. study and ours on gender are examples of empirical research, or research based on observations of the world or *data, which is just a term for facts about the world*.[10] The data we and La Porta et al. happened to collect were numerical or quantitative data; that is, we and they took information about cases and court systems (among other things) and translated the information into numbers that we analyzed using statistical tools. In our study we began with a large pile of court cases—8,895—and converted them into pre-established numbers: a decision in favor of the party claiming sex discrimination (the plaintiff) became a "1"; a decision against the plaintiff was a "0." But both studies could have used qualitative data, as we just hinted. For example, we could have extracted information from the text of court decisions. The data in this case would be words, not numbers, that we could interpret, organize into categories, and use to identify patterns. This too would qualify as empirical research *because empirical evidence (i.e., data) can be numerical (quantitative) or non-numerical (qualitative)*, despite some tendency in the legal community to associate empirical work solely with "statistics" and "quantitative analyses." The truth of it is, neither is any more "empirical" than the other. This holds to such an extent that almost everything we say in Parts I, II, and (some of) Parts III and IV of this book applies with equal force to qualitative and quantitative work.[11]

So if the qualitative–quantitative division isn't all that meaningful for differentiating empirical projects from other types of legal research, what is? Not the types of data deployed but the very idea of bringing

---

[9] See, e.g., Hayek (1960). See also Klerman and Mahoney (2005) for a review of the relevant literature.

[10] Epstein and King (2002, 2–3).

[11] Note we do not include all of Part III on this list because some tools designed to perform (principled) statistical analysis require that data be quantified.

data to the table is the chief point of distinction. Think about it this way. Many doctrinal studies, lawyers' briefs, and even judicial decisions start with a hunch[12]—what amounts to the author's best guess about the answer to a question concerning law and legal institutions. Juries are biased against corporations, minorities receive harsher sentences in criminal cases, privately retained attorneys are more effective than public defenders, to provide just a few examples. Empirical projects are no different. We had a hunch that female and male judges reach different decisions. La Porta et al. theorized that independent judiciaries are more effective at ensuring economic freedom. In both, as in almost all empirical work, theory does (and should) play a crucial role in informing the analysis.[13] But neither La Porta et al. nor we stopped with our theories or hunches; we collected data to assess them.

This is not to say that ours or La Porta et al.'s or any other data project, for that matter, will end with data instead of the sort of policy recommendations or normative conclusions that often appear in traditional legal research. On the contrary. For reasons that we hope will become clear, well-executed research with a data component is likely to make more important, influential, and, frankly, better contributions to policy and law because the study's authors can accurately gauge the uncertainty of their conclusions.

1.2 Conducting Empirical Research in a World Without Constraints

Because most empirical studies contain theoretical and data components, it sometimes helps to visualize them as consisting of two transparent slides. On the first slide we write down our hunches about the answer to a research question. The second includes all the data we've collected to answer the question. The (usual) hope is that when we put the two slides together (that is, when we analyze the data), they will align: the data will support our hunches.

We devote the rest of this book to describing how researchers go about creating the two (metaphorical) slides, aligning them, and

---

[12] Or "theories," which we define as "a reasoned and precise speculation about the answer to a research question" (Epstein and King, 2002; King et al., 1994, 19). We flesh out this definition in Chapter 2.

[13] We make this point with force in Chapter 2.

communicating their contents. Before moving forward, though, let's take a brief but important detour. We want you to perform a thought experiment—one designed to illustrate the difficulty of this process, along with the work-arounds social scientists have developed.

The experiment is this: If you were endowed with the combined powers of the world's superheroes—the Avengers, Batman, Superman, Spider-Man, Wonder Woman, and all the rest—how would you create and match up the two slides? To make the experiment more concrete, think about how La Porta et al. might have answered their research question about the effect of an independent judiciary on economic freedom if they were superhuman and had no constraints.

We can tell you what we'd do. We'd start by randomly selecting a country from all the countries in the world.[14] Then we'd randomly assign the country a judicial type—say, an independent judiciary—and observe whether the country enjoys economic prosperity. Next, we'd reverse time (remember, we're superheroes) to the precise moment we assigned the country a judicial type; only this time we'd assign the country—the same country—the other type: a judiciary lacking in independence. If we observe the same level of economic freedom in both versions of the same country, we would conclude that the judiciary has no effect on the economy. If we observe the version of the country with an independent judiciary flourishing economically and the version without an independent judiciary faltering, we'd conclude that an independent judiciary generates greater economic freedom.

Why would we proceed in this way if we had no constraints? To arrive at the answer, consider the many other things that could affect whether a country will experience economic freedom *other than the state of the judiciary*. A very short list might include the country's geography (the healthier the climate, the better the institutions and outcomes), ethnic heterogeneity (the more heterogeneity, the more likely that the ruling regime limits the production of public goods), and overall wealth.[15] Because we concocted a plan for comparing precisely the same country at precisely the same moment in time we don't have to worry about these other factors; we've held them constant so that we can focus on the factor of interest: the type of judiciary.

---

[14] As we explain in some detail in Chapters 4 and 6, a random probability sample is one in which each element—here, a country—in the total population—here, all countries—has a known probability of being selected.

[15] For more detailed explanations, see La Porta et al. (2004, 457–8).

Of course, ours is a research plan that no mere mortal can ever implement. Because we aren't superheroes, we can't assign a country a type of judiciary and then reassign it another; and we certainly don't have the power to rerun history. This limitation is known as the fundamental problem of causal inference,[16] and it simply means that researchers can only observe the factual (e.g., the economic freedom of a country with an independent judiciary if, in fact, the country has an independent judiciary) and not the counterfactual (e.g., the economic freedom of a country without an independent judiciary if, in fact, the country has an independent judiciary).[17] Without being able to observe both the factual and counterfactual at the same time, we can never know *for sure* whether there is a causal effect of independent judiciaries on economic freedom. (A causal effect is just the contrast between the factual and counterfactual, as we explain in more detail later.)

Unless (until?) humans develop the power to reverse time, this is a problem without a solution, but scholars have developed various fixes. The gold standard solution is a proper experiment—that is, an experiment with two key conditions: the researcher (1) randomly selects subjects from the population of interest (all countries, in the La Porta et al. study) and then (2) randomly assigns the subjects to treatment and control conditions (a judiciary is or is not independent).[18] Very few experiments in empirical legal research satisfy the first condition (random selection from the population) but some scholars have tried to meet the second (random assignment of control conditions). When the second condition is met, we can often compare the outcomes in the treatment and control groups to estimate the causal effect. Rachlinski and his colleagues, for example, recruited (not randomly selected) bankruptcy judges to participate in an experiment designed to detect whether the race of the debtor affects their decisions.[19] The researchers asked the judges to read exactly the same case materials, but unbeknown to the judges, the researchers randomly assigned them to one of two groups. The judges in the first group, the "control" group, were led to believe that the debtor was white; those in the second group, the

---

[16] Holland (1986, 947).
[17] For a more formal account of these ideas in the context of empirical legal scholarship, see Boyd et al. (2010); Epstein et al. (2005).
[18] Ho et al. (2007).
[19] Rachlinski et al. (2006).

"treatment" group, were led to believe that the debtor was black.[20] It turned out that the debtor's race did not affect the judges' decisions.[21]

While this is a reasonable approach to the fundamental problem of causal inference, it is sadly infeasible for many empirical legal projects, including studies of judicial independence and economic growth (not many, if any, countries would allow us to assign them a legal system). The Rachlinski et al. study aside, it is not even feasible for many analyses of how judges make decisions. To return to our example of the effect of gender on judging, suppose we wanted to understand whether the presence of a female judge affects the decisions of her male colleagues.[22] We know of no court that would allow us to manipulate its composition so that we could identify a possible gender effect (and we've asked!). Our original project of determining whether male and female judges reach different decisions faces an even higher hurdle because it's impossible to assign a gender to a judge to see if the male and female versions of the same judge reach different decisions.

1.3 Conducting Empirical Research in a World With Constraints

The upshot is that most empirical legal researchers simply do not have the luxury of performing experiments. And even if we could conduct them, some would question whether they are worth undertaking. A few judges we know cringe when they hear about Rachlinski et al.'s experiments, claiming they are too artificial to replicate decisions in a real courtroom.[23]

---

[20] The researchers did not identify the race of the debtors but instead gave them white- or black-sounding names. See Rachlinski et al. (2006, 1247).

[21] But see Rachlinski et al. (2008), who, using a different set of judges, identified some racial bias in favor of or against criminal defendants of different races.

[22] See note 6.

[23] More formally, these judges question the experiment's "ecological validity." Psychologists use this term to refer to "the extent to which behavior . . . studied in one environment [usually in a laboratory setting] can be taken as characteristic of (or generalizable to) an individual's cognitive processes in a range of other environments" (Cole, 2004). This is an important consideration in experimental design because it focuses attention on how well an experiment approximates the look and feel of real-world conditions. In empirical legal studies, questions of ecological validity often arise in jury simulation research. Major validity concerns are "the mock juror sample (i.e., undergraduates vs. community-dwelling adults), the research setting (i.e., laboratory vs. courtroom), the trial medium (i.e., written summaries vs. more realistic simulations), the trial elements included (e.g., the presence

For these reasons, the vast majority of studies of law and legal institutions make use of data the world, not they, created—the decisions reached by a female *or* a male judge in an actual case or the degree of economic freedom in actual countries with an independent *or* non-independent judiciary. The problem is that the use of this sort of *observational* data substantially complicates the task confronted by empirical legal researchers.[24] To see why, think about the data we cooked up in our thought experiment, or that Rachlinksi and his colleagues generated in their lab. Because these data were produced by the random assignment of an independent/non-independent judiciary (as in our thought experiment) or of black/white debtors (as in Rachlinski et al.'s), they minimize the effect of other factors on economic freedom or the judge's decision. The same cannot be said of observational data. In our study of gender and judging, something else—surely not us—assigned a gender to the judges; the same holds for La Porta et al.'s analysis of economic freedom. When the assignment of subjects to treatment and control groups is determined by the world and not the researcher, as it is in our study of gender and judging, it makes it difficult to determine whether gender or other factors could lie behind the differences in judicial decisions we observe in the data.

So what do we do? We attempt to approximate as closely as possible our thought experiment by taking three steps: (1) designing our project, (2) collecting and coding data, and (3) analyzing the data.[25] We also think researchers should (though they don't always) take a fourth, which entails giving careful consideration to how to present results.

These four steps or, more accurately, components of the research process are the focus of the chapters to come and so require only

---

or absence of deliberation), the dependent variables used (e.g., dichotomous verdicts vs. probability-of-guilt judgments), and the consequentiality of the task (i.e., making a hypothetical vs. a real decision)" (Bornstein, 1999).

[24] Rosenbaum (2002) defines observational studies as those in which researchers estimate the effects of some treatment that is not under their control. His taxonomy provides a third type of study that does neither. For our purposes, we refer to all non-experimental studies as observational.

[25] Because observational datasets are so much more common in empirical legal research, we focus on strategies for working with them. Still, you should know that much of what we have to say applies with equal force to experimental research. (The chief exceptions are issues of data generation and control.) For example, empirical projects almost always start with a question the researcher wants to answer. This is true in experimental *and* observational studies.

a preview here.[26] The important thing to keep in mind is that their purpose is to move us as close as possible to our superhero experiment.

1.3.1 Designing Research

Designing research principally, though not exclusively, involves the process of moving from the conceptual to the concrete to clarify the project. To return to the La Porta et al. study, the researchers had a hunch that the more independent the judiciary, the greater the country's economic freedom. However plausible this hunch, it's impossible to assess on its face because "judicial independence" and "economic freedom" are both concepts that we cannot observe.

A design challenge confronting La Porta et al.—and indeed virtually all empirical researchers—was to define these concepts in concrete terms so that they could observe them. They met the challenge by defining judicial independence (in part) by the tenure of the country's judges. They created a scale such that tenure = 2 if judges serve for life, 1 if tenure is more than six years but not for life, and 0 if tenure is less than six years.[27] The researchers clarified economic freedom, their other key concept, through four indicators: a subjective index (which ranges from 1 to 5 in their data) of the security of property rights; the number of steps that a start-up business must take to obtain legal status (from 2 to 19 in their data); a scale of worker protection through labor laws (from .77 to 2.31); and the share of the assets of the country's top banks owned by the government (from 0 to 1).[28]

These were not the only concepts requiring clarification by La Porta et al. Because they aren't superheroes and couldn't reverse time or randomly assign legal systems to countries, they had to consider all the other factors that affect economic freedom—the country's wealth and climate, for example. These and many other possibilities had to

---

[26] In what follows we describe these "steps" in order, from designing research to presenting results. Nonetheless, because empirical legal scholars rarely regard their research as following a singular, mechanical process from which they can never deviate, it is more accurate to refer to them as components, rather than steps. For more on this point, see the opener to Part I.

[27] They considered only judges serving on their country's highest court and the highest-ranking judges who rule on administrative cases. To derive their final measure of judicial independence, they computed the normalized sum of the tenure of the highest court judges, the tenure of administrative judges, and a case law variable, which takes on a value of 1 if the country's judicial decisions are a "source of law" and 0 if they are not. See La Porta et al. (2004, 450–1).

[28] See La Porta et al. (2004, 450–2).

be clarified too. In their study, a country's wealth became per capita gross domestic product; climate was the absolute value of the country's latitude.

A question you might ask is why these definitions, and not others? For example, you might think that a country's average temperature is a better measure of its climate, or that judicial independence relates more to legal provisions preventing the government from reducing the judges' salaries than to the length of their terms. There is no automatic answer. The choice of which proxy (or proxies) is not just a crucial part of the design process; it is a choice that researchers must justify with reference to accepted criteria. We explore these in Chapter 3.

1.3.2 Collecting and Coding

The long and short of it is this: before researchers can answer legal questions empirically—actually before they can collect even the first piece of data—they must devise ways to clarify the concepts of interest so that they can observe them. All of this and more appears on that first (metaphorical) transparent slide.

Collecting and coding data are the makings of the second slide. Collecting data entails several steps, beginning with a consideration of the possible sources of information necessary to answer the research question and the methods available to extract the information. There are numerous possibilities, from interviewing people to analyzing documents, and we consider many in Chapter 4. The researcher must also contemplate whether to study all the elements of interest (e.g., all countries, all cases) or draw a sample of them; and, if the latter, how to draw the sample as well as how much data to collect. The La Porta et al. study and ours on gender display some of the options. We drew samples of cases decided by the U.S. Courts of Appeals; they studied all seventy-one countries (with stable economies) whose constitutions were included in the book, *Constitutions of the Countries of the World*.[29] Chapter 4 examines these and other alternatives for selecting data.

Once researchers decide how and how much data to collect, they must code the data—that is, translate information into a usable form for analysis. For our study of the effect of gender on judicial decisions, we began with piles and piles of judicial decisions (or, more accurately, thousands of pdfs on a hard drive). If we were unable to transform those

---

[29] Maddex (2005).

piles into data that we could analyze—that is, to code the cases—we would have been unable to proceed with our study. Ditto for La Porta and his team. To assess the length of judicial tenure, they started with legal documents, mostly laws and constitutions. It was the information in the documents that required translation.

There is some art to collecting and coding data but, frankly, the science part is more crucial. For the reasons we explain in Chapter 5, following some time-honored standards will yield high-quality results, as well as save time and resources.

1.3.3 Analyzing Data

If research design is the first transparency, and collecting and coding data the second, then data analysis is about comparing the two. When the overlap between the hunches and data is substantial, analysts may conclude that the real world confirms their hunches; if the overlap is negligible, they may go back to the drawing board or even abandon the project altogether.

This process of comparing the slides—analyzing data—typically involves two tasks. The first amounts to *summarizing* the data the researcher has collected. For our gender study, suppose we drew a random sample of 1,000 cases of employment discrimination out of a total of 10,000 decided in the U.S. federal courts. For these 1,000 cases, we might summarize the data by comparing the fractions in which a male versus a female judge voted for the party alleging discrimination. As you already know, La Porta et al. also summarized their data. When we described how they clarified the concepts in their hunches, we gave you their ranges; for example, for the countries in their dataset the number of steps that a start-up business must take to obtain legal status ranges from 2 to 19. The range too is a way to summarize data.

Generating fractions or ranges requires only school-level mathematics. No specialized training is needed if all you want to do is summarize data (or understand reports of data summaries).[30] The more typical goal of data analysis, however, is far more difficult to achieve. It is the goal of making statistical inferences, which means using facts we know or can learn (for example, the decisions of the courts in our sample of 1,000 cases) to learn about facts we do not know (decisions in all 10,000 cases).

---

[30] As we explain in Chapter 6, the range is simply the minimum and maximum values. In La Porta et al.'s data, two steps is the minimum, and 19 steps the maximum.

Because we spend many pages on inference in Part III, suffice it to make two points here, on (1) the types of inference and (2) the task of performing inference.

The Types of Inference.   In empirical research, statistical inference comes in two forms: descriptive and causal. Descriptive claims themselves can take several forms but, at first blush, most seem to bear a family resemblance to summarizing data. Return to the La Porta et al. study, which proxies economic freedom (in part) as the number of steps a start-up business must take to obtain legal status. Now suppose that across all 71 countries, the average number is ten. This figure of ten probably isn't all that interesting in and of itself to most of us. What we want to learn about is the number of steps in all 195 countries in the world.[31]

This is the task of drawing a descriptive inference. We do not perform it by summarizing facts; we make it by using facts we know—the small part of the world we have studied (the 71 countries in La Porta's)—to learn about facts we do not observe (the 195 countries). Researchers call the "small part" a sample and the "world" a population. (An important part of performing descriptive inference is quantifying the uncertainty we have about the inference we draw. We'll get to this in a minute.)

Causal inference too is about using facts we know to learn about facts we do not know. In fact, with observational data a causal inference is the difference between two descriptive inferences: the average value of whatever it is we are trying to explain, say, economic freedom (as measured by the number of steps) when there is an independent judiciary and when there is not. Because each country *either* does or doesn't have an independent judiciary, we can only observe the factual and not the counter-factual. The causal effect—the goal of the process of causal inference—is the difference between the factual and the counter-factual, here the difference between the number of steps when a country does or does not have an independent judiciary. As we'll see later on, making this comparison requires a careful research design and appropriate tools to perform it.[32]

---

[31] As of January 2012, according to the U.S. Department of State's count of independent countries (at: <http://www.state.gov/s/inr/rls/4250.htm>).

[32] It may—and it's important to stress the word may—be easier to perform causal inference with experimental data because of random assignment to treatment and control groups. Even experimental data require explicit assumptions and proper tools to draw causal inferences.

The Task of Performing Inference.   How do empirical researchers go about making descriptive or causal claims? In many studies, as we just suggested, they make use of statistical inference, which entails examining a sample to learn about the population, along with evaluating the quality of the inference they reach.

Conceptually, statistical inference is not all that hard to understand; in fact, we confront such inferences almost every day in the form of survey results. Consider a Gallup poll that asked people living in one of the 27 member countries of the European Union (EU) whether they "feel safe walking alone at night in the city or area that you lived." Of the respondents, 69% answered yes.[33]

To arrive at the 69% figure, did Gallup talk to all 500+ million people living in EU countries? Of course not. Their researchers drew a sample of about 1,000 people per country, for a total of about 27,000. And from this sample they drew an inference (in this instance, a descriptive inference) about the percentage of people who feel safe walking alone at night.

Now, it is one thing to say that 69% of the *respondents in the sample* feel safe (this is summarizing or describing the data); it is quite another to say that 69% of *all citizens* in EU countries feel safe. So how did the researchers at Gallup go about making the statistical inference that 69% of the 500+ million, and not merely the 27,000 in their sample, feel safe? It turns out that all they—or any empirical researcher—need do is tally (i.e., summarize) the responses to their survey. That's because our best guess about the views of the population is also 69%, assuming the sample has been properly drawn. We explain why in Chapter 6.

But there's more. We know that Gallup interviewed only a sample and not the entire population so, surely, there is some uncertainty about the 69% figure. Gallup expresses the uncertainty in terms of a margin of error, which for this poll is about 95% CI ± 4.[34] Non-technically, this means that we can be 95% confident that the percentage of all respondents believing they are safe in the neighborhoods lies somewhere between (69% - 4% =) 65% and (69% + 4% =) 73%. (More technically, we would say that the true percentage of people feeling safe will be captured in 95 out of 100 applications of the same procedure to sample

[33] Gallup World, August 2012, at: <http://www.gallup.com/poll/156236/Latin-Americans -Least-Likely-Worldwide-Feel-Safe.aspx>.
[34] CI stands for confidence interval. We explain these names and calculations in Chapter 7.

from the population and to compute the margin of error. But don't worry about this now. We'll get to it in Chapter 7.)

This example shows that statistical inference involves not merely estimating the quantity of interest—the fraction of people who feel safe or the number of legal steps for start-ups in the La Porta et al. study—but also our level of uncertainty about the inference. Gallup and most other pollsters typically report the margin of error; empirical legal researchers use many other measures of uncertainty, and we explore some of the most prominent in Part III.

Even from this brief discussion, we hope that you see that inference is easy to understand as a conceptual matter. Performing it is harder. This is especially true of causal inference, which some say is so difficult with observational data that we should never frame research in terms of causality; we should talk only about associations. Rather than say an independent judiciary *causes* greater economic freedom, we should say that an independent judiciary *is associated* with greater economic freedom.

We disagree. Yes, causal inference is hard but it's not impossible. Besides, scholars, lawyers, and judges need to make causal claims and so giving up is not an option. What we advise instead is that researchers proceed with great care.[35] To this end, in Part III we provide the statistical tools to begin to perform and understand inference. The tools we describe presuppose that the study is well designed and the data are up to the task. If the design is poor or the data are inadequate, researchers can't reach inferences of high quality, nor will they be able to assess their uncertainty (e.g., the 95% CI $\pm$ 4 in the Gallup poll) about the inferences they reach. Without a proper design no statistical method can provide reliable answers.

The broader lesson is this: if the goal is to make causal inferences, researchers should not be deterred (nor should judges and lawyers be wary) assuming they follow the best scientific practices. Those include practices not just for statistical analysis but for design (Part I) and data collection (Part II) as well.

1.3.4 Communicating Data and Results

Once analysts have drawn inferences from their data, they must present their results so that others can understand them. To a greater extent

---

[35] Epstein and King (2002) and King et al. (1994) make much the same point.

than other components of the process, effective communication blends art and science. It also requires careful consideration of the intended audience.

Many treatments of empirical research neglect this component in the hope, we suppose, that researchers will figure it out for themselves. But we think the omission is such a big mistake that we devote two chapters to the topic (Chapters 10 and 11).

Why? Two reasons. First, legal scholars (perhaps more than most others) hope to affect the development of law and policy. We certainly do. We want judges, lawyers, and policy makers to read and understand our work. The problem is that these people often lack any training in empirical methods and so have trouble translating the results into meaningful information. This is as regrettable for them (they will miss out on research that may bear directly on their concerns), as it is disappointing for the scholar who invests time and resources into producing high-quality, policy-relevant work.

Happily, though, the problem is completely avoidable because scientists have made substantial progress in developing approaches to convey empirical results in accessible ways—progress facilitated by the revolution in micro-computing and statistical software. By providing information and examples of these advances, we hope that researchers will take advantage of them. Both they and their audience will be the beneficiaries.

This takes us to the second reason for our emphasis on communicating results. The advances can be abused, resulting not in more accessible and elegant forms of communication but in messy and even misleading graphs. We offer guidance to help researchers create useful (and truthful) data displays.

1.4 (Revisiting) The Goals of Empirical Research

Almost all empirical research seeks to accomplish one or more of three ends: summarizing data, making descriptive or causal inferences, and creating public multi-user datasets. We have already discussed the first two, with emphasis on inference because inference is the ultimate goal in most empirical studies (and so the focus of this book too). Still, we think it's worthwhile to say a word or two about the creation of public multi-user datasets as a research objective.

Table 1.1 Crosstabulation of U.S. Court of Appeals votes in a sample of sex discrimination cases over the gender of the judge.[36]

	Judge		
	Male	Female	Total
Judge Votes in Favor of Party Alleging Discrimination	564	140	704
Judge Votes Against Party Alleging Discrimination	994	162	1,156
Total	1,558	302	1,860

In some sense, creating public datasets resembles collecting and coding data, that is, translating or amassing information in such a way that researchers can make use of it. This is a component of almost all empirical projects, but the goals of public or multi-user databases tend to be different.[37] Rather than collect data to answer particular research questions—for example, do male and female judges reach different decisions?; do independent judiciaries lead to greater economic freedom?—the idea is to amass a dataset so rich in content that multiple users, even those with distinct projects, can draw on it.

In addition to opening access to many researchers, large multi-user databases have what is known as a *combinatoric advantage*. To see this, consider one useful method of analyzing data, the crosstabulation, or a table that summarizes information about various quantities of interest. Table 1.1 provides an example. There we show a sample of votes cast for or against the party alleging sex discrimination in cases before the U.S. Courts of Appeals, by whether the judge is a male or a female. Note that the table produces four "cell" values: the number of votes in favor of the party alleging discrimination when the judge is a male (n = 564) and when the judge is a female (140); and the number of votes against when the judge is a male (994) and when the judge is a female (162).[38]

The important point is that the two factors most relevant to our project—the judges' votes and their gender, each with two categories—produce information on (2 × 2 =) 4 cells. Now suppose another team of researchers comes along and they too want to study

---

[36] Source: Boyd et al. (2010).

[37] We adapt some of this material from Epstein and King (2002).

[38] This is in addition to information about vote and gender taken separately—for example, the fraction of total votes in favor of the defendant (1,156/1,860) and the fraction cast by male judges (1,558/1,860).

votes in sex discrimination cases. What they want to know, though, is whether the judges are more likely to affirm (rather than reverse) the lower court's decision. So now we have two teams of researchers both interested in sex discrimination cases but focused on different factors to explain votes: us, on the judge's gender (male or female) and them, on the lower court's decision (for or against the party alleging discrimination). Further suppose the teams are not working together, but rather each drawing its own sample and collecting data on the factor of interest (gender for us and the lower court's decision for them), along with three other factors each team suspects affect judges' votes; that is, each team selects its own three factors. The result is that crosstabulations for each study could produce as many 32 cells. Note, though, that because we and the other team drew our samples independently, crosstabulations of the factors in one sample with the factors in the other wouldn't be possible. Combining them would amount to mixing apples and oranges.

Now consider what would happen if we and the other team joined forces and collected the ten factors on the same set of cases in one large dataset. A combinatoric advantage accrues: if the ten factors were collected on the same cases, the ten factors of two categories each would generate $2^{10} = 1,024$ different cells, or

$$\left[\frac{2^{10}}{2 \times 32} \right] = 16$$

times as much information as the two independent databases produced separately.

Aware of these advantages, researchers have created many multi-user databases related to law and legal institutions worldwide.[39] Because Chapter 4 describes some of the more influential ones, two examples suffice for now: the Comparative Constitutions Project,[40] which houses information on the characteristics of constitutions written since 1789 in 184 countries; and the U.S. Supreme Court Database,[41] which contains over 200 attributes of Court decisions handed down since 1946, including information on the lower court's decision, the parties to the suit, and how the justices voted. The researchers who developed

---

[39] Including, by the way, one on the U.S. Courts of Appeals. The U.S. Appeals Court Database, at: <http://artsandsciences.sc.edu/poli/juri/appct.htm>.

[40] <http://www.comparativeconstitutionsproject.org/index.htm>.

[41] <http://supremecourtdatabase.org>.

these databases have made extensive use of them, but so too have a multitude of other scholars—including ourselves. Throughout this book we employ these and other multi-user datasets to illustrate particular concepts, statistical techniques, and methods for communicating research results.

Even so, it is important to keep in mind what we said at the beginning of this section. Despite the many advantages of multi-user databases, they are, after all, just datasets. To have value, they must meet the standards of good science no less than those developed for a particular research project.

$$* * * * * * * *$$

With this, we've finished our introduction to the contours of empirical legal research. It's now time to flesh them out.

PART I

Designing Research

Designing empirical research involves: (1) asking research questions, (2) theorizing and extracting observable implications from the theory, (3) identifying rival hypotheses, and (4) developing measures—and we discuss each in turn, the first three in Chapter 2 and measures in Chapter 3.

Now, in some texts on research design, the authors display these four components, along with other features of the research process, in a flow chart that begins with "Asking Questions," moves to "Invoking Theory" and "Developing Measures," and ends with "Reaching Conclusions."[1] The suggestion here is that research design, and indeed empirical research more generally, is a singular mechanical process from which the analyst can never deviate.[2] Charts of this sort imply that the researcher is akin to a baker who must follow every step in the recipe or else the cake will fall.

We reject this approach.[3] The process is not a recipe; researchers do and should have the flexibility of mind to deviate, to overturn old ways of looking at the world, ask new questions, revise their blueprints as necessary, and collect more (or different) data than they might have intended. Imagine that after their study, the researchers find an imperfect fit between the data and their research question or

---

[1] E.g., Kellstedt and Whitten (2009) use a flow chart; Le Roy and Corbett (2009) outline "stages" of the process; Gravetter and Forzano (2012) identify the steps of the scientific method.

[2] We adopt and adapt some of the material to follow from Epstein and King (2002), King et al. (1994).

[3] This is so even though one of the authors has used it in the past (Epstein, 1995). Live and learn!

hunches. Rather than erase months or even years of work, they will almost always return to the drawing board and design more appropriate procedures or even recast the original question. More often than not, when they find that data are inconsistent with their original expectations, they immediately see a new hypothesis that apparently explains the otherwise anomalous empirical results.

Suppose, hypothetically, that La Porta et al.,[4] in testing their hunch that an independent judiciary fosters economic freedom, find that the data support their hypothesis for Germany, France, and Spain but not for Argentina, Australia, and the United States. Should they wave a white flag in defeat? We wouldn't. Instead we'd consider an alternative explanation for the findings. Perhaps the original hunch holds only for countries where a single constitutional court has the authority to invalidate laws in abstract disputes brought by elected officials—here Germany, France, and Spain but not Argentina, Australia, and the United States, where review generally occurs in concrete disputes. Perhaps abstract review is more effective at keeping the government on its toes.[5]

It would be perfectly acceptable for the La Porta (or any other) team to test this alternative account because they, and indeed all empirical researchers, should and must be flexible. What we can't do is make post-hoc adjustments in our theories to fit the data. This would amount to fooling ourselves into thinking that our adjustments constitute confirmation of the new theory when they do not. Confirmation requires vulnerability, that we could prove ourselves wrong. To see this, imagine a criminal justice system that allowed only the government to present its case, with no cross-examination. The government would likely win at very high rates—not necessarily because its theory of the case was right but because there was no truth-testing process.

The lesson for empirical research is that using insights from data is a good way to develop a new hunch. But investigators should interrogate the new hunch against fresh data, in La Porta et al.'s case, information on the countries that were not in their original dataset.[6]

---

[4] La Porta et al. (2004).

[5] See, e.g., Stone (1992); Vanberg (1998).

[6] Another takeaway is this: because even the best designs occasionally fall apart after the researcher collects the very first bits of data, we recommend that researchers work sequentially: amass that first piece and consider whether it comports with the research question and the hypotheses. If it does not, they may want to rethink their expectations but, more likely, they will come to see that the type of evidence they intended to collect is not as well suited to answering the research question as they anticipated.

With that, let's turn to the components of research design, keeping in mind that they are part of a dynamic process of inquiry, not steps on a flow chart. On the other hand, clear rules govern each component and the process itself, as we'll soon see.

2

Questions, Theories, Observable Implications

As its title suggests, this chapter examines three of the four components of designing empirical research: (1) asking research questions, (2) developing theories and observable implications, and (3) assessing rival hypotheses. Chapter 3 takes up the fourth: measurement. Again we remind you that even though we present the components in sequential order, the process is never quite as orderly in practice. Analysts should and often must deviate but even as they do it is always a good idea to follow best practices—the tried-and-true standards for conducting research that we flesh out in this and the chapters to follow.

2.1 Research Questions

Almost all empirical legal research starts with a basic question or set of questions that the author wants to answer.[1] In the study of law and legal institutions, questions can be as broad in scope as "what leads people to obey the law?"[2] to the narrower, "do gun control laws reduce violent crime?"[3] Questions can center on aggregates—"Are courts more likely to rule in favor of the government during war time?"[4]— or individuals—"Are individual judges more likely to decide in the

---

[1] The chief exception here is research aimed at creating public databases. See Chapters 1 and 4.

[2] E.g., Alm et al. (1992); Eigen (2012); Tyler (2006).

[3] E.g., Dezhbakshs and Rubin (1998); Duggan et al. (2011); Loftin et al. (1991), Miron (2001).

[4] E.g., Clark (2006); Epstein et al. (2005).

government's favor?"[5] And they may focus on events occurring at a specific point in time ("What explains economic prosperity today?"[6]) or over time ("What explains economic prosperity since 1960?"[7]). Some questions are causal in nature, others are descriptive. None is any less legitimate than the other.

How do empirical legal scholars develop their questions? In nearly uncountable ways and from everywhere and anywhere, as a glance at any disciplinary journal would confirm. Often, the researchers want to contribute to good legal or public policy, which may entail asking very fundamental questions—for example, the way policy makers should understand "how well an individual's life is going" in their attempts to enhance well-being.[8] There is now a cottage industry of research addressing this question by measuring "happiness" worldwide.[9]

Sometimes research is driven by gaps in the existing literature, such as the study we've discussed by La Porta et al.[10] Although several scholars had theorized that an independent judiciary promotes economic freedom, almost no one bothered to assess this hunch against data. The La Porta team did just that. Other times, scholars undertake projects because they think the existing literature is wrong, incomplete, or inconclusive. Posner and de Figueiredo's study of the International Court of Justice (ICJ) provides an example.[11] Some experts argue that judges serving on international tribunals reach decisions "impartially," without regard to their home country's interests.[12] Others contend quite the opposite.[13] In an effort to clarify the existing literature, Posner and de Figueiredo explored whether ICJ judges are biased toward their home countries, its allies, or even countries that resemble theirs. Conflicting research findings also motivated our study of gender and judging.[14] By our count, social scientists and legal academics had produced over 30 (quantitative) empirical studies asking whether

---

[5] E.g., Howell and Ahmed (2014).

[6] E.g., Dougherty and Jorgenson (1996); Frankel and Romer (1999); Hall and Jones (1999); La Porta et al. (2004).

[7] E.g., Barro (1996).

[8] Dolan and Peasgood (2008, 5).

[9] For an overview, see, e.g., Posner and Sunstein (2008). In Chapter 5, we discuss one of these studies (Kahneman and Deaton, 2010).

[10] La Porta et al. (2004).

[11] Posner and de Figueiredo (2005).

[12] E.g., Franck (1995); Alter (2008); Helfer and Slaughter (1997).

[13] See, e.g., Hensley (1968); de Bertodano (2002); Garrett and Weingast (1993).

[14] Boyd et al. (2010).

female and male judges decide cases differently. Of these, roughly one-third found differences, one-third reported mixed results, and the final third identified no differences.[15]

Relatedly, sometimes discrepancies between what scholars think they know and what they observe motivate research. This was the driving force behind a study one of us (Epstein) conducted on dissent in the U.S. Supreme Court.[16] During the 1800s and early 1900s, there were very few dissents; today, the justices write dissents in about two-thirds of the cases. The cause of the increase seemed obvious to most lawyers and scholars (including Epstein): after the passage of a law in 1925 that gave the Court more discretion to select the disputes it would resolve,[17] the justices were less able to agree over the outcomes of specific cases. This seemed a perfectly plausible explanation—except that the facts suggested otherwise. The rise in dissent appears to have come much later than 1925 as Figure 2.1 shows. The gap between what we thought we knew and what the data indicated gave rise to the research question: If the 1925 law did not lead to increased dissent, what did?[18]

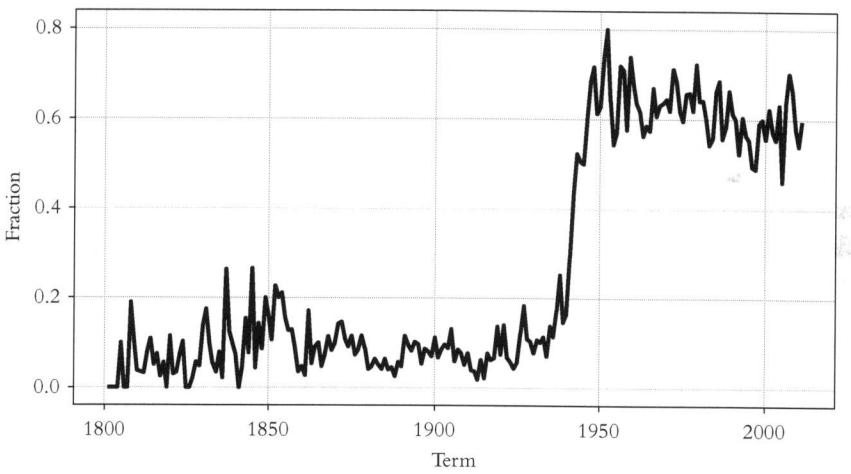

Figure 2.1 Fraction of U.S. Supreme Court cases with at least one dissenting opinion, 1801–2011 terms.[19]

---

[15] A list of these studies is available at: <http://epstein.wustl.edu/research/genderjudging.html>

[16] Walker et al. (1988).

[17] Judiciary Act of 1925 (43 Stat. 936).

[18] We're still not sure. Compare Walker et al. (1988) and Corley et al. (2013).

[19] Sources: 1801–1945 from Epstein et al. (2012, Table 3-2); 1946–2011 calculated from the U.S. Supreme Court Database.

Current events too can generate research questions, such as whether a law is having the desired (or any) effect or whether a court decision is efficacious. The gun control studies tend to fall into this category, including a now famous one conducted in 1991 by Loftin et al.[20] To answer the question of whether restricting access to guns would reduce deaths, the research team examined the number of gun-related homicides and suicides before and after the District of Columbia (in the United States) enacted a very restrictive handgun law.[21] It turned out that the adoption of the gun-licensing law coincided with a sharp decline in homicides (by 3.3 per month, or 25%) and suicides (0.6 per month, or 26%) by firearms.

Then there are researchers who are paid to produce studies, whether for a law firm, a non-governmental organization (NGO), or a corporate interest. This seems fairly common in empirical legal research (though it is hard to know for sure because many legal journals, unlike medical publications, do not have disclosure policies. They should.[22]) To provide a few examples: the Exxon Corporation has funded studies on the amount of damages awarded by juries;[23] pharmaceutical companies support research on the approval of drugs by government agencies[24] and the legality of mandatory vaccinations;[25] and left- and right-leaning foundations have commissioned studies on a wide range of policy matters including racism, racial integration, environmental protection, democratization, and inequality.[26] Although some judges and even scholars balk at funded studies because they think the researchers' conclusions will reflect the benefactors' interests,[27] we don't. There may be reasons to be cautious about the conclusions of funded work because, as you'll soon see, every empirical project requires the researcher to make scores of decisions—many of which

---

[20] Loftin et al. (1991).

[21] The U.S. Supreme Court invalidated the law over 30 years after its passage, in *Heller v. District of Columbia*, 554 U.S. 570 (2008).

[22] For more on this point, see Epstein and Clarke (2010).

[23] See, e.g., Schkade et al. (2000); Sunstein et al. (2002).

[24] Grabowski and Wang (2008).

[25] Dowling (2008).

[26] On the left, e.g., the Open Society Institute (see, e.g., Lobao et al., 2007; Mason and Kluegel, 2000; Payne-Pikus et al., 2010; Roberts, 2001); on the right, the John Olin Foundation (see, e.g., Buccafusco and Sprigman, 2010; D'Souza, 1995; Thernstrom and Thernstrom, 1999; Viscusi, 2006).

[27] E.g., in *Exxon Shipping Co. v. Baker*, 554 U.S. 471 (2008), the U.S. Supreme Court "decline[d] to rely on" several studies because they were funded by Exxon.

could go either way. Why not make them in favor of the group that is funding you?[28] On the other hand, skepticism should not give way to outright rejection. As long as the researchers follow best practices, there is no more reason to doubt the integrity of their final product than there is for any non-funded study.[29] Imagine the consequences of medical researchers declining industry money or of medical journals rejecting articles solely because the authors received commercial support. Many valuable studies would never see the light of day (that is, if they were undertaken in the first place). Empirical legal research is no different.

The contents of any socio-legal journal would provide evidence of these and other motivations for research. We assume that you too have interests that will generate research questions or that have drawn you to questions in studies you would like to evaluate, so we need not say too much more about the source of questions. There are, however, two issues that require some attention: (1) the criteria that good research questions should meet and (2) their conceptual nature.

2.1.1 The Criteria for Research Questions

When developing questions two criteria should move to the fore.[30] The first is that the question has a potential implication—normative, policy, or otherwise—for the real world. For most empirical legal research, this is rarely a concern. A, if not the, goal of many studies is to provide guidance to members of legal and policy communities. Consider, for example, Elkins, Ginsburg, and Melton's work, which puts a new spin on an age-old question: why do some constitutions survive for decades, even centuries, while others endure for little more than a year?[31] If we assume that long-lasting constitutions are desirable,[32] isolating the characteristics of an enduring document could offer important insights for future drafters.

---

[28] As *Nature*, the science journal, summarizes it:

[E]vidence [on commercial sponsorship of research] is consistent with the truism that although, in principle, science may be objective and its findings independent of other interests, scientists can be imperfect and subjective. There are circumstances where selection of evidence, interpretation of results or emphasis of presentation might be inadvertently or even deliberately biased by a researcher's other interests.

Nature.com, Competing Financial Interests, <http://www.nature.com/authors/policies/competing.html>.

[29] For more on this point, see Epstein and Clarke (2010).

[30] See Epstein and King (2002); King et al. (1994).

[31] Elkins et al. (2009).

[32] A debatable assumption, it turns out. See Elkins et al. (2009, Chapter 4).

The second characteristic of a good research question is that it seeks to engage the existing literature. Again, for many projects this is not an issue because the literature played a role in generating the question; perhaps the author spotted a gap, as in La Porta et al.'s study of economic freedom, or took note of conflicting answers, as in Posner and de Figueiredo's work of the ICJ[33] and ours on gender and judging.[34] For other types of empirical legal research—say, a report prepared for a law firm, a corporation, a government body, or an NGO—this characteristic may seem irrelevant. We assure you it is not. Understanding the existing literature minimizes the chances that an informed audience will question whether the researchers are up on the "state of the art" in whatever area they're studying. In other words, engaging with the literature enhances the credibility of the research, which may be especially important for studies that will be subject to cross-examination. Imagine a researcher called to testify about a study purporting to find that judges who are elected by the people are more likely to rule against criminal defendants on the theory that voters don't like judges who are soft on crime.[35] Because we know that laws governing the selection of judges across countries (or U.S. states) are non-random occurrences (and we can't randomly assign the laws), empirical assessments will need to take into account other factors that may affect the judge's vote (recall the thought experiment from Chapter 1). Now suppose that one of those factors is the judge's attitude toward criminal defendants but the researcher is so unfamiliar with the existing literature that he neglected it in his study. This would be a point of vulnerability, opening up the study to attack by the opposing side.

Relatedly, scouring the relevant literatures decreases the odds of reinventing the wheel. This is not to say that scholars should necessarily avoid raising the same questions as others, reanalyzing the same data, pursuing new ways of looking at old problems, or bringing fresh data to bear on them. It is rather to say that if they are addressing existing

---

[33] Posner and de Figueiredo (2005).

[34] Boyd et al. (2010).

[35] Although judicial elections are common in U.S. states, they are quite rare elsewhere. According to Shugerman (2010, 1351) only in France, Switzerland, and Japan are some judges elected; and even there the numbers are small and the elections limited. In Japan, for example, "the cabinet initially appoints high-court judges, and they run once for election unopposed." In 2011, after Shugerman published his study, Bolivia began conducting contested elections for all national judges (see Driscoll and Nelson, 2012).

questions, they should take into account the lessons of past studies. Failure to do so is more than wasteful; it also decreases the odds that the "new" research will be as successful as the original because the researcher is, in effect, ignoring the collective wisdom gained from earlier work.

Finally, following the advice that research engages existing scholarship ensures that someone will be interested in the results—an important goal for many scholars. If a body of literature exists, however slim and underdeveloped, it suggests that the question is important to at least some others. Generating interest among those others is a real benefit to analysts. It also increases the chances that someone will examine their research question, reevaluate their evidence from a new angle, or introduce new evidence of a closely related problem—with the result being more certain knowledge about communal concerns.

2.1.2 Their (Typically) Conceptual Nature

In offering these criteria, we want to be clear: we are not suggesting that researchers should raise questions and answer them in precisely the same way as others. We are rather recommending that new studies engage the existing literature. So doing might lead to asking questions that are important to the legal community but that no other scholar has tackled (the La Porta et al. study of economic freedom[36]); that attempt to settle a question that has evoked conflicting responses (the Posner and de Figueiredo article on the ICJ[37]); that raise an "old" question but address it from a fresh perspective and with better data (the Elkins et al. study on why constitutions endure[38]); or that use new methods to reanalyze existing data (our study on gender). This helps explain why, even when researchers follow the advice of engaging a body of literature, their questions will be unique and varied.

Even amid all the variation, most research questions are similar in one respect: as conceived, they are conceptual in nature.

Return to La Porta et al.'s study,[39] which asks:

1a. Do independent judiciaries promote economic freedom?

---

[36] La Porta et al. (2004).
[37] Posner and de Figueiredo (2005).
[38] Elkins et al. (2009).
[39] La Porta et al. (2004).

However important, this question is not one that even the best empirical legal project can address. Rather, the question the study will eventually answer comes closer to this:

> **1b.** In 71 countries, do longer tenures for judges lead to fewer steps that a start-up business must take in order to obtain legal status?[40]

Consider too Posner and de Figueiredo's article on the ICJ.[41] The research question of interest is in the title of their paper:

> **2a.** Is the International Court of Justice biased?

The question they answer is this:

> **2b.** Do ICJ judges favor applicant countries with a democracy score, ranging from 0 (authoritarian) to 10 (democracy), close to theirs?[42]

Note that the first form of both questions (1a, 2a) contains several concepts that the researchers cannot directly observe, such as "independent judiciaries" (La Porta) or "biased" (Posner and de Figueiredo). Only by clarifying these concepts, as in the second form (1b, 2b), can the researcher empirically answer the question. As we noted in Chapter 1, this is more or less true of every empirical project (including our own), and so a major research challenge is to tighten the fit between the question asked and the question actually answered. If it is too loose the researchers cannot claim to have answered the question they initially posed.

How to ensure a good fit? We turn to this question when we tackle the subject of measurement in Chapter 3.

2.2 Theories and their Observable Implications

Once analysts have settled on a research question, they usually begin *theorizing* about possible answers they can use to develop *observable implications* (sometimes called *hypotheses* or *expectations*).

"Theory" and theorizing are words researchers often bandy about, but what do they mean? They probably mean different things

---

[40] Recall from Chapter 1 that the number of steps is one of their indicators of economic freedom. See La Porta et al. (2004, 450).

[41] Posner and de Figueiredo (2005).

[42] The authors invoked other measures of bias. We consider these later.

depending on the discipline and the project.[43] As a general matter, though, "theorizing" entails the development of "a reasoned and precise speculation about the answer to a research question."[44] By "observable implications," we mean things that we would expect to observe in the real world—that we expect our data to unearth—if our theory is right.

There is nothing magical or mystical about these activities. In fact, we engage in them every day. After a professor teaches the first few sessions of a course, she might develop a simple theory, say, that the new students are better than those she taught the year before. Observable implications of this theory are easy enough to develop: we might expect the students to perform unusually well on the exams, to write especially cogent essays, or to say notably smart things in class. Like our professor, judges develop theories (and observable implications) about lawyers and juries; and lawyers, about judges and juries too.

In what follows we flesh out these ideas, though one point is worth underscoring at the outset. Some might argue that these steps are unnecessary in research motivated purely by policy concerns—say, a study designed to assess the effect of gun laws on crime or the effect of gender on salaries. Not so. Because the statistical methods we describe in Part III are aimed at testing hypotheses, even the hired researcher should develop some observable implications ultimately to assess.

2.2.1 A Few Thoughts on Theory

Theorizing is a big topic deserving of a book all of its own.[45] For our purposes, two points are worth underscoring. First, theorizing in empirical legal scholarship comes in many different forms. Sometimes it involves little more than reviewing the relevant literature or doctrine to identify existing answers. This is common in work that asks whether

---

[43] As Friedman (1998, 68) observed:

In legal scholarship, "theory" is king. But people who talk about legal "theory" have a strange idea of what "theory" means. In most fields, a theory has to be testable; it is a hypothesis, a prediction, and therefore subject to proof. When legal scholars use the word "theory," they seem to mean (most of the time) something they consider deep, original, and completely untestable.

[44] King et al. (1994, 19).

[45] And, in fact, there are many. For a tiny list of books offering and testing theories related to law and legal institutions, see Clark (2011); Elkins et al. (2009); Epstein et al. (2013); Helmke (2005); Rosenberg (2008); Segal and Spaeth (2002); Simon (2012); Staton (2010); Staudt (2011).

a law or court decision had its intended (or unintended) effect—for example, whether a law allowing people to carry handguns affects the crime rate or whether a court decision legalizing abortion increases the number of abortions. Rather than offering a theory of "impact," the researchers often review other studies, reports, and essays that address the effect of the same or similar laws or cases.[46]

For other projects, analysts might develop their own theories but they will be simple, small, or tailored to fit particular problems. Such is the example of the professor theorizing about the quality of her students. Then there are theories that are grander in scope, seeking to provide insight into a wide range of phenomena. Take an increasingly common one in legal scholarship: positive political theory (PPT), which consists of "non-normative, rational-choice theories of political institutions" and so could be seen as part of the law and economics program.[47] Employing PPT, researchers have sought to address a long list of diverse research questions—from why judges (with discretion over their docket) agree to hear certain cases and reject others,[48] to whether the preferences of the existing or incoming government influence judicial decisions,[49] to what circumstances (in common law systems) lead lower courts to deviate from precedent established by higher courts,[50] to why judges sometimes write vague rather than clear decisions.[51]

2.2.2 Observable Implications

The upshot is that theories come in many types, levels of abstraction, and substantive applications. But—and this is our second point—for

---

[46] We don't mean to imply that researchers can't or shouldn't develop grander theories of impact; in fact, some have (see, e.g., Rosenberg, 2008; Spriggs, 1996; Canon and Johnson, 1999). It is rather to say that most empirical legal studies seem content with the literature review approach. Depending on the purpose of the study and its intended audience, this is not an unreasonable way to proceed.

[47] Farber and Frickey (1992, 462). More precisely, PPT (in most law applications) assumes that goal-directed actors operate in a strategic or interdependent decision-making context. Seen in this way, it is quite akin to "strategic accounts" in the social-scientific literature. On this account, (1) social actors make choices in order to achieve certain goals, (2) social actors act strategically in the sense that their choices depend on their expectations about the choices of other actors, and (3) these choices are structured by the institutional setting in which they are made (see, e.g., Epstein and Knight, 1998, 1–21).

[48] E.g., Caldeira et al. (1999); Flemming (2004); Owens (2010).

[49] E.g., Eskridge (1991); Helmke (2005); Segal et al. (2011).

[50] E.g., Caminker (1994); Gennaioli and Shleifer (2007); Kornhauser (1995).

[51] Staton and Vanberg (2008).

the purposes of conducting an empirical study, the distinctions among them may not be all that important.

Why not? It turns out that just as analysts almost never actually answer the question they pose, they almost never directly test their theory; they only indirectly assess it by evaluating the observable implications that follow from it. The professor will never be able to test her theory that her new students are better than those she taught last year. But she will be able to assess whether they are more prepared for class, ask better questions, and earn higher grades, to name just a few observable implications following from her theory.

This plays out in research too. Let's reconsider Posner and de Figueiredo's study of whether ICJ judges are biased toward their home country. They offer several different theories,[52] including the two depicted in the left-hand column of Table 2.1.

Note, though, that in neither instance—no matter how good their design, data, or methods—will Posner and de Figueiredo be able to conclude that their theory is right or wrong (that impartiality leads

Table 2.1 The relationship between theories and observable implications in Posner and de Figueiredo's study of the ICJ.

Theory		Observable Implication
Neutrality Theory. Because they are judges, members of the ICJ will "seek to rule in the manner dictated by law."	→	If this theory is correct, we should observe judges reaching decisions that reflect no bias toward their home country or its allies (all else equal).[53]
Attachment Theory. Because they are nationals with strong ties to their countries and have spent "their careers in national service," ICJ judges will "have trouble seeing the dispute from the perspective of any country but that of their native land."	→	If this theory is correct, we should observe judges reaching decisions in favor of their home country, or countries that resemble their home country or are otherwise allies (all else equal).

[52] See Posner and de Figueiredo (2005, 608). The terms "neutrality" and "attachment" are ours.

[53] "All else equal" takes us back to the thought experiment in Chapter 1. Because we can't conduct an experiment on ICJ judges, we need control for the many other factors that might affect their decisions, other than their country of origin (and the country of origin of the applicants). We return to this point at the end of the chapter, where we consider rival explanations.

to unbiased judgment or that strong home attachments lead to biased judgments). All they will be able to say is whether their data are consistent with one or the other observable implication shown in the right-hand column of Table 2.1.

The point of this example is to underscore why our focus should be on observable implications; it is they, not the underlying theory, that empirical researchers ultimately assess. We can't test the idea that judges will "see the dispute from their perspective," but *ultimately* we can examine whether they rule in favor of their home country. (We emphasize "ultimately" because observable implications too contain concepts that require clarification; for example, how should we operationally define "resemble their home country"? This is the subject of the next chapter.)

If observable implications are so important, how do we go about developing them? And what form do they take?

Extracting Observable Implications from Theory.   When it comes to developing observable implications, there's no single right way. Sometimes researchers simply think through their theory. Again, return to Posner and de Figueiredo's study. It's not much of a leap to go from the idea that judges "see disputes from the perspective of their home country" (attachment theory) to the implication that judges will rule in favor of their home country.

Sometimes researchers derive observable implications more formally. To provide a very simple example applying positive political theory (PPT), consider Figure 2.2. There, we depict the choice confronting a high court judge over whether or not to vote to hear a case. Were we to think about this problem solely in terms of the judge's preference, the figure would include only "Judge," and not "Court." But under PPT accounts the judge's decision over whether to vote to hear the case would be contingent on whether, in this example, the majority of his colleagues ("Court") ultimately would rule for or against the government, assuming the judge cares about being on the winning side of the case. If this assumption holds, we can use the theory to develop several implications. To wit: if the judge prefers to rule for the government, he will vote to hear the case only if he thinks the majority of his colleagues agree that the government should win; otherwise, he will vote against hearing the case. Alternatively, if he prefers to rule against the government, he will vote to hear the case if he thinks he

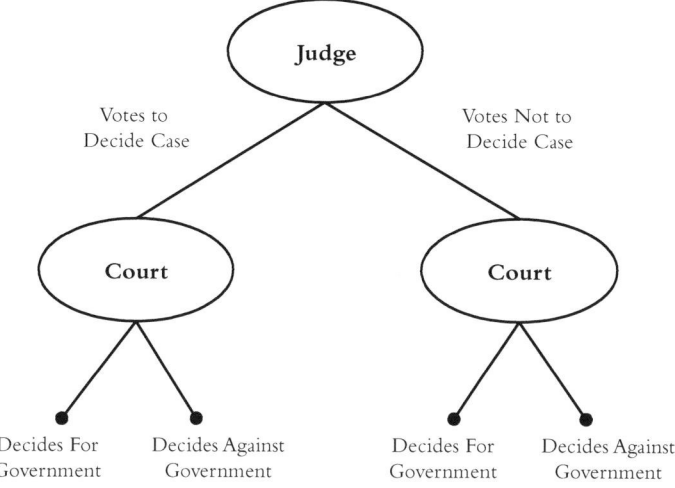

Figure 2.2 The judge's decision over whether or not to hear a case is contingent on the court's decision on the merits of the dispute.

has a majority for his view; otherwise he will vote against hearing the case. The idea is that it's better not to hear the case than to give the government a victory in his Court.

The Form of Observable Implications: Dependent and Independent Variables. Whatever the method for extracting them from theory, observable implications tend to take a common form: as a claim about the relationship between (or among) *variables* that we can, at least in principle, observe.

Variable is a word that sounds technical but it has a straightforward definition. It is something that varies. Again, consider a (simplified) implication from Posner and de Figueiredo's study:

If attachment theory is correct, we should observe judges *voting* for countries with *governments* that most resemble theirs, such that judges from democratic countries cast their votes in favor of litigants from democratic countries and judges from authoritarian countries, for litigants from authoritarian countries.

In this example, voting or Votes is a variable: ICJ judges can vote for or against the applicant country. Government too is a variable: the applicant country can be a democracy or an authoritarian regime. If all the votes of ICJ judges were always, now, and forever more in favor of the applicant country, Votes would not be a variable but a constant. We would say the same of Government if the only countries permitted to come before the ICJ were democracies. (From this point forward, we use this font to indicate a variable.)

Variables come in two general forms. *Dependent variables* are the things (or outcomes) we are trying to explain, here: a judge's votes. *Independent variables* are those things (or inputs, such as events or factors) we think account for the dependent variable, here: the type of government. Again, note that the possible inputs and outcomes are variables that take on different values (that is, they vary). Votes are for or against the applicant; the Government is a democracy or an authoritarian regime.[54]

Because the concepts of dependent and independent variables are so important, let's consider a few other examples. Test yourself to be sure you can identify which variable is the independent and which is the dependent. (The footnotes supply the answers.)

From the La Porta et al. study: The more independent a country's judiciary, the greater the economic freedom its citizens will enjoy (all else equal).[55]

From Our Study on Gender and Judging: Female judges are more likely than male judges to favor the litigant claiming sex discrimination (all else equal).[56]

From (Some) Studies of Gun Violence: The looser a country's gun control laws, the higher the murder rate (all else equal).[57]

---

[54] Recall that in Posner and de Figueiredo's study, government type is bit more complicated because they use a scale rather than a dichotomy (whether the government is or is not a democracy). We return to these sorts of measurement issues in Chapter 3.

[55] La Porta et al. (2004). Because they are trying to explain economic freedom, it's the dependent variable. Whether the country has an independent judiciary is a factor they think explains variation in economic freedom so it's an independent variable. Note: We state this and the other implications in conceptual terms. Here, economic freedom and judicial independence both require clarification if we are to observe them. We take this up in more detail in Chapter 3.

[56] Boyd et al. (2010). The judge's gender is the independent variable (social science studies almost never explain gender!); the judge's vote in sex discrimination cases is the dependent variable.

[57] In impact studies, an act of government or the decision of a court is always the independent variable, meaning here gun control laws are the independent variable. Murder rate is the outcome or dependent variable. Of course, some studies hypothesize the opposite: the stricter the gun control laws, the higher the murder rate. For a review of this literature, see Kates and Mauser (2007).

From the Elkins et al. study. The more flexible a constitution, the more likely it will be able to adopt to changing circumstances and so will endure longer (all else equal).[58]

Note that we have phrased the implications in somewhat varying terms, and the relationship between the variables differs too. For some, the relationship is positive (e.g., the more independence, the greater economic freedom), for others it is negative (the looser the gun laws, the higher the murder rate or, if you prefer, the looser the restrictions on guns, the lower the murder rate, which would be a positive relationship). This is fine; there's no one right way to specify a hypothesis so long as the independent and dependent variables are clearly delineated.

2.3 Rival Explanations

In each of these examples, there is one independent variable—the independent variable of primary interest (or what studies seeking to make causal inferences call the causal variable). This reflects the fact that in many empirical legal studies the researcher is especially interested in one observable implication containing one particular explanation in the form of one independent variable; for example, in our study, the gender of the judge. But—and this is a very important but—in almost no compelling empirical study is it sufficient to consider only one explanation and thus only one independent variable. That's why, for each of the hypotheses above, we add the parenthetical "all else equal." If we were able to conduct a proper experiment on countries, judges, crime rates, or constitutions, all else would be equal for different levels of our independent variable of interest. But for observational data, we need to control for all the other factors that might affect the outcome, in addition to the independent variable of primary interest.

This was the chief point of the thought experiment in Chapter 1,[59] and let's reinforce it here with an example. Imagine we produced a study showing that male judges reach decisions in favor of the party alleging sex discrimination in 25% of the cases and female judges in 75%. Should we conclude that there's a difference between the females and males? No, and by now you probably know why: gender

---

[58] Elkins et al. (2009). Flexibility is the independent variable and endurance is the dependent variable.

[59] And one we revisit in some detail in Chapter 8.

is not the only variable that explains judicial decisions (more generally, could one variable possibly explain any human behavior!?). It may be that when we take into account alternative explanations, the effect of our favored explanation—here, gender—could vanish entirely. Suppose that 75% of the male judges, but only 25% of the females, were business-friendly types who viewed sex discrimination claims as costly to firms. Further suppose that these males and females were equally likely to rule against the sex discrimination claim, while the anti-business males and females were equally likely to rule for it. In this case, we might say that attitudes toward business, and not the gender of the judge, provides a more satisfactory explanation of judicial decisions (though we might want to investigate why the males tend to be more business-oriented).

Of course, if we could conduct our thought experiment from Chapter 1, this problem wouldn't exist. We would randomly assign a sex to a judge and ask the judge to decide the case. We'd then reverse time and change the sex of the same judge and ask the judge to decide exactly the same sex discrimination case at exactly the same moment in time. That way, we wouldn't worry at all about features of the judges (perhaps their world views, ideology, or other background characteristics) or features of the cases (perhaps the gender or race of the party claiming discrimination or the quality of the attorney, assuming non-random assignment of cases to judges), or anything else that could lead to differences between the decisions of males and females. But because we can't reverse time and clone judges, we must worry about all these "rival" explanations if we are to produce compelling work. To state it even more strongly, when using observational data, researchers cannot claim to have supported the observable implication of their theory (i.e., their hypothesis) without consideration of alternative explanations. In fact, their neglect makes their work appear all the weaker and more open to attack, whether in the faculty lounge, a courtroom, or a legislative hearing.

Avoiding this problem requires researchers, first, to comb the existing literature for, and to think hard and imaginatively about, explanations that do not square with the theory they are offering. Doing so now is far easier than ever before. The vast majority of socio-legal journals, law reviews, and, increasingly, books are available on line and in searchable formats. The result is that the excuse of not knowing about a particular study has grown less and less credible. Second, authors should alert readers to the fruits of those exercises—in other words, to any existing rival explanations—and, ultimately, build them into their research.

From a statistical perspective, this last step is critical because if scholars ignore competing explanations, their work will suffer from what is known as *omitted variable bias*, making suspect any causal inferences they reach.[60] We have more to say about avoiding this type of bias in Chapter 9, but note the gist of this point: in selecting variables for their study, scholars cannot stop with those following directly from the observable implications of their theory. They will in all likelihood have to incorporate variables designed to control for the implications of other theories that do not necessarily square with theirs (in other words, rival explanations).

Devising measurement and data collection strategies for variables favored by potential critics is a great way to minimize vulnerability, and ultimately, maximize inoculation against attack. It is to these topics of measurement (Chapter 3) and data collection (Chapter 4) that we now turn.

---

[60] As we'll see in Chapter 9, there are limits here. For example, when performing causal inference, we wouldn't want to account for explanations occurring after the causal variable of interest.

3

Measurement

In the last chapter, we made the point that empirical researchers rarely directly test their favored theories; they instead assess whether their data are consistent with the observable implications (hypotheses) following from their theory or with rival explanations.

Yet even assessing these manifestations of theory requires hard work. The problem, once again, is that observable implications, along with rival explanations, are conceptual claims about the relationship between or among variables. Take the Elkins et al. study on the endurance of constitutions in 200 different nations between 1789 and 2005.[1] To address the question of why some constitutions last far longer than others, they offer a theory of constitutional renegotiation. The idea is that constitutions will generally endure until society experiences a shock, such as a financial crisis or a militarized conflict. At that point, some constitutions will die; others will be more durable, though not necessarily because of any great acumen on the part of the country's leaders. Rather, features within the document itself can make it more resilient. Among these are the constitution's level of specificity, such that constitutions that are less loosely drafted, and so more specific, are more likely to endure in part because they "will more easily generate shared understandings of what [the constitutional contract] entails."[2] Put another way, an observable implication of the theory of constitutional renegotiation is this: all else equal, the greater a constitution's specificity, the more likely it is to endure.[3]

---

[1] Elkins et al. (2009, especially Chapter 4).

[2] Elkins et al. (2009, 84).

[3] As we imply in the text, other observable implications follow from Elkins et al.'s (2009) theory, including one we considered in Chapter 2: the more flexible a constitution, the more likely it is to endure. For pedagogical purposes, we'll focus on specificity here.

This is a fine hypothesis, but Elkins et al. can't assess it without first translating the variable "specificity" into some precise indicator of specificity. The same is true of the La Porta et al. study. The authors hypothesize that an independent judiciary will lead to greater economic freedom (all else equal).[4] But how do they define judicial independence—a concept that is also not directly observable—so that they can assess its effect on economic freedom? Economic freedom too must be delineated in concrete terms.

In both studies, determining whether the hypothesis holds requires the researchers to move from abstract ideas ("specificity," "independent judiciary," "economic freedom") to something far more concrete. They must do the same for any rival explanations too (the "all else equal" part of the hypotheses).

This movement from the abstract to the concrete is known as measurement or, more formally, the task of comparing an object of study (for example, a real world event, subject, or process) with some standard, such as exists for quantities, capacities, or categories.[5] We typically measure height by comparing an object to a standard such as meters or feet. We could measure a country's economic freedom by asking financial experts to tell us whether they think the country provides economic freedom; or we could examine the number of steps that a start-up business must take to obtain legal status. Either is a measure of the concept of economic freedom, a concept that we cannot observe without clarifying it.

As we noted in Chapter 1, measurement is a critical step in designing research. That's because, as we now know, we can't usually draw comparisons among the variables as conceptualized in our observable implications; we cannot compare the level of "specificity" of constitutions or the "independence" of judiciaries. All we can do is compare the levels (or degrees) of specificity or independence we obtain from some measure of them. This means that our comparisons and, ultimately, our answers to research questions are only as valid as the measures we've developed. If the measures do not adequately reflect the concepts contained in our hypotheses, the conclusions we draw will be faulty. To put it another way, if, say, the opinion of financial experts is not a very good way to define "economic freedom," the study's results will be vulnerable to attack. As well they should be.

---

[4] La Porta et al. (2004).
[5] We adapt some of the material in this chapter from Epstein and King (2002).

Because this holds for virtually all empirical projects, in what follows we consider, first, the task of measurement and, second, the standards empirical researchers (and their readers) use to assess the measures they've developed to proxy the variables in their hypothesis.

3.1 Measuring Concepts

As we just noted, measurement is about comparing an object of study with some standard. Making the comparison usually involves two interrelated steps: (1) delineating how the concepts can be measured and (2) identifying the values of the measure. Figure 3.1 illustrates this process for an observable implication—a hypothesis—from the La Porta et al. study. The researchers' job, to reiterate, is to ensure that the measures of the variables in their hypothesis capture their underlying concepts as precisely as possible. (Keep in mind that the analyst will need to go through this process for all observable implications, as well as rival explanations.)

To see how La Porta et al. perform it, let's recall their core conceptual argument: when judges enjoy independence from the government, they are better able to prevent the government from infringing on people's economic liberty. To analyze this argument, they measure judicial independence (in part) by a scale indicating the tenure for the country's highest court judges.[6] To them, this is a good measure because "When judges have life-long tenure, they are both less susceptible to direct political pressure and less likely to have been selected by the government currently in office."[7] The dependent variable, partly measured by the steps to create a start-up,[8] also, they believe, well taps the concept of economic freedom because high barriers to entry tend to benefit the regulators (politicians and bureaucrats) rather than greater societal interests.[9]

---

[6] We emphasize again that this is one of two measures they use to assess judicial independence. The other is whether or not "judicial decisions . . . are a source of law" (La Porta et al. 2004, 451). We focus on tenure because it is a fairly common measure of judicial independence.

[7] La Porta et al. (2004, 453).

[8] Again, this is only one of their measures of economic freedom. See Chapter 1 for the others.

[9] For more details, see Djankov et al. (2002).

What about the second task—assigning values to the measure? Note that in the example depicted in Figure 3.1, the researchers assigned numbers to values of the measures of the independent and dependent variables. The independent variable ranges from 0 (tenure less than six years) to 2 (life tenure). For the measure of the dependent variable—the number of steps necessary for a new business to obtain legal status—the values are the number of steps (ranging, across their 71 countries, from 2 to 19).

Observable Implication

(Identify the relationship between the Independent Variable X and the Dependent Variable Y)

The more independent a country's judiciary, the greater the level of economic freedom.

Measurement 1

(Delineate how the concepts in the Independent Variable X and the Dependent Variable Y can be measured)

The longer judicial tenure, the easier it is for a business to begin operating as a legal entity. So:
• For the independent variable: tenure of judges
• For the dependent variable: ease of starting up a new business

---

Measurement 2

(Identify the values of the measures of the Independent Variable X and the Dependent Variable Y)

• For the independent variable: tenure of country's highest court judges, such that:
  o 2 = tenure is lifelong
  o 1 = tenure is more than six years but not lifelong
  o 0 = tenure is less than six years.
• For the dependent variable: the number of different steps with which a start-up must comply to obtain legal status, i.e. to start operating as a legal entity (ranges from 2–19 in the dataset).

Figure 3.1 The process of moving from an observable implication (or hypothesis) to measures.

In the case of La Porta et al.'s dependent variable, the measure itself implies the values—the number of steps. (It wouldn't make much sense to assign the values of, say, 2,000 to 2 steps, 2,001 to 3 steps, etc. when 2 and 3 are not only simpler but convey meaning too.) The same holds in the Elkins et al. study. A key observable implication in their study is:

The greater the specificity of a constitution in terms of the scope of the topics covered, the more likely it is to endure.[10]

They translate this hypothesis to:

The higher the percentage of topics covered in the constitution (out of 92 possible topics), the greater the number of years the constitution will endure.

So for their purposes, a good measure of "specificity" is a percentage: the percentage of topics the Constitution covers from a potential total of 92.[11] The higher the percentage, the greater the specificity. Theoretically, the percentage could range from 0% (the constitution covers none of the 92 topics) to 100% (all topics covered), though in their dataset the minimum is about 10% and the maximum 79%.[12] The dependent variable—the number of years the constitution endured—ranges from 0 to 217 in their data.[13]

It isn't always the case that the values follow directly from the measure.[14] Recall an observable implication of Posner and de Figueiredo's analysis of the International Court of Justice (ICJ): ICJ judges are partial to countries that are structured as their own, such that judges from democracies favor democracies and judges from authoritarian states favor authoritarian states.[15] To measure the government type—an independent variable—Posner and de Figuerido assigned a

---

[10] Specificity also includes "the level of detail in the constitution." For the sake of pedagogy, we'll stick with scope.

[11] Elkins et al. (2009, 104).

[12] Elkins et al. (2009, 226).

[13] Our numbers here are slightly off because 189 of the 746 constitutions in their dataset are still in force (Elkins et al., 2009, 51). Also, for reference, "The median survival time (the age at which one-half of constitutions are expected to have died) is nineteen years" (p. 129).

[14] It may not even hold for La Porta et al. (2004) and Elkins et al. (2009). In both, the researchers could have chosen to group their measure; for example, in La Porta et al., instead of the actual number of steps, the values could have been: +1 = "many steps," 0 = "average number of steps," -1 = few steps. For the reasons we provide in Chapter 5, collapsing data in this way is generally not advisable, at least not when the researcher is developing a dataset. But there are circumstances when grouping data in this way is quite sensible, as we shall see.

[15] Posner and de Figueiredo (2005).

type-of-government score to each country, which ranged from 0 (authoritarian) to 10 (democracy).[16] They could have added even more values, say, from –10 to +10; or fewer, say, –1 to +1.[17]

Then there are instances where values would seem to follow directly from a measure; for example, it might seem more natural to measure judicial term length as the number of years, rather than proceed as La Porta et al. did: 0 (less than six years), 1 (greater than six years but not life tenure), and 2 (life tenure). It is possible that year was the value unit when La Porta et al. collected the data but later, for the analysis, they collapsed it into three categories. For the reasons we explain in Chapter 5, this can be a sensible approach. (Chapter 5 also addresses the question of how researchers develop the values of their variables when the matter isn't entirely obvious, as in the Posner and de Figueiredo study, because creating values is an issue intimately associated with collecting and coding data.)

Finally, measurement need not involve assigning numbers to values. In qualitative research, categories such as "Autocracy," "Anocracy," and "Democracy" or "Constitution is Not Specific," and "Constitution is Specific" are reasonable assuming researchers sufficiently define the standard for measurement so that they (or others) can unambiguously apply it. This last point goes to a study's reproducibility, which we develop in more detail in Part II.

3.2 Evaluating Measures and Measurement Methods

As you can probably tell by now, common to all measurement exercises (regardless of the values of the measure) is that everything about the object of study is lost except the dimension or dimensions being measured. Summarizing, say, the European Union by saying it consists

---

[16] Posner and de Figueiredo (2005, 612). The scores come from the Polity IV Project (at: <http://www.systemicpeace.org/polity/polity4.htm>). The Polity IV dataset defines a democracy as "conceived [of] three essential, interdependent elements. One is the presence of institutions and procedures through which citizens can express effective preferences about alternative policies and leaders. Second is the existence of institutionalized constraints on the exercise of power by the executive. Third is the guarantee of civil liberties to all citizens in their daily lives and in acts of political participation."

[17] In fact, there are Polity scores (see note 16) that range from –10 (hereditary monarchy) to +10 (consolidated democracy) and those that use a three-party categorization: autocracies, anocracies, and democracies. See the Polity IV Project, at: <http://www.systemicpeace.org/polity/polity4.htm>.

of 27 member states obviously leaves out an enormous amount of information, as does claiming that economic freedom exists when there are fewer legal steps for start-ups or that a country's constitution is more likely to endure when the percentage of topics covered is high.

All measurement schemes are susceptible to the critique of oversimplication. Instead of understanding economic freedom in 71 countries or the level of specificity in the 935 constitutions promulgated in 200 different countries between 1789 and 2005 or the 1,437 votes of ICJ judges by looking at the countries or constitutions or votes all at once, we can greatly simplify the task by summarizing each with 71 or 935 or 1,437 numbers—one for each country, constitution, or vote. Even more to the point, understanding the real world always requires a certain level of abstraction. The key is that we abstract the right dimensions for our purposes, that we measure enough dimensions of each subject to capture all the parts that are essential to our research question, and, perhaps most crucially of all, that we carefully evaluate our choices and procedures.

How do researchers make these evaluations? To put it more concretely, why did La Porta et al. rely in part on the "the length of tenure" as a measure of judicial independence and not one of the many other plausible indicators including: restrictions on the removal of judges, frequency of changes in the size of the judiciary, fluctuations in the court's budget, the protection and adequacy of judicial salaries, public perception of the degree of judicial independence, and an absence of corruption and bribery, to name just a few?[18]

The answer to this question lies in the two criteria researchers use to assess their measures and measurement procedures: *reliability* and *validity*. Reliability is the extent to which it is possible to replicate a measure, reproducing the same value (regardless of whether it is the right one) on the same standard for the same subject at the same time. Measures of high reliability are preferable to those with lower levels. Validity is the extent to which a reliable measure reflects the underlying concept being measured. To assess this, we might start by considering whether the measure comports with prior evidence or existing knowledge (in which case it would be "facially valid"), among other criteria.

---

[18] For a longer list, see Ros-Figueroa and Staton (2014). The power to review the constitutionality of laws is another obvious measure of judicial independence. But because judicial (constitutional) review is a separate concept in the La Porta et al. study, they develop measures to distinguish independence and review.

3.2.1 Reliability

To understand reliability, think about a bathroom scale. If any one of us stepped on the scale 100 times in a row and it gave us the same weight 100 times in a row we'd say the scale was reliable (though not necessarily accurate; that gets to validity). A measure is reliable when it produces the same results regardless of who or what is actually doing the measuring. Conversely, suppose we stepped on the scale 100 times in a row and it gave us 100 different weights. We'd deem the scale unreliable, and either get it fixed or buy a new one.

The same is true in research. Recall that Posner and de Figueiredo expect ICJ judges to vote in favor of their home country when their home country is an applicant.[19] Suppose that the researchers devised the following values of the measure: if the judge voted for his home country, assign the value 1; if the judge voted against his home country, assign the value 0. Further suppose, hypothetically, that the researchers assign a vote as "1" in a particular case, but that we (in an effort to replicate their data) classified the same vote as "0." This would provide some evidence that their measurement procedure was unreliable—and, in fact, unreliable in a way that was biased toward their theory. (Recall that they expect ICJ judges to favor their home country.)

That's why, when researchers produce unreliable measures, it is the researchers' problem; they, not the replicators, must take responsibility. But what specifically has gone wrong for the researchers? How could this happen? Well, to continue with our ICJ hypothetical, suppose the judge's vote was ambiguous—ruling for the home country but only in part, or ruling for neither party.[20] If the researchers create a simple dichotomy—the judge voted for or against his home country—then

---

[19] Posner and de Figueiredo (2005).

[20] For a case that may provide an example of various possibilities for classifying votes, see Request for Interpretation of the Judgment of 15 June 1962 in the Case Concerning the Temple of Preah Vihear (Cambodia v. Thailand), Provisional Measures (Int'l Ct. Justice July 18, 2011). In this case, Cambodia asked the ICJ to hold that the territory of the Temple of Preah Vihear belonged to Cambodia; Thailand argued that only the Temple belonged to Cambodia and that there was no dispute (and so no ICJ jurisdiction). The Court ordered "[b]oth Parties [to] immediately withdraw their military personnel currently present in the provisional demilitarized zone." It also ordered Thailand not to "obstruct Cambodia's free access to the Temple" and ordered both parties to "continue the cooperation which they have entered into" to "refrain from any action which may aggravate or extend the dispute." See Cogan (2012); Shulman (2012).

ambiguity could emerge over how to classify a vote that does not fall squarely into either.

To combat unreliability of this kind, researchers must attempt to remove human judgment from measurement or, when judgment is necessary, they must make their measures wholly transparent to others who may want to reproduce, backdate, or update their study—including themselves. Months or even weeks after researchers finish their study, they will forget their own procedures. (We know; we've been there.) In the case of judicial votes, a possible approach would be to include another value, such as "judge voted in favor of his home country but only in part." Another would be to write a rule that says "any vote, whether partially or fully in favor of the home country, counts as a vote in favor of the home country."

In Chapter 5 we offer more advice for minimizing judgment. For now, it is worth re-emphasizing the importance of creating reliable measures. If you ever forget, just return to the metaphor of the bathroom scale and remember what you would do with a scale that gave you a different weight each time in a row that you stepped on it.

You should also keep reliability in mind when you read about measures that seem "worse" than others—say, the length of tenure of a country's highest court judges in years as a measure of judicial independence. In terms of reliability, this one strikes us as quite sound. If we used the same set of documents as the researchers, we should be able to reproduce their measure—the number of years—exactly for each country. The same may not hold for some of the other measures of judicial independence, say, an absence of corruption, even if they seem better in some way.

Of course, ideally, we would like measures that are both reliable *and* better (or even the best available). It is to this idea of "better"—or validity—that we now turn.

3.2.2 *Validity*

We know that if your bathroom scale registered a weight of, say, 120 kilograms (about 265 pounds) 100 times in a row, we would probably deem it a reliable scale. Now suppose that right after you weighed yourself on the bathroom scale, you stepped on the most accurate scale in the world—the gold standard scale—and it registered a weight of 70 kilograms, or 50 kilograms *less than* the bathroom scale! If this happened, you wouldn't think much of the bathroom scale because it didn't report your true weight. This is where validity comes in. A scale that is both reliable and valid will give you your true weight of 70 kilograms 100 times in a row.

Validity, in other words, implicates accuracy. It is the extent to which a reliable measure reflects the underlying concept being measured. A scale that is both reliable and valid displays the weight of 70 kilos 100 times in a row; a scale that displays a weight of 120 (or 50 kilos higher than the truth) 100 times in a row is reliable but not valid, and we would no more use this scale than we would a scale that was unreliable.

Just as a bathroom scale can be reliable but not valid, so too can the measures used by researchers. Evaluating validity, though, is more difficult than assessing reliability. If we want to know whether Elkins et al.'s measure of "specificity" is reliable, we could try to reproduce it by obtaining a list of their 92 topics and applying it to the constitutions in their study. The degree to which our application differs from theirs would provide some indication of the reliability of their measure.[21] We could do the same with La Porta et al.'s measure of judicial independence. But determining validity is a different story. In the social sciences, as opposed to the physical world, there are few benchmarks or "gold standards." What is the true measure of a constitution's specificity? The gold standard indicator of judicial independence? There is none.

To compensate, researchers have developed a number of criteria that valid measures should satisfy. In what follows, we explore three—facial validity, unbiasedness, and efficiency—with the caveat that meeting all of them isn't always necessary, and together they are not always sufficient even though collectively they are often helpful in understanding when a measure is more or less valid.[22]

Face Validity. Face validity is perhaps the most common of the three criteria. A measure is facially valid if it is consistent with prior evidence of all sorts—including all quantitative, qualitative, and even

---

[21] Several statistics help us compare how two or more individuals apply the same coding rules to the same data. The most common is Cohen's κ (Cohen, 1960). For more information about κ and other measures of inter-coder reliability, see Landis and Koch (1977); Lombard et al. (2002), along with the research design textbooks listed on our website.

[22] See Quinn *et al.* (2010, 216–18) for a discussion of additional types of validity.

impressionistic reports or anecdotes. But do not take this to mean that assessing face validity is unsystematic. It demands not a casual armchair judgment of plausibility but instead a careful comparison of the new measure and extant evidence. To return to our bathroom, imagine you have good evidence to believe that you weigh 70 kilos and have no prior evidence to believe your weight has changed (your clothes fit as they always have, you have not modified your diet, and you are doing no more or less exercise). Now suppose you stepped on a scale and weighed 120 kilos. On the face of it you have reason to believe that the scale isn't valid.

Assessing the face validity of measures in empirical legal research is much the same. We know that La Porta et al.'s measure of judicial independence, which in part relies on tenure as specified in the countries' legal documents, has three values: 0 = the judge's tenure is less than six years; 1 = more than six years but not life tenure; 2 = life tenure. Table 3.1 shows the score assigned to each country in their dataset.

Is tenure length a facially valid measure of judicial independence? Does it comport with existing knowledge? Perhaps not.[23] Over two centuries ago, James Madison, a framer of the U.S. Constitution, was skeptical about bills of rights, believing they are little more than "parchment barriers"—mere words on paper that have little bearing to actual practices.[24] Many students of constitutions not only concur but have provided data to support the view that law as specified in the constitution provides at best only a partial explanation of law on the ground.[25]

We shouldn't be surprised then that studies often distinguish between de jure (in law) and de facto (in fact) judicial independence, and more

---

[23] Again, this is not a criticism of the La Porta et al. (2004) study because it does not rely solely on tenure as a measure of judicial independence.

[24] See, e.g., James Madison to Thomas Jefferson (October 17, 1788): "[E]xperience proves the inefficacy of a bill of rights on those occasions when its controul is most needed. Repeated violations of these parchment barriers have been committed by overbearing majorities in every State." Available at The Founders' Constitution: <http://press-pubs.uchicago.edu/founders/documents/v1ch14s47.html>). Still, for various reasons, Madison became a supporter of (and even drafted) the U.S.'s Bill of Rights (see Rakove, 1985).

[25] E.g., Feld and Voigt (2003); Helmke (2005); Herrona and Randazzo (2003); Keith (2002).

Table 3.1 The tenure of highest court judges in 70 countries, as reported by La Porta et al.[26]

Tenure for Highest Court Judges is Less Than Six Years		
1. Algeria	4. Honduras	7. Vietnam
2. China, PR	5. Iraq	
3. Cuba	6. Korea, DPR	

Tenure for Highest Court Judges is Greater Than Six Years but Not for Life		
1. Colombia	4. Korea, Rep.	7. Panama
2. Haiti	5. Mexico	8. Switzerland
3. Japan	6. Nicaragua	9. Venezuela

Life Tenure for Highest Court Judges		
1. Argentina	20. Indonesia	39. Philippines
2. Australia	21. Iran	40. Portugal
3. Austria	22. Ireland	41. Saudi Arabia
4. Bangladesh	23. Israel	42. Singapore
5. Belgium	24. Italy	43. South Africa
6. Brazil	25. Jordan	44. Spain
7. Canada	26. Kenya	45. Sweden
8. Chile	27. Kuwait	46. Syria
9. Denmark	28. Lebanon	47. Taiwan
10. Ecuador	29. Liberia	48. Thailand
11. Egypt	30. Malaysia	49. Turkey
12. Ethiopia	31. Mozambique	50. Uganda
13. Finland	32. Nepal	51. United Kingdom
14. France	33. Netherlands	52. United States of America
15. Germany	34. New Zealand	53. Zambia
16. Ghana	35. Nigeria	54. Zimbabwe
17. Greece	36. Norway	
18. Iceland	37. Pakistan	
19. India	38. Peru	

often than not favor de facto measures.[27] Even from the small sample of 71 countries in the La Porta et al. study we can spot problems with the de jure measure of tenure length as a proxy for judicial

[26] Source: Dataset accompanying La Porta et al. (2004), at: <http://scholar.harvard.edu/files/shleifer/files/jcb_data.xls>. La Porta et al. includes 71 countries; tenure data are not provided for Libya. Judicial tenure of high court judges is only a part of La Porta et al.'s measure of judicial independence. They also include two others: the tenure of administrative court judges and whether judicial decisions are "a source of law."

[27] See Ros-Figueroa and Staton (2014, 112), outlining 13 measures of judicial independence. Only three are de jure.

independence: chiefly, because over 75% of the countries give life tenure to their high court judges, we would say that their judges are "independent." This seems inconsistent with other evidence, whether across all the countries or for particular societies.

Let's start with the cross-national evidence. According to an authoritative source, about a third of La Porta et al.'s 71 states are non-democratic regimes.[28] The good news for studies that rely in part or in full on tenure to measure judicial independence (including La Porta et al.) is that six of the seven countries that have the lowest level of judicial independence (the shortest tenure) in Table 3.1 are not democracies. (Honduras is the exception.[29]) On the downside, of the 54 countries that give life tenure to their judges, over a quarter ($n = 14$) are not considered democracies—including Syria, Saudi Arabia, Kuwait, and Iran.[30]

Perhaps it is possible that countries with authoritarian regimes have independent judiciaries but this seems unlikely, and, in fact, de facto measures of judicial independence tell a different story. Consider Howard and Carey's study, which also contains three categories: the high court is fully independent (= 2), partially independent (= 1), or not independent (= 0).[31] Rather than rely on the constitution and other legal documents, though, Howard and Carey make use of the U.S. State Department's annual country reports on human rights practices to determine if a high court *in practice* is (1) independent of the executive and legislative and/or (2) is relatively free of corruption and bribery, and provides basic protections to criminal defendants.[32] If the country's court meets both criteria, it is independent; if neither, it is not independent; if one or the other, it is partially independent.

Comparing the de jure (La Porta et al.) and de facto (Howard and Carey) measures of judicial independence, as we do in Table 3.2, unearths some important overlaps. All of the countries with low levels of judicial independence as measured by term length also fall into Howard and Carey's lowest category, "Judiciary is Not Independent."

---

[28] The source is Polity, which is the same source that Posner and de Figueiredo used to define the types of government in countries litigating before the ICJ. See note 16. Democracies have Polity scores between +6 and +10. Note: Iceland isn't rated in the Polity data.

[29] Of the seven countries with the shortest tenure in Table 3.1, only Honduras is a democracy according to the Polity data.

[30] Polity scores between -6 and -10.

[31] Howard and Carey (2004). What we are calling a " not independent" judiciary, they label a "dependent" judiciary.

[32] The reports are available at: <http://www.state.gov/j/drl/rls/hrrpt/>. Of course, it is possible that the experts rely in part on de jure measures in making their assessments.

Table 3.2 A comparison of a de jure and a de facto measure of judicial independence. The de jure measure is the tenure of the highest court judges as reported in La Porta et al. (2004); the de facto measure comes from an analysis of U.S. State Department country reports conducted by Howard and Carey.[33]

		De Facto Measure			
		Non-independent	Partially Independent	Independent	Total
De Jure Measure	Non-independent	7	0	0	7
	Partially Independent	3	1	5	9
	Independent	12	15	26	53
	Total	22	16	31	69

Moreover, 26 of the countries with life tenure are in Howard and Carey's highest category, "Judiciary is Independent." But there are equally important disjunctures, chiefly: a greater number (27) of the life tenure societies have judiciaries that are not fully independent (according to Howard and Carey's de facto measure) than are independent (26). All in all, for only about 50% of the countries do the two measures completely align (i.e., short tenure = judiciary is not independent, medium tenure = judiciary is partially dependent, and tenure for life = independent judiciary).

This amounts to a facial validity check *across* countries. Turning to individual countries, it seems difficult to categorize the Argentine Supreme Court as independent on the basis of a constitutional guarantee of life tenure when we know from Helmke's work[34] that justices have historically left the bench (one way or another) when there is a change in the government. Life tenure there—a classic example of a parchment guarantee—might be better characterized as tenure for the life of the regime rather than for the life of the justice. On the other hand, although there are reports that promotions in the Japanese judiciary depend on pleasing the ruling party,[35] it is still hard to square

---

[33] Sources: Dataset accompanying La Porta et al. (2004) at: <http://www.economics.harvard.edu/faculty/shleifer/dataset>; Howard and Carey (2004) data provided by Jeffrey A. Staton. See also notes to Table 3.1.

[34] Helmke (2005). See also Pérez-Liñán and Castagnola (2009).

[35] Ramseyer and Rasmussen (2001).

treating Japan as less independent than, say, Argentina simply because the latter guarantees life tenure. The de facto measure may be more consistent with existing knowledge, at least for some societies.

These problems with using tenure length as a measure of judicial independence could be so severe that the measure may not pass the test of facial validity. Still, we would want to go further and compare it with other measures, as we did with Howard and Carey's measure, before we reach any firm conclusions (either over whether judicial tenure is invalid or whether Howard and Carey's is better). This is part of the process of assessing facial validity because it uses what we know—including other measures that researchers have developed—to validate the measure we have selected.[36]

Approximately Unbiased.   In addition to meeting the criteria of facial validity, measures should be approximately unbiased. A measurement procedure is unbiased if it produces measures that are right on average across repeated applications; that is, if we apply the same measurement procedure to a large number of subjects, sometimes the measure will be too large and sometimes too small, but on average it will yield the right answer. Let's suppose that we weighed 100 people on the world's most accurate scale, recorded their weight, and then asked each to step on our bathroom scale. Some might weigh a bit more and some might weigh a bit less, but as long as the errors that were too heavy were about the same in number and size as the errors that were a bit too light, we would say that our scale was unbiased.

An example of a biased procedure would be to ask people to report their weight. In all probability, some would give accurate answers, or answers that were right on average; others would respond to the social situation and underestimate their weight.[37] Since the overestimates would not be cancelled out by the underestimates, the result would be a biased measure.

In fact, often the quickest way to create a biased measure is to develop a procedure that relies in a biased way on responses from the

[36] Ros-Figueroa and Staton (2014), among others (see, e.g., Adcock and Collier, 2001), refer to this as convergent validation. Performing it requires a comparison of different measures of the same concept to see if they yield similar results.

[37] See, e.g., Andrade et al. (2012), showing that about a third of the respondents (Mexican college applications between the ages of 18 and 20) were actually overweight but less than 20% perceived they were overweight. And although only 7.4% of the respondents were underweight, 15.9% reported that they were underweight.

population under analysis. Imagine we asked judges whether they were independent. Just as people tend to underestimate their weight, we suspect that many judges too would likely overestimate their degree of independence proclaiming that they vote on the basis of what the law—and not the government or public opinion—demands.[38] More generally, as it turns out, asking someone to identify his or her motive is one of the worst methods of measuring motive.[39] Asking others, though, is not necessarily an invalid strategy; and scholars have developed several measures of judicial independence that rely on the perceptions of experts.[40] Some might argue that the Howard and Carey approach falls into this category because it relies on expert reports produced by the U.S. State Department.

Efficiency. Bearing a relationship to unbiasedness, efficiency is the third approach to assessing validity. Efficiency helps us choose among several unbiased measures, such that we would choose the one that minimized errors. If we had two bathroom scales that were each unbiased but one registered smaller errors in any one measurement, we would choose that scale.

To see the implications for empirical research, let's return to the problem of measuring judicial independence. As we now know, La Porta et al. rely (in part) on the length of tenure of high court judges,[41] while Howard and Carey make use of information gleaned from official reports on whether the judiciary is (1) independent of

---

[38] Actually, we don't have to guess. In a survey conducted by the State Bar of Texas, a U.S. state that elects its judges, fewer than half of the state's judges believed that campaign contributions had "fairly" or "very" significant influence on judicial decisions, while 69% of court personnel and 79% of attorneys said that campaign contributions had a "fairly" or "very" significant influence on judicial decisions. Survey at: <http://www.courts.state. tx.us/pubs/publictrust/execsum.htm>. Likewise a survey of judges in ten U.S. states where judges must be retained by the public to keep their seat found that only 27.6% of the judges believed that retention elections make them more responsive to public opinion (Aspin and Hall, 1994). This is despite a fair amount of social science evidence indicating that judges who must face the electorate tend to reach decisions designed to increase their chances of reelection or retention (see, e.g., Berdejó and Yuchtman, 2013; Canes-Wrone et al., 2012; Gordon and Huber, 2007). Just as some people do not underestimate their weight there are exceptions, as the 27.6% figure indicates. Perhaps they believe it or perhaps (ironically) they are afraid to say otherwise out of fear of reprisal.

[39] See, e.g., Nisbett and Wilson (1977); Rahn et al. (1994).

[40] For a list, see the appendix to Ros-Figueroa and Staton (2014).

[41] La Porta et al. (2004).

the executive and legislative and (2) relatively free of corruption and bribery and provides basic protections to criminal defendants.[42]

We know from their scholarly studies (and our own analysis of the data) that both measures, on average, are able to predict the level of economic freedom in various countries, that is, they will yield the same answer for at least some societies. But we also know that sometimes the predictions produced by the tenure measure will be way off,[43] perhaps because it omits important information about judicial independence: that sometimes constitutional provisions are mere parchment guarantees and so we must consider how they work in fact. Discarding such information is the definition of inefficiency.

This is why we suggest that whenever researchers are confronted with two unbiased measures, they should normally select the more efficient one. Individual applications of the measurement procedure based on more information yield measures that cluster more narrowly around the true answer than do the ones based on less. The result is that any one application of the measure with more information will be likely to yield an answer closer to the truth than any one application of the measure with less information.

* * * * * * * *

As we have now seen, face validity, unbiasedness, and efficiency are the criteria we use to assess the validity of a measure—in our running example, tenure length as a measure of judicial independence. Worth reiterating, though, is that even after we complete this process, we still may be unable to conclude whether any particular measure is more valid than any other precisely because there is no gold standard measure of judicial independence. More to the point, it is entirely possible that "there is no single best choice of measurement,"[44] whether for judicial independence or any other concept.

For these reasons, scholars may create one measure to tap each of their independent and dependent variables—the measure that they think is especially reliable and valid—but in practice they will likely develop many more. The hope is that regardless of which measure they use, their statistical analysis will return the same (or similar) results.

---

[42] Howard and Carey (2004).

[43] For three of their four measures of economic freedom, the Howard and Carey measure explains more of the variation in economic freedom and produces smaller errors.

[44] Ríos-Figueroa and Staton (2014).

At the very least, they will be able to answer a question that emerges about all empirical studies, whether in the courtroom, legislative halls, or faculty commons: "If you had used measure A instead of measure B, would the same results obtain?"

But we are getting ahead of ourselves. Before moving to statistical analysis, which this question most directly implicates, we need to consider issues associated with data: collecting and coding them. We take these up in the next two chapters.

PART II

Collecting and Coding Data

In Chapter 1 we introduced the metaphor of two slides to describe empirical research. On the first slide, we write down our hunches about the answer to a research question, as well as the measures we've developed to interrogate our hunch; the other slide includes the data we've collected to answer the question. The (usual) hope is that when we put the two slides together—that is, when we analyze the data—they will align: that the data supports our hunches.

In the following two chapters we turn to the makings of that second slide: collecting and coding data. Here, we merely want to offer a simple though crucial piece of advice that applies to all the remaining aspects of empirical research: researchers must keep careful records of how they go about collecting, coding, and analyzing their data, and evaluators of the research should not hesitate to ask for their records.

Put more generally, all empirical studies should adhere to the *replication standard*: anyone should be able to understand, evaluate, build on, or reproduce the research without any additional information from the author.[1] This standard does not actually require anyone to replicate the results of a study; it only requires that researchers provide information—whether in the study itself, on the internet, or in some other publicly available or accessible form—sufficient to replicate the results in principle.[2]

Why is such documentation a requisite step in conducting empirical research, regardless of whether the work is qualitative or quantitative in nature? There are two answers to this question, with the first centering on the ability of outsiders to assess the research and its

---

[1] We adopt and adapt some of this material from Epstein and King (2002).
[2] Epstein and Clarke (2010); Hazelton et al. (2010); King (1995).

conclusions. In a broad sense, the point of the replication standard is to ensure that research held out as authoritative—a published article or book, an expert witness's report, a consultant's study—stands alone so that readers can consume what it has to offer without any necessary connection with, further information from, or beliefs about the status or reputation of the author. The replication standard keeps empirical inquiry above the level of ad hominem attacks or unquestioning acceptance of arguments by authority figures.

To provide an example of why this is so important, recall the study that we, your authors, conducted to determine whether female and male judges reach different decisions in similar cases.[3] Now suppose that this was the description of our procedures:

Before we started the study, we recognized that results finding no difference between male and female judges wouldn't be very interesting. So, to ensure that we found differences, we went to the cases and located those in which males and females (serving on the same panel) disagreed; we ignored the cases in which they agreed.

Of course, this statement is ludicrous. No researcher would ever write such words. But do they proceed in this way without saying so? To answer this question, readers need to know precisely what the researcher did in practice so that they can decide what merits their attention, what is worth further research, and whether it makes sense to base future public policy or law on the study. For these reasons, we were very explicit about the procedures in our gender research:

Our data on judges' votes come from Sunstein et al.'s project on the U.S. federal appellate courts.[4] The Sunstein team developed a database containing the decisions of appellate court judges in 13 areas: abortion, affirmative action, disability law, campaign finance, capital punishment, the Contract Clause, environmental protection, federalism, piercing the corporate veil, sex discrimination in employment, sexual harassment, the Takings Clause, and race discrimination. Sunstein et al. provide the information necessary to replicate their procedures;[5] the appendix to our study provides the number of observations and years of inclusion for each of the 13 areas.[6]

---

[3] Boyd et al. (2010).
[4] Sunstein et al. (2006).
[5] Sunstein et al. (2006, footnotes 20–35).
[6] Boyd et al. (2010, 397). Edited for pedagogical purposes.

Without statements to this effect, researchers leave readers without a clue of how to interpret their results—other than by an illegitimate appeal to authority and their reputations. This is precisely what the replication standard is designed to prevent.

Which takes us to the second reason why scholars must record and make their procedures public: those procedures may, and in most instances do, influence the outcomes reported in research. The sample of cases we selected led us to include some (those falling into one of the 13 areas) and exclude others (those outside the 13 areas). Because we based our results only on the cases we included, a selection procedure that excluded some of the cases we included and included some we excluded might produce different findings. The same holds for any study that seeks to make claims or inferences about the real world.

The replication standard applies to all the phases of the research process, though as you can probably tell it has special relevance to collecting data. Regardless of how researchers perform this task—and there are many approaches, as you'll soon see—valid inferences require information about the process researchers used to generate their data.[7] A study that gives insufficient information about how the investigator came to observe the data cannot be replicated and thus stands in violation of the replication standard. Equally important, it breaks the assumed link between the facts we have and the facts we would like to know, and so is of no use in making inferences about the population. Finally, only by understanding the data-generation process can researchers determine whether bias afflicts their inferences.

Because we cover these points in some detail in the next chapter, suffice it here to provide a simple example of the problems that can accrue when researchers are not clear or do not record the procedures they used to generate their data. Suppose the Elkins team[8] described their procedure for studying the endurance of constitutions in this way: "We started with a list of 1,000 constitutions and read 100 of them to understand why some last longer than others." It turns out that this (fake!) description of Elkins et al.'s procedures is no better than the fake description of our study above, even though the bias seems more overt in ours. In fact, if this were the description of their study (again, *it is not*), we might suspect that certain predilections inflict

---

[7] See King et al. (1994, 23).
[8] Elkins et al. (2009).

their sample of 100—for example, because Elkins and his colleagues work at English-speaking universities, a bias toward constitutions available in English. We would be unable to rule out this possibility or any other type of bias because the one-sentence description provides virtually no information about the data-generation process. Think about all we don't know. How did they produce the list of 1,000 constitutions? What time period and countries does it cover? How did they select the sample of 100? And on and on.

The lack of answers to these questions would not affect the researchers' ability to draw conclusions from their sample of 100 constitutions (which are probably of little interest in and of themselves), but it would impede their ability to draw inferences about all constitutions, much less the 1,000 with which they started. The only link between the population (all constitutions for all time) and the ultimate sample (the 100) is the process by which the data came to be observed. All inferential methods that seek to learn about the population with data from a sample require knowledge of this process. Without this knowledge, we are left making unjustified theoretical assumptions about easily knowable facts and substantive conclusions that are far more uncertain than necessary.

Among our goals in the two chapters to follow is to provide this knowledge; it is that important for conducting and evaluating empirical research. We start with collecting data and then turn to coding the information so that researchers can analyze it.

4

Collecting Data

The topic of this chapter—collecting data—centers on deceptively simple questions: how should researchers select the observations to include in their studies, and how should we evaluate their choices? We know that Elkins et al. are interested in why some constitutions endure longer than others.[1] How should they decide which constitutions in what countries to examine, and what criteria should we use to appraise their decision? Or to return to our project exploring whether male and female judges reach different decisions:[2] Which judges and cases—and how many judges and cases—should we include in our study?

Just as we saw in Chapters 2 and 3, the answers to these questions turn not on anecdotes, guesses, or impressions but rather on rules or best practices. We describe many in the course of discussing the four topics that are central to the task of collecting data: (1) Identifying the Target Population, (2) Locating or Generating Data, (3) Deciding How Much Data to Collect, and (4) Avoiding Selection Bias.

As you read about them, keep in mind the replication rule we discussed a few pages back. This chapter provides the knowledge necessary to adhere to it as it applies to amassing data.

4.1 Identifying the Target Population

Way back in Chapter 1, we explained that making inferences is the primary goal of empirical work. In a nutshell, the idea is to use facts

---

[1] Elkins et al. (2009).
[2] Boyd et al. (2010).

we know (or can gather) to draw conclusions about facts we don't know (or didn't collect). Suppose we were interested in learning about what all adults living in Europe today think about gun control. Making an inference about their views would involve examining a *sample* (of say 1,000 European adults) to generalize about the *population* (all 401.3 million adults living in Europe[3]).

When we collect data to make inferences, a critical step is to identify this population, known as the target population (or "population of interest"). This is the population about which we would like to make the inference. It is *all* people, cases, judges, constitutions, countries, or other units in a specified timeframe on which we would collect information if we had unlimited time and resources. If the goal is to understand what all adult Europeans think about gun control then, once again, the population of interest is all adult Europeans. Likewise, if the objective is to estimate the average *age* of every existing *constitution* in every *country today*, then the population of interest is all existing constitutions in all countries today. The task for the researcher is to define, plainly and precisely, the concepts of "age," "constitution," "county," and "today." In principle if not in practice, it should be possible to collect data on all constitutions in this population, and the definition of the population should be sufficiently clear that no ambiguity exists as to what is included and excluded.

Identifying the target population may seem a trivial matter but often it is not. Return to our study of whether males and female judges reach different decisions. To conduct it, and for others to evaluate our results, we must clarify the target population. Do we want to make an inference about all male and female judges in all countries for all years? If so, then the population of interest is "all judges" in "all countries" for "all years"—and we would have to define what we mean by these terms (and draw a sample that represented this population, as we discuss below). Or are we interested only in U.S. appellate court judges serving between, say, 1990 and 2010? We'd still have to be clear about the terms (e.g., does appellate include only the courts of appeals or the Supreme Court too? Is "serving" limited to judges who are "active" or does it also include those who have taken "senior status"?[4]). But the target

---

[3] Adults are between the ages of 15 and 65. Source: <http://www.wolframalpha.com>.

[4] In the United States, federal life-tenured judges may take "senior status" if their age plus years of service add up to 80, provided they are 65 years of age and have served on the bench for at least ten years. When judges take senior status, they free up their seat on whatever court they are serving but they continue to hear cases (though usually fewer than they would if they kept their active status) and perform other judicial duties.

population would be very different, as would the sample we would draw and the inferences we might reach. If we conducted the first study appropriately, we could draw conclusions about all judges for all time; for the second, our inferences would be limited to U.S. appellate judges serving between 1990 and 2010.

How do researchers make these decisions? In part, they should follow from the research question. If the question is why some constitutions endure for decades, even centuries, and others fail within a few years, then the target population must be something broader than the "U.S. Constitution," which has been in effect since 1789. Identifying the target population also relates to theory. In our study of gender and judging, life tenure plays an important role because we assume that judges do not need to please the public or elected officials to retain their jobs. Because we proceed from this premise, we should restrict our target population to societies that give judges lifelong tenure. Finally, data play a role. It might seem attractive to generalize about every constitution ever promulgated or all judges with life tenure, but if the data are difficult or even impossible to collect, this too will force the researcher to narrow the target population.

For all these reasons, identifying the target of inference is a crucial decision that researchers must make before they collect even the first piece of data. Investigators, not to mention their audience, should never have to guess about the population of interest and, ultimately, the breadth of the inference the study can reach.

4.2 Locating and Generating Data

Identifying the target population is only the first step. Thinking through the project's data needs and then locating (or generating) the data come next. We devote this section to the latter, but we should say a word or two about data needs. No more than that is necessary because measures of the observable implications will often dictate (or, at the least, imply) the requisite data. To see this, turn back to Figure 3.1, which outlines an observable implication (and measures) from the La Porta et al. project.[5] The data needs are obvious. The researchers require information on the tenure of judges and the legal steps necessary to create a new business. Likewise, to test the hypothesis

---

[5] La Porta et al. (2004).

that constitutions that are more specific are more likely to endure, the Elkins et al. study demands data drawn from constitutions.[6]

In short, from their measures researchers usually know the data they require. The more challenging matters boil down to locating or generating the data, and it is to those that we now turn.

4.2.1 Locating Data

Scholars new to empirical research often tell us that their project requires the collection of lots and lots of data (which they almost invariably want to generate through surveys or interviews). Our response is always the same: "Are you sure?". This reflects the fact that an enormous number of datasets relating to empirical legal studies already exist, and we strongly recommend that you investigate whether someone has already amassed the information you need prior to launching an expensive and time-consuming data collection project.

Before identifying the types of datasets out there, let's clarify what we mean by a *dataset*. It is simply a collection of data that someone has organized in a form that is susceptible to empirical analysis. Datasets relating to law come in different forms—and formats (e.g., Excel, Stata, SPSS)—and we consider these soon.[7] For now, Figure 4.1 supplies a snapshot of a dataset familiar to you. It's the dataset from the La Porta et al. study on the relationship between judicial independence and economic freedom,[8] which, it turns out, is fairly typical of datasets centering on law and legal institutions. Note that the units of study (often called the *units of analysis*) are on the rows. Here they are countries,[9] but they could be people, cases, constitutions, and so on. Further note that the variables are in the columns, such that here, they supply information on the number of steps that a business must take to obtain legal status (the dependent variable) and on the tenure of the highest court judges in each country (an independent variable) ($0 = $ less than six years; $1 = $ more than six years but not for life; $2 = $ life tenure). The dots represent missing data. Perhaps they couldn't find information on the number of steps in Algeria or perhaps it doesn't exist.

---

[6] Elkins et al. (2009).

[7] In Chapter 5 we discuss statistical software. The book's website has even more information and tutorials about using statistical software.

[8] La Porta et al. (2004).

[9] We show only the first 20 of the 71 countries in the dataset.

	country	steps	tenure
1	Algeria	.	0
2	Argentina	13	2
3	Australia	2	2
4	Austria	8	2
5	Bangladesh	.	2
6	Belgium	7	2
7	Brazil	11	2
8	Canada	2	2
9	Chile	10	2
10	China, PR	10	0
11	Colombia	17	1
12	Cuba	.	0
13	Denmark	3	2
14	Ecuador	16	2
15	Egypt	11	2
16	Ethiopia	.	2
17	Finland	3	2
18	France	15	2
19	Germany, FR	8	2
20	Ghana	10	2

Figure 4.1 A snippet from the La Porta et al. dataset. Countries, the units in their study, are on the rows; the variables are on the columns. steps: the number of steps for a start-up to obtain legal status. Tenure (of the highest court judges): 0 = less than six years; 1 = more than six years but not for life; 2 = life tenure; · represents missing values.

La Porta et al.'s study is an example of a dataset created for a specific project, and these abound. In Chapter 1, we also discussed "multi-user" datasets—those designed to answer many research questions rather than being tailored to a particular study. Either way, good places to check for existing datasets are repositories or archives, such as the

Inter-University Consortium for Political and Social Research.[10] You could also check the book's website, where we include a list of existing databases that cover courts throughout the world and their decisions, features of constitutions, measures of governance, and public opinion in the United States, Europe, and Latin America, among other regions. Finally, a well-formulated internet search can unearth datasets that scholars maintain on their own websites.

However they conduct their search, the larger point is that it is entirely possible (even probable in some areas of empirical legal studies) that researchers can locate a database suitable to their goals without having to invest in costly from-scratch data-collection efforts. And even if an existing dataset doesn't house every variable the analyst requires, it can nonetheless serve as a foundation for the research project. Suppose you were interested in studying the Supreme Court of India. The National High Courts Judicial Database contains a good deal of information on the Indian Court's decisions between 1970 and 2000.[11] Following the Database's protocols you could update or even backdate the dataset. You could also create new variables. For example, while the Database provides information on how the judges voted and whether they wrote an opinion, it does not include data on the judges' background characteristics (e.g., age, gender, previous positions). Because this information is available on the Indian Supreme Court's website[12] (and perhaps from other sources), you could add it to the dataset.

Finally, even if you can't find a dataset ready for analysis, you may well be able to locate the information you need to build your own dataset. This should not come as much of a surprise. Each day the world generates 2.5 quintillion bytes of data,[13] at least some of which pertains to

---

[10] <http://www.icpsr.umich.edu/>. The book's website lists others.

[11] The National High Courts Database (<http://artsandsciences.sc.edu/poli/juri/highcts. htm>) is a multi-user resource that provides information on decisions rendered by the high courts in 11 countries. The courts (and years covered) are: High Court of Australia (1969–2003); Supreme Court of Canada (1969–2003); Supreme Court of India (1970–2000); Supreme Court of Namibia (1990–1998); Supreme Court of the Philippines (1970–2003); South Africa—Supreme Court of Appeal (1970–2000) and Constitutional Court (1995–2000); Court of Appeal of Tanzania (1983–1998); Judicial Committee of the House of Lords (Law Lords) of the United Kingdom (1970–2002); Supreme Court of the United States (1953–2005); Supreme Court of Zambia (1973–1997); Supreme Court of Zimbabwe (1989–2000).

[12] <http://supremecourtofindia.nic.in/judges/judges.htm>.

[13] Zikopoulos et al. (2013).

law and legal institutions. People file lawsuits, governments promulgate laws, police make arrests, innovators apply for patents (and offices issue them), and on and on. Governments and agencies have compiled at least some of this information, including data on population demographics, economic indicators, and court caseloads. For example, the statistical office of the European Union (Eurostat) maintains data on crime, finance, international trade, and the environment, to name just a few areas.[14] The U.S. Central Intelligence Agency releases annual fact books on the history, government, geography, and military (among other topics) of 250 world entities.[15] And the United Nations[16] and World Bank[17] collect a wealth of cross-national data. Many countries also retain their own databanks that house useful information.

Of course, it should (almost) go without saying, that simply because a dataset or data exist doesn't mean you should rely on it; you should first learn how the data came to be observed. For these purposes, reproducing the data isn't necessary (although you might want to do so to assess its reliability, as we'll discuss shortly). But you must understand how you could reproduce the data or dataset—that is, adhere to the replication rule—if you so desired. This requires treating each piece of information in the dataset as if it were part of a chain of evidence, asking how the variables were generated, and ultimately whether they are reliable and valid.

To highlight the point, let's reconsider the La Porta et al. dataset (again, partially reproduced in Figure 4.1). We'd certainly want to know how the researchers created the two variables, steps and tenure. It turns out that steps (the number of procedures for a start-up to obtain legal status) was generated by another team.[18] So we'd need to determine how this other team amassed the data. La Porta et al. themselves created tenure (the tenure of judges on the country's highest court) from constitutions and other sources. But knowing this doesn't end the matter. Before we used their dataset, we'd want to know more; for example, in what year did they look at the constitutions? We

---

[14] <http://epp.eurostat.ec.europa.eu/portal/page/portal/eurostat/home>.
[15] <https://www.cia.gov/library/publications/the-world-factbook/index.html>. Along similar lines, the U.S. State Department issues annual human rights reports for each country. These are the reports that Howard and Carey (2004) used to create their measure of judicial independence (see Chapter 3).
[16] <http://data.un.org>.
[17] <http://data.worldbank.org>.
[18] Djankov et al. (2003).

know from Elkins et al.'s study[19] that in some countries, constitutions don't last very long, making the year an important piece of information. Also, we know the dataset contains 71 countries even though there are nearly 200. Why these 71 countries? How did La Porta et al. select them? (Questions of this sort implicate sampling, which we take up momentarily.)

Once we've established the chain of evidence for the data, we should move to the matters of reliability and validity that we covered in the last chapter. Assessing reliability might lead us to draw a small sample of the data in an effort to reproduce it, as we suggest above. Validity also implicates the quality of the data, but it has greater bearing on the question of whether the particular measure developed by one researcher is valid for your project. Along these lines, and as we hope Chapter 3 made clear, we agree with Collier and Adcock: "Specific [measurement] choices are often best understood and justified in light of the theoretical framework, analytic goals, and context of research involved in any particular study."[20]

Running through this inventory is crucial when researchers rely on existing datasets or data. Always in the back of their mind should be the old adage "garbage in, garbage out." Researchers should also understand that they, and not the original data collectors, will be held responsible for problems with the data in their studies even if they didn't collect the information. Imagine a study that relied on a government's recording of its per capita rate of violent crime to conclude that the rate had increased by 200% over the last 50 years. This is an important finding—unless of course the researcher failed to realize that, say, during that period the government expanded its definition of violent crime to include not just physical violence against a person but also stealing by force (or threat of force).

4.2.2 Generating Data

All the advice in the previous section applies to any data that researchers themselves generate, which they may need to do if, even after a massive search, the information they require simply does not exist. How researchers go about creating their own data varies from project to project depending on the questions, theory, observable implications,

---

[19] Elkins et al. (2009).
[20] Collier and Adcock (1999, 539). See also Ros-Figueroa and Staton (2014).

and measures—though four approaches are common in empirical legal research: *performing experiments*, *surveying*, *observing*, and *analyzing text*.

Before describing each, a couple of provisos are in order. First, the strategies are not mutually exclusive as we'll see, nor should they be for the reasons we discuss in the next section on how much data to collect. Secondly, we keep the descriptions brief as a way of telegraphing a cautionary message: making effective use of any data collection strategy requires far more than we can capture in this one book; it requires you to learn about the specific strategy through detailed study because deploying them successfully requires specialized knowledge. Without this knowledge, you are bound to waste time and resources. We hope the material that follows makes this crystal clear.

With these qualifications in mind, let's turn to the approaches themselves: (1) experiments; (2) surveys; (3) observation; (4) textual analysis.

Experiments.   Of the four, experiments are perhaps the least likely in empirical legal research (though this may be changing), and proper experiments are virtually non-existent.[21] In a proper experiment, the researcher randomly selects a large number of the units of study (e.g., people) and randomly assigns them to either a treatment or control group.[22] For example, in a study of the effectiveness of a drug, some people will be chosen at random to receive the drug (the treatment condition) and others might receive another drug that is commonly used for the disease (often called the control condition).[23]

Because this comes the closest to the superhero thought experiment we outlined in Chapter 1, it is the "gold standard" for generating data. But, once again, you can see why a proper experiment is so rare in studies of law and legal institutions. We can't draw a random sample of a large number of judges and assign them a gender (as we would have liked to do in our study); we can't randomly assign to countries an

---

[21] In a Westlaw search of the academic literature, the word "experiment" appears 2,180 times in 2002 and 5,335 in 2012. This is an increase of 145%, which may be suggestive of an increase in experiments in empirical legal studies.

[22] In more complicated experiments there might be more than one treatment group, or there might be variation within the treatment group.

[23] Ho et al. (2007). As the text suggests, key to a proper experiment is random selection and then random assignment to the treatment values. In the next section, we discuss (and define) random selection in the context of drawing a sample from the relevant population. Random assignment to treatment is similar except that it concerns the assignment of people (or other units) in the (randomly drawn) sample to different treatments.

independent or a dependent judiciary (as the La Porta et al. team might have desired); and we can't bestow on some states a specific or more general constitution to determine which is more durable (an impossible dream for Elkins et al.).

Still, some legal phenomena are susceptible to experimentation, and there are ingenious cases of experimental research in this sphere. Zink and his colleagues were interested in the question of whether people are more likely to agree with a unanimous, rather than a divided judicial decision.[24] Rather than ask people directly, the Zink team ran an experiment. They created two newspaper articles describing the same case (and were otherwise identical), except that in one article the decision was reported as unanimous and in the other as divided. The researchers then randomly assigned undergraduate students to read one article or the other. It turned out that the students were more likely to agree with (and accept) the decision that was reported as unanimous.[25] Recall too from Chapter 1 that Rachlinski et al. performed experiments on judges who were attending various conferences. The team asked the judges to read vignettes of court cases and then reach a decision. In some vignettes, Rachlinski et al. varied the race of one of the parties;[26] in others, they were interested to see if judges fall prey to cognitive biases. (They do.) As a final example, consider Greiner and Pattanayak's study of the efficacy of legal representation.[27] This is a bit different from the first two because the researchers conducted their experiment not in a lab, a classroom, or at a conference but rather in the "field."[28] When potential clients phoned a legal aid bureau operated out of the Harvard Law School, the research team randomly assigned the clients to one of two conditions: they received an offer of representation or they did not (and were given the names of other legal service providers in the area).[29] The researchers then looked to see whether an offer of representation increased the probability that the client would win. (It did not.)

---

[24] Zink et al. (2009). Their study also considered whether the court was reported as following or overturning precedent.

[25] And that did not overturn precedent. See note 24.

[26] Rachlinski et al. (2008).

[27] Greiner and Pattanayak (2012).

[28] For a general analysis of field experiments, see Harrison and List (2004).

[29] The clients were all told about the study when they called. For more details, see Greiner and Pattanayak (2012, 2143–4).

None of these three is a "proper" experiment.[30] The teams did not randomly select subjects (people or judges) from the population of people or judges; they instead relied on samples of convenience: in Zink et al.'s study, students at their school;[31] in Rachlinski et al.'s study, judges attending conferences;[32] and in Greiner and Pattanayak's study, people who asked a law school clinic for assistance.[33] Nonetheless, the research teams benefitted from the nice properties of experiments because they were able to randomly assign their subjects to different conditions—for example, to the newspaper article that reported either a unanimous or divided decision. Assuming that random assignment "worked," meaning that the students who read the unanimous article and those who read the divided article were similar on variables that might also affect their inclination to agree with a court decision (e.g., their attitudes toward the underlying issue in the case), the researchers didn't need to control for those variables. (This is an assumption that researchers can check, as we'll see in Chapter 9.)

Experiments in empirical legal research have their share of detractors. Some question whether college students—the guinea pigs in many of these studies—are representative of the target population (say, all people in a given society). Using subjects in the population of interest, as the Rachlinski team does, deflects some of these criticisms. It is one thing to demonstrate that undergraduates or even law students exhibit certain biases;[34] it is quite another to show that actual judges do too.[35] Still, some contend that the Rachlinksi et al. experiments are artificial because the case vignettes don't come close to approximating cases in

[30] But they are better than so-called "natural experiments, a study 'in which assignment of treatments to subjects is haphazard and possibly random'" (Sekhon and Titiunik, 2012, 35). In empirical legal research, these sorts of studies often (though not always) explore whether a "naturally" occurring intervention—a change in laws or legal standards, for example—generated change in behavior. For examples, see Drago et al. (2009) (on the effect of an Italian clemency bill on recidivism) and Coates (2012) (on the effect of a Supreme Court decision, *Citizens United v. Federal Elections Commission*, 558 U.S. 310 (2010) on corporate political activity). Whether these are "natural," "experiments," both, or neither is a question that requires testing (see Sekhon and Titiunik, 2012).

More to the point: though properly constructed studies of this sort (or any other, for that matter) can yield valuable information, we agree with those who say that the term "natural experiment" is an oxymoron. That's because natural experiments lack the hallmark of an experiment—random assignment to treatment values.

[31] Zink et al. (2009).
[32] Rachlinski et al. (2008).
[33] Greiner and Pattanayak (2012).
[34] E.g., Braman (2009).
[35] Guthrie et al. (2007).

a real courtroom.[36] Greiner and Pattanayak's field experiment, while an important advance, is not necessarily immune to similar charges. Some critics claim that it fails to replicate the way real lawyers operate because real lawyers usually consider whether representation will affect the outcome before they agree to take a case; here, the student-lawyers were forced to "cede[] to a randomizer control over which among the eligible set would receive an offer of representation."[37] Moreover, because field experiments are conducted in the real world, and not a lab, the world can conspire to create headaches for the researcher. In Greiner and Pattanayak's study, the possibility existed that clients offered representation would decline it; and that those rejected would find it elsewhere.[38]

Surveys. A second data-collection method, surveying, is more common, not only in scholarly research but also in the courtroom. Diamond notes that at least in the United States:[39]

... courts have accepted survey evidence on a variety of issues. In a case involving allegations of discrimination in jury panel composition, the defense team surveyed prospective jurors to obtain their age, race, education, ethnicity, and income distribution. Surveys of employees or prospective employees are used to support or refute claims of employment discrimination. . . . In ruling on the admissibility of scientific claims, courts have examined surveys of scientific experts to assess the extent to which the theory or technique has received widespread acceptance. Some courts have admitted surveys in obscenity cases to provide evidence about community standards. Requests for a change of venue on grounds of jury pool bias often are backed by evidence from a survey of jury-eligible respondents in the area of the original venue. The plaintiff in an antitrust suit conducted a survey to assess what characteristics, including price, affected consumers' preferences. The survey was offered as one way to estimate damages.

---

[36] As we noted in Chapter 1 (see note 27), these complaints center on the experiments' ecological validity.

[37] Symposium on "What Difference Representation," <http://www.concurringopinions.com/archives/category/representation-symposium>. Greiner and Pattanayak (2012, 2202) address this critique in their paper and report that they are skeptical but nonetheless "actively pursuing" a study that would respond to it.

[38] See Greiner and Pattanayak (2012, 2121).

[39] Diamond (2011, 365). We omit the original footnotes, which point to case examples.

The surveys used in these cases, and in scholarly work more generally, have several common features. First and foremost, they involve generating data about people's attitudes, opinions, behavior, motivations, and emotions by asking people about their attitudes, opinions, behavior, motivations, and emotions. To provide an example, consider a survey commissioned by a company and introduced in a trademark dispute, *Victoria's Secret Stores Brand Management, Inc. v. Sexy Hair Concepts, LLC.*[40] In a nutshell, Sexy Hair Concepts (SHC) had secured a U.S. trademark for several hair care products, all of which used the word SEXY (e.g., SEXY HIGHLIGHTS, SEXY HAIR, STRONG SEXY HAIR). When Victoria's Secret Stores (best known for retailing lingerie) applied to register the mark SO SEXY, SHC objected on the ground that people would be confused between its SEXY mark and SO SEXY. After a trademark board denied Victoria's Secret's application,[41] the company appealed the decision to a U.S. federal court where it introduced the results of a survey designed by a consultant to explore whether the word SEXY had attained a secondary meaning in relation to hair care products. The key question on the survey was: "Do you associate the word SEXY with hair care products from more than one company, one company, no company, you don't know, or you have no opinion?"[42]

Gibson et al.'s study provides another example of survey research.[43] To learn about what people think about their courts, Gibson and his colleagues fielded a survey in 18 countries, asking each respondent: "From what you have read or heard, would you say that you are very satisfied or not satisfied with the way [the highest court of the country] has been working."[44]

Although there are obvious differences in the goals and breadth of the two surveys, in both the researchers were trying to gauge public sentiment. There's another commonality too. Each survey asked respondents the *same* question. Now, of course it's possible that people interpreted the question differently—a point we'll return to shortly—but at least the question to which they responded was the

---

[40] Not reported in F. Supp. 2d. The Westlaw cite is 2009 WL 959775 (S.D.N.Y. Apr. 8, 2009).

[41] The Trademark Trial and Appeal Board, which is a body within the U.S. Patent and Trademark Office.

[42] In Part III, we make use of this survey to illustrate how to analyze tabular data.

[43] Gibson et al. (1998).

[44] This was just one of the questions they asked. For others, see Gibson et al. (1998).

same.[45] Standardization is key if the researcher is to make inferences about the target population. To see this, imagine if Gibson et al. asked some people whether they were "very satisfied or not satisfied with their high court" and others whether they were "very satisfied or not satisfied with the way their high court treated criminal defendants." Both questions are fine standing alone, but combining the two isn't a good idea. Some respondents might be very satisfied with their high court generally but not with the way the judges decide criminal cases. These respondents would answer "very satisfied" to the first question but "not satisfied" to the second. And vice versa for people who aren't satisfied with their court generally but satisfied with its handling of criminal disputes.

On the other hand, some standardized surveys, while not necessarily asking subjects different questions, *deliberately* change the situation to which the subjects are asked to respond. This is the idea of embedding an experiment in a survey, and it is increasingly common because it takes advantage of the nice features of surveys (primarily the large number of subjects) and of experiments (the ability to randomly assign subjects to various conditions). An example is Eigen's study of compliance with contracts.[46] Eigen hypothesized that people who participate in the negotiation over a contract will be more likely to comply with it. To test it, he ran a internet-based experiment in which individuals were randomly assigned to sign one of four kinds of contracts, ranging from form-adhesive agreements (those that are "unilaterally drafted and offered on a take-it-or-leave-basis") to those that gave room for greater negotiation on the subject's part.[47] (The study validated the hypothesis.)

These are some common features of surveys but there are differences too, especially in the strategies (or modes) survey researchers use to

---

[45] It is certainly possible to gauge people's beliefs and attitudes without asking them a standardized set of questions; the researcher could conduct open-ended or unstructured interviews. In contrast to standard survey research, in unstructured interviews the questions are not established in advance but can be adapted to the respondent; the interview itself can be conversational and informal. Using the various approaches to text analysis we describe below, it is possible to generate data useful for inference from unstructured interviews (much as it is possible to do so from observational methods). Still, it seems to us and many others, that the greater value in this approach lies in theory building, developing other methods of data collection (including standardized surveys), and generating observable implications (Rubin and Rubin, 2004; Weiss, 1995).

[46] Eigen (2012).

[47] Eigen (2012, 67).

generate their data.[48] Sometimes they conduct in-person interviews with the respondents; sometimes they mail them a survey or contact them by phone. Growing in popularity are surveys conducted via the internet (Eigen's is an example), corresponding to the increasing number of people who have access to it.[49] Generating a sample from which to draw a valid inference can be challenging for internet-based surveys (we'll get to drawing samples in the next section) but researchers have devised clever solutions—for example, asking people randomly selected for a mail or telephone survey to fill out the questionnaire online; or embedding experiments in internet surveys so that they need not worry too much about whether the sample is representative. Again, Eigen's study provides an example, but there are others.[50]

Surveys have some obvious advantages. We already mentioned one: for researchers who require information on attitudes, opinions, behavior, motivations, and emotions of a *large* number of people, surveys may be the only way to gather the data. Another is that researchers can often field surveys quickly, meaning that they can be used to capture attitudes toward events almost immediately after they occur (or before if the date is known). Less than two weeks after the U.S. Supreme Court handed down its historic decision upholding the Affordable Care Act (i.e., the 2010 health care law or "Obamacare"),[51] the *New York Times* and CBS News (a major TV network in the United States) fielded a survey. Among the interesting results was that only about 30% of the respondents believed that the Court's decision "was mainly based on legal analysis," while 53% thought that it "was mainly based on the justices' personal or political views."[52]

---

[48] For a recent review of the various modes, see Couper (2011). Note that in addition to the sorts of surveys we mention in the text, the types of questions can vary. In many, perhaps most, surveys, there are at least some "closed-ended" questions. Gibson et al. (1998) is an example: respondents can be "very satisfied" or "not satisfied" with their court. Gibson et al. could have also asked: "Please list two reasons why you are very satisfied [or not satisfied] with your high court." This is an example of an open-ended question.

[49] See, e.g., Pew Research Center, Internet Surveys, <http://www.people-press.org/methodology/collecting-survey-data/internet-surveys/>.

[50] Researchers have used survey experiments to study topics as diverse as public opinion on eminent domain policies (Nadler and Diamond, 2008), the persuasive ability of the Russian judiciary (Baird and Javeline, 2007), and the effect of high-profile campaigns on the legitimacy of U.S. state courts (Gibson, 2008, 2012).

[51] *National Federation of Independent Business v. Sebelius*, 132 S.Ct. 2566 (2012).

[52] Poll conducted between July 11–16, 2012. Available at: <http://www.anytimes.com/2012/07/19/us/politics/publics-opinion-of-court-drops-after-health-care-law-decision.html>.

The downsides of surveying are multiple, in part because respondents may supply unreliable or downright inaccurate answers. Ask people in the United States if they intend to vote in a presidential election, and nearly 80% say yes, though fewer than 60% actually vote.[53] Or, to return to an earlier example, we know that many people will underestimate their weight when asked. More generally, the quickest way to get a biased response is to ask people, as we noted in Chapter 3. This is why it is often better, if possible, to rely on other measures—actual behavior or revealed preferences (Did they actually vote? What's their weight on a valid and reliable scale?). At the very least, we probably should never treat what people say as a fact, though it seems reasonable to treat that they said it as a fact—and one possibly worthy of investigation.[54] It is not a fact that 80% of the people who say they will vote will, in fact, vote. That they said they would vote, though, is a fact, and one we might want to explore.[55]

Another problem with surveys is the difficulty in replicating them if things go wrong. This is true of other data collection methods. But surveys can be especially frustrating because, without expending lots of time and resources, there's no second bite at the cherry. You can re-run an experiment and, as we'll see, you can usually return to whatever text you're analyzing. But refielding a survey may not only be cost-prohibitive but actually impossible if it's time dependent (such as gauging people's reactions to an event immediately after it occurs).

What can go wrong? Just about everything, at every decision point from identifying the target population, to selecting the sample (more on this below), to ordering and phrasing the questions, to dealing with non-responses. Question wording is especially tricky. As we intimated earlier, it's not enough that the questions are the same; to the extent possible, the respondents must interpret them the same way. This is the researcher's job, but it is often hard to do because even seemingly clear questions can admit multiple interpretations. Fowler points to this example: "What is the average number of days each week you have butter?"[56] This may seem plain enough but, apparently, some of the respondents did not know whether margarine counted as butter.

---

[53] See, e.g., Ansolabehere and Hersh (2012).

[54] See Bertrand and Mullainathan (2001).

[55] Another way to remove bias from surveys is to combine information from multiple surveys that ask the same or similar questions. Nate Silver takes this approach when forecasting the electoral college vote in the United States. See Silver (2012).

[56] Fowler (1992, 222, 225). Example also cited in Diamond (2011, 387).

When the researcher revised the question—"Not including margarine, what is the average number of days each week you have butter"—there was a decrease in the number of respondents who said they used butter.

In this case, the word "butter" (without the clarifying exclusion of "margarine") generated unreliable responses. But there are more fundamental ambiguities in question design. Suppose we want to learn whether citizens in Great Britain support reinstatement of the death penalty for murder.[57] In addition to matters of sampling, the kind of survey to field (e.g., telephone, internet), and questionnaire design, we would have to write the question. This would seem a simple matter:

> All things considered, would you support or oppose reinstating the death penalty for murder in Great Britain?

We can assure you, though, that it is not so simple because question wording can make a big difference in the response. When a polling company asked the question above to a random sample of 2,009 British adults in September of 2011, 64% responded that they supported reinstatement.[58] But suppose we asked it this way:

> All things considered, which of these two approaches would you prefer as a punishment for convicted murderers in Great Britain? The death penalty or life imprisonment?

Well, in fact the same survey company did phrase it this way, and support for the death penalty fell to 51%, at least in part, it would seem, due to question wording.[59] The larger lesson is that relying on the results of a survey without understanding how question wording might affect responses can lead to unreliable conclusions. And for those

---

[57] Great Britain eliminated the death penalty in 1969.

[58] Online survey conducted by Angus Reid Public Opinion between September 11 and September 12, 2011. Of the 2,009 respondents, 28% strongly supported reinstatement, 36% moderately supported, 10% moderately opposed, 18% strongly opposed, and 8% weren't sure. Survey results available at: <http://www.angus-reid. com/polls/46891/two-thirds-of-britons-would-bring-back-capital-punishment/>.

[59] 35% selected life imprisonment and 13% weren't sure. Similar results obtain in the United States. When asked if they are "in favor of of the death penalty for a person convicted of murder," over 60% of respondents say yes. When asked "which they think is the better penalty for murder—the death penalty or life imprisonment"—fewer than 50% select the death penalty. Data at: <http://www.gallup.com/poll/1606/death-penalty.aspx>.

with nefarious intentions, in many cases it's possible to manipulate conclusions by manipulating the way the questions are framed.

Observation.   The third method for generating data, observation, can be desirable because it may be able to overcome the artificiality of some experiments and the inaccurate self-reporting that we know occurs on questionnaires. Like the other methods, observation comes in different forms. Its variants tend to hinge on the degree of contact with the study's subjects.[60] Sometimes researchers will directly observe the units in their sample; and the units will know they are being watched. To examine how solicitors in England and Wales deal with their clients (and one another) in divorce cases, Eekelaar et al.[61] observed the lawyers at work. Likewise scholars have ridden along with police to determine how they investigate crimes and whether they comply with the rights accorded to defendants.[62] Somewhat less intrusive was the Arizona Jury Project, in which a team of researchers were able to videotape jury deliberations to learn how jurors respond to expert testimony and to evaluate the quality of their discussions, among other things.[63] The researchers were not in the room during the deliberations but all participants—the attorneys, parties, and jurors themselves—were told that they would be videotaped "for research purposes."[64] In still other studies, the subjects don't know the researcher is watching them. This was the case in Retting et al.'s work, which investigated whether red light camera systems placed around a city deterred drivers from running red lights even at intersections where the systems were not installed.[65] To conduct the study, the researchers observed drivers at intersections where the driver knew there were cameras and intersections where there were no cameras. The latter is a form of unobtrusive observation, and it was designed to overcome an obvious problem with (some) observational methods.

---

[60] Axinn and Pearce (2007). We mention only the kinds of observational approaches that seem most common in empirical legal research. For others see Bates et al. (1998); King et al. (1994); Lofland et al. (2006); Rubin and Rubin (2004); Weiss (1995).

[61] Eekelaar et al. (2000).

[62] Bayley and Garofalo (1989); Gould and Mastrofski (2004).

[63] See, e.g., Diamond et al. (2003); Diamond (2007). Arizona is a U.S. state.

[64] For more details, see Diamond et al. (2011, 158–9).

[65] Retting et al. (1999). Red light camera systems are designed to capture speeding and running red lights. The camera takes a photograph of the driver, who then may be charged with violating traffic laws.

The jurors—or Eekelaar et al.'s solicitors or, for that matter, any subjects—may alter their behavior in response to being watched.[66]

Observation poses a related difficulty for the researcher. Because subjects are not checking off boxes on a questionnaire or otherwise recording their own choices, it's up to the analyst to document their behavior. This raises the possibility of various biases (consciously or unconsciously) intruding into the process, such as when researchers record statements that support their hypothesis and ignore those against it. We should say too that, even if observers generate reliable and valid notes, they will need to translate the text of their notes into useable data should they desire to make inferences.

Textual Analysis. Which brings us to the fourth method: analyzing text. This involves extracting information from textual content that the researcher can use to draw inferences. The content (or text) can come from a multitude of sources: newspaper articles, websites, legal documents, field notes, and so on. Text analysis of various forms is everywhere in law, and in fact you've already seen numerous examples. La Porta et al. read laws and other documents to determine the tenure of high court judges; Elkins et al. studied constitutions to code their degree of specificity; Posner and de Figueiredo pored over ICJ cases to identify which party won; and the Arizona Jury Team analyzed transcripts of video taped jury deliberations to assess their quality.

You might be thinking: aren't all of these things—legal documents, transcriptions, field notes, etc.—already data? The answer is yes, but in their raw form they aren't susceptible to systematic analysis and thus are hard to use to draw inferences. There's not much La Porta et al. could have done with a stack of laws or Posner and de Figueiredo with a bunch of court cases or the Arizona Jury Project with transcriptions from videos. Only by extracting the information from these piles of laws, cases, and videos could they generate data ready for analysis. In other words, we can think of the documents, transcriptions, and other text as sources of data rather than data themselves.

Generating or extracting data from texts too takes various forms, from the simple to the more sophisticated. Falling into the former category is Elkins et al.'s use of constitutions to generate information about their specificity. The researchers manually (or hand) counted whether the document covered a particular topic. Ditto for La Porta et al.,

---

[66] This is often referred to as an observer effect. See <http://www.aqr.org.uk/glossary/?term=observereffect>.

who went through the legal documents for each country to locate the information they needed. On the more sophisticated end, text analysis can derive simple facts—such as coverage or tenure length—but also the underlying theme or sentiment in the documents.[67]

In between would be some form of systematic content analysis. Segal and Cover's work on justices of the U.S. Supreme Court provides an example.[68] To create an exogenous measure of each justice's ideology—that is, a measure not based on the votes the justices cast or other choices they made—Segal and Cover collected newspaper editorials written between the time of each justice's nomination to the U.S. Supreme Court and their confirmation. With the editorials in hand, they coded each paragraph in each editorial for political ideology as follows:

Paragraphs were coded as liberal, moderate, conservative, or not applicable. Liberal statements include (but are not limited to) those ascribing support for the rights of defendants in criminal cases, women and racial minorities in equality cases, and the individual against the government in privacy and First Amendment [speech, press, and religion] cases. Conservative statements are those with an opposite direction. Moderate statements include those that explicitly ascribe moderation to the nominees or those that ascribe both liberal and conservative values.[69]

Segal and Cover then measured judicial ideology by subtracting the fraction of paragraphs coded conservative from the fraction of paragraphs coded liberal and dividing by the total number of paragraphs coded liberal, conservative, and moderate. The resulting scale of policy preferences ranges from 0 (an extremely conservative justice) to .5 (a moderate justice) to 1 (an extremely liberal justice).[70]

In this example, Segal and Cover extracted the data by "hand coding," that is, without the help of a computer. Increasingly, researchers are making use of computer software to *help* generate the data for them. But note our emphasis on "help." In many applications, the researcher

[67] For example, Quinn *et al.* (2010) have estimated the topic of every speech in the U.S. Congress with models that use the text of the speeches as data. A similar approach could be used to determine the topic of judicial opinions, litigant briefs, statutes, and so on.

[68] Segal and Cover (1989).

[69] Segal and Cover (1989, 559).

[70] Many researchers have used these "Segal–Cover" scores to measure the ideology of justices in the United States. See, e.g., Epstein et al. (2013); Cameron and Park (2009); Casillas et al. (2011). Some have tried to use Segal and Cover's procedure to measure the ideology of judges in other contexts. E.g., Ostberg and Wetstein (2007) and Traut and Emmert (1998).

must do some hand coding to help train the software. Such is the case with ReadMe,[71] a software package developed by Hopkins et al. (and just one of many of its kind). To use it, the researchers start by developing a categorization scheme, say, an ordering of ideology from most liberal to most conservative, to use Segal and Cover's subject as an example. Next, they select the documents they would like to analyze (say, newspaper editorials) and draw a small sample of the documents to hand code to train the software. Once the software understands the underlying categorization scheme, it will analyze the documents and, in this example, yield an ideology score for each justice (along with other statistics of interest).

This is but one example; there are many others we could develop to show the possibilities of sophisticated textual analysis for empirical legal research, and the many other software packages available. Still, we should emphasize that the software rarely does all the work. Often the researcher must supervise the software so that it learns the underlying scheme. This is why we devote Chapter 5 to coding data, which entails establishing protocols for translating the information in texts (and other sources) into data.

Chapter 5 should provide you with sufficient information to develop high-quality schemes designed to yield reliable data. Even so, we want to reiterate the caution we offered at the beginning of the chapter. Deploying more complex forms of textual analysis requires specialized knowledge developed through detailed study—far more knowledge than we can convey in this introductory book. That goes double for performing experiments, observing, and surveying, as we're sure you can tell by now.

So how might you proceed? First, for the academics and students among our readers, we recommend that you take a course in whatever data-collection method is of interest. Departments of psychology (and increasingly economics and political science) are good places to look for courses on experimental design. Creating and fielding surveys is a mainstay in political science and sociology departments; and observing is a core activity of sociologists and anthropologists. Extracting information from text via computers is a subject now taught in many departments of computer science, social science units, and schools of engineering (and, occasionally, business). Short of formal

---

[71] Freely available at: <http://gking.harvard.edu/readme>.

study, there are good books and guides on each of these topics that researchers, along with lawyers and judges, can consult.[72]

Second, don't hesitate to locate experts. For the academics, it should be possible to obtain help from colleagues on your campus. Better yet, you might enter into a collaboration, maximizing your substantive knowledge of law and legal institutions and your colleagues of a particular data-collection strategy. There are numerous examples of such fruitful collaborations in the sciences, the social sciences, and, increasingly, law. Many law firms already follow a model along these lines, retaining experts when necessary; the survey commissioned for the *Victoria's Secret* trademark case is only one of hundreds of examples to which we could point. Judges should, and occasionally do, follow suit with the appointment of special masters or their own experts.[73] But still, it's crucial that lawyers, judges, and researchers understand enough about empirical research so that they know at the very least what questions to ask their expert.

Third, if neither of the first two suggestions are appealing, we recommend returning to our earlier advice of conducting a search to see if the data or a dataset already exists. If not, you could hire experts to amass it for you. In the case of surveys, there are plenty of operations that will, for a price, help researchers develop and field surveys. One of many is the scientific and academic branch of YouGov,[74] which now has offices throughout the United States and Europe.

Finally, if you choose to ignore us altogether (you wouldn't be the first among our former students!) and embark on your own data-collection expedition, be sure to pre-test whatever method you are using. We offer the same advice in the next chapter on coding data and it holds here too. You could gauge the reaction of a focus group to

---

[72] On experimental methods, we recommend Dunning (2012); Friedman and Sunder (1994); Gerber and Green (2012); Kagel and Roth (1997); Kinder and Palfrey (1993); Mutz (2011). On surveys, see Bradburn et al. (2004); DeVellis (2011); Groves et al. (2009); Rea and Parker (2005); Tourangeau et al. (2000). On observation, Bates et al. (1998); Lofland et al. (2006); Rubin and Rubin (2004); Weiss (1995). On text analysis, Allen (1994); Bird et al. (2009); Jurafsky and Martin (2008); Manning and Schuetze (1999); Manning et al. (2008).

[73] See, e.g., Judge Richard A. Posner's opinion in *ATA Airlines v. Federal Express Corp.*, 665 F.3d 882, 889 (7th Cir. 2011), noting that "a judge can always appoint his own expert to assist him in understanding and evaluating the proposed testimony of a party's expert. . . . If he worries that the expert he appoints may not be truly neutral, he can ask the parties' experts to agree on a neutral expert for him to appoint." We return to Judge Posner's opinion in this case in Chapter 12.

[74] <http://research.yougov.com>.

your questions; you could even draw a small random sample from your target population. Either way, you should be able to get some feedback on the reliability and validity of your instrument, which may (or may not) force you back to the drawing board. Even a small, simple pre-test could save substantial money, time, and effort.

4.3 Deciding How Much Data to Collect

The most oft-asked question at the empirical legal workshop we run for law professors is easily this: "How much data do I need?" The answer is simple: inference—learning about facts we do not know by using facts we do know—requires some facts. Knowing more of these facts should make for better inferences. If scholars base their inferences on relatively little information, then any conclusions will be on especially shaky ground (or "uncertain"). If, however, they are able to marshal a massive quantity of information, then the answer to their research question may be certain enough to change the course of (or at least make a contribution to) legal scholarship or to recommend policies that affect many people.

To bottom line it: *as a general rule, researchers should collect as much data as resources and time allow* because basing inferences on more data rather than less is almost always preferable. When an opportunity exists to collect more data, we should *usually* take advantage of it.

Even so, we do not mean to imply that scholars should spend years collecting data for every individual research project; we recognize that many other constraints, personal and professional, quite reasonably affect research decisions. There are also scientific reasons that cut against the claim that more data are always better, and that's why we say "as a general rule" and not "always." Think about a study designed to probe Australians' opinions about same-sex marriage. The more people included in the study, the more certain the conclusions we can reach. As a practical matter, however, diminishing returns kick in and settling on a sample size (as opposed to including all Australians) is good enough. To see why, suppose we drew a random sample of 2,400 Australians and asked them this:

If a referendum took place tomorrow in Australia, and you only had these two options on the ballot, how would you vote? To define marriage as between two people or to define marriage as between a man and a woman.

Further suppose that 52% selected the first option, which indicates support for same-sex marriage.[75] Given our sample size of 2,400, it turns out that mathematically the margin of error (a measure of uncertainty) is ±2%.[76] This means that we are reasonably certain that somewhere between (52%-2%=) 50% and (52%+2%=) 54% of Australians would define marriage as between two people, rather than as between a man and a woman. Now suppose we surveyed 9,600 Australians (again finding that 52% support the same-sex marriage option), the margin of error declines to only ±1%. This means that instead of saying that we are reasonably certain that somewhere between 50% and 54% support same-sex marriage we can now say that between 51% and 53% support it—not much of a difference. This is why most public opinion surveys sample a couple of thousand respondents at most.

But, as a general matter, our advice still holds: if they have the option, researchers should amass as much information as they can. Because the goal of empirical research is to make inferences, basing them on more data in an appropriate way will not hurt. If researchers have an easy way of collecting data even partially relevant to their project, they should do it. If the procedures for gathering data for another project can be slightly amended to be relevant to the researchers' project without much trouble, then do this too.

And it can be useful to collect data of different types from different sources rather than collecting more of the same type (such as increasing the number of observations, as in the Australian example). This counsels for researchers to undertake broad searches for diverse types of data even over a particular observable implication. If we are interested in whether and why judges on the International Court of Justice (ICJ) are biased toward their home country or their home country's allies (as were Posner and de Figueiredo[77]), then the sorts of data we might collect (in addition to the judges' votes) and the data-collection mechanisms we could deploy are wide-ranging: analyzing the judges' opinions to gauge their sentiment toward the litigant, surveying people

[75] In fact, in an online survey conducted between February 21 and 29, 2012, 52% of Australians said they would define marriage as between two people; 43% would define it as between a man and a woman; 10% weren't sure. Poll results available at: <http://www.angus-reid.com/wp-content/uploads/2012/03/2012.03.12_SameSex.pdf>.

[76] For more on the margin of error (sometimes called *sampling error*) and other measures of uncertainty (such as *confidence intervals*), see Part III.

[77] Posner and de Figueiredo (2005).

familiar with the court's work, and even drawing comparisons with other supranational courts. Some refer to this as *mixed methods* research, which, in many ways, is just a fancy term for collecting different types of data from different sources using different data collection mechanisms.[78]

4.3.1 Avoiding Selection Bias in Studies with a (Fairly) Large Number of Observations

Speaking of Posner and de Figueiredo's analysis of the ICJ, recall that the population of interest was all votes cast by all ICJ judges, and the researchers collected this information for the entire population of cases in which the ICJ decided substantive, rather than administrative or procedural, questions.[79] Likewise, to explain why some constitutions last longer than others, Elkins et al. examined all 935 constitutions promulgated between 1789 and 2005 in all countries. This is rare. Usually, researchers do not or cannot examine all members of their target population. Can you imagine surveying all 493 million EU inhabitants to assess their views on gun control? Or even talking with the 23.2 million Australians to learn what they think about same-sex marriage? Of course not. Even in smaller-scale studies it may be difficult to collect data on the entire population. Recall that La Porta et al. learned about the link between judicial independence and economic freedom in 71 countries and not all 195 independent states in the world.[80]

But how should researchers decide whom to survey or study? To put it more generally, if circumstances prevent researchers from collecting data on all members of the population, what should they do? If they want to make valid inferences about the population of interest—here, all Europeans or all Australians or all countries—they must invoke a selection mechanism that avoids selection bias, meaning a mechanism that doesn't bias their sample for or against their theory. If they have the resources to collect a relatively large number of observations (that

---

[78] Scholars continue to debate the definition of "mixed methods research" (for various definitions, see Johnson et al., 2007b). This one, from a text on the subject, seems to be as common as any other: "Mixed method data collection strategies are those explicitly decided to combine elements of one method . . . with other methods . . . in either a sequential or a simultaneous manner" Axinn and Pearce (2007, 1).

[79] Posner and de Figueiredo (2005).

[80] According to the U.S. Department of State, at: <http://www.state.gov/s/inr/rls/4250.htm>.

is, they are conducting a large-*n* study, where *n* is the number of observations), then the only mechanism that meets this criterion is *random probability sampling*.[81]

We have used this term colloquially throughout and it is now time to formally define it: a random probability sample is a sample in which each element in the total population has a known (and preferably the same) probability of being selected. Developing it involves identifying the population of interest (all Europeans) and selecting a subset (the sample of Europeans) according to known probabilistic rules. To perform these tasks, the researcher assigns a probability of being selected to each member (person, case, country, etc.) of the target population, and selects each member into the sample according to these probabilities. Happily, statistical software will do the work for us using a random number generator, which is just a way for a computer to approximate the process of pulling numbers out of a hat.[82] (There are different approaches to drawing a random sample. We consider them soon.)

Why do we advise using random sampling if researchers have a large number of observations in the population? After all, just a few pages back we asserted that "more data are better," so why do we now suggest ignoring any information we have about potential observations to be selected, and selecting according to some random number generator guaranteed to be ignorant of all this auxiliary information? The main reason is that random selection is the only selection mechanism in large-*n* studies that automatically guarantees the absence of selection bias. When we use random sampling we are, by definition, assuring the absence of any association that may exist between selection rules and the variables in our study.

Return to our study of gender and judging and suppose we devised the following selection rule: include in our sample only those cases in which a male judge ruled against the party alleging sex discrimination and in which a female judge ruled in favor of the party alleging sex discrimination. If we had adopted this rule, you would (or should!) say:

---

[81] The number of observations (*n*) to select depends on the type of analysis you wish to perform. Although the computations are intricate, the basic idea is to find a sample size that will give you an estimate that is precise enough to answer your research question.

[82] By the way: collecting all the observations is a special case of random selection with a selection probability of 1.0 for every element in the population. Dealing with data collected on a population raises some foundational statistical issues—chiefly, should researchers draw inferences (via traditional statistical tools) about a population when the data themselves represent the population? We address this in Chapter 7.

wait a minute. You've adopted a rule that biases your sample in favor of your hypothesis, and you did so by selecting your observations (here, cases) on the basis of your dependent variable (the judge's vote): you've chosen only those values of the dependent variable (for or against the party alleging discrimination) that support your hypothesis.

This is not the only way to bias a sample. Imagine trying to gauge public opinion in the EU about same-sex marriage by surveying only people in Denmark or Sweden (the two countries most supportive of same-sex marriage in the EU[83]) or public confidence in Barack Obama by stopping people in the street of his home town in Chicago, IL (where Obama is very popular). More to the point, a selection rule that draws randomly from the population of interest is the only way not to bias a sample whether intentionally or unintentionally. It is the only approach that guards against including (or excluding) observations favorable (or unfavorable) toward the researcher's thesis, again whether or not on purpose. When appropriately applied, random selection prevents bias except by chance, and a large n means that the chance is exceptionally small. There is another reason too for drawing random samples. Many statistical procedures for analyzing data—including all those we'll explore in Part III—operate under the assumption that the data were randomly drawn.[84] Violating this assumption makes any inferences suspect.

This is a point we explore in more detail soon enough, beginning in Chapter 6. For now, we want to emphasize just one last time (we promise!) that unless the researcher collects all observations in the population and that population itself was created in an unbiased manner, random sampling is the only selection rule that safeguards against choosing observations in which the selection rule is related (or correlated) with the dependent variable or indeed any variable, except by chance. No matter how carefully a selection rule is designed, when it is based on human knowledge it may be related, however inadvertently, to the outcome variable and thus may introduce bias. So, yes, it is true that selecting observations randomly (instead of using whatever knowledge we have about the data to make the selection) violates the fundamental rule that "more data are better," but we must live with

---

[83] <http://yougov.co.uk/news/2013/01/11/french-opposed-gay-adoption/>.

[84] The methods we cover in Part III also assume that we have an equal probability sample. Using appropriate weighting, they can all be adapted to deal with more complicated samples, but the assumption that the data came from a random sample remains.

discarding some information to avoid the inadvertent introduction of selection bias.

While we have talked so far in general terms about random sampling, it's important to realize that researchers take multiple approaches to drawing the sample they will ultimately analyze. Three are especially prominent in empirical legal studies: equal probability sampling, stratified random sampling, and clustering sampling. There are differences among the three, as you'll see. But keep in mind that the goal is the same: to produce a random sample by identifying the population of interest and selecting the units according to known probabilistic rules.

In *equal probability sampling* all observations in the target population have an equal chance of being included in the study.[85] Reconsider our research on whether female and male judges reach the same decisions in cases involving discrimination based on gender, and imagine we had a list of the 1,000 sex discrimination cases decided in all 94 U.S. federal trial courts (called U.S. district courts).[86] Further suppose that we wanted to include 100 (or 10% of the cases) in our study's sample. Equal probability random sampling involves assigning every case the same probability of selection and selecting only 100. One way to do this would be to draw a set of 1,000 numbers from what is known as a "uniform distribution on the integers 1 to 1,000." This process is equivalent to writing the numbers 1 to 1,000 on poker chips, mixing them all up in a barrel, randomly choosing one, writing down the number, throwing the chip back in, and repeating the process until the investigator obtains a list of 100 numbers.[87] Many statistical software packages perform this task for us, as we noted earlier.[88]

A potential problem with equal probability sampling comes when the researcher has in mind a key causal variable, and worries that the sample will include too few members of one of the values of the variable. This is a real possibility in our study of gender and judging. Keep in mind that we are interested in the effect of the judges' gender on the probability of ruling for the party alleging sex discrimination (the plaintiff), hypothesizing that females, relative to males, are more likely to decide in favor of the plaintiff. If resources permit us to select,

---

[85] We adapt the next few paragraphs from Epstein and King (2002).

[86] 1,000 is a hypothetical figure.

[87] This is an example of sampling with replacement. In most studies, especially surveys, the researcher samples without replacement. So long as the population is large, this difference is inconsequential.

[88] The book's website shows you how to do this in both Stata and R.

say, only 100 cases and we did so at random with equal probability of selection, we might by chance end up with no female judges because there are fewer females than males (especially in earlier decades). This would make inference impossible. Even if our sample contains many more males than females, our inference would be less efficient than it would be with a sample of equal numbers of each.

To guard against the inefficiencies of chance occurrences, scholars often use a technique called *stratified random sampling*. The idea is to draw separate equal-probability-of-selection random samples within each category of a variable. In the present example, stratifying by the key explanatory variable (gender) would be especially useful since it guarantees a fixed number of observations (presumably an equal number) within categories of female and male judges. To implement this strategy, we would first divide (stratify) the cases according to the gender of the judge (that is, create two lists, one of cases decided by male judges, the other by female judges). Second, assuming we want a sample of 100, with an equal number of cases decided by male and female judges, we would draw an equal probability sample of 50 from each list (or stratum).

Drawing equal probability and stratified random samples supposes that the researcher can generate a list of every unit in the population—in our example, all sex discrimination cases, but it could be all countries, individuals, constitutions, and so on. For many kinds of studies, however, it may be too time-consuming or even impossible to create such a list. Imagine identifying by name every adult living in an EU country! Even enumerating all sex discrimination cases decided by a particular kind of court in one country could be impractical. In these circumstances, researchers use a technique called *cluster sampling*. While it may be impractical to create a list of all sex discrimination cases in all 94 U.S. federal trial courts, it is surely possible to create a list of the 94 courts. From this group (or cluster) of all trial courts, we would draw an equal probability sample of, say, ten courts and then generate a list of all the sex discrimination cases in the ten. This list might constitute our sample; or we could draw a random sample (either stratified or equal probability) from the cases in the ten courts. Cluster sampling also would be appropriate for studying public opinion in EU countries. We could start with a list of countries and then draw a random sample of countries. If we could not generate a list of all persons living in the sample, we might consider adding a cluster such as towns within the countries and then drawing a sample of towns. The idea is to arrive at a cluster for which it is possible to list àll the relevant units (here people) but to do so by random sampling at each stage.

4.3.2 Avoiding Selection Bias in Studies with a (Very) Small Number of Observations

To our admonition of using random selection strategies in large-n studies, note the caveat: it applies only to large-n studies.[89] The reason a large n is useful is that it makes correlations by chance extremely unlikely, in fact less and less likely as the number of observations increases. But random selection does not help to avoid selection bias in studies with a very small n, because correlations between the selection rule and the dependent variable can occur by chance, even with fairly high probabilities.

Suppose we were conducting a study to explain why, in some countries, the judiciaries are highly independent, and in others, highly dependent and, in yet a third group, somewhere in-between.[90] Further suppose we have identified three countries, each with a different level of judicial independence (high, medium, and low), but we can study only two of the three. The question is how to select the two. If we use random selection, there is a two-thirds probability of selection bias. That's because there are only three possible ways to select two of the three countries to study: include the two countries with high and medium levels of judicial independence (and exclude the one with a low level), include the two with medium and low levels (and exclude the one with a high level), or include the low and high level countries (and exclude the medium level). Only for the latter (high and low) is the selection rule uncorrelated with the dependent variable—judicial independence. Put another way, for two of the three—both of which are as likely to result from random selection as the uncorrelated rule—bias is possible.

Perhaps you can now see the magnitude of the problem when we are dealing with very small samples. On the one hand, we know that random selection is the only selection mechanism that avoids selection bias; on the other, it can be a perilous approach for small-n studies. So how should researchers proceed if they have only a few observations?

---

[89] We adopt and adapt much of the material in this section from Epstein and King (2002, 112–14).

[90] We adapt this example from King et al. (1994, 124–28).

The answer is that they must guard against bias inadvertently introduced into their study when they substitute random selection for some form of intentional choice. Achieving this requires them to design a selection mechanism that is not related to the dependent variable, including, by the way, selecting on the dependent variable itself. To return to our example of judicial independence: if we are trying to explain why some countries have a very high level and others a very low level, we wouldn't want to select only countries that we know have the highest level. (If the countries in our sample don't vary on the dependent variable, there's nothing to explain!)

In this example, we have some knowledge of the levels of judicial independence. In many other studies, however, the values of the dependent variable are typically unknown prior to any sampling (that is, we may not know the level of judicial independence in each country). This makes the process of generating a selection rule that is uncorrelated with the dependent variable even more difficult.

Fortunately, there are methods for overcoming it. Consider a research team at the University of Oxford that wants to understand the degree to which police currently working in England comply with a suspect's right to silence,[91] and hopes to do so by observing their behavior. They could probably identify all police officers in England and draw a random sample of those they will include in the study. But assume that the members of the research team, like many of us, have constraints on their time and ability to travel such that they can only observe police in the station closest to Oxford. In other words, they have intentionally, and not randomly, selected their sample, thereby risking the possibility that the station they have chosen may be different for all others in the way it enforces the right to silence.

How can they minimize this risk? Ideally, the research team should collect more data. Given constraints, however, one good approach is to identify a measurement strategy that is easy or inexpensive to apply across a wider range of observations, one that complements the detailed examination of the neighborhood police station. Perhaps the research team could draw a random sample of, say, 100 police stations in England and learn from public records the number of challenges to the

---

[91] Under the Criminal Justice and Public Order Act 1994, police must caution a suspect with these words: "You do not have to say anything. But it may harm your defence if you do not mention when questioned something which you later rely on in court. Anything you do say may be given in evidence."

application of the right to silence involving officers in those stations. No doubt these data will be different and less valid indicators than those the researchers would collect from their detailed case study; but equally true is that they may help the team to determine whether their local station is representative of the others (for example, a ranking of three out of 100 on challenges would suggest something very different than, say, a ranking of 50 out of 100).

Another productive strategy might be to conduct the analysis from public records first and then choose a more representative police station to observe for detailed study. With this sort of information in hand the researchers could be more (or less, as the case might be) certain of the inferences they make from the smaller, intentionally drawn sample.

Whatever the procedure the team uses to select their sample, they will find themselves in the same situation as researchers who have drawn a large-n sample: with piles and piles of information or, more likely, computer files full of field notes, interview transcriptions, court cases, and so on. In the next chapter we confront squarely the question that we have mostly skirted until now: how to translate these piles and files into useful data that the investigator can analyze and, ultimately, use for inference.

5

Coding Data

You've probably noticed that empirical legal researchers approach their projects in myriad ways. Some develop hypotheses as implications from sophisticated models; others, from intuition. Some researchers collect information from primary sources; others rely primarily on secondary archival data. And, as we'll see in Part III, there are some analysts who simply categorize or describe the information they collect, while others deploy complex statistical methods.

Seen in this way, it might appear that researchers producing empirical work have little in common (beyond following the basic rules and procedures we outlined in the previous chapters). Their data come from innumerable sources; and their tools for making use of the data are equally varied.

Even so, there is at least one task in empirical scholarship that is universal—that virtually all researchers undertake no matter whether their data are quantitative or qualitative, from where their hypotheses and data come, or how they plan to analyze the information they have collected. That task is coding data, which is the process of translating properties or attributes of the world (variables) into a form that is susceptible to systematic analysis. The process itself entails, first, developing a precise scheme to account for the values of each variable and, second, methodically and physically assigning all units a value for each variable. To provide a very simple example: for our study of the effect of gender on judging, the variable `judge's gender` can take on the value of male or female; that is the scheme. To complete the second task, we would assign each judge the value "male" or "female" based on his or her gender. (Remember: we're using `this font` to represent variables.)

Surprisingly, despite the common and fundamental role it plays, most volumes on empirical research mention coding only in passing; the subject has received almost no attention in empirical legal studies.[1] Why this is the case we can only speculate, but an obvious answer centers on the seemingly idiosyncratic nature of the undertaking. For some projects researchers may be best off coding inductively, that is, collecting their data, drawing a representative sample, examining the data in the sample, and then developing their coding scheme. For other projects, investigators proceed in a deductive manner, that is, they develop their schemes first and then collect and code their data.

Note that we use the generic terms, "some projects" and "other projects." Some authors would be more specific because they tend to associate inductive coding with qualitative data, and deductive coding with quantitative data. Given the (typically) dynamic nature of the processes of collecting and coding, however, these associations do not always or perhaps even usually hold. Many researchers, we suspect, use some combination of deductive and inductive coding regardless of whether their data are qualitative or quantitative. We do.

There is another reason for the omission of coding in most accounts of empirical legal research. Not only do distinctions exist between inductive and deductive coding but the relative ease (or difficulty) of the coding task itself can vary, depending on the types of data with which the researcher is working, the level of detail for which the coding scheme calls, and the amount of pre-testing the analyst has conducted, to name just three.

Nonetheless, we believe it is possible to develop some generalizations about the process of coding variables and, more importantly, guidelines for so doing. This much we attempt to accomplish below, with our discussion divided into two sections corresponding to the two key phases of the coding process that we just noted: (1) developing a precise scheme to account for the values of the variables and (2) assigning all units a value for each variable.

In line with earlier chapters, and those to follow, our goal is to offer best practices for performing both in an effort to help researchers produce reliable data and to provide evaluators with a set of standards to assess their efforts. For the researchers, though, we want to offer a

---

[1] There are some exceptions. See, e.g., Lawless et al. (2010). We wrote a section on coding for the *Handbook of Social Measurement*, and draw on it in this chapter.

special piece of advice that will become clearer as you read the material to come: following best practices will help if and only if you have a strong sense of your project, particularly about the piece of the legal world you're studying and how that piece generated the data you'll be coding, as well as the observable implications of the theory you'll be assessing.

5.1 Developing Coding Schemes

Regardless of the type of data they collect, the variables they intend to code, or even whether they plan to code inductively or deductively, *at some point* empirical researchers require a coding scheme, that is, a detailing of each variable of interest, along with the values of each variable—such as the variable `judge's gender`, with the values "male" and "female."

Providing another example is Posner and de Figueiredo's analysis of the International Court of Justice (ICJ).[2] Among the observable implications of their theory is that ICJ judges will favor states whose culture is similar to the dominant culture in their own state. Because `culture` is an abstract concept, the researchers must clarify or measure it, as you know by now. To do so, Posner and de Figueiredo use the proxy of religion so that their hypothesis becomes: "Judges are more likely to vote for states with the same . . . religion as their home state."[3] And the variable for which they must develop a coding scheme is `religion`, with the values corresponding to the dominant religion of every country's judge and applicant-country in the dataset. Something like:

1. Buddhist
2. Catholic
3. Hindu
4. Jewish
5. Muslim
6. Protestant
7. None[4]
8. Other

---

[2] Posner and de Figueiredo (2005).

[3] Posner and de Figueiredo (2005, 610). They also use language to measure culture.

[4] E.g., China is officially atheist. See, e.g., the CIA's world factbook, at: <https://www.cia.gov/library/publications/the-world-factbook/fields/2122.html>.

With this sort of coding scheme in hand, investigators can prepare codebooks or guides they employ to code their data and others can use to replicate, reproduce, update, or build on the variables in their database and any analyses they perform on the data.

In the next section, we have much more to say about codebooks. For now let us hone in on this first phase—developing a coding scheme—and offer two introductory notes, one on timing and the other on difficulty. The note on timing follows from our emphasis above on developing schemes "at some point" in the process. In terms of research design many steps typically precede "developing a coding scheme", such as devising research questions, theorizing about possible answers, generating observable implications, and so on. But sometimes "developing a coding scheme" follows from the data (inductive) and sometimes it precedes the data (deductive). It may even occur after the researchers have created a full-blown database because they or others decide to change or even add variables. The general point is that there is variation over when in the process researchers develop their scheme. What does not vary is that both the original researchers and anyone who uses their database will perform this task during the course of a project's life.

As to the difficulty of developing coding schemes, the level ranges from really easy to really hard depending on the types of variables under investigation. In our gender and judging study, it was trivial to develop a coding scheme for the variable judge's gender: the judge could be a "male" or "female." Likewise, if we were conducting a survey of students, all of whom were between the ages of 18 and 21, then it would be simple to develop a coding scheme for the variable age: it could take on the values of "18," "19," "20," and "21."

Devising values for many other variables is not as straightforward. To see this, return to the example of the variable religion. Above we listed eight possible values: "Buddhist," "Catholic," "Hindu," "Jewish," "Muslim," "Protestant," "None," and "Other." This scheme may work well for some studies, but we can imagine others for which it would not. Consider a project on the views of Canadians who are members of one of the country's 280 Jewish synagogues.[5] Assuming that nearly all the subjects are Jewish, the eight values of religion we list above

---

[5] Number calculated from the National Synagogue Directory, maintained by the Canadian Jewish Congress Charities Committee, <http://www.cjccc.ca/en/community-faq/jewish-life-in-canada/synagogue-directory/>.

would not be very informative; nearly 100% would fall into the "Jewish" category. This is an example of "heaping," which occurs when a large amount of data fall into one value. Heaping presents problems for any statistical analysis because the variables start to resemble constants, leaving little or nothing to explain. In this case the investigator would want to alter the scheme, perhaps by incorporating finer divisions of "Jewish": "Jewish-Orthodox," "Jewish-Conservative," "Jewish-Reformed," "Jewish-Reconstructionist"—or whatever enables the analyst to capture the information relevant to the project.

Heaping may not be the only problem with our original eight values of religion for a study of Canadian synagogue members. For example, what of respondents who are inter-denominational in their religious preferences? Perhaps they belong to a Jewish synagogue and a Protestant church. They would be forced to choose among the eight values of religion; or perhaps respond with "Other," even if their preference is one that combines Jewish and Protestant tenets. And, for that matter, what should we make of the "Other" category? It's a necessary category in most projects but if too many respondents fall into it, this also would amount to heaping (and an especially pernicious form for the reasons we explain momentarily).

Even for Posner and de Figueiredo's study our eight values may not work all that well. Take the value "Muslim." Should we include all Muslim countries in this category when some are majority Sunni (e.g., Jordan) and others Shia (e.g., Iraq)? The answer may seem obvious: create new categories. But what if reliable data aren't available? The U.S. Central Intelligence Agency's World Factbook reports that Muslim is the plurality religion in Nigeria but it doesn't specify whether the majority of Muslims there are Sunni or Shia,[6] and other sources don't provide much help.

We could go on, but the more general point should not be missed: accounting for the values of the variables of interest, even for seemingly straightforward ones like religion, can be a difficult task.

To help researchers accomplish it, we offer three recommendations: ensure that the values of the variables are exhaustive; create more, rather than fewer, values; establish that the values of the variables are mutually exclusive. These guidelines reflect standard practice, along

---

[6] According to the CIA's Factbook, 50% of Nigerians are Muslim, 40% Christian, and 10% hold indigenous beliefs. At: <https://www.cia.gov/library/publications/the-world-factbook/fields/2122.html>.

with our own experience. But, again, they presuppose that researchers understand their project. Because we made this point at the outset, we will not belabor it here. We only wish to note that even adhering to our three basic rules will be difficult, if not impossible, without a deep understanding of the objects of study and an underlying theory about whatever feature(s) of their behavior is of interest.

5.1.1 Ensure that the Values of the Variables are Exhaustive

The recommendation here is that the values for each variable must exhaust all the possibilities. To see why, consider a simple example: enumerating the values of the variable marital status as "married," "single," "divorced," "widowed." This is not an exhaustive list because it fails to include "living together but not married" and so would cause confusion for coders (and survey respondents) who must make a decision about the marital status of an individual living with but not married to someone.[7]

Were we to use our original list of eight values of religion to code the ICJ data, we might face this problem too because our list is not inclusive of the dominant religions in all countries—for example, there's no value for "Armenian Apostolic," the religion of 94.7% Armenians, or for "Lutheran Church of Finland," the major religion in Finland (82.5%). For Posner and de Figueiredo's study, it would be easy enough to add these values if the researchers came upon a court case in which the judge or the party was from Armenia or Finland. For other studies, though, it's more cumbersome to add values along the way. Suppose a team of scholars wanted to code laws according to the type of issue they covered. Further suppose the scholars created a list of 50 issues (that is, 50 values of the variable law type)—such as "criminal," "environmental," "immigration"—and then went about the task of assigning a type (value) to each law. What would happen if the scholars came upon a law for which there was no value, say "bankruptcy"? They could try to fit it into an existing category (thus expanding

---

[7] This example shows up another important point: even though this is a fairly common set of values of marital status, it is now obsolete, as Bourque (2007) points out. For example, the U.S. Census Bureau reports that there were 6.8 million unmarried partner households in 2010 (up from about 5.2 million in 2000). In Britain, the number of unmarried couples living together has doubled since 1996 and cohabitation is the fastest growing category of families in the country, according to the Office for National Statistics. See <http://www.ons.gov.uk/ons/rel/family-demography/families-and-households/2012/cohabitation-rpt.html>.

the definition of the category). That would be fine unless there were many bankruptcy laws, in which case the researchers probably would conclude that bankruptcy deserved a value of its own. If so, they would need to go back through all the laws in the category to which they added bankruptcy.

This sounds tedious, but at least the researchers could pull it off by returning to the laws. Ditto for Posner and de Figueiredo, who coded religion from a set of documents. Imagine, though, if they were coding not from a text but a survey. How would a Scientologist respond if we asked him if he was a "Buddhist," "Catholic," "Hindu," "Jewish," "Muslim," or "Protestant"? He would be stymied, and the research project along with it.

To skirt problems of this sort, investigators typically include the value "other," as we did in our original eight values of religion. This is not only acceptable but, frankly, necessary. It may be that researchers cannot anticipate every value of a particular variable however well they know their project and however well developed their theory. Moreover, even if they did know every value, it may be impractical or inefficient to include each and every one because they show up infrequently in the data. At the same time, though, because we can learn very little from a dataset full of variables mostly coded "other," researchers should avoid its overuse. Only by having a thorough understanding of their project—or at least an understanding sufficient enough to be able to write down an exhaustive list of the likely-to-occur values—will they steer clear of this pitfall. If investigators are studying the religious preferences of Europeans and they include Armenia, they should know enough about their subject to create the value "Armenian Apostolic."

In addition to understanding the subject, pre-testing or conducting a pilot study (when possible) is often a useful way to detect potential problems of all sorts, including the overuse of "other." As a rule of thumb, when pre-testing shows that more than 10% of the data for a given variable fall into the "other" value, the researcher should create new values.[8]

5.1.2 Create More, rather than Fewer, Values

To the extent that this next recommendation counsels "when in doubt, include a value rather than exclude it," it follows from the first as it will

---

[8] See Shi (1997).

help to avoid the problem of too many "other" codes. It also implies that analysts should generally create values that are more rather than less detailed.

To see why, let's consider a research team that wants to understand why higher courts sometimes reverse the decisions of lower courts and sometimes affirm them. There are many studies along these lines,[9] perhaps because they are of great interest (and even consequence) to members of the legal community—including judges.[10]

For such a project the researchers need to enumerate the values of the variable `disposition`, which they could merely list as "affirm" or "reverse" as these are the dispositions that concern them. The problem here is that higher courts do not always simply affirm or reverse; they have many other options available to them. The High Courts Judicial Database, which contains information on the high courts in 11 countries,[11] identifies five possibilities but, perhaps out of necessity, the Database lumps together several types of dispositions; for example, "reversed or vacated or remanded" are all in one value. Hewing closer to our recommendation of creating more values, the U.S. Supreme Court Database codes `disposition` more finely, into 11 categories, as Table 5.1 shows.[12] Now we know the research team is interested solely in a court's decision to affirm or reverse, but the guideline of "creating more, rather than fewer, values" commends that they start with all possible values of `disposition`. (This is so even though the researchers should know which values of `disposition` ought to count as an "affirm" and which should count as "reverse"; and we should require them to specify this. In Table 5.1, for example, values 3, 4, 5, 6, 7, and 8 might be considered "reverse" or, at the least, a victory in part or full for the appealing party.)

---

[9] See, e.g., Atkins (1990); Flemming (2004); Hilbink (2007); McCormick (1992); Schneider (2005); Scott (2006); Songer et al. (1994).

[10] The judges' interest may reflect empirical studies demonstrating a relationship between reversals and promotion. See, e.g., Salzberger and Fenn (1999) providing evidence that the lower the reversal rate, the higher the judge's prestige and thus the higher the likelihood of promotion from a court of appeals to the House of Lords in England (now the Supreme Court). See also Ramseyer and Rasmussen (2001), showing that Japanese judges who are reversed receive less prestigious responsibilities.

[11] Australia, Canada, India, Namibia, the Philippines, South Africa, Tanzania, United Kingdom, United States, Zambia, and Zimbabwe. Dataset available at: <http://www.cas.sc.edu/poli/juri/highcts.htm>.

[12] <http://supremecourtdatabase.org/>.

Table 5.1 Values of the variable `disposition` for the U.S. Supreme Court.[13]

Value	Value Label
1	stay, petition, or motion granted
2	affirmed
3	reversed
4	reversed and remanded
5	vacated and remanded
6	affirmed and reversed (or vacated) in part
7	affirmed and reversed (or vacated) in part and remanded
8	vacated
9	petition denied or appeal dismissed
10	certification to a lower court
11	no disposition

Beginning with detailed values has two clear advantages, both of which have more direct bearing on assigning values to each unit (the second phase of the coding process, which we cover in the next section) but they have relevance here as well. First, whoever eventually codes the data will make fewer errors. Think about it this way: if our investigators tell their coder in advance to report values 3, 4, 5, 6, 7, and 8 as "reversals" and values 2 and 9 as "affirmances," the coder must take two steps: identify the disposition by examining the court's decision and, then, identify whether it is a reversal or affirmance. But if the researchers simply ask the coder to identify the disposition, then the coder has only one step to take. Because each step has the possibility of introducing error, researchers should seek to reduce them.

A second set of advantages accrue when the investigators turn to analyzing their data. Because they have now coded the variable `disposition` quite finely, they can always collapse values (e.g., they can create "reverse" from values 3, 4, 5, 6, 7, and 8 in Table 5.1 and "affirm" from 2 and 9) to generate a new variable, say, `dispositionRevAff`, which would house the two categories of primary interest to them ("reverse" and "affirm"). At the same time, and again because the researchers have coded `disposition` finely, they will be able to discover whether any particular coding decision affects their conclusions. Suppose, for example, that, in collapsing values of

[13] Source: U.S. Supreme Court Database.

disposition, they count value 6 as a "reverse," even though the Court affirmed in part. Because this represents a judgment on their part (though one they should record, thereby enabling others to replicate their new variable, dispositionRevAff) and because the converse coding (counting value 6 as an "affirm") is plausible, they will be able to examine the effect of their judgment on the results. Coding data finely, in short, allows the researcher to encode a greater amount of information—and information that may well turn out to be quite valuable as the project progresses.

Researchers realize none of these advantages if they start with only two values of disposition ("reverse," "affirm"), and this we can't emphasize enough: one can never go from fewer to more categories without returning to the original data source (which sometimes, say in survey research, may be impossible). But it is always possible to move from more to fewer.

This noted, and despite all the advantages of creating more values, limits do and should exist. Consider Kahneman and Deaton's contribution to the long-standing debate in law, economics, and sociology over whether "money buys happiness."[14] Of course, the researchers needed a measure of "happiness"[15] but, more relevant for our purposes, they also required a measure of the variable income ("money"). Following the recommendation of creating detailed values might have led them (or, more accurately, the Gallup survey on which they relied) to ask respondents to report, say, the precise amount of their income in €s (or $s or whatever the currency). This would provide the finest possible level of detail on the variable income. But very few reputable pollsters operate in this way because they realize that individuals may not know that exact dollar amount or may not want others to know it. So rather than running the risk of reliability problems down the road, researchers typically create values representing income categories (e.g., "under €10,000;" "€10,000–19,999;" "€20,000 to 29,999;" and so

---

[14] Kahneman and Deaton (2010).

[15] They were interested in subjective well-being, including emotional well-being and life evaluation. To measure the former, they used survey questions that tapped into whether the respondent experienced enjoyment, stress, etc. yesterday. For life evaluation, they used Cantril's Self-Anchoring Scale, with the following wording: "Please imagine a ladder with steps numbered from 0 at the bottom to 10 at the top. The top of the ladder represents the best possible life for you, and the bottom of the ladder represents the worst possible life for you. On which step of the ladder would you say you personally feel you stand at this time?" Kahneman and Deaton (2010, 16492).

on). This was true of the Gallup survey that Kahneman and Deaton used, which asked respondents to report their monthly income in one of 11 categories.

We can imagine other variables for which our recommendation of developing detailed values would not be advisable.[16] But, in general, more rather than less detail is a principle worth remembering.

5.1.3 Establish that the Values of the Variables are Mutually Exclusive

Under this guideline, researchers should ensure they have created values such that whatever unit is under analysis falls into one and only one. It is easy to see how failure to follow this recommendation could lead to confusion on the part of respondents and coders alike but, unfortunately, it is also easy to violate it. Consider the variable student living arrangements for which the investigator has created four values: "live in residence hall," "live with parents," "live off campus," "live with spouse."[17] To the extent that the values seem exhaustive and detailed, this scheme meets the two other recommendations but not the one here: because a student could "live with parents" and "live off campus"—or, for that matter, live off campus with a spouse, live with parents and a spouse, or (at some universities) live in a residence hall with a spouse—the values are not mutually exclusive.

Closer to our concerns with empirical legal research, reconsider Table 5.1 and imagine that "vacated and remanded" (value 5) was broken into two separate values, "vacate" and "remand." This too would violate the rule of mutually exclusive values because a high court could "vacate and remand" a lower court's decision. If coders came upon a case in which the court vacated and remanded, they would not know whether to code it as "vacate" or "remand." This is just the kind of choice coders should not have to make because unreliable data will result (one coder may select "vacate;" another, "remand").

Guarding against the problem requires researchers, once again, to understand their project. Pre-testing also is a useful step.

---

[16] For example, when the variables could reveal confidential information about a respondent, researchers will develop values to mask the information. E.g., rather than asking respondents to identify the city or town where they live, they might ask: do you live in an urban or rural area? For a discussion of these sorts of issues, see <http://www.census.gov/acs/www/methodology/housing_questions/>.

[17] Example adapted from Frankfort-Nachmias and Nachmias (2008, 306).

5.2 Assigning a Value to Each Unit Under Study

After or perhaps concurrently with developing a coding scheme, analysts must methodically assign all units under study a value for each variable. So doing typically requires them to (1) create a codebook to house the scheme and other relevant information and (2) determine how they will ultimately enter their data into a statistical software package so that they can analyze them.

5.2.1 Codebooks

In line with our earlier definition, codebooks provide a guide to the database that the researcher is creating. The guide should be sufficiently rich so that it not only enables the researchers to code their data reliably but also allows others to replicate, reproduce, update, or build on the variables housed in the database (and any analyses generated from it). That's because the primary goal of a codebook is to minimize human judgment—to leave as little as possible to interpretation. A researcher using your data should not have to contact you in order to replicate your study, nor, for that matter, should a lawyer or judge who wants to understand how you collected and coded your data.

For codebooks to serve this function, they should house the basic coding scheme, that is, the variables and the values that each variable can take. But this is the minimum requirement. Many codebooks contain much more, including information about features of the research process (e.g., information about the sample and sampling procedures, data sources, and the time period of the study).[18] If all the variables come from the same source (say, a survey), investigators might provide this sort of detail at the beginning of the codebook as it will apply to all variables. If the data are from different sources, the analyst might also offer some general notes at the front end of the codebook, but much of the more finely grained information will appear in coding notes.

---

[18] If you intend to archive your data with an organization (such as the Inter-University Consortium for Political and Social Research) you should consult the organization's requirements. You should also be aware of the Data Documentation Initiative (<http://www.ddialliance.org>), which "is an effort to create an international standard for describing data from the social, behavioral, and economic sciences" and the Dataverse Network, which is a "web application for sharing, citing, analyzing and preserving research data" (<http://thedata.org>).

Table 5.2 A modified and embellished coding scheme for the variable disposition. (Compare with Table 5.1.)

disposition: how the U.S. Supreme Court treated the decision of the court it reviewed

1	affirmed
2	petition denied or appeal dismissed
3	reversed
4	reversed and remanded
5	vacated and remanded
6	affirmed and reversed (or vacated) in part
7	affirmed and reversed (or vacated) in part and remanded
8	vacated
9	other
555	not clear: stay, petition, or motion granted
666	not applicable: certification to a lower court
777	not applicable: case started in the Supreme Court.
888	not applicable: no disposition
999	missing

Coding Notes:
1. The variable disposition contains the treatment the Supreme Court accorded to the decision of the court it reviewed (that is, of the court directly below it).
2. The information relevant to disposition may be found near the end of the summary that begins on the title page of each case, or preferably at the very end of the opinion of the Court.
3. disposition encodes the specific language used by the Supreme Court.
Source: The *United States Reports*.

Let's reconsider the example disposition (from Table 5.1), only now we've embellished and modified the coding in Table 5.2 so that it will better serve the investigators and their audiences. Note that in addition to listing the source of the data, this coding scheme creates (or relabels) (1) variables and (2) value labels. It also adds (3) a missing value and (4) coding notes. Because all four are relevant to the coding process, we discuss each in turn.

Variables. When researchers enumerate the values of their variables, the variables themselves have (or should have) precise meaning to them. In the example in Table 5.2, we named our variable disposition, which we understand to mean "how the Supreme Court treated the decision of the court it reviewed" (see also Coding Note 1 in the table). Likewise, to return to the "happiness" study, perhaps Kahneman and Deaton called their variable income but knew it to signify "total monthly household income."

Codebooks contain both a short variable name (e.g., `disposition`) as well as the investigator's more descriptive name—sometimes called a label, such as "how the U.S. Supreme Court treated the decision of the court it reviewed." One reason for the short name is that some statistical software packages (into which researchers enter their data) limit the length of the variable name to some fixed number of characters.[19] (Depending on the software there may be other restrictions. In Stata, for example, spaces or special characters, such as & or %, are prohibited, and you can't begin a variable name with a number.)

Conventions for naming variables abound. Especially useful is this suggestion from the Inter-University Consortium for Political and Social Research (a major repository of datasets): "It is important to remember that the variable name is the referent that analysts will use most often when working with the data. At a minimum, it should convey correct information, and ideally it should be unambiguous."[20] This is indeed the case, and so advice worth taking.

In addition to the shortened variable name, researchers should supply the longer, descriptive names (labels) for each variable. For variables created from survey questions, the label may be the exact question asked of respondents. For variables generated by other data-collection procedures, it's up to the researcher to supply a descriptive label. In the example above, we gave our variable `disposition` the name "how the U.S. Supreme Court treated the decision of the court it reviewed." The name should convey a sense of the contents of the variable, and it ought to be listed in the codebook and in the database. (Most statistical packages allow the user to enter such a longer variable identifier as a "variable label.")

Values. When researchers develop their coding schemes, they create values—usually in the form of value "labels"—for each variable. In Table 5.2, for example, we created 14 descriptive labels corresponding to the 14 values of the variable `disposition`. After or concurrently with creating the labels, they assign a unique number to each value; e.g., for `disposition` the number 1 stands for "affirmed."

---

[19] About a decade ago most packages required variable names to be eight characters or less. Modern software provides more flexibility but there still is a limit, and for the purpose of analyzing data, it can be useful to keep variable names reasonably short.

[20] Inter-University Consortium for Political and Social Research (2012, 22).

The codebook should contain both the value labels and the value numbers. The database too houses both but it is typically the number that the coder enters for each unit of analysis (in our example, each case).

Just as they do for variable names, conventions for assigning numbers to the values of variables abound.[21] A few of the more important include, first, that value numbers should be convenient, logical, and intuitive. For example, because matters of size and order are irrelevant (and the numbers themselves convey no information), the values of the variable gender could be 1010 = male and 5020 = female.[22] But the convention of "convenient, logical, and intuitive" counsels that the researcher should begin with, say, 0 or 1, and increase by 1 (e.g., male = 0; female = 1 or male = 1; female = 2).

Note that we follow this rule in coding disposition in Table 5.2. Though we could have started with the value 10,000, we begin with 1 and increase by 1 for each subsequent label. The exceptions here are the four "not applicable"/"not clear" codes of 555, 666, 777, and 888 and "missing," which is 999. These values provide no information about "how the Supreme Court treated the decision of the court it reviewed" because there was either no lower court, no treatment of its decision, or the information is unenlightening or doesn't exist. To distinguish these "not applicable" and missing values from those that convey information about the Court's treatment, we gave them different numerical values. (And we should follow that scheme for all other variables in the dataset where "not applicable" or "missing" is a possibility. For purposes of coding and codebooks, consistency is a virtue.)

We have more to say about these kinds of codes below, under missing values. For now, we only wish to note that our general advice of starting with the lowest values with the fewest digits for variables where size and order don't matter need not come at the expense of sophistication. Suppose we were conducting a survey for a sample of respondents who were either Protestant or Jewish. Adhering to the rule of coding the data finely, we would ask them to identify their denomination if they are Protestant denominations (say, Baptist, Methodist, Presbyterian, Lutheran) or the form of their Judaism if they are Jewish (say, Orthodox, Conservative, Reform). We could

---

[21] See, e.g., Inter-University Consortium for Political and Social Research (2012).
[22] Gender is an example of a nominal variable, as we explain in Chapter 6.

simply number each value consecutively: e.g., Baptist = 1, Methodist = 2, and so on. A more refined and intuitive scheme would classify numbers in a logical, meaningful way: 10 = Baptist, 11 = Methodist, 12 = Presbyterian, 13 = Lutheran; 20 = Jewish Orthodox, 21 = Jewish Conservative, 22 = Jewish Reform).[23] Once again, we tried to follow this rule in creating the values for disposition, such that 1 and 2 are clear wins for the appellee (respondent) and 3–8 at least partial victories for the appealing party (appellant or defendant).

As we just noted, the variables disposition and religion do not have any particular order or size, nor do the numbers themselves convey useful information. That's not the case for many other variables; a survey respondent's age or weight provide two examples.[24] But ease of use, intuition, and logic should still guide the assignment of numbers to these sorts of variables. This means that researchers usually should use the actual values of the variable, and not create new numbers. For the variable age: if a person is 27, then the value of the variable age for that person should be 27, and not 0 even if 27 is the youngest age in the dataset. Along similar lines, researchers should record the original value even if they intend to transform it. Suppose you know you'll use the logarithm of the variable age in your analysis. You should still code the raw values of age.

Two other rules of thumb are, first, wherever and whenever possible, researchers should stick with standard values. For example, if zip codes of respondents is a variable in a study of the United States, it would make little sense to list the codes and then assign numerical values to them (11791 = 1; 11792 = 2; 11893 = 3; and so on) when the government has already done that. In other words, the researcher should use the actual zip codes as the values. The same holds for other, less obvious variables, such as industry (or economic activities), to which the researcher can assign the values developed by government agencies: 10.13 = production of meat and poultry meat products; 20.13 = manufacture of other inorganic basic chemicals; 35.13 = distribution of electricity; etc. The values in this example are from the statistical classification of economic activities in the European

---

[23] Example adopted from Brians et al. (2010, 252–3). Under this system, each major category of religion (Protestant and Jewish) receives the same first digit, with the second digit representing a subdivision. As Inter-University Consortium for Political and Social Research (2012, 24) explains, "Such a coding scheme permits analysis of the data using broad groupings or more detailed categories."

[24] These are examples of interval variables. See Chapter 6.

Community (usually abbreviated as NACE);[25] governments elsewhere have created their own codes.[26]

The second rule is simple enough, and follows from virtually all we have written thus far: avoid combining values. The researcher who creates a variable gender and religion and codes a male (value = 0) Baptist (value = 10) as value = 010 is only asking for trouble. Besides working against all the other recommendations we have offered, such values can be difficult to separate for purposes of analyses (but when coded separately as gender and religion, are simple to combine in most software packages).

Missing Values. However carefully researchers plan their project, they will almost inevitably confront the problem of missing values. A respondent may have failed (or refused) to answer a question about her religion, information about a court case that should appear in the official records is missing, data simply may be unavailable for a particular county, and so on. Investigators should be aware of this problem from the outset and prepare accordingly. This is so even if they plan to invoke a statistical method to deal with missing data because the various solutions to the problem assume that researchers treat appropriately "missingness" when they create the original database.[27]

The suggestion here is that investigators must incorporate values to take into account the possibility of missing data, with those values distinguishing among the different circumstances under which missing information can arise. As Table 5.2 indicates, these can include "not applicable" and "missing" but also (especially for surveys), "don't

[25] These are NACE Rev. 2. Available at: <http://epp.eurostat.ec.europa.eu/statistics_explained/index.php/Glossary:Statistical_classification_of_economic_activities_in_the_European_Community_(NACE)>.

[26] E.g., the North American Industry Classification System (NAICS), used by statistical agencies in the United States, Mexico, and Canada. Details available at: <http://www.census.gov/eos/www/naics/>.

[27] Our primary concern here is with coding variables to be included in an initial and original database, and not with strategies for handling missing data or even with recoding or otherwise transforming variables. If, however, the research team has imputed (or filled in) missing values (using one of the many existing approaches to imputation (Gelman and Hill, 2007, Ch. 25), they should indicate this in the final version of the codebook. Along these lines, the Inter-University Consortium for Political and Social Research (2012) suggests one of two possible approaches: (1) "include two versions of any imputed variables: the original variable, including missing data codes, and the imputed version that contains complete data" or (2) "create an 'imputation flag,' or indicator variable, for each variable subject to imputation, set to 1 if the variable is imputed and 0 otherwise."

know," "refused to answer," and "no answer." Whatever the circumstances, researchers should assign values rather than leave blank spaces. At the very least, blanks raise all sorts of questions, especially: is the observation truly missing, or has the researcher failed or forgotten to code it? Using an explicit missing value code eliminates confusion, and can also provide an explanation for the missing data.[28]

Coding Notes. As we noted earlier, the overriding goal of a codebook—and indeed the entire coding process—is to minimize the need for interpretation. Human judgment should be removed as much as possible or, when judgment is necessary, the rules underlying the judgments should be clarified enough to make them wholly transparent to the coders and to others who will examine the study. Only by proceeding in this way can researchers help to ensure the production of reliable measures.

To accomplish this in practice, analysts must be as clear as possible in delineating the values of the variables. But they should also write down a very precise set of rules for the coders and researchers in their wake to follow—and include that information for each variable housed in their codebook, as we have done in Table 5.2.[29] Such a list should be made even if the investigators code the data themselves because without it, others wouldn't be able to replicate the research. Along these lines, an important piece of advice is to imagine that the researcher assigned an assistant the task of coding a variable (in Table 5.2 classifying each case by its disposition), and that the only communication permitted between the researcher and the assistant was through a written appendix to the work detailing the coding scheme. This is the way to conduct research and how it should be judged.[30]

---

[28] Some software packages allow for multiple missing value codes. Stata, for example, enables each dataset to have up to 27 missing value codes. This function is helpful because the reason for missingness is encoded in the dataset and the software can handle missing data appropriately in the analysis.

[29] In a lecture at the University of Southern California (March 15, 2013), Professor Justin Grimmer recommended very concise coding rules, along with a flow chart to help coders make decisions. Though we agree with Grimmer on the value of a flow chart, the length or the degree of detail will vary by project.

[30] See Epstein and King (2002). Again, given the scope of our concerns, coupled with space limitations, we gloss over the topic of transforming original variables (see note 27). But, of course, if the researchers create new variables from existing ones, they should note this somewhere in the codebook.

5.2.2 Data Entry and Software

Once researchers have devised their codebook, they must turn to the tasks of (1) employing the codebook to assign a value for every variable for each unit under study and (2) entering these values into a statistical software program. They can perform these tasks concurrently or separately. Analysts making use of certain kinds of computer-assisted telephone surveys, for example, do not separate the two; direct data entry occurs. At the other extreme, researchers who code their data from a host of sources may record the assigned values on coding sheets and then transfer the information to a software program. Why? Return to the example of analysts coding court disposition and suppose that, in addition to the values of this variable, the project also required them to collect data on the age of the judges deciding the case. Because judges do not list their age in their opinions, the researchers can't obtain information on disposition and age from the same source. To overcome this obstacle, they might create a coding (or transfer) sheet, assign values to each case on the variable disposition, and then do likewise for age. Once they've collected and coded all the data, they can enter the information (now on coding sheets) into a software package (be it Excel, SAS, SPSS, Stata, among others).

We are not proponents of this physical coding-transfer approach. The problem is that every extra step has the potential to create error, such that recording information onto coding sheets and then transferring that information into a computer introduces a step that is not necessary in direct data entry. We say this even though we understand that coding and data entry are often two separate tasks and so performing them concurrently can lead to errors in one, the other, or both. Using a data entry program, though, can help ameliorate the problem. There are a number of different types of data entry systems. Some are stand-alone applications, such as Microsoft Access or FileMaker. Others are systems that run on the internet and interact with a database through the web browser.[31]

---

[31] Common database management systems (DBMSs) include Oracle Database, Microsoft SQL Server, and MySQL. Some websites that use these DBMSs are custom systems designed for a specific project, such as the one we designed for the U.S. Supreme Court Database (<http://supremecourtdatabase.org>). Others, including Zoho Creator (<https://www.zoho.com/creator/>), are off-the-shelf systems that can be used to build web-based data entry pages.

The advantages of these kinds of programs or systems are, first, their ability to validate data as they are being entered, ensuring that whoever enters the data can't, for example, type the letter "A" if the values of the variable are limited to numbers. Second, they allow developers to create drop-down menus or checkboxes to code variables, safeguarding against typographical errors. Finally, sophisticated systems allow multiple coders to enter information into the same dataset. The drawbacks are the sometimes steep learning curve and the need to anticipate where coders are likely to make mistakes. If you don't set up the right validation before the coders begin, then the system won't be very useful. Of course, thinking carefully about each variable and the values it can take *before* collecting and coding data has some real benefits.

Whatever data-entry choices researchers make, they can and should evaluate them. Reliability checks on the coding of variables are now standard. Drawing a random sample of cases in the study and asking another person(s) to recode them is a simple way to conduct them. So too analysts must assess the reliability of the data-entry process even if they've made use of sophisticated software to input the information. Although such programs may make it difficult, if not impossible, for investigators to key in wild or out-of-range values (e.g., a "7" if the only values for gender are $0 = 1$ male, $1 =$ female), the programs on their own will not perform consistency or other checks.

Researchers can undertake the process of error-checking or "cleaning" their dataset in any number of ways. For example, if they haven't used a data entry program, they can still employ their software to spot wild codes. And, regardless of how they've entered the data, they can run consistency checks. Imagine, in addition to coding the disposition of a case, we also coded the vote (e.g., 5–4) and whether or not the justice voted with the majority. If the vote is 5–4, then we should see 5 justices in the majority; if there are 6 or only 4, then we know there's a problem.

We could provide other examples but we don't want you to miss the larger point: error-checking is a key part of the process, for as Rubin and Babbie well state, " 'dirty' data will almost always produce misleading research findings."[32] The same, of course, is true of data that have been

---

[32] Rubin and Babbie (2011, 508).

collected and coded via asystematic, unthinking means—that is, means the recommendations contained in this chapter are designed to thwart.

* * * * * * * *

Once we've entered our data, the final step is analysis—the subject of Part III. Before moving there, though, a word or two is in order about what it is researchers are analyzing and how statistical software can help.

We just mentioned data entry systems. Foregoing them is fine, but researchers need to enter their data into something—say, an Excel sheet or a Word file—and then transform that something into a dataset, which can be stored in a number of file formats.[33] Unlike a spreadsheet or text file, binary data files house all the information we need to analyze our data—including variable names, long descriptions of each variable, and, where appropriate, value labels. They also contain information about missing data, and, of course, the data themselves.

The point of creating a data file is that statistical software packages[34] can read them, and using these packages for data analysis is a near essential for several reasons. First, they make the user clearly delineate data manipulation and data analysis. Unlike a spreadsheet where it's *very* easy to change a data value accidentally, in these packages analysis takes place after manipulation, and would need to be repeated if the underlying data change. Second, statistical packages make it very easy to implement the tools in chapters to come. As their name suggests, they are designed for statistical analysis, and it's just more efficient to use them for this purpose. Third, all the packages support doing analysis in "batch" mode—submitting a set of commands and getting results back. While using software interactively is very important for exploratory preliminary analysis, researchers should conduct all final analyses in batch mode so that they (and others) can replicate each and every step of the process. We've both wasted many hours not following this

---

[33] The product StatTransfer (<http://stattransfer.com>) makes it easy to transform one file type into another.

[34] Some commercial packages, as we've noted throughout, are SAS (<http://www.sas.com>), SPSS (<http://www.ibm.com/software/analytics/spss/>), and Stata (<http://www.stata.com>). The R language is a popular open source option (<http://www.r-project.org>). The book's website contains tutorials and replication materials for both Stata and R.

guidance, and now do so religiously. Finally, these statistical packages offer higher quality graphics capabilities, and many more statistical models than a general purpose spreadsheet.

We hope you follow this advice. It will make implementing the material to come much easier and more intuitive.

PART III

Analyzing Data

After researchers design their studies and collect their data, they try to make sense of what the data tell them—that is, they analyze their data. They usually begin this process by summarizing the sample of data that now resides on their hard drive (if we were writing this book 15 years ago we would have said "floppy disk" and 30 years ago, "punch cards") so that they can learn about it. We cover methods for summarizing (or describing) data in Chapter 6.

However important this first step, it's usually just that—a first step. More often than not, researchers also want to know what their sample of data tells them about some broader population of interest: they'd like to learn about the facts they don't observe (the entire population) using facts they do observe (the sample). To return to an earlier example, we might be interested in what all adults living in Australia think about same-sex marriage by collecting survey data about what 1,500 Australians think. We usually don't care so much about the 1,500 in our sample, but we care a lot about what that sample can tell us about all 14.6 million adult Australians.[1]

This process of learning about populations from samples of data is called *statistical inference*. In Chapter 7 we cover the basics of statistical inference, focusing on how we can perform descriptive inference using random samples of data. Empirical legal scholars deploy many tools to perform statistical inference with observational data (remember: data we don't produce in a lab but that the world creates), though regression models are the most common. Chapters 8 and 9 focus on these models

[1] Wolfram Alpha, 2013 <http://www.wolframalpha.com/input/?i=adult+population+australia>.

with the goal of understanding what they can, and cannot, tell us about causal relationships.

In presenting the material to come we move sequentially—from summarizing in Chapter 6 to making inferences in Chapters 7–9—but in practice the process of analyzing data is as dynamic as the process of designing research. Sure, we usually start by summarizing the data we have collected and then turn to making inferences, but the truth of it is that even after we estimate, say, a regression model, we may turn back to summarizing data. Perhaps we've added a new variable from fresh data; or maybe we've created a new variable from existing data. Either way, we return to learning about the new variables before turning to inference, meaning that summaries and inferences are best conceptualized as components in a dynamic process rather than as steps in a recipe.

We should add one other note before moving forward. Actually, it's a point we made in the Preface—about the material in this book amounting to a true primer, an introduction to important concepts. This holds with particular force for Chapters 7–9. Covering the topics in these chapters rigorously and comprehensively would take many more books, or two to three semesters worth of seminars in a Ph.D. program. The chapters are certainly not meant to be exhaustive, but designed instead to provide a foundation on which you can build if you so desire. On the other hand, after reading the material to come, you should be able to evaluate empirical studies, understand claims based on statistical evidence in expert reports, and begin to summarize and perform inference on your own dataset.

Please keep in mind these notes as we turn to the task of analyzing data. You'll find it challenging but interesting, satisfying, and, yes, even enjoyable. Trust us.

6

Summarizing Data

Once researchers have designed and executed their study, they're left with a dataset. The focus of this chapter is on the usual first component of the data-analytic process: summarizing and exploring a sample of data—in other words, understanding the data that the researcher (or someone else) has collected.

To put summarizing data in context, consider a hypothetical study of eligible jurors in a large city. Let's suppose the city has a population of two million eligible jurors. Further suppose we randomly select 1,000 eligible jurors for our study. Figure 6.1 depicts the population and sample.

For any study there are features or characteristics about the population we would like to understand—say, for this study, the proportion of eligible jurors that have been victims of a crime. Any characteristic of the population that we care to learn about is called a *parameter*. Parameters are sometimes referred to as "quantities of interest." The proportion of eligible jurors in the population of our city who were victims of a crime is one parameter. Because we do not have information about all the jurors in the population, it is impossible for us to observe the parameter directly; in other words, we don't know the precise proportion of crime victims among the two million eligible jurors. Nonetheless, because we have drawn a random sample of eligible jurors, we could make a good guess about the parameter by developing a *statistic* from our sample.

What is a statistic? Sometimes people use the term "statistic" as a synonym for "data." Newspapers regularly publish survey statistics, governments release demographic statistics, corporations provide financial statistics, and the like. We use the term "statistic" to refer to a quantity or a number computed using a sample of data. We typically

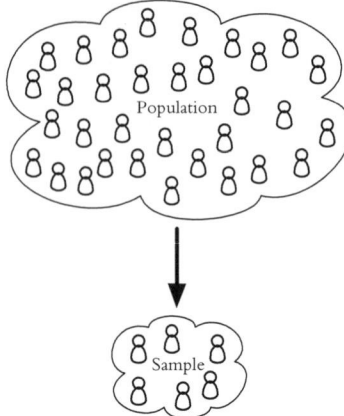

Figure 6.1 A hypothetical population and sample of eligible jurors.

choose a statistic that will give us a good estimate of the parameter of interest. (In the following chapters, we'll discuss what makes for a good statistic.)

So what statistic might we use to estimate the proportion of eligible jurors in the population who were victims of a crime? The simplest—and, it turns out, the best—statistic is the proportion of eligible jurors *in our sample* who were victims of a crime. Because we drew a random sample from the population, the proportion of crime victims in the sample provides an estimate of the proportion of crime victims in the population. The bigger the sample, the better the estimate will be. But it will only be an estimate, and we'll need to figure out how good of a job our statistic does. This process of learning about a population from a sample is called descriptive inference—the topic of Chapter 7.

For the remainder of this chapter we'll set aside the population and just focus on our sample. We won't say any more about parameters and populations until the next chapter. But we'll talk about statistics because they're our focus when summarizing the data in our sample.

6.1 Variables

In our hypothetical study of eligible jurors, each juror that appears in our sample is a single *unit of analysis*. We can think of any sample as a collection of units of analysis, whether jurors, cases, decisions, votes, or anything else. For each unit of analysis, we collect various pieces of information about each of those units (here, eligible jurors). Each piece of information we collect is called a *variable*. As we know from Chapter 2, variables are characteristics that vary across units of analysis in the population, such as whether or not a juror was the victim of a crime.[1] Because we're dealing with a random sample (rather than the entire population), these characteristics might not vary in the sample, but they do need to vary in the population.

We can organize data in many ways, but typically we would put the units of analysis on the rows and the variables on the columns. In Figure 4.1, we showed you how La Porta et al. organized their data. Table 6.1 provides a similar display for the hypothetical data in our eligible juror study. There we show five of the eligible jurors in this dataset, each with a unique identification number (ID). Each row in the table corresponds to one eligible voter—one unit of analysis. The five columns of data each house a variable. Besides the identification number, there is a variable indicating whether the individual has been the victim of crime (Victim), the juror's age (Age), the juror's level of education (Education), and the township of the juror's primary residence (Township).

When deciding what types of tools to use to perform descriptive and statistical inference, it is necessary to consider the type of variable that we or another researcher has collected. In Chapter 2, we distinguished between independent variables (inputs) and dependent variables (outputs). This distinction is important for statistical analysis as we'll soon

Table 6.1 Hypothetical data for a study of eligible jurors. Here we show information on five of the eligible jurors in our sample of 1000. Each unit of analysis (eligible juror) is on a row; information about each unit (the variables) is in the columns.

ID	Victim	Age	Education	Township
1	Y	47	Some College	Perry
2	N	68	College	Wea
3	Y	25	High School	Perry
4	Y	77	High School	Wabash
5	N	31	Some High School	Wabash

---

[1] If a characteristic didn't vary in the population, it would be a constant and wouldn't be worth collecting. For our study of eligible jurors, it wouldn't be worth collecting the information that each eligible juror is of the species *homo sapiens*.

see, but so is another: how the independent and dependent variables are measured. There are three possibilities: nominal (sometimes called categorical), ordinal, and interval. Further, for the reasons you'll understand momentarily, nominal variables are a type of *qualitative* variable, and the other two, *quantitative* variables. (Regardless of these labels, we can perform statistical analysis on all three.)

In Table 6.1 Township and Victim are examples of *nominal* variables. Note that for both, every value comes from some unordered, exhaustive list of possible values. The city from which we drew the sample consists of a number of townships, and each eligible juror has a primary residence in one and only one. The table encodes this information using the name of the township. Victim is another nominal variable. Eligible jurors either were ("Y") or were not ("N") victims of a crime. Because Victim has only two categories, it is a special type of nominal variable, sometimes called a *dichotomous* or "*dummy*" variable. They are called dummy variables because the values 0 or 1 are used to stand in for something else—in this case whether or not someone was the victim of a crime—just as a dummy would stand in for a person in a clothing store.

The ID variable is also nominal. Do you see why? Even though the information is encoded using numbers—perhaps to protect the identity of each individual in the sample—the numbers themselves don't carry any intrinsic meaning other than the assignment to each person in the sample.

Sometimes variables appear to be nominal but, in fact, the categories they contain follow some logical ordering. Education provides an example. Those who have completed high school ("High School") have more education than those who have some high school ("Some High School").[2] Because it is often necessary to finish high school before attending college, we know that those with some college ("Some College") probably have more education than those in the "High School" category, and those who graduated from college ("College") have more education than those with just some college. In short, the categories are ordered: "Some High School" < "High School" < "Some College" < "College." Education or any other

---

[2] In most parts of the world, high school marks the end of (often compulsory) secondary education. Our variable distinguishes among those with just some secondary education ("Some High School"), those who graduated from secondary education ("High School"), and those who have gone on to higher education ("College").

Table 6.2 A taxonomy of types of variables.

Type	Description	Category
Nominal	Categories	Qualitative
Ordinal	Ordered categories	Quantitative
Interval	Differences between values are equal	Quantitative

variable with ordered categories is called an *ordinal variable*. Ordinal variables are a type of *quantitative* variable as we just mentioned, but the distances between each of the categories in the orderings need not be the same.

Interval variables are also quantitative variables. They resemble ordinal variables to the extent that their values are ordered but the differences between values are equal to one another. Take Age in Table 6.1: the one-year difference in age between 50- and 51-year-olds is the same as the difference in age between a 5- and a 6-year-old.[3] Other interval variables are measured in equally familiar units including euros, dollars, kilograms, pounds, centimeters, and inches.

What we're left with is a taxonomy, as depicted in Table 6.2. Nominal variables are qualitative and capture labels of categories. Ordinal and interval variables are quantitative, the latter measured in units where the differences are the same between categories. You should study this table carefully because the tools and statistics that we use to summarize our variables depend on their type. In fact, some tools are only appropriate with certain types of variables, as we'll soon see.

6.2 An Introduction to Tools for Summarizing Variables

Imagine that the dataset displayed in Table 6.1 contained not five eligible jurors but all 1,000 in our sample, and someone asked us: "how old are the jurors in your sample?" Just looking at the column of data won't be much help. That's because the alternatives—in this example,

---

[3] In the physical sciences there are *ratio* variables, which are just interval variables with a true zero point. In empirical legal studies, the distinction between an interval and ratio variable is rarely important.

the varying ages of 1,000 jurors—are beyond the direct comprehension of most human beings. We can't even hold this many numbers in our head at one time, much less simultaneously interpret them. And the task grows exponentially more difficult as the size of the dataset increases. For some people remembering 10 numbers is difficult; for nearly all of us, 1,000 (or 10,000 or 100,000) is impossible.

This is where tools for summarizing variables come into play. Not only do they help researchers learn about their data; they communicate to others what the data are about.

In the two sections to follow, we examine two kinds of tools: displays and statistics. To animate our discussion, we make use of the International Criminal Tribunals (ICT) dataset amassed by Meernik and his collaborators.[4] The ICT dataset contains information on defendants brought up on charges between 1994 and 2010 in three international criminal courts: the International Criminal Tribunal for Rwanda, the International Criminal Tribunal for Yugoslavia, and the Special Court for Sierra Leone. Meernik and his co-authors used these data to examine the determinants of the sentences handed down by these courts (and in this way the research mirrors the Posner and de Figueiredo study of the International Court of Justice that we explored in previous chapters[5]). For each case, the ICT dataset contains variables on the charge leveled against the defendant (including both the number and types of charges), the presence of various aggravating and mitigating factors, and the length of the sentence, both at trial and on appeal.

6.3 Displays

Summarizing variables takes different forms. With numerical data, we often summarize many numbers with only a few, and indeed this activity accounts for much of the academic field of statistics. Simple summary (or descriptive) statistics include the mean, median, mode, range, and standard deviation. We'll get to these in the next section. For now, we want to focus attention on two types of displays for

---

[4] See Meernik et al. (2005); Meernik and Aloisi (2007); Meernik (2011). The most current data is at: <http://bit.ly/UDOMPD>. The book's website contains all the datasets and other material necessary to replicate the analyses presented here.

[5] Posner and de Figueiredo (2005).

summarizing variables: *frequency distributions* and *histograms*. Often these can convey the information we need without losing much of value.[6]

Let's start with *frequency distributions*, which researchers often use to summarize nominal or ordinal variables. A frequency distribution is a table that contains the number of observations that fall into each of the variable's categories. To see how it works, consider `Criminal Rank`,[7] a variable in the ICT dataset identifying the highest (or most severe) crime of which the court found the defendant guilty.

Table 6.3 shows the frequency distribution for `Criminal Rank`. Note that "crimes against humanity" is the most frequently occurring value: 69 times out of the 139 total observations. The Percent column in the table contains the percentage of observations that fall into each category. Just shy of 50% of the defendants were found guilty of crimes against humanity, while not quite 14% were convicted of war crimes. The rest were genocide. Researchers can report frequency distributions in a table as we do here, or in a bar chart (see Chapter 10 for details).

The ICT database also contains a variable `Sentence Length` that identifies the sentence (in months) imposed on convicted defendants. This is the dependent variable in many studies, and one we use too as an outcome in the chapters to come. For now, we're just interested in describing `Sentence Length`. But how should we do it? For an interval variable, which this is, a frequency distribution won't be terribly useful because the variable can take on many unique values,

Table 6.3 Frequency distribution of `Criminal Rank`, the most severe crime of which courts in the ICT dataset found that defendant guilty.[8]

Criminal Rank	Frequency	Percent
War crimes	19	13.7%
Crimes against humanity	69	49.6%
Genocide	51	36.7%

[6] Part IV makes clear that we strongly prefer using graphs rather than tables to summarize data (and results). Histograms are graphs; frequency distributions are often presented in tabular form (Table 6.3 provides an example). We explore graphical approaches here and, in more detail, in Part IV.

[7] In the ICT dataset, the name of the variable is `crimRank`.

[8] Source: ICT data.

making a table unwieldly and difficult to use to spot any patterns. (In fact, for Sentence Length there are 33 different sentence lengths in the dataset.)

A handy and common solution to this problem is a histogram—a visual representation of the distribution of a variable. Such depictions are desirable because, in addition to describing a variable, they allow us to explore its underlying distribution.[9]

Before we consider distributions, let's think about how to construct a histogram. We always start with an interval variable, which we chop up into a set of categories. For Sentence Length we might create categories that range from 0–50 months, 51–100 months, etc., and then count the number of observations that fall into each category. Once that's complete, we can create a figure showing the counts within each category. (Histograms are nice because they're easy to construct. It's possible to make one with just a pencil and a piece of graph paper, although it's easier to use a computer.)

Figure 6.2 shows the result—a histogram for Sentence Length. Note that the y-axis (vertical axis) displays the number of observations that fall within the range. This is fairly standard, though sometimes the y-axis will show the percentage or proportion rather than the raw count. Note too that there are some gaps, one around 450 months

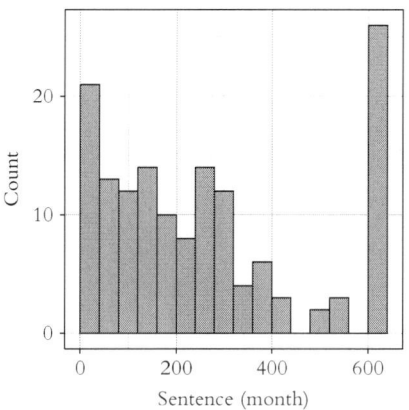

Figure 6.2 Histogram of sentence length (Sentence Length) for convicted defendants.[10]

---

[9] This is one of many graphical tools we can use to summarize data. See Part IV for others, including violin and kernel density plots.

[10] Source: ICT data.

and another at 550. This means that there are no observations in these ranges.

We answer the question of how to interpret this and other histograms momentarily. First, though, you might wonder about the best approach to choose the number and width of categories. Statistical software packages provide default options based on various heuristics. Most will make a good initial choice but will also provide options that researchers can override as they wish. (So, too, most histograms have categories of equal width, though that's not a requirement.) As a general matter there is no best number of categories, but there are some bad choices. A histogram with just one category would be useless. It would show that all the observations fall between the largest and smallest value in the dataset! On the other hand, if there are too many categories, the number of observations that fall within each would be small, maybe just one or two, making it difficult to detect the shape of the underlying distribution. This would be a serious problem because it undermines an important goal of making a histogram: to unmask the underlying distribution of a variable of interest.

How should we go about exploring this underlying distribution? First, we should consider the location of the most frequently occurring values—the regions where there are big "bumps." Often called *modes*, these bumps are the places where most of the data are located. In Figure 6.2 there appear to be two modes—a group of very short sentences and a group of very long sentences. (It turns out that the researchers coded life sentences as 624 months, which is the longest sentence observed in the dataset.) The histogram also tells us that very few sentences fall between 400 and 600 months.

In addition to exploring the number and location of modes, a histogram can help us uncover the shape of the underlying distribution of a variable. We can think of a shape as a curve, and a histogram as a "fuzzy" picture of the underlying curve. If we could make the categories in our histograms really, really small, and we had an enormous amount of data, we could find these curves. In statistics, we use the term *density* for a curve that summarizes a variable.[11] To illustrate some of the shapes that we might uncover with a histogram,

---

[11] Probability density functions are non-negative functions that integrate to one over their domain. We can compute various probabilities by integrating these functions.

from this point forward we'll plot curves rather than categories, but you can think of them as histograms too.[12]

When it comes to detecting the shape of our variable, we are primarily interested in whether it follows a symmetric or skewed distribution. Figure 6.3 shows three shapes that we might see in a histogram. The top panel is symmetric; around the mode there is roughly the same proportion above and below. The second panel shows

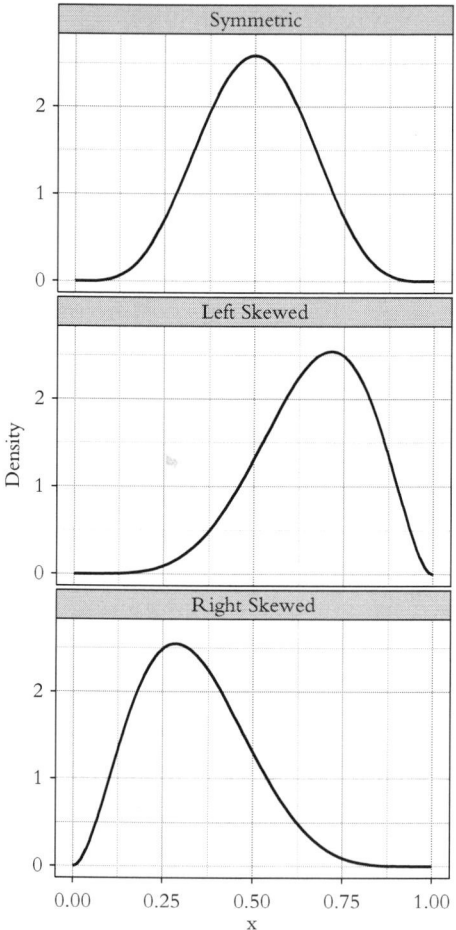

Figure 6.3 Illustration of symmetric and skewed distributions. The top panel is an example of a symmetric distribution; the second panel is left skewed and the third, right skewed.

[12] One alternative to constructing a histogram is something called a kernel density plot, which estimates these smooth curves rather than the stair-step depiction produced by a histogram (see Chapter 10).

a left-skewed distribution; the third shows a right-skewed distribution. Skew is defined by where the outlier observations fall. (Outliers are observations or groups of observations that are different from the rest.) Most of the data in our left-skewed panel are actually on the right!

Why would we care about skew? If the sentences in the ICT data were heavily right skewed, it would suggest that most sentences are relatively short, with a small number that are very long. If, hypothetically, the distribution was symmetric, it would tell us that the sentences handed down by these three courts clustered around a single mode, such that none in the data was extraordinarily short or long.

Finally, we can use histograms to visualize the dispersion of a variable. Dispersion is the amount of homogeneity or heterogeneity in a variable. For example, if one of the international criminal tribunals regularly imposed the same sentence, then Sentence Length would be fairly homogeneous—that is, less dispersed—and would look something like the bottom panel in Figure 6.4. If, on the other hand, a court's sentences were all over the map, Sentence Length would be more dispersed, as in the top panel of Figure 6.4. Were we to create histograms for each of the three courts in the International Criminal

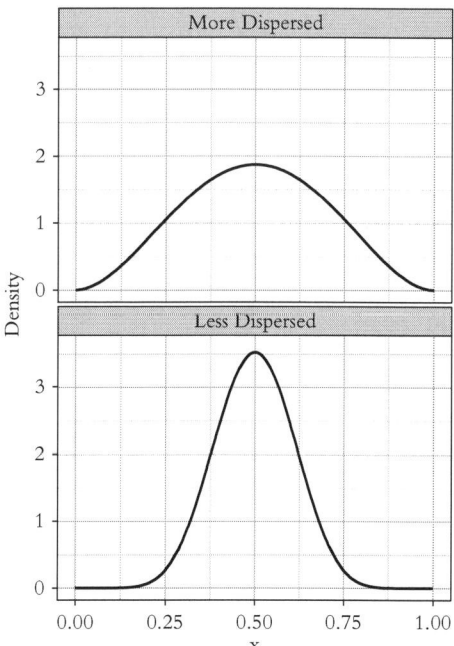

Figure 6.4 An illustration of two distributions, one more dispersed (top panel) and one less dispersed (bottom panel).

Court dataset, it would be possible to ascertain which is more dispersed; that is, which imposes the most heterogeneous sentences.

6.4 Descriptive Statistics

In addition to frequency distributions and histograms,[13] we can use statistics to summarize a variable of interest. Remember that a statistic is just a number we calculate from our sample of data. The statistic we choose to calculate (or that statistical software will calculate for us) depends on what we're interested in learning from our sample. Our concern here is with statistics developed to summarize or describe various aspects of a variable. Not surprisingly, these are called *descriptive statistics*. Some common examples include the mean and the standard deviation, as we'll soon see.

Before going further, you might ask: why bother with descriptive statistics at all? There are several reasons, with the first taking us back to a point we made earlier. With datasets larger than a few observations (that is, most datasets), it's virtually impossible to look down a column and interpret the variable of interest. Can you imagine staring at thousands of criminal sentences and learning very much? Probably not. A descriptive statistic, like the mean, allows us to distill (summarize) the data to a single number that can convey a lot of information. Second, because we can use descriptive statistics to estimate the values of population parameters, they allow us to learn about the population from our sample of data, as we explain in Chapter 7. Finally, some statistics allow us to assess the degree to which an independent and dependent variable are related (or associated) and so can help us to test hypotheses. We discuss these in Chapters 8 and 9.

To understand descriptive statistics, it's necessary to develop some mathematical notation. Bear with us! This won't be hard. We begin by letting n denote the size of our sample. n is just a natural number that tells us how many rows there are in our dataset. Or, if you prefer, n is simply the number of units we're studying. At present we're interested in just a single variable, Sentence Length, and we'll use this notation to describe the values of that variable:

$$Y_1, Y_2, Y_3, \ldots, Y_n$$

---

[13] And other graphical tools we discuss in Chapters 10 and 11.

Table 6.4 Sample of sentence length data (in months) for cases in the ICT dataset.[14]

Observation (ICT Case)	Sentence Length
Y_1	624
Y_2	96
Y_3	624
Y_4	420
Y_5	180
Y_6	180
Y_7	360

The subscripts represent each observation (here, case) in the data. The first observation gets a subscript 1, the second observation a subscript 2, and so on. We count up to n because that's how many observations we have.

On our computer, we usually store each variable in its own column. Table 6.4 contains a sample of sentence length data from the ICT dataset. You'll see that Y_1 corresponds to the first observation (a case in which the defendant received a sentence of 624 months), Y_2 corresponds to the second observation, and so on. With this notation in hand, we can define statistics that measure central tendency and dispersion. Central tendency tells us about the center (or middle) of a distribution—about its "typical" values. Dispersion tells us how wide a distribution is—or the degree to which the data are spread around the typical values.

6.4.1 Central Tendency

In many studies, it is important to know the values of a typical observation. In the ICT dataset, for example, we might want to know how long sentences are in the middle of the distribution of the variable Sentence Length. There are many ways to describe the middle, each with its advantages and disadvantages.

The most commonly used measure of central tendency is the *sample mean* or just the mean. It's also sometimes called an average because it's

[14] Data are a subset of the ICT data.

the simple average of all the values of a variable. Usually denoted $\bar{Y}$, the sample mean is easy to compute: we simply add up all the values and divide by the number of observations. Equation 6.1 shows the calculation using our notation:

$$\bar{Y} = \frac{Y_1 + Y_2 + \cdots + Y_n}{n}$$

$$= \frac{1}{n} \sum_{i=1}^{n} Y_i \qquad\qquad (6.1)$$

The first line of the equation shows adding up each observation and dividing by the number n. In the numerator Y_1 is the first observation, Y_2 the second, and so on. In the denominator n denotes the sample size; i.e., the number of observations in our dataset. To get the sample mean you just take the sum of all the observations and divide by n. To save some space—and to impress your friends—the second line of the equation expresses the summation using a capital sigma. Here's how it works. We start by setting i to 1 and count to 2, 3, 4, and so on until we get to n. Σ tells us that for each of those values, we sum, or add, the values to each other. The values we add are Y_i, which just represents each observation in our data as we count i from 1 to n.

For our sentence length data in Table 6.4, we would compute the sample mean as follows:

$$\bar{Y} = \frac{96 + 180 + 180 + 360 + 420 + 624 + 624}{7}$$

$$= \frac{2484}{7} = 354.86$$

In other words, 354.86 months is the on average sentence length for the data in our sample (shown in Table 6.4).

The sample mean is only appropriate for interval variables (such as Sentence Length). We can't compute a mean for most nominal variables because the values of the variable aren't numeric.[15] For example, even if we were to label the values of the variable Township with numbers (such as 1 = Perry, 2 = Wea), computing a sample mean isn't going to tell us anything about the middle. As for ordinal variables

---

[15] We can compute the mean of a dummy variable, that is, a nominal variable with two categories with values either 0 or 1. Taking the mean of a dummy variable will give the proportion of 1s in the sample.

(for example, Education as depicted in Table 6.1), although they often correspond to numeric values, computing a mean could be misleading because the values aren't equally spaced.

For interval variables, though, researchers often use the mean to summarize central tendency, as we just did for Sentence Length. It's easy to calculate, it provides a lot of information for variables that follow the empirical rule (which we discuss in the next section), and it's easy to use to perform statistical inference from a population average (as we'll see in Chapter 7). These positive features notwithstanding, the sample mean is a statistic that has an undesirable property: it is non-robust. A statistic is non-robust when a small change in just a handful of observations can result in a dramatic change in the statistic. Suppose you were interested in computing the average family income in a neighborhood. Further suppose that just about every family in that neighborhood has an income around €100,000 except for one person: a professional athlete who earns €25 million per year from his team and endorsements. If our sample included just the "regular" individuals in this community, the sample mean would give us a clear picture of the middle. It would be around €100,000. But if our sample happened to include the athlete, our sample mean could be greater than €1 million (if our sample contained only 25 families or so)! By including just this one individual in our sample, our statistic changed dramatically.

For variables that have substantial skew—such as family income, house prices, and the like—the sample mean is not the ideal measure of central tendency. Better is another statistic called the *median*. Computing the median is easy: you sort the values from smallest to largest and pick the one right in the middle (or, again, let the computer do it for you). What happens if there's an even number of observations? Software packages handle it differently, but most would define the median as the midpoint between the two central values. For example, if our dataset was {1, 2, 3, 4}, most software would report a median of 2.5.[16] For our sample data in Table 6.4, the median is 360. Three observations are smaller than 360 (96, 180, and 180), and three are greater than 360 (420, 624, and 624). Unlike the sample mean, the median is a robust statistic. We could change our top value from 624 to 624 million and the median would be exactly the same.

---

[16] Technically, any value that falls between 2 and 3 inclusive is a median of these four observations. As such, medians are non-unique.

We've just computed a median for interval data. Since ordinal variables are ordered, it is possible to compute a median for them as well. For our hypothetical jurors in Table 6.1, we could find the median level of education for the five in the sample by (1) sorting the observations of Education from its lowest ("Some High School") to highest values ("College") and (2) picking the observation in the middle: "High School." Here, either person 3 or person 4 in the dataset would represent the median observation.

However useful, the median has a real downside as a measure of central tendency. In contrast to the mean, it is quite difficult to perform descriptive inference using the median, as we'll see in the chapters to come. This may explain why the mean tends to receive more play in empirical legal studies.

If means help us summarize interval variables and medians, interval and ordinal variables, how might we measure the central tendency of nominal variables? This is where the *mode* comes in. It is simply the most frequently occurring value of the variable. The mode is especially useful for nominal (and ordinal) variables because it is easy to spot by looking at a frequency distribution. In our data in Table 6.4, there are two modes: 624 and 180.

6.4.2 *Dispersion*

The mean, median, and mode tell us something about the typical value or category of a variable. We also might care about the variable's level of homogeneity or heterogeneity—in other words, about its amount of dispersion or variability. When assessing the dispersion of an interval variable, the standard deviation is the most common measure.

To understand how to compute the standard deviation, let's start with calculating the deviation. We begin with the sample mean $\bar{Y}$ and subtract it from each of our observations. (Remember: we're letting Y_i denote the variable of interest.)

$$\left(Y_i - \bar{Y}\right)$$

For an example, look at the second and third columns of Table 6.5. The second column contains the raw data; the third column contains the deviations. Note that observations above the sample mean $\bar{Y} = 354.86$ have positive deviations, while observations below the sample mean have negative deviations.

Table 6.5 An illustration of computing a standard deviation from our sample of sentence length data. Deviations are the difference between each observation and the sample mean. Total shows the sum of each column.[17]

Observation	Sentence Length	Deviation	Deviation²
Y_1	624	269.14	72,437.88
Y_2	96	-258.86	67,007.02
Y_3	624	269.14	72,437.88
Y_4	420	65.14	4,243.59
Y_5	180	-174.86	30,575.02
Y_6	180	-174.86	30,575.02
Y_7	360	5.14	26.45
Total	2,484	0	277,302.9

How are deviations related to dispersion? If a variable is not very dispersed, the observations will fall pretty close to the mean, so the deviations too will be smaller, on average, than a more dispersed variable.

Now, you might think that one way to create a measure of dispersion is simply to add up the deviations and divide by the sample size. But this won't work, as the third column in Table 6.5 shows. If we add up the deviations, they will always sum to zero. This makes sense because the deviations above the mean (the positive ones) offset the deviations below the mean (the negative ones).

The solution to this problem is to square the deviations.[18]

$$\left(Y_i - \bar{Y}\right)^2$$

This ensures that deviations above and below the mean are treated the same. The fourth column of Table 6.5 contains the squared deviations for our sample of sentence length data.

The next step is to add up the squared deviations and divide by something. Our intuition would suggest that we should divide by n, just as we did for the sample mean. But our intuition would be misleading.

[17] Data are the subset of the ICT data in Table 6.4. Columns 2 and 3 show rounded values; all calculations are carried out to full precision.

[18] There are other solutions. One is to take the absolute value of the deviations and average them. This produces another statistic that measures dispersion: the mean absolute deviation.

When computing the sample standard deviation, we should divide by $(n-1)$. (Why? We can't provide a complete answer until the next chapter, where we discuss statistical inference. For now, just go with us.) Of course, for very large samples, there will be little difference dividing by n or $(n-1)$. This results in the following equation:

$$\frac{1}{n-1}\left[(Y_1 - \bar{Y})^2 + (Y_2 - \bar{Y})^2 + \cdots + (Y_n - \bar{Y})^2\right]$$

There's one last step to defining the standard deviation. Our variable of interest is sentence length measured in months. Once we square each deviation and add them all up, the units are months-squared. It would be far more pleasing to return our statistic back to the original units. To do this, we need to take the square root, which results in the standard deviation:

$$s = \sqrt{\frac{1}{n-1}\left[(Y_1 - \bar{Y})^2 + (Y_2 - \bar{Y})^2 + \cdots + (Y_n - \bar{Y})^2\right]}$$

$$= \sqrt{\frac{1}{n-1}\sum_{i=1}^{n}(Y_i - \bar{Y})^2}$$

Throughout this book we'll use s to denote the standard deviation.[19] For our sample sentence length data:

$$s = \sqrt{\frac{277,302.9}{(7-1)}} = 214.98$$

Measures of dispersion are relative. Without any context it's difficult to say whether a standard deviation is "big" or "small", that is, is 214.98 a lot or a little? Nonetheless, the standard deviation will be larger for variables that are more dispersed, and smaller for variables that are less dispersed. If we had a sample of sentences from a domestic criminal court with a standard deviation of 100, we would say that those sentences were more homogenous than the sentences from the international criminal tribunals, where $s = 214.98$.

---

[19] As we'll see in the next section, the standard deviation plays an important role in the empirical rule for understanding normally distributed variables.

One property of the sample standard deviation s is that it must be greater than or equal to zero. Do you see why? Because we're squaring deviations they must be greater than or equal to zero, and then we're just adding them up, dividing by a positive number, and taking a square root. Indeed, the sample standard deviation will only take the value zero when our variable is a constant. Of course, it's not terribly interesting to look at the dispersion of a variable that doesn't vary.

There are other measures of dispersion in addition to the standard deviation. Some analysts look at the *variance*, which is computed in the same way as standard deviation, just without taking the square root. For our sample of sentence length data, the variance $s^2 = 46,217.14$. Another, more common measure is the *range*. It is defined as the difference between the largest (maximum) and smallest (minimum) value in the sample. For our data, the range is $(624 - 96) = 528$.

The range is of limited value because it doesn't take into account the amount of dispersion in the middle of the variable; it only considers the ends of the distribution. As a result, many researchers report the *interquartile range*. The interquartile range is the difference between the 75th and 25th percentile. It is computed in the same way as the median (and so can be used for interval and ordinal variables): we sort the observations and pick the one with 25% of the data above and below. Variables that are more dispersed will have larger interquartile ranges; those that are less dispersed will have smaller interquartile ranges. The interquartile range for our sample sentence length data is 342.

The mean, median, and mode as measures of central tendency and the standard deviation and (interquartile) range as measures of dispersion are among the most common in empirical legal research. But two qualifications are worth noting. First, each provides researchers and their audience with a feel for the distribution of a variable but necessarily excludes other features. A simple example is the median, which includes information about central tendency, but omits information about variation. In other words, knowing the median sentence length tells us nothing about the degree to which sentences deviate from that median. Were they tightly clustered around 360 months (the median value) or not? This counsels for supplying several (appropriate) descriptive statistics for each variable but even then information will be lost, including the exact sentence length in each case. That's why graphical representations of the data (such as histograms) can be useful, in addition to descriptive statistics.

Second, though we have described the most common measures of central tendency and dispersion, statisticians have developed many others for all sorts of purposes.[20] We saw one of these at the very beginning of the chapter—the sample proportion. Some, like the geometric or harmonic mean, are used to measure central tendency. Others, including the mean absolute deviation or median absolute deviation, are ways to measure dispersion. Statistics can also tell us whether variables are skewed and the direction of the skew, and even how heavy the tails are of a particular variable. (The technical term is kurtosis.) Then there are statistics that allow us to examine whether two or more variables are related to one another. We explore these in Chapter 8.

6.5 The Empirical Rule

All the statistics we've reviewed so far have their uses, but as we foreshadowed, the sample mean $\bar{Y}$ and sample standard deviation s can provide even more information about a variable when the variable is normally distributed. Sometimes called the bell curve (or, in some circles, the Gaussian distribution), the normal distribution plays an important role in statistical inference, in part because so many variables are, in fact, normally distributed. (The variables height, weight, and test scores follow this distribution in nature.) Just because a variable doesn't follow the normal distribution doesn't mean that it's untrustworthy, bizarre, or just plain wrong. The term normal doesn't carry any normative bite; it's just a term used to represent a precisely defined mathematical function.

We'll talk much more about the importance of the normal distribution for inference in the next chapter. For now, we simply want to introduce it and explain its value for summarizing data.

Let's start with the introduction. Figure 6.5 shows three different normal distributions. Each is characterized by two parameters: its mean μ and standard deviation σ. (Why are these represented by Greek letters rather than the formulas described in the previous section? Because these are parameters, not statistics, and so we typically use Greek letters to represent them.) The top panel of Figure 6.5 contains a normal distribution with a mean of 0 and a standard deviation of 1. The location of the normal distribution can be shifted. The middle panel has the same standard deviation, but the mean has been moved to 2.

---

[20] Agresti and Finlay (2009); Dodge (2006).

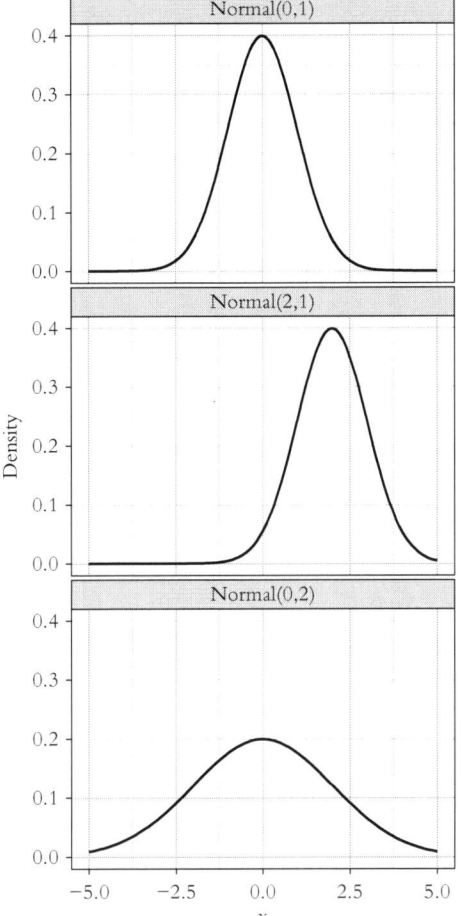

Figure 6.5 Three different normal distributions. The top panel has
a mean of 0 and a standard deviation of 1. The middle panel has a mean of
2 and a standard deviation of 1. The bottom panel has a mean of 0 and a
standard deviation of 2.

In the bottom panel, the mean remains at 0 but the dispersion of the
distribution has been increased to 2. All of these curves are normal
distributions.[21]

---

[21] The normal distribution is defined by the following formula:

$$\phi(x|\mu,\sigma) = \frac{1}{\sigma\sqrt{2\pi}}e^{-\frac{(x-\mu)^2}{2\sigma^2}}$$

Where $\pi \approx 3.14159$ and $e \approx 2.71828$ are transcendental numbers.

We can use the normal distribution in a number of ways. First, any variable can be transformed into a *z-score* by subtracting off the sample mean and dividing by the sample standard deviation:

$$z = \frac{Y_i - \bar{Y}}{s}$$

Why would we want to do this? z-scores are useful because they allow us to see where each observation in a dataset falls *relative* to other observations in the dataset. Suppose a student scored 80 points on a mathematics test, and a different student scored 80 on a sociology exam. In the mathematics course the average score was $\bar{Y}_{math} = 70$ and in the sociology course the average score was $\bar{Y}_{soc} = 85$, and, let's suppose, the standard deviation for both exams was $s = 5$. If we turned the mathematics student's test score into a z-score we would get 2.0 because this student performed better than the average z-score value of zero. The sociology student, on the other hand, gets a z-score of -1.0, which is below average. The mathematics student should be pleased while the sociology student should be disappointed even though their raw scores were the same.

z-scores are a tool that we can use to standardize scores across different classes to facilitate comparison. But what do they have to do with summarizing data? If we know that a variable follows an approximately normal distribution—which a histogram will reveal—we can invoke something called the *empirical rule*. The empirical rule tells us how much data we would expect to find within particular ranges. We compute the ranges with just two statistics: the sample mean $\bar{Y}$ and the sample standard deviation s.

To see how the empirical rule works, imagine that we gave an examination to our students and computed the mean to be 75 and the standard deviation, 5. Suppose we also created a histogram and saw that the variable looked to be normally distributed. Given these two statistics and a normal distribution, what can we say about the distribution of test scores? The empirical rule, as illustrated in Figure 6.6, tells us that about 68% of our data fall within one standard deviation of the sample mean. For our exam this means that 68% of the data fall between 70 and 80. The figure shows that if we go out two standard deviations in either direction ($\bar{Y} \pm 2s$) we would expect to see 95% of the observations. For this example, 95% of the data would fall between 65 and 85. Finally, 99.7% of the data fall within three standard deviations of the mean; in this example, 99.7% of the data fall between 60 and 90.

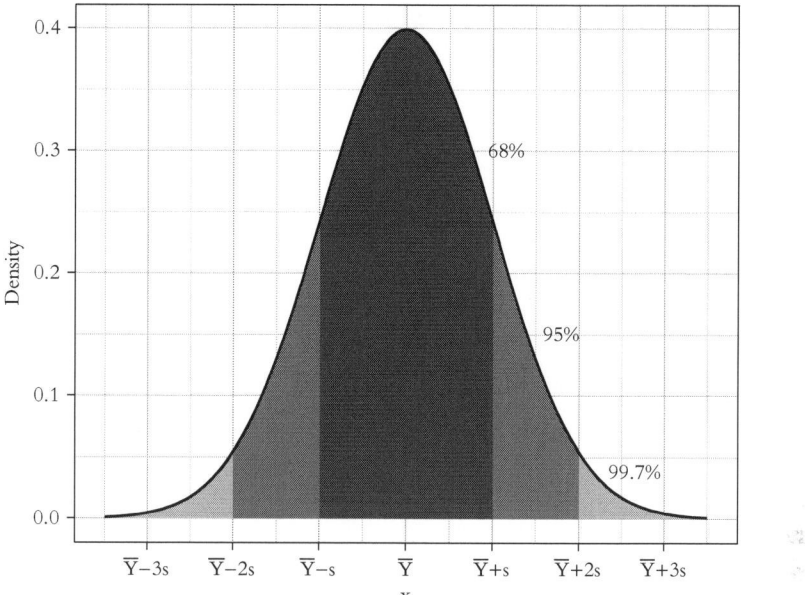

Figure 6.6 Illustration of the empirical rule. $\bar{Y}$ denotes the sample mean; s denotes the sample standard deviation.

The upshot is that the empirical rule is quite powerful. When the values of a variable are normally distributed, the rule provides a lot of information with just two measly statistics. Suppose we knew that the amount of damage awards for a particular tort followed a normal distribution. With just the sample mean and sample standard deviation, we could quickly understand what percentage of damage awards fall in particular ranges by applying this simple rule.

* * * * * * * * *

In this chapter we've considered many tools for summarizing the data that reside on our hard drive. But summarizing is only a small component of most empirical projects. It's now time to turn to the bigger and more consequential component: making inferences. This takes us back to the population of interest and what descriptive statistics might tell us about it.

7

Statistical Inference

We've come a long way in just short of 145 pages. We've carefully designed our study, collected our sample of data, and summarized it. The next step is learning about a broader population of interest from the sample. This is *statistical inference*—the process of using something we actually observe (the sample of data) to learn about something we do not (the entire population)—and it comes in two flavors: descriptive inference and causal inference.

Before exploring these, let's take a step back and review the role of statistical inference in empirical legal studies. As we discussed in Part I, research projects are motivated by questions about a population of interest. But we typically do not collect data on the entire population; we rather design a data collection protocol to draw a random sample of data from the population. Because the sample was random, if we were to use the same protocol over and over we'd get a slightly different sample. If this doesn't make sense to you, try the following. Take 26 index cards, and on each card write one letter of the alphabet. Shuffle the cards and randomly select five of them. Perhaps your sample was: V, G, S, Q, and N. Now put the five cards back, shuffle again, and choose another five cards. Would you expect to get the same five letters again? Of course not. Because we're randomly sampling from a population (the 26 cards), every sample we draw will be somewhat different. This is why we need to perform statistical inference.

To answer whatever research question we've asked, we must determine what our sample does—and does not—tell us about our population of interest. Most of the time we don't care so much about the observations in our sample (even though they're what we analyze); it's the population that motivates our work. The goal of statistical inference is to make a principled guess about what's going on in the population from our sample of data, and to quantify how certain or uncertain we are about the guess we make.

This chapter begins our journey into the world of statistical inference. In what follows, we start with the logic of inference, illustrating how we use random samples from populations to answer research questions. Next, we develop the two different tools that analysts use to perform statistical inference: confidence intervals and hypothesis tests.

7.1 The Logic of Statistical Inference

To understand the logic of statistical inference, let's start with an example. As we mentioned earlier, in the United States, some states elect their judges and others appoint them.[1] Tabarrok and Helland studied the effect of these different methods of judicial selection on damage awards in tort suits.[2] In particular, they were interested to know whether, in states that elect their judges, awards were higher in cases where an in-state plaintiff brought suit against an out-of-state defendant. Their prediction was that elected judges would be more likely than appointed judges to rule in favor of plaintiffs because redistributing "wealth from out-of-state businesses to in-state plaintiffs" would help them win re-election.[3] To test their hypothesis—here to compare awards in states that do and do not elect their judges—Tabarrok and Helland collected data from thousands of cases from 48 of the U.S. states. Using a variety of statistical methods, they report that their hypothesis holds: "the expected total award in ... elected states with out-of-state defendants is approximately $240,000 higher than in other states."[4]

---

[1] See Chapter 2.

[2] Tabarrok and Helland (1999).

[3] Tabarrok and Helland (1999, 157). Their story is a little more complicated than this because they compared awards in partisan elected states (where judges identify their partisan affiliation), non-partisan states (where judges run for re-election but not on a partisan ballot), and non-elected states. For pedagogical purposes, we'll stick with the basic distinction between elected and non-elected.

[4] Tabarrok and Helland (1999, 186).

7.1.1 *Exploring Sampling Distributions with a Known Population*

Let's set aside the results of the Tabarrok and Helland study for a minute and explore what could happen if we were to conduct the same study. We begin with Figure 7.1, which shows two possible scenarios about the broader population of all tort suits. In Scenario A there are no differences, on average, in the amount of damages awarded by elected and non-elected judges; that is, the Tabarrok and Helland hypothesis is just plain wrong. In Scenario B there is, in fact, a difference in the population of awards between those made by elected and non-elected judges. That difference is $240,000 in size. For the sake of illustration, assume that either Scenario A or Scenario B is true; i.e., there is either no difference or a difference of $240,000 in the population.[5] These two scenarios are about populations. Remember that characteristics of populations are called *parameters*. In both scenarios the parameter of interest is the difference in average damage awards between elected and non-elected judges. In Scenario A the parameter takes the value $0 and in Scenario B the parameter takes the value $240,000. This is hypothetical because we would have to be an omniscient superhero to actually know what's true in the population. But walking through these scenarios will allow us to understand how statistical inference works.

If we were to conduct this study, how would we learn about the parameter? We'd draw a random sample of data and then compute a *statistic*—in fact, we'd use a statistic based on the sample mean. We'd compute the sample mean for states with elected judges, the sample mean for states with judges that don't stand for election, and then take the difference. That (sample) statistic would give us our best guess for the value of the (population) parameter.

In Figure 7.1 we show the statistics that might be computed for each of our two scenarios with the small bubbles labeled Sample 1, Sample 2, and Sample 3. Let's start with Scenario A. If there are no differences on average in the population, what would we expect to see? Intuition might suggest that we'd expect to see a precise difference of zero in each of our samples, but this intuition is wrong. Do you see why? Because we're *randomly* sampling from the population, each of our samples will be different. And because each of our samples is

---

[5] This is obviously artificial because the difference could be $100,000, or $240,001, or -$125,000 in the population. We restrict it to these two possibilities to make the illustration easier.

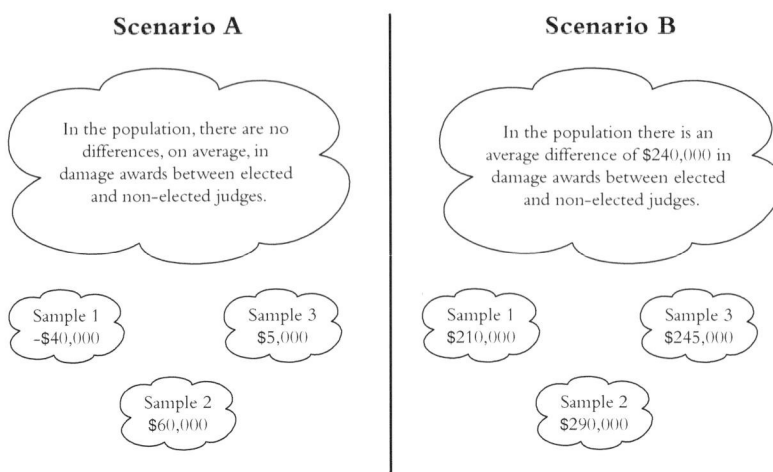

Scenario A

In the population, there are no differences, on average, in damage awards between elected and non-elected judges.

Sample 1
-$40,000

Sample 3
$5,000

Sample 2
$60,000

Scenario B

In the population there is an average difference of $240,000 in damage awards between elected and non-elected judges.

Sample 1
$210,000

Sample 3
$245,000

Sample 2
$290,000

Figure 7.1 An illustration of a sampling distribution for a hypothetical tort award study. The large clouds on the top depict populations; the small clouds on the bottom represent samples. The numbers in the small clouds are the means of the samples.

unique, our statistics will be distinct for each sample. In Scenario A, the statistics are pretty close to zero. In one sample, elected judges awarded damages that are on average $40,000 *lower* than appointed judges. In the other two, the damage awards are higher for elected judges, in one $60,000 higher and in the other $5,000 higher. All in all, they approximate the population parameter zero. If we were to sample over and over again from the population in Scenario A, we would expect the statistics to be reasonably close to zero, with some positive and some negative.

We see something different in Scenario B. Here, when sampling over and over again from the population with a parameter of $240,000, we see our statistics are quite far from zero. In fact, they are close, but not equal to, $240,000. Some, like Sample 1, fall below the population parameter. Some, like Samples 2 and 3, fall above the population parameter.

Why are we drawing multiple samples from the same population? To show how statistics vary from sample-to-sample. Because it's crucial to have a random sample of data from the population, the statistics we compute from those data are random themselves. Actually, statistics are random variables. This seems odd because we usually just draw a single sample and compute a statistic once. But *if* we were to repeat sampling over and over again—as we did in Figure 7.2—our statistics would vary.

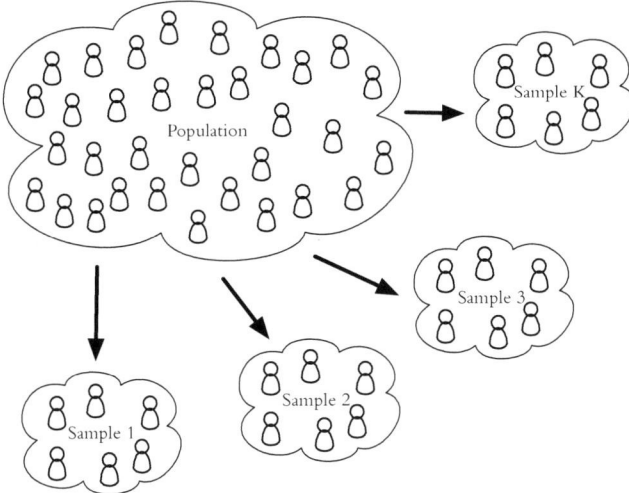

Figure 7.2 An illustration of repeatedly sampling from the same population.

Rather than drawing just three samples from a population, suppose we did it over and over again K times (where K just denotes the number of samples that we draw), as in Figure 7.2. If we wrote down a statistic for each of these samples, say, their mean, and plotted a histogram, we would be able to see the *sampling distribution*. A sampling distribution is the distribution a statistic takes after repeatedly drawing from the same population. Because we're randomly sampling from the population, the statistic in each sample will be different, just as we show in Figure 7.1. In this case, the sampling distribution of the statistic in Scenario A was centered around zero. The sampling distribution of the statistic in Scenario B was centered around $240,000.

There are two quantities of the sampling distribution that are of interest. One is the mean of the sampling distribution. A "good" statistic is one where the mean of the sampling distribution is the population parameter of interest.[6] In our example, if we computed the mean for Samples 1, 2, and 3 in Figure 7.2, it should equal the mean in the population. All the statistics we discuss in this book have this property; on average, across a bunch of samples, they get the population

---

[6] "Good" could mean unbiased or consistent, depending on the particular statistic. An unbiased statistic is one where the expected value of the statistic equals the population parameter. A consistent statistic is one where the statistic converges to the population parameter as the sample size gets infinitely large.

parameter right. Remember back in Chapter 6 when we discussed the sample standard deviation? When we computed that statistic we divided by $(n - 1)$ rather than n. We did this to ensure that we're getting the right estimate of the population parameter. If we computed the sample standard deviation by dividing by n, we'd get a "bad" (i.e., biased) estimate of the population parameter.

The other quantity of the sampling distribution that is important is its *standard error*, which is the standard deviation of the sampling distribution. Remember that the standard deviation tells us about the amount of dispersion. The standard error conveys how much, or how little, we expect our statistics to vary across a bunch of samples. Look back at Figure 7.1. Within each scenario there is variability across the statistics. The amount of variability is determined by the standard error. It tells us how much certainty, or uncertainty, we have about the estimate provided by our statistic. Because more is preferable to less, all else equal, we prefer statistics that have the smallest possible standard error.[7]

Although it's not always the case, the sampling distribution for most statistics follows a particular distribution. Any idea what that might be? If you guessed the normal distribution you would be correct. For most statistics, the sampling distribution follows a normal distribution with a mean centered on the population parameter of interest, and the smallest standard error possible.[8] We'll now use this information to perform inference using a sample of data.

7.1.2 Using the Sampling Distribution to Perform Inference

In the two scenarios in Figure 7.1 we just happened to know the population parameter of interest and explored what would happen if we sampled from the same population over and over again and computed a statistic each time. But this isn't how things work in practice. First, we never know the population parameter of interest. If we did, there would be no reason to perform statistical inference because we'd already know the answer to the question we're asking! Second, we rarely, if

[7] There is, in fact, a lower bound for how small a standard error can be for a particular statistic. This is the Cramér-Rao lower bound (DeGroot and Schervish, 2012, 520).

[8] This is the result of the Central Limit Theorem. This theorem states that the distribution of the sum of just about any random variable follows the normal distribution as the sample size gets large. Because many statistics consist of sums—both the sample mean and the sample standard deviation involve summing—the Central Limit Theorem implies that sampling distributions are normal in large samples (DeGroot and Schervish, 2012, 360).

ever, sample from the same population multiple times; we almost always draw a single random sample from the population.

So, how much can one measly sample from a population tell us? A great deal as long as one condition holds: *that we drew a random sample from the population of interest.* If this holds, it is possible to determine mathematically what the sampling distribution would look like were we to draw more samples. The technical details are far beyond the scope of this book,[9] but the idea is pretty simple. With a random sample and the formula used to compute the statistic, it is possible to figure out the shape of the sampling distribution, along with its mean and its standard deviation (which, remember, is called the standard error since we're dealing with a sampling distribution).[10]

For the single sample of data on our hard drive, the statistic itself is our best guess of the population parameter of interest. As we saw in Chapter 6, the sample proportion is the best statistic for the population proportion, and the sample mean provides us with a good estimate of the population mean. Along similar lines, the sample standard deviation—dividing by that pesky ($n - 1$)—gives us an unbiased estimate of the population standard deviation. For all of these statistics we can also compute their standard errors, which is crucial for computing confidence intervals and performing hypothesis tests (as we'll see soon).

If you take a step back and think about it, these calculations are pretty magical. Relying solely on the fact that our one sample is randomly drawn from a population, we can leverage information from it not only to provide a principled estimate of the population parameter of interest (such as the mean), but also to quantify how certain we are of that estimate by computing a standard error. So, magical? Yes, but such is the logic of statistical inference.

7.2 Confidence Intervals

The goal of statistical inference is to learn about population parameters given a sample of data. Consider an example from the International

---

[9] See DeGroot and Schervish (2012, Chapter 8) on how to compute a sampling distribution. There are other ways to compute a sampling distribution that do not rely on the Central Limit Theorem, including resampling methods like the bootstrap (Efron 1981).

[10] Statisticians have developed "good" statistics for just about every context. You'll have to take our word for it that the statistics we show you in this book are, in fact, the right ones.

Criminal Tribunal dataset. Suppose we've drawn a random sample of cases and then collected data on the length of sentence in each case. From the sample, we can produce an estimate of the average length of sentences using a statistic, the sample mean, $\bar{Y}$, which is 190.128 months. This is our best guess about the population mean, which is μ. (As is customary, we use Greek letters to denote population parameters.) We still need to quantify the reliability of (or uncertainty about) this estimate of the population mean.

To state the reliability of our estimate, we'll use a *confidence interval*. A confidence interval is a range of values where we would expect the population parameter, here the mean, to fall some percentage of the time. As researchers, we get to choose the percentage, called the *confidence level*, though for reasons you'll understand soon it's 95% in most studies.

How do we get a confidence interval? It turns out that once we know the sampling distribution, it is straightforward to write down a confidence interval. The sample mean $\bar{Y}$—just like every other statistic we discuss in this book—is a "good" statistic in that it has a sampling distribution centered on the population parameter μ. Our confidence interval then will be centered at our best guess for the population parameter, which you already know is our statistic the sample mean, or $\bar{Y}$ (=190.128).

The sample mean provides the middle of the confidence interval. To capture the reliability, or lack thereof, of a particular statistic, we rely on the standard error. Remember that the standard error tells us how much variability we're likely to see in our statistic just because we're taking a random sample from some broader population. The standard error for $\bar{Y}$ is $\frac{s}{\sqrt{n}}$. (You'll have to take our word on this, too.) For the International Criminal Tribunal data $s = 149.242$, so our standard error is:

$$\frac{s}{\sqrt{n}} = \frac{149.242}{\sqrt{125}} = 13.349$$

How do we use the standard error? It depends on the shape of the sampling distribution. As we discussed in the previous section, most of the time the sampling distribution follows the normal distribution. And that's the case here, too, because the sample size (n) is larger than 30. When the sample size is smaller than 30 and the population is normal, the sampling distribution takes the shape of Student's t-distribution, which is a bell-shaped symmetric distribution with tails just a bit fatter than the normal. (Student was William Gosset's pseudonym.[11])

For any confidence interval, we choose a confidence level and construct an interval based on that choice. Most of the time, as we just mentioned, we choose a 95% confidence level. But what does that mean exactly? Earlier we provided an informal definition[12] but it's now time to be more precise. A 95% confidence interval is such that if we were to draw sample after sample, the interval would contain the population parameter (here, the mean) 95% of the time. In other words, the interval would correctly contain the population mean for about 19 out of 20 of our samples. If you think back to the Empirical Rule, about 95% of the data fall within two standard deviations of the mean. Similarly, a 95% confidence interval is roughly the sample mean plus or minus two standard errors (remember, the standard deviation of the sampling distribution).

Two standard errors, though, is just a guess. We can get more accurate by using this formula to compute a confidence interval for 95% (or any other confidence level):

$$\bar{Y} \pm t_{(n-1)} \left(\frac{s}{\sqrt{n}} \right) \tag{7.1}$$

This looks complicated, but it just formalizes our discussion above. The confidence interval is centered on the sample mean $\bar{Y}$. The expression $\pm$ means plus or minus. The quantity to the right of the $\pm$ is the *margin of error* (discussed in Chapter 1). The margin of error is composed of two parts. The standard error is on the far right. $t_{(n-1)}$ comes from the *t*-distribution with $(n-1)$ degrees of freedom. The degrees of freedom parameter represents the number of values that are free to vary when computing a statistic. Think of it as telling us what type of t-distribution to use. We use the t-distribution for this confidence interval so it works

---

[11] Gosset worked at the Guinness Brewery in the early twentieth century. He was not allowed to publish trade secrets in academic journals, but went ahead and published his result: the sampling distribution of the sample mean (Student, 1908). Alas, we don't know the population standard deviation σ so we must estimate it with the sample standard deviation s. The *t*-distribution is a symmetric distribution just like the normal distribution, but it has slightly thicker tails to capture some additional uncertainty caused by the fact that we're estimating both the population mean and population standard deviation when computing the confidence interval. The *t*-distribution has a special parameter: a degrees of freedom parameter. For this confidence interval, Gosset showed that the appropriate degrees of freedom was $(n-1)$.

[12] See the related discussion about margin of error in Chapter 1.

for both small and large samples. A t-distribution with a large number of degrees of freedom is indistinguishable from the normal distribution. The precise number depends on the confidence level. Back in the twentieth century we used to look up these numbers in the back of the book (every statistics book had such a table). Today, our statistical software packages can return the appropriate values.

For the International Criminal Tribunal data, we would start by computing the degrees of freedom. Here it would be $(125 - 1) = 124$. We would then pick a confidence level, such as 95%. With the degrees of freedom parameter and the confidence level, we could obtain the appropriate t statistic from a table or by using statistical software. For this application the value is 1.979 (just about 2, as we'd expect). That results in our 95% confidence interval:

$$190.128 \pm 1.979 \cdot 13.349 \text{ or } 190.128 \pm 26.418$$

We also might choose to write the confidence interval in the following way: 95% $CI : [163.71, 216.55]$.

How do we interpret this range of values? We could say this: In our sample, the mean sentence length is 190.128 months. Because of the way we constructed the interval around that sample mean, we are 95% confident that the population mean sentence length lies between 163.71 and 216.55. We would not say that the interval $[163.71, 216.55]$ contains the parameter with 95% probability. Though tempting, this would be incorrect. Population parameters—the things we're interested in learning about—are fixed, unknown quantities. Statistics, on the other hand, are random variables because they are computed from data that are randomly selected from the population. Every sample will yield a slightly different statistic. We construct confidence intervals such that in some percentage of *samples* the interval will contain the true population parameter.

To see how this works, consider Figure 7.3. Here we have a population with a known mean $\mu = 240$. We randomly draw 50 samples from this population, each of size $n = 50$. We then compute and plot the 95% confidence intervals for the population mean. If you look carefully at the figure you'll see that 47 out of the 50 confidence intervals contain the known population parameter. This is just what we'd expect; in about 95% of the 50 samples we'll find the population parameter. For any given sample the probability that the confidence interval contains the population parameter is either zero (it doesn't) or one (it does). As an analyst it's impossible to know for certain because

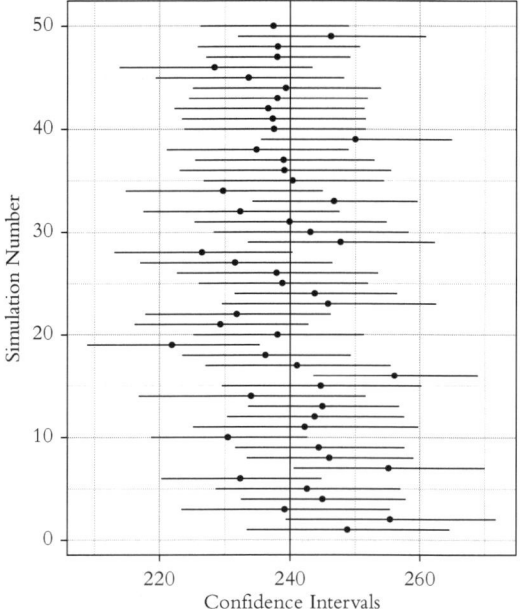

Figure 7.3 Confidence intervals for the population mean from 50 random samples of size $n = 50$. The population mean $\mu = 240$ is shown with the vertical line.

we never know what the population parameter is. The other thing to notice is that the confidence interval is different for each sample. Confidence intervals are random variables too because we compute them from random samples of data.

This implies that confidence intervals will be misleading some percentage of the time. Indeed, 95% confidence intervals will be misleading in about 1 out of every 20 studies (or 5% of the time). Is there any way to obtain a 100% confidence interval? Only in a substantively useless way. For the population mean μ, the interval $(-\infty, \infty)$ contains the population parameter with certainty (∞ is the mathematical symbol for infinity). But that doesn't really tell us much of anything. Of course, we could choose levels of confidence higher than 95%, perhaps 99%. This would result in confidence intervals that are larger, and so are more likely to capture the population parameter correct. We could also choose intervals with a lower confidence level, say 80%, which would make the confidence interval narrower. One reason that more data are almost always better is that confidence intervals narrow as our sample size n gets larger. Narrower conference intervals imply greater confidence in our estimate of the population parameter. If you look at Equation 7.1 you'll see that $\sqrt{n}$ is the denominator of the margin of error. So as n gets bigger and bigger, the margin of error gets smaller and smaller. This is why we said in Chapter 4 that more data are almost always better. The more observations, the clearer the picture of the population.

Our discussion of confidence intervals makes a lot of sense when talking about something like survey research where there is a large, well-defined population and we've been able to sample a small number of individuals from the population to study. But what about datasets that contain the entire population? We've seen several in this book, including Elkins et al.'s on *all* constitutions.[13] We could create confidence intervals around the variables in this dataset (for example, the length of constitutions), but it's hard to think of it as a sample because it includes information on every constitution.

Is it still appropriate to compute confidence intervals in this situation? Our answer is that "it depends."[14] If the goal of the study is merely to describe the sample and nothing more, then there is no reason to compute confidence intervals or anything else; that is, if all we cared about was the average length of constitutions in the dataset, we could just report the mean and be done with it. But, in empirical legal studies, the goal is to make inferences about some broader population, which might include future constitutions. In this situation, where we recognize that all sorts of idiosyncratic factors contribute to the particular observations we observe, it makes sense to use tools like confidence intervals (and hypothesis tests) because they allow us to capture the uncertainty we have about quantities of interest.[15] For this reason, we continue to use the nomenclature of population and sample in the chapters to come, recognizing that we often use these tools when we haven't drawn a sample but, in fact, have collected all the data (the population) for analysis.

[13] Elkins et al. (2009).

[14] For a slightly different answer, see Gill (1999).

[15] Technically, to use population data to extrapolate to a different context or a future context, Bayesian statistics are the appropriate method. Bayesian statistics treat data as given and parameters as the things about which we have uncertainty. All the inferential tools described in this book are close approximations to Bayesian methods as long as we have sufficiently large samples, which provides justification for their use. In other words, it is appropriate to use hypothesis tests or confidence intervals as part of a process of extrapolation to different contexts or different time periods as an approximate Bayesian solution to the inferential problem.

7.3 Hypothesis Testing

So far we've focused on the population mean, but it's worth noting that statisticians have developed confidence intervals for just about every parameter imaginable, including the population standard deviation, differences in means between two groups, and, as we'll see in Chapter 8, regression coefficients.

Confidence intervals, though, are not the only tool we use to perform statistical inference. There's also *hypothesis testing*. Hypothesis tests are a formal way to examine a *null hypothesis*, which is a statement about population parameters. The easiest way to understand a null hypothesis is to think about a criminal trial. In the United States, a criminal trial starts with the null hypothesis that the accused is not guilty. For a hypothesis test, we also start with some assumption—for example, that in the population, the mean number of hours that people spend at work per day is eight. In other words, the population mean is $\mu = 8$.

In a criminal trial, the jury looks at the evidence to see whether it's consistent with the null hypothesis that the accused is not guilty or whether it is consistent with some alternative hypothesis (say, the accused is guilty beyond a reasonable doubt). In hypothesis testing, we look at the data to see whether they are consistent with the null hypothesis or some alternative hypothesis. Here the null hypothesis is that in the population people work eight hours per day on average ($\mu = 8$ hours). The alternative is that the average work day is something else ($\mu \neq 8$ hours).

In a criminal trial we would usually examine the evidence, put it all together, and draw one of two possible conclusions. One option would be to find the accused not guilty. The other option would be to find the accused guilty beyond a reasonable doubt. So, too, in hypothesis testing. We obtain some data, process it, and then draw one of two possible conclusions. We could fail to reject the null hypothesis that the average work day is eight hours long, concluding that there just isn't enough evidence to draw the opposite conclusion (this would be the same as finding a criminal defendant not guilty). Or we could reject the null hypothesis and conclude that the average work day is likely *not* eight hours long (this would be the same as finding a criminal defendant guilty beyond a reasonable doubt). It's important to note that we never accept a null hypothesis, just like we never proclaim the accused innocent. Rather, we conclude that the accused is not guilty.

Table 7.1 The steps of hypothesis testing.

- Formulate a null hypothesis that speaks to your research question; e.g.:

$$H_0 : \mu = 8 \text{ (hours)}$$

- State the alternative hypothesis; e.g.:

$$H_1 : \mu \neq 8 \text{ (hours)}$$

- Compute the appropriate *test statistic*
- Translate the test statistic into a *p-value*
- Draw a conclusion

Now that you understand the null, the formal process for hypothesis testing outlined in Table 7.1 should make sense. After noting some technical assumptions about the population,[16] the next step is to formally state a null hypothesis, typically denoted H_0, as well as the alternative, denoted H_1. The remaining steps involve weighing the evidence in the appropriate way. To illustrate how this works, let's turn to a test about the population mean.

7.3.1 One-sample t-test

Once we have stated the null and alternative hypotheses, the next step is to compute a *test statistic*. Not surprisingly, a test statistic is a statistic used to conduct a hypothesis test. To generate the test statistic we need to decide on a test. We'll use the one-sample *t*-test, which is a hypothesis test about a population mean (for example, whether people work eight hours per day on average). It's called one-sample because we're looking at just a single sample of data. Later, we'll see a two-sample test that we can use to compare population means across two groups (or, if you prefer, sub-populations).

The test statistic for our one-sample *t*-test is:

$$t = \frac{\bar{Y} - \mu_0}{s/\sqrt{n}} \sim t_{n-1}$$

---

[16] Technically, the data generating process; that is, the statistical model presumed to have generated the data.

We've seen just about all of this before. $\bar{Y}$ is the sample mean (for example, the mean number of work hours in a random sample we might draw of workers). μ_o is the only thing we've not seen before. This represents the hypothesized value of the parameter in the null hypothesis. For the example above, $\mu_o = 8$. s denotes the sample standard deviation, and n the sample size. It turns out that this test statistic follows (that's what the $\sim$ means) the t-distribution with $(n - 1)$ degrees of freedom—the same t-distribution developed by Gosset.[17] This comes from the sampling distribution. Here the sampling distribution follows the shape of the t-distribution, which is bell-shaped and symmetric like the normal distribution. It's interesting to note that nearly every test statistic takes a common form. An observed value ($\bar{Y}$) minus a hypothesized value (μ_o) divided by the standard error.

Computing the test statistic is easy. It's just a matter of grinding through the formula (or letting the computer do it for you). But how do we translate the statistic into a conclusion? We need to compute something called a *p-value*. Let's suppose for our work day study we drew a sample of $n = 15$ individuals and computed a sample mean of $\bar{Y} = 9.65$, or 9.65 hours of work per day. The p-value we'd like to compute will tell us the probability of observing a statistic of $\bar{Y} = 9.65$ or further away from the hypothesized value of eight hours, assuming that the null hypothesis of a population average of an eight-hour work day is true. A large p-value implies that the hypothesized value and the sample statistic are pretty close to one another. Alternatively, a small p-value would suggest that the hypothesized value and sample statistic are far apart. We'll leverage this in just a bit to draw a conclusion.

So how do we perform the computation to obtain a p-value? For our sample with $\bar{Y} = 9.65$,[18] we could compute our test statistic $t = 1.6$. Figure 7.4 shows how we convert the test statistic to a p-value. For our test statistic of $t = 1.6$, we compute the p-value by seeing how much probability falls above 1.6 or below -1.6. Those are the ranges of values that are as far or farther away from the hypothesized value of $\mu_o = 8$. In this case, the total probability in the two tails is $p = 0.132$, by adding 0.066 from the left tail to 0.066 from the right tail.

To see how this works for different test statistics, Figures 7.5 and 7.6 show similar calculations. In Figure 7.5 our test statistic is much closer to zero. Indeed, with the same sample size[19] and a sample mean

[17] Student (1908). See also footnote 11.
[18] And, let's suppose, a sample standard deviation $s = 4.0$.
[19] And the same sample standard deviation.

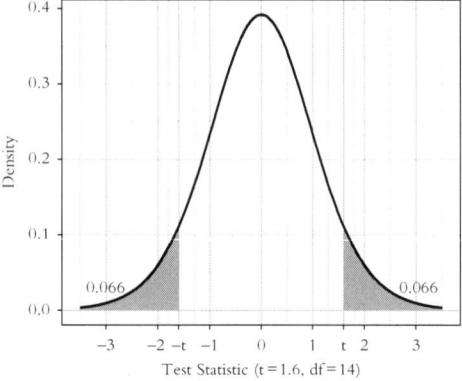

Figure 7.4 An illustration of computing a p-value with $t = 1.6$ for a one-sample t-test ($p = 0.132$, $df = 14$). The dark regions are those that contribute to the p-value.

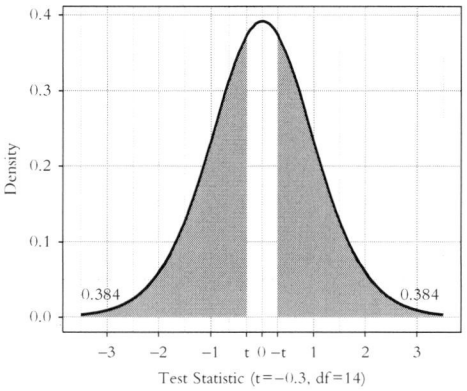

Figure 7.5 An illustration of computing a p-value with $t = -0.3$ for a one-sample t-test ($p = 0.769$, $df = 14$). The dark regions are those that contribute to the p-value.

of $\bar{Y} = 7.70$ we get a test statistic $t = -0.3$. As we would expect, since $\bar{Y} = 7.70$ is closer to the hypothesized value ($\mu = 8$), it produces a much larger p-value; in this case $p = 0.769$. What would happen if our sample means was $\bar{Y} = 10.27$?[20] Not surprisingly, since 10.27 is further away from 8 than 9.65, we get a larger test statistic. Here the test statistic is $t = 2.2$. What's the resulting p-value? In this case, it is $p = 0.045$, as shown in Figure 7.6.[21]

[20] Again, with the same sample standard deviation.
[21] It is possible to conduct hypothesis tests where the alternative hypothesis is stated as a > or < rather than ≠. These are called one-tailed tests, and can be used in the situation where

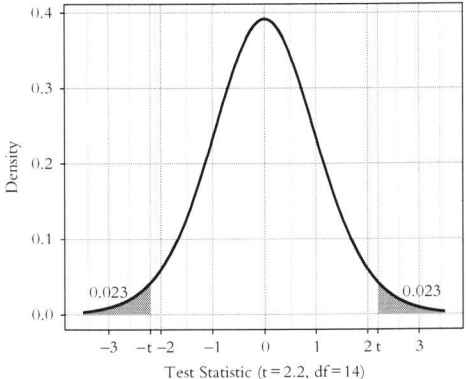

Figure 7.6 An illustration of computing a p-value with $t = 2.2$ for a one-sample t-test ($p = 0.045$, $df = 14$). The dark regions are those that contribute to the p-value.

So now we're able to compute a p-value. How do we use it to draw a conclusion? As you've just seen, the further the sample mean is from the hypothesized value ($\mu_0 = 8$), the smaller the p-value. The smallest p-value we observed ($p = 0.045$) came from the sample with $\bar{Y} = 10.27$—pretty far from 8. If the p-value is so small that it is quite unlikely that the sample data we observed came from the population, then we can conclude that the null hypothesis probably isn't true. This is an argument by contradiction. In general, if the observed sample data look really different from the hypothesized value, then we should conclude that the hypothesized value is likely wrong. On the other hand, if the observed sample data look a lot like the hypothesized value, then we don't have any reason to reject the null hypothesis. The p-value that we just computed tells us how close or how far the observed data are from the null hypothesis. When p-values are large, we would tend to favor the null. When they are small, we would tend to favor the alternative hypothesis.

How small? Before conducting a hypothesis test we must choose a significance level. Most of the time, it's $\alpha = 0.05$. (As you might guess, this relates to the confidence level when computing a confidence interval. We'll see in the next section that a 95% confidence interval

ex ante it is possible to entirely rule out half of the parameter space. Because that's nearly impossible in most empirical legal studies, we focus our attention solely on two-tailed tests. We suspect that some analysts choose to use one-tailed tests because they effectively cut the p-value in half for a given test statistic. So doing makes it more likely to conclude that an effect is statistically significant. We're highly skeptical of their use in empirical legal research.

relates to $\alpha = 0.05$.) If the p-value is less than α, we reject the null hypothesis and conclude that the alternative hypothesis is likely true. On the other hand, if the p-value is greater than or equal to α, we fail to reject the null hypothesis. When we reject a null hypothesis we conclude that the effect is *statistically significant*. Failing to reject a null hypothesis is synonymous with statistical insignificance.

To see how this works in practice, let's return to our International Criminal Tribunal dataset and consider the differences in sentence lengths between the trial and appellate courts in non-death penalty cases. Suppose we suspect that trial courts will, on average "get it right" and sentence defendants appropriately. If so, we would expect the differences, on average, between trial and appellate sentences to be zero. In other words, we would expect the average of this variable to be zero. We could state our null hypothesis $H_0 : \mu = 0$ and our alternative $H_1 : \mu \neq 0$. To compute our test statistic, we just apply the formula:

$$ t = \frac{\bar{Y} - \mu_0}{s/\sqrt{n}} = \frac{190.13 - 0}{149.24/\sqrt{125}} = 14.2 $$

Our statistical software reports our p-value to be very, very small, less than 0.001, in fact. In other words, our p-value is $p < 0.001$. Because it's less than 0.05, we *reject* the null hypothesis and conclude that the differences in sentences between the trial and appellate levels are statistically significantly different from zero. Hypothetically, if our p-value had been greater than or equal to 0.05, we would fail to reject our null hypothesis and conclude that there is a statistically insignificant difference; that is, the data didn't persuade us that the difference is significantly different from zero. In practice, of course, we needn't perform the computation by hand. Statistical software will report the test statistic (along with the p-value) for this and many other hypothesis tests.

7.3.2 Errors

Because we're making a choice when conducting a hypothesis test—reject the null hypothesis or fail to reject a null hypothesis—it is always possible that we can make the wrong choice. The same, of course, is true of a criminal trial. What are the chances of making a wrong choice? Thankfully, we can quantify the probability (and, along the way, understand why most researchers choose a 95% confidence level).

Table 7.2 Possible mistakes when conducting a hypothesis test.

		Decision	
		Reject Null	Fail to Reject Null
Truth	Null False	OK	**Type II Error**
	Null True	**Type I Error**	OK

Table 7.2 shows the four results that can obtain when we conduct a hypothesis test. On the rows is the truth: the null hypothesis is either true or false. On the columns is the decision that we reach when conducting the test: we either reject the null hypothesis or we fail to reject it.

Let's start with what can happen if the null hypothesis is true. If we fail to reject the null hypothesis, then we've made the right decision. Conversely, if we reject the null hypothesis we've made a mistake called a *Type I error*. This would be the same mistake as convicting an innocent person. What's the probability of committing a Type I error? It turns out that this is equal to the significance level α we choose to use to conduct our test. For $\alpha = 0.05$, we will commit a Type I error 5% of the time.

If the null hypothesis is false and we reject it, we've made the correct decision. If we don't reject it, we commit a mistake called a *Type II error*. This is the same error we would make if we found a guilty person not guilty. How do we determine the amount of Type II error? These calculations are quite difficult as the amount of error will depend on the value of the parameter. Because alternative hypotheses are stated for ranges of values, the amount of Type II error will vary across the range of parameter values. Type II error relates to *statistical power*. A hypothesis test is powerful if it could possibly detect a difference if it were to exist. While rarely used in empirical legal studies, statistical power is of utmost importance in medicine as it dictates the design of many experiments.[22]

Hopefully, you see the trade-off between Type I and Type II errors. Could we devise a system that would eliminate the possibility of committing a Type I error? Yes, we could never reject that null hypothesis!

---

[22] Computing statistical power is beyond the scope of this book. For information on computing the power function for a test, see DeGroot and Schervish (2012, 533).

This would be the same as a criminal justice system that never found anyone guilty. Just as it's impossible to send an innocent person to jail when you send no one to jail, it's impossible to commit a Type I error if you never reject a null hypothesis. So we shouldn't choose $\alpha = 0.000$. Similarly, if we always rejected the null hypothesis, we would never commit a Type II error. A criminal justice system that convicted everyone would never let an innocent person go free, but would, of course, wrongly convict some innocent people. When thinking about a criminal justice system we tend to be conservative and try to minimize Type I errors. As William Blackstone said, it's "... better that ten guilty persons escape than that one innocent suffer."[23] The same holds for empirical studies. That's why our conventional level (.05) for assessing statistical significance is so low. Sometimes we might want to be more conservative and reduce our significance level to $\alpha = 0.01$ or even lower. But keep in mind that so doing will increase the number of Type II errors, thus reducing the power of the test.

7.3.3 Two-sample t-test

One-sample t-tests are quite useful when there is some conventional wisdom or baseline that can be used to formulate a null hypotheses (such as an eight-hour work day or whatever the standard is in your country). A more commonly used (and more useful) test allows us to compare population means for two groups (often called sub-populations)—for example, to compare whether doctors and lawyers work the same number of hours per day on average. What's nice about this type of test is that there is an obvious null hypothesis: there is no difference in the population means between the two groups (doctors and lawyers work the same number of hours). Rejecting that null hypothesis would tell us that there was indeed a statistically significant difference between the population means of the two groups (doctors work longer hours than lawyers or vice versa).

We can state our two-sample t-test as follows:

$$H_0 : \mu_1 = \mu_2$$

$$H_1 : \mu_1 \neq \mu_2$$

Note that μ_1 denotes the population mean for group one (lawyers) and μ_2 denotes the population mean for group two (doctors).

---

[23] Blackstone (1769, 352).

Many different two-sample tests are available. All require different assumptions about the shape of the distribution of the data in the population and the population standard deviations in the two groups. The test we'll describe here, developed by Welch, is the most flexible one.[24] For Welch's two-sample t-test, it is not necessary to assume that the standard deviations are the same in the two groups. Group 1 (say, the lawyers) might, for example, have a much higher dispersion than group 2 (the doctors). You also don't have to assume that the distributions of data in the population follow a normal distribution; as long as there are 30 or so observations per group, the test performs just fine.

Welch derived the following test statistic:

$$t = \frac{\bar{Y}_2 - \bar{Y}_1}{\sqrt{\frac{s_1^2}{n_1} + \frac{s_2^2}{n_2}}} \sim t_{WS} \tag{7.2}$$

We label the sample means for the two groups $\bar{Y}_1$ and $\bar{Y}_2$ and the sample standard deviations for the two groups s_1 and s_2. n_1 and n_2 indicate how many observations there are in each of the two groups. Just as with the one-sample t-test, this test statistic is the observed value $(\bar{Y}_2 - \bar{Y}_1)$ minus the hypothesized value (0), divided by a standard error. Welch showed that this test statistic follows a t-distribution with degrees of freedom computed from the complicated Welch–Satterthwaite equation.[25] We denote that with t_{WS}. Once we have our test statistic we (or our software) converts it into a p-value and we can draw the appropriate conclusion.

As an illustration, let's return to sentence lengths in cases decided by the international criminal tribunals. We might hypothesize that defendants who cooperate with the prosecutors receive a lighter sentence than defendants who do not. This gives us have two groups of defendants: those who cooperated and those who did not. What's the dependent variable here? And what about the independent variable? If you answered "sentence length" and "whether or not the defendant cooperated with prosecutors", respectively, you would be correct. Sentence length, recall, is an interval variable. Whether or not the defendant cooperated is a dichotomous nominal variable, often called a "dummy" variable.

---

[24] Welch (1947).
[25] Satterthwaite (1946); Welch (1947).

If we just look at the sample means of these sentences we see that the average sentence length for defendants who did not cooperate is $\bar{Y}_2 = 274.03$. For defendants who did cooperate, the average sentence length $\bar{Y}_1 = 189.931$.[26] Clearly sentences are shorter in our sample for defendants who cooperated but is the difference statistically significant? When we run through the calculation in Equation 7.2 for these data, we get a test statistic $t = 2.496$ with 62.8 degrees of freedom. Converting this to a p-value we get $p = 0.015$, meaning that the difference we've observed is statistically significant. This is a way of saying: the pattern we see in our sample is consistent with a population where there are different average sentences for defendants who cooperate and for those who don't—differences that we cannot attribute to the one random sample of data we draw. This gives us good reason to believe that those who cooperate with prosecutors receive, on average, shorter sentences. But how much shorter? The average difference between the two sentences is 84.1 months. We also could compute a confidence interval for the difference. Here, that interval is: $95\% \: CI : [16.77, 151.43]$. Note our estimate isn't terribly precise because we have a small sample (especially for the group of defendants who cooperated with the prosecutors).

At this point you might have some questions. First, what's the relationship between confidence intervals and hypothesis testing? We've already foreshadowed the answer. Remember that a 95% confidence interval corresponds to a significance level of $\alpha = 0.05$. Because both confidence intervals and hypothesis tests are derived from the same sampling distribution, they capture precisely the same amount of uncertainty about the quantities of interest; they just present the information in different ways. If you have a 95% confidence interval for some parameter of interest, you will fail to reject any null hypothesis where the hypothesized value is *inside* the confidence interval, and you will reject any null hypothesis *outside* of the confidence interval.[27] Just by looking at the confidence interval we'd know we could reject the null hypothesis if the confidence interval doesn't contain zero.

This procedure wouldn't provide an exact p-value, just an indication of how the test would turn out. Hypothesis tests give us answers about whether or not an effect exists; confidence intervals often tell us how

---

[26] The other quantities are: $s_1 = 219.00, s_2 = 145.71, n_1 = 119, n_2 = 29$.

[27] This result will not hold for hypothesis tests where the computation of the test statistic differs slightly from the confidence interval calculation, such as with a two-sample test for proportions where a pooled estimate is used to compute the standard error.

big the effect is. In most applications we care about both: the existence of an effect and an effect size. In practice, we recommend reporting both even though a hypothesis test and a confidence interval provide the same information.

Second, is statistical significance the only thing we should care about? Absolutely not (especially not when our sample is very large, making it easy to find statistically significant differences). The size of the effect, or *substantive significance*, is equally important. More to the point, we believe that decisions about whether the size of the difference is substantively, and not just statistically, significant merits explicit thought and discussion.[28] Imagine that we found a statistically significant difference of 0.25 months (just under a week) in sentence length between defendants who cooperated and those who did not. Substantively this difference isn't very important not only because it's small but also because the average sentence length in the dataset is greater than 15 years.

Third, what if you have more than two groups to compare? Suppose you wanted to compare average sentence length for all three of the internal criminal tribunals? Here we would turn to a generalization of the two-sample *t*-test called the analysis of variance (or ANOVA) model.[29] We won't discuss the model here, other than to note its existence and to point out that it's a special case of the linear regression model we cover in the next two chapters. Suffice it to say that there is a method to compare population means for multiple groups.

7.4 Cross-Tabulation and Tests for Tables

As the sentencing example illustrates, the two-sample *t*-test can be used when the dependent variable is interval and the independent variable is dichotomous.[30] The final hypothesis test in this chapter looks at the situation where both our independent and dependent variables are nominal.

The example we'll use comes from *Victoria's Secret Stores Brand Management v. Sexy Hair Concepts*,[31] a trademark case that we considered

---

[28] Part IV delves into this point in some detail.
[29] DeGroot and Schervish (2012, 754).
[30] The ANOVA model can be used when there are more than two categories.
[31] No. 1:07-CV-05804 (S.D.N.Y. filed June 19, 2007). The docket for this case is available at: <http://archive.recapthelaw.org/nysd/308471/>.

earlier when we discussed survey research.[32] To refresh your memory, a trademark board denied Victoria's Secret's application to register the mark "SO SEXY" for its hair care products based on the objections of another business, Sexy Hair Concepts, LLC. Victoria's Secret appealed this decision and one of their expert witnesses, a marketing research consultant, designed a survey to explore whether the word "SEXY" had attained a secondary meaning in relation to hair care products.[33] We'll call the consultant's data the Trademark Survey dataset.

The Trademark Survey dataset contains 308 survey responses. The variable of interest asks respondents how many hair care companies they associate with the word "SEXY." Respondents could choose one of the following answers: one company, more than one company, no company, don't know, or no opinion. The answers were presented to each respondent on a card. In order to ensure that the order of the options presented did not bias the responses, the consultant randomly ordered the "One company" and "More than one company" responses on the cards. In the first version, "One company" was presented first. In the second version, "More than one company" was presented first. The last three options remained the same in both versions of the survey. If respondents were more likely to pick the option at the top of the list, we would expect more "One company" responses in the first version and more "More than one company" responses in the second version. The dependent variable is the response to the question; the independent variable is the version of the survey presented to the respondent. Both variables are nominal. What we're trying to ascertain is whether the version of the survey led to different responses.

To show the relationship between these two nominal variables we've created a special table called a cross-tabulation (or just a cross-tab) in Table 7.3.[34] By convention, the dependent variable goes on the rows and the independent variable goes on the columns. (The reason for this will become apparent in Chapter 8, where we start our discussion of regression models.) Each row has its own label, as does each column. Within each of the ten squares or cells are two numbers. The top number is the number of observations (here, survey respondents) that appear in each cell. We can see, for example, that there are

---

[32] See Chapter 4.

[33] The expert report is available at <http://ia600401.us.archive.org/28/items/gov.uscourts.nysd.308471/gov.uscourts.nysd.308471.21.1.pdf>.

[34] We introduced cross-tabs in Chapter 1. Here we provide more detail.

Table 7.3 Cross-tabulation of the number of companies associated with the word "SEXY" and the version of the survey respondents received, with column percentages.[35]

	Version		
	One	Two	
One company	24 15.7%	34 21.9%	58
More than one company	19 12.4%	29 18.7%	48
No company	45 29.4%	33 21.3%	78
Don't know	36 23.5%	33 21.3%	69
No opinion	29 19.0%	26 16.8%	55
Total	153	155	308

24 individuals who responded "One company" when shown the first version of the card, 29 individuals who responded "More than one company" when shown the second version of the card, and so on.

The other numbers that appear in each cell are column percentages. Why column percentages? It might be tempting just to divide the number in each cell by the total size of the sample, in this case $n = 308$. This would tell us what percentage of respondents fell in to each cell; e.g., $\frac{24}{308} = 7.8\%$ of respondents received the first version of the card *and* responded "One company." But that's not the comparison we want to make. In order to ascertain whether the version of the card provoked different responses, we'd like to compare the relative percentages across columns. The percentages in the first row of the table tell us this: of the people who received the first version of the card, what percentage answered "One company" (15.7%) and of the people who received the second version of the card, what percentage answered "One company" (21.9%). This is the comparison we'd like to make.

The table also provides numbers called "marginals" because they are in the margins of the table. The row marginals convey the number of total respondents who answered "One company," "More than one company," and so on (58, 48, etc.). The column marginals tell us the number of individuals who received each version of the card. In this case 153 received the first version and 155 received the second. It's not surprising that these numbers aren't identical because the expert used randomization to decide which card each person received. The total number of observations (308) is to the right of the column marginals and below the row marginals.

If we look at the percentages in each cell we see that our initial hypothesis doesn't look to be correct. People who received the second version of the card were *more likely* to have answered "One company" (21.9%) than those who received the first version (15.7%). For some reason, those who received the first version of the card were more likely to answer "No company," "Don't know," or "No opinion" than those who got the second version of the card. All in all, it appears that there are some differences in response patterns related to the version of the card presented.

If you're thinking "hold on a minute," you're on the right track. All respondents came from a broader population. Perhaps the differences we're seeing in Table 7.3 simply trace to the vagaries of the sample the expert happened to draw. Or, perhaps, they're indicative of something far more substantial in the broader population. What we need to do is perform a hypothesis test to ascertain whether or not the observed differences are statistically significant or just noise that occurred because of sampling. To state this in a way familiar to us, here's the hypothesis we'd like to test:

H_0 : Variables are statistically independent

H_1 : Variables are statistically dependent

The two variables of interest here are (1) the response to the "number of companies" question and (2) the version of the survey the respondent received. The null hypothesis is that the variables are unrelated to one another; i.e., they are statistically independent. The alternative is that the variables are, in fact, meaningfully related to each other; i.e., they are statistically dependent. Remember that these statements are about the broader population. We observe only a sample.

The hypothesis test we'll use was developed over 100 years ago by Karl Pearson.[36] The title of the article Pearson wrote to introduce this method pretty much sums it up: "On the criterion that a given system

---

[36] Pearson (1900).

of deviations from the probable in the case of a correlated system of variables is such that it can be reasonably supposed to have arisen from random sampling."

Pearson called the test the χ^2-test (chi-squared) based on something called the χ^2-distribution. The χ^2-distribution characterizes the sum of the squared normal random variables. It has a degrees of freedom parameter just like the t-distribution. Since it characterizes the sum of squared variables, this distribution is defined on the non-negative real numbers (that's a fancy way to say that the statistic must be greater than or equal to zero). Here's the test statistic, which we'll immediately unpack:

$$\chi^2 = \sum \frac{(f_o - f_e)^2}{f_e} \sim \chi^2_{(r-1)(c-1)} \qquad (7.3)$$

In this equation f_o denotes the observed counts and f_e denotes the expected counts. r denotes the number of rows, and c denotes the number of columns. Three of these numbers are easy. The observed counts f_o are just the interior counts in each cell, and for our table $r = 5$ and $c = 2$.

How do we compute the expected counts f_e? It turns out that if two variables are independent—which is the case if the null hypothesis is true—the expected count is equal to the product of the respective row and column marginal divided by the sample size. For example, for the upper left-hand cell, we would compute the expected count:

$$f_e = \frac{58 \times 153}{308} = 28.812$$

As you can see, these expected counts won't necessarily be whole numbers (integers). But they are the counts we would observe in extremely large samples if the variables are, in fact, independent. Table 7.4 contains the same table as before, only this time we replace the column percentages with the expected counts.

With these expected counts in hand, we can turn back to the test statistic in Equation 7.3. If the observed and expected counts are close to each other—which we would expect if the null hypothesis is true—the numerator of the fraction will be close to zero, and even closer to zero when dividing by the expected count. We then sum across all of the cells to get a test statistic that follows the χ^2-distribution with, in our case, $4 \times 1 = 4$ degrees of freedom. If we carry out this calculation for the cross-tabulation in Table 7.4 we end up with a test statistic $\chi^2 = 5.935$.

Table 7.4 Cross-tabulation of the number of companies associated with the word "SEXY" and the version of the survey respondents received, with expected counts ($\chi^2 = 5.935; p = 0.204$).[37]

	Version		
	One	Two	
One company	24 28.812	34 29.188	58
More than one company	19 23.844	29 24.156	48
No company	45 38.747	33 39.253	78
Don't know	36 34.276	33 34.724	69
No opinion	29 27.321	26 27.679	55
Total	153	155	308

The final step is to convert our test statistic into a p-value. There are tables of χ^2 statistics to perform this translation, and statistical software will do so as well. Intuitively, though, as the observed and expected counts get further and further apart—meaning that the alternative hypothesis is likely true—the statistic will get bigger and bigger. If the observed and expected counts are the same, then the null hypothesis is likely true. The p-value will allow us to make the determination of how big the difference really is. For our table, $p = 0.204$. This is greater than 0.05, so we would fail to reject the null hypothesis. In other words, the small differences in percentages in our observed sample notwithstanding, we can't reject the null hypothesis that the variables are independent. There are no significant differences in our sample based on the version of the survey the respondent received.

One nice feature of the χ^2-test is that it will work for tables of any size. The only restriction is that the expected number in each cell (f_e) must be greater than or equal to five. Some software packages print a warning message if this condition doesn't hold (but be careful: some don't). If it doesn't hold there are some alternative tests for tables. In fact, there are whole courses devoted to analyzing tabular data.[38]

More generally, because this book is a primer, we covered just a handful of statistical tests. Suffice it to say that scores have been

---

[37] Source: Trademark Survey data.
[38] See, e.g., Agresti (2007).

developed for just about any inferential problem imaginable. Comprehensive statistics texts by Agresti and Finlay[39] and DeGroot and Schervish[40] (and many others) provide details about some of the other most commonly used tests, including:

- A one-sample χ^2-test for the population standard deviation.
- A two-sample F-test to compare population standard deviations in two groups. The F-test is also commonly used in the ANOVA model.
- A variety of tests for proportions, including one-sample tests against a baseline and two-sample tests. Some of these are exact tests based on the binomial distribution. Others are approximations using the normal or χ^2-distribution.
- Exact tests, like Fisher's exact test for small tables, which can be used for tables if the criteria to use the χ^2 test is not met.
- Tests for all sorts of tabular data, including situations where one or both variables is ordinal rather than nominal.

* * * * * * * *

In this chapter we've explored a test we can use if our dependent variable is interval and the independent variable is nominal (the two-sample t-test[41]), and methods for dealing with independent and dependent variables that are both nominal (the χ^2-test). What should we do when both the dependent and independent variables are interval-level? We'll find out in Chapter 8, where we cover regression analysis. And what about when we have more than one independent variable, which is very common in empirical legal studies? That's the topic of Chapter 9, where we describe the multiple regression model.

---

[39] Agresti and Finlay (2009).
[40] DeGroot and Schervish (2012).
[41] And ANOVA.

8

Regression Analysis: The Basics

This is the first of two chapters that examine the *linear regression model*. In its simplest form, linear regression is a statistical tool we can use to explore the relationship between two interval variables: a dependent variable, which, following convention, we label Y, and an independent variable, X. As long as the relationship is linear—that is, a line characterizes the nature of the relationship—the linear regression model will allow us to perform inference.

Why does this model merit two chapters? Because it's the workhorse of empirical legal studies. This may seem surprising because many variables of interest are nominal; for example, is the defendant guilty or innocent, is a judiciary independent or not, is the judge male or female? But the fact of it is that the basic regression model can be adapted to deal with non-interval dependent variables. We'll see how in Chapter 9. Moreover, and perhaps more important, the model allows us to include more than one independent variable in our analysis, and, depending on our research design, draw causal inferences.

Here we focus, first, on lines and how we can use them to summarize the relationship between variables. Next we describe ordinary least squares, which is a method to find the line that best fits the data. We also define the linear regression model and show how to use it to perform statistical inference. We conclude with a discussion of model performance.

8.1 Lines and Linear Relationships

To interpret the results of a linear regression analysis, it's important to understand the properties of a line. This is probably something you learned in middle school, but a refresher may be in order. (If you're familiar with the equation $Y = mX + b$, please skip to the next section.)

Let's start with some hypothetical data. Our dependent variable Y is the sentence length (in months) imposed on criminal defendants in the international criminal courts. The independent variable X is the number of crimes (or counts) the defendant was found guilty of committing. We might expect a positive relationship between the two: all else equal, the more counts, the longer the sentence. Figure 8.1 shows our hypothetical data. (These data are obviously fake because the points fall so nicely along a straight line.)

This figure, called a *scatterplot*, represents each observation in our dataset (a defendant in a given case) as one point. The points scatter because both Y and X vary. For example, the first defendant (located in the lower left corner) was found guilty of one count and sentenced to 120 months; the next defendant was found guilty of two counts and sentenced to 140 months. In other words, each point on this graph is an ordered pair (X, Y) where X denotes the location on the x-axis, and Y the location on this y-axis. In this scatterplot, we can easily fit a straight line through all of the points, as in Figure 8.2.

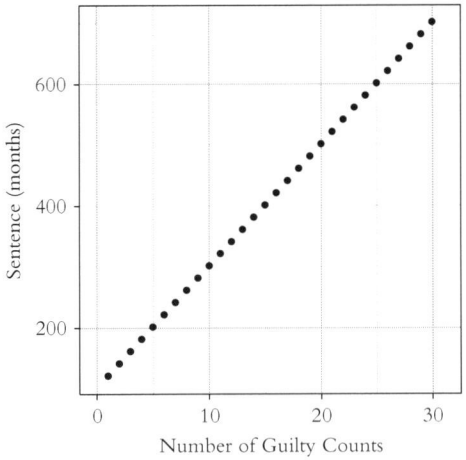

Figure 8.1 Scatterplot of hypothetical sentence length data.

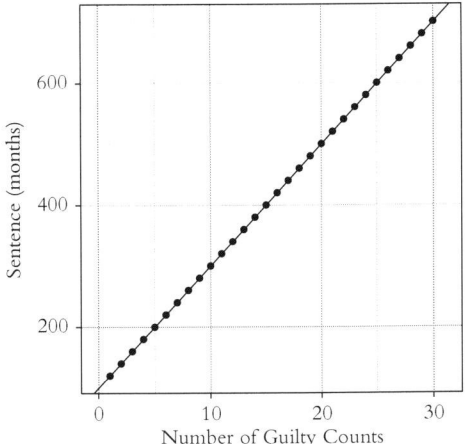

Figure 8.2 Scatterplot of hypothetical sentence length data with a best-fitting line.

At some point, you learned the equation of a line. It was probably this:

$$Y = mX + b$$

Two parameters characterize the line. m is the slope, and b is the y-intercept. The slope tells us how much we expect Y to increase for a one-unit increase in X. In other words:

$$m = \frac{\text{rise}}{\text{run}}$$

For these data, we'd expect Y to increase m units for each additional guilty count. The y-intercept b tells us where the line crosses the y-axis, or the value of Y when $X = 0$. You'll see in Figure 8.2 that at no point does $X = 0$. This makes sense: if a defendant is convicted of zero counts (or crimes) the court will not impose a sentence. Nonetheless, because lines continue on infinitely in both directions, every line has a y-intercept whether or not $X = 0$ is a value in the dataset (or even makes sense for the data).

When we use linear regression, we write the equation of a line slightly differently. Rather than the familiar $Y = mX + b$, we use

$$Y = A + BX$$

A represents the y-intercept and B represents the slope. (In the next section we'll use Greek letters to denote population parameters that correspond to these two values.) What's the equation for the line in Figure 8.2? It's this:

$$Y = 100 + 20X$$

The slope $B = 20$. This tells us that the expected sentence goes up 20 months for each additional guilty count. If the slope had been negative, perhaps -10, it would mean that for each additional guilty count sentences go down by ten months. Our y-intercept, $A = 100$, tells us, counterfactually, that someone convicted of zero counts would expect a sentence of 100 months. It's a counterfactual, of course, because someone convicted of nothing won't receive a sentence. This is an example of the slope falling outside the range of the data, and as such, we won't interpret it. Nonetheless, we can't eliminate it entirely because it is part of the equation that characterizes the line that runs through these points.

We can generate predictions once we have the equation of a line. For example, if a defendant is convicted of ten counts, how long a sentence can he expect to receive? To derive the answer, all we need to do is plug 10 in for X:

$$Y = 100 + 20 \cdot 10 = 100 + 200 = 300$$

The line tells us the sentence would be 300 months. Visually, this would be the same thing as drawing a vertical line at 10 in Figure 8.2 up to the line. You'll see that the line at that point corresponds to 300 on the y-axis. What if the number of counts increased to 11?

$$Y = 100 + 20 \cdot 11 = 100 + 220 = 320$$

If someone is convicted on 11 counts, the sentence will be 320 months. This is precisely what we'd expect to see with a slope $B = 20$. A one unit increase in X yields a 20-unit increase in Y. In other words, for every additional count, the sentence length should increase by 20 months.

8.2 Ordinary Least Squares

Figures 8.1 and 8.2 display data we cooked up; Figure 8.3 shows the real sentence length data from the International Criminal Tribunals

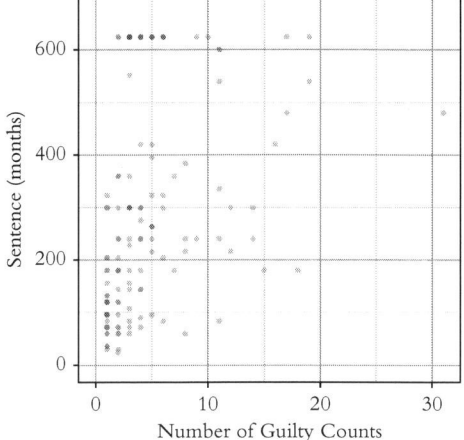

Figure 8.3 Scatterplot of sentence length on number of guilty counts.[1]

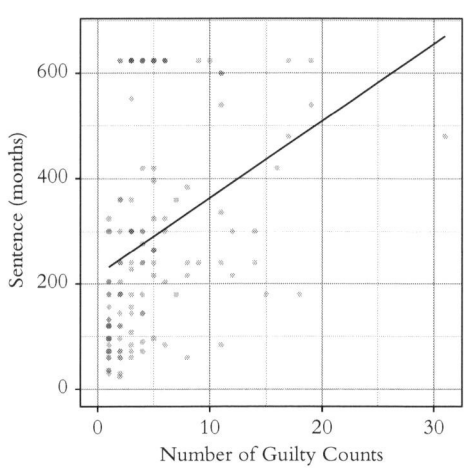

Figure 8.4 Scatterplot of sentence length on number of guilty counts with linear regression line, estimated using ordinary least squares.[2]

(ICT) dataset. Once again, the points represent defendants in the dataset.

As you scan Figure 8.3 note, first, that in contrast to Figures 8.1 and 8.2, the data are messier; they no longer fall along a single straight line. This is to be expected. While the fake data in Figure 8.2 suggest that the number of guilty counts perfectly predicts sentence length,

---

[1] Source: ICT data.
[2] Source: ICT data.

the real world is not so neat. Because many factors affect sentence length beyond just the number of guilty counts, you will almost never see scatterplots that look like Figure 8.2 in studies of law and legal institutions.

Even so, there appears to be a positive relationship between these two variables. Although it is not as close as it is in Figure 8.2, it does seem that as the number of counts increases (looking from left to right in the graph), the sentences appear to get longer. We'll soon put a line through these points to see whether or not our intuition is correct.

You might also notice that some of the points in the figure are darker than others. Why? They depict different defendants who were convicted on the same number of counts and receive the same sentence. This means that in the dataset there are some (X, Y) pairs that are exactly the same. In Figure 8.3 we chose to make the dots light grey so we could depict multiple points on top of one another with darker grey. Another alternative is to slightly "jitter" (that is, move) each point by adding a little bit of random noise to both X and Y to make each point visually distinct. The choice isn't consequential; it is really up to you and your software.

Finally, note that there are "flat" regions of the scatterplot: one on the left, and one on the top. On the left, there are simply no data points when the number of guilty counts is zero or less. This makes sense for the reasons we just discussed. But there are a number of defendants who were convicted on just one count, and one defendant (to the far right) who was convicted of 31. The other "flat" region is at the top of the figure. In this dataset, defendants who receive life sentences are coded as having received a sentence of 624 months, which corresponds to the longest sentence in the dataset. This coding choice produces the "flat" region on the top.

What line characterizes the relationship between our dependent and independent variables? With our hypothetical data, it was easy to get a line: put down a ruler and connect the dots. But with these real data it's not so easy. In Figure 8.4 we plot the best fitting line using something called ordinary least squares. We'll discuss why this line is the best possible line in just a bit. For now, please take our word that the line summarizing the relationship between these two variables is:

$$Y = 217 + 14.6X$$

We can interpret these numbers for the real data in just the same way as we did for the hypothetical data. Our slope of 14.6 tells us that, for every additional count, the defendant's sentence increases, on average, by 14.6 months. The y-intercept of 217 is the average sentence of someone who was convicted on zero counts, but, of course, that's an implausible counterfactual.

We can use the equation to predict as well. Here is how we'd compute the predicted sentence for someone convicted of ten counts:

$$Y = 217 + 14.6 \cdot 10 = 217 + 146 = 363$$

And what about 11 counts? We could perform the computation again:

$$Y = 217 + 14.6 \cdot 11 = 217 + 160.6 = 377.6$$

Just as we'd expect, because we're increasing X by one charge, Y increases by the magnitude of the slope: 14.6 months.

You might be wondering: how did we get the line? *Ordinary least squares* (OLS)—which was developed over 200 years ago!— is the method we used.[3] To set the stage for what's to come, let's assume that our line has the following equation:

$$Y_i = \alpha + \beta X_i + \varepsilon_i \qquad (8.1)$$

Three features of this equation are worthy of note. First, rather than calling the intercept A and the slope B, we're now using Greek letters α and β. As we'll see in the section to come, these are population parameters we'd like to estimate. Think of them as the population intercept and the population slope.

Second, notice the subscript letters i beside X and Y. i denotes our observations. For the sample of size n the letter i goes from 1 to n; i.e., $i = 1, 2, \ldots, n$. The first observation in the dataset is (X_1, Y_1), the second observation in the dataset is (X_2, Y_2), and so on. The parameters α and β don't have subscripts because the intercept and slope don't change across observations. We estimate the slope and intercept for the entire dataset.

Third, as we just suggested, unless we're really, really lucky—or we've cooked up data—not all of our data points will fall precisely on the line. What remains, what's left over between each point and the regression line, is: ε_i. We call this the *residual*. We need to add the residual to Equation 8.1 to make sure that everything adds up. Without a residual, we'd have to assume that every point falls along the line, which is an unrealistic assumption.

---

[3] Carl Friedrich Gauss is credited with inventing least squares in 1795 (Sorenson, 1970).

We'll use these residuals to derive the OLS line. Since the residual is just the difference between each point and the regression line, it's easy to draw them on a scatterplot. Take a look at the upper left-hand panel in Figure 8.5. This panel shows a scatterplot of (hypothetical) data and a line with a slope of -3 and an intercept of 70. We've connected each point with a vertical line: a residual. The residuals are the collection of these vertical lines for each data point. The way OLS works is to try to find the line that makes the set of squared residuals as small as possible.

(Why squared residuals? Just as we saw when we computed standard deviations, some residuals are positive and others are negative. If we added up all the residuals, the positive ones would offset the negative

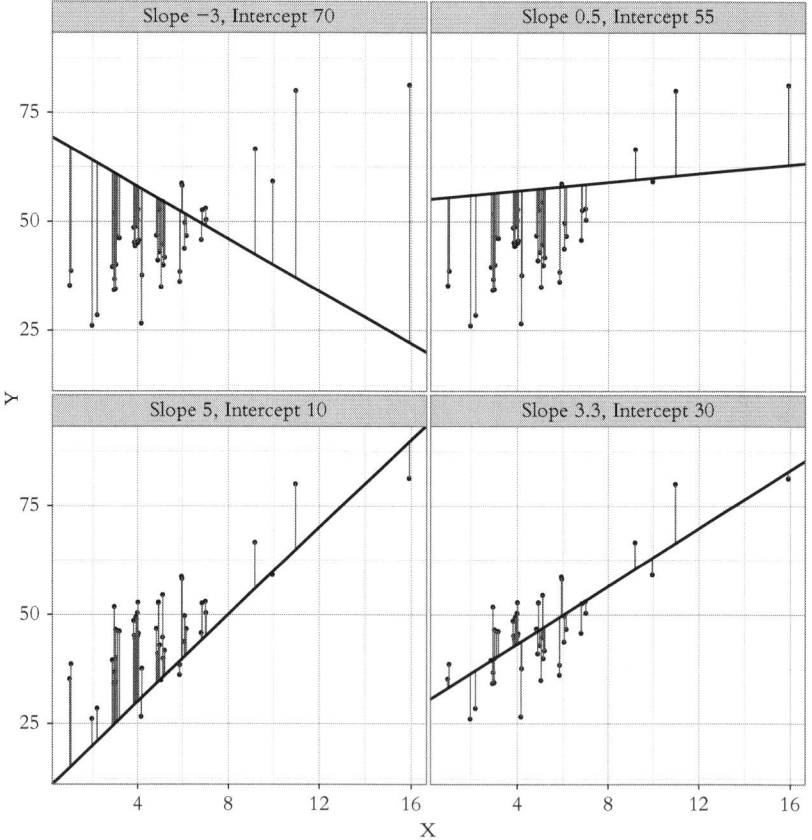

Figure 8.5 Demonstration of OLS with some hypothetical data. Each panel shows the same scatterplot with different lines and, thus, different sets of residuals. The lower right-hand panel is the best fitting line.

ones. So we square them in order to treat positive and negative residuals the same way.)

Now look at the line of the same data in the upper right-hand panel, the one with a slope of 0.5 and an intercept of 55. All in all, this set of residuals looks smaller but the lower left-hand panel (with a slope of 5 and an intercept of 10) is smaller still. Even better is the bottom right panel, with a slope 3.3 and an intercept of 30. In fact, this is the "best" (OLS) line—the one that produces the smallest set of squared residuals.

Instead of sitting around and trying out line after line, we can mathematically determine the best fitting line using a little calculus. We'll spare you the details, but the way it works is pretty straightforward. All we need to do is find the slope and intercept that minimizes the sum of the squared residuals. This leads to the name "least squares:" we pick the line that gives us the least total amount of squared residuals. These estimates are the least squares estimates, using $\hat{\alpha}$ and $\hat{\beta}$ to denote the intercept and slope respectively. We use the little hats (^) to show that these are estimates of parameters (a subject we take up in the next section). With this notation the residual is just:

$$\hat{\varepsilon}_i = Y_i - (\hat{\alpha} + \hat{\beta} X_i)$$

In other words, it's the difference between the observed value Y_i and the expected value $\hat{Y}_i$, which is produced by the equation $\hat{\alpha} + \hat{\beta} X_i$. If you sum up these across all observations, you get a function that you can minimize using differential calculus.

Except for the pathological case when the independent variable X does not vary, the solution to the OLS problem is unique. We compute the slope using this formula:

$$\hat{\beta} = \frac{\sum_{i=1}^{n}(X_i - \bar{X})(Y_i - \bar{Y})}{\sum_{i=1}^{n}(X_i - \bar{X})^2}$$

While this looks pretty intimidating, it's not that complicated. All we're doing is taking the X deviations (remember deviations—the difference between each observation and the average) and the Y deviations, multiplying them, and adding them all up. We divide this by the sum of the squared X deviations, which is related to the standard deviation of X. The slope that minimizes the sum of the squared residuals is what results.

The formula for the y-intercept is much easier. Once you have solved for $\hat{\beta}$, you can compute the intercept with this:

$$\hat{\alpha} = \bar{Y} - \hat{\beta}\bar{X}$$

Remember that $\bar{Y}$ and $\bar{X}$ denote the averages of those two variables.

Given these formulas, it's possible to compute the best fitting line for any scatterplot. But the line we calculate comes from our sample of data. Indeed, our estimates $\hat{\alpha}$ and $\hat{\beta}$ are just statistics because we compute them entirely from a random sample of data. Just as with other statistics, we use these to draw inferences about the broader population. This is the subject of the next two sections, where we perform statistical inference for this model and assess the model's performance.

8.3 Simple Linear Regression and Statistical Inference

OLS allows us to put a best fitting line through a scatterplot of points. This provides a good summary of the relationship in the sample, but what about in the population?

The *linear regression* model allows us to perform inference about linear relationships between interval variables in a population. The term "regression" comes from Francis Galton,[4] who studied the heights of parents and their children. Think of a scatterplot with the heights of the parents on the x-axis and the heights of the children on the y-axis. What Galton discovered is that the heights of children of very tall people tend to regress down toward the average height in the population. Similarly, children of very short people tend to regress up toward the average height in the population. He called this phenomenon "regression" and the name stuck.

Here we focus on "simple" linear regression. It's called simple because it considers only one independent variable. In Chapter 9 we extend the model to the more complicated case of multiple independent variables.

But, truthfully, if you've followed the discussion to this point, you've already seen just about all of the linear regression model—with one exception. We have not yet needed to make any assumptions about

---

[4] Galton (1885).

the distribution the residuals take. OLS will produce a best fitting line regardless of the distribution we assume. But in order to perform inference, we need to make an assumption about the residuals. Can you guess what distribution we'll use? Here's the answer:

$$Y_i = \alpha + \beta X_i + \varepsilon_i \quad \varepsilon_i \sim N(0, \sigma^2)$$

You'll see that everything looks the same as before except the assumption at the very end. Here we assume that our residuals ε_i follow a normal distribution with a mean 0 and a standard deviation σ. The symbol $\sim$ means "distributed as" and N denotes a normal distribution with two parameters: a mean and variance (the square root of which is the standard deviation). The parameter σ is called the *residual standard deviation*, and we'll return to it a little later when we assess model fit.[5]

We've seen the formulas to estimate the intercept $\hat{\alpha}$ and slope $\hat{\beta}$. What about the residual standard deviation? For the simple linear regression model we compute it as follows:

$$\hat{\sigma} = \sqrt{\frac{\sum_{i=1}^{n}(Y_i - \hat{Y}_i)^2}{n-2}} = \sqrt{\frac{\sum_{i=1}^{n}(Y_i - (\hat{\alpha} + \hat{\beta} X_i))^2}{n-2}}$$

Look carefully at this formula. You'll see that we're taking the difference between the observed values and expected values, squaring to treat positive ones and negative ones the same, summing across all observations, dividing by $(n-2)$ to account for the number of observations, and taking the square root to make this a standard deviation.[6]

With all of this in mind, let's return to our ICT data. We've already seen a scatterplot in Figure 8.4 that shows a positive relationship between sentence length and the number of counts on which a defendant is convicted. In Table 8.1 we provide the linear regression

---

[5] How strong is this assumption of normally distributed residuals? In many cases it's a good one. One nice thing is that once we fit a regression line with OLS we can obtain a set of observed residuals. In an advanced regression course you would learn about a host of diagnostic tests to ascertain whether or not this assumption is reasonable. If it's not, there are a variety of other regression models you could use.

[6] We divide by $(n-2)$ to get an unbiased estimate of the population residual standard deviation. For the multiple regression model in the next chapter, the denominator of this formula is $(n-k-1)$, where k is the number of independent variables.

results as they might appear in an article, expert report, or working paper.[7]

Table 8.1 Linear regression of sentence length (in months) on the number of guilty counts.[8]

	Sentence Length
Intercept	216.92^*
	(23.36)
Number Guilty	14.61^*
	(3.40)
n	132
R^2	0.12
Resid. sd	187.64

Standard errors in parentheses. * indicates significance at $p < 0.05$

Let's unpack this table, starting with its caption. When writing about linear regression the custom is to talk about regressing Y on X. So, in this case, we're regressing sentence length on the number of guilty counts. It's also important to note that we call these numbers the results of a "linear regression," not an "ordinary least squares" or an "OLS." The term *linear regression* refers to the model we're using; OLS is the method we use to obtain parameter estimates.[9]

Many of the other features in the table we've seen before. *Intercept* is $\hat{\alpha}$ (the y-intercept) and *Number Guilty* is $\hat{\beta}$ (the slope). This table tells us that for every additional guilty count, defendants receive, on average, an additional 14.6 months on their sentence. We can't interpret the y-intercept in this model because someone convicted of zero counts won't get a sentence at all. In general, y-intercepts, recall, tell us that the average value of Y when X equals zero. The table also contains n, which denotes the size of the sample.[10] With these estimates we can put together a prediction equation:

---

[7] In Part IV we suggest ways to present regression results that aren't as off-putting to non-specialists. For now, we stick with standard practice.

[8] Source: ICT data.

[9] Though beyond the scope of this primer, there are other ways to obtain parameter estimates for the linear regression model.

[10] We explain the "Resid. sd." (the residual standard deviation) and R^2 in the section on Model Fit at 8.3.2.

$$\hat{Y}_i = 216.92 + 14.61 \cdot X_i$$

For any plausible value of X_i we can obtain the expected value for $\hat{Y}_i$. It's important to keep in mind that this works only for plausible values—values that we observe in the range of the data. Although it might be fun to predict the length of sentence for a defendant convicted of one million charges or negative 1,000 charges, such predictions would be meaningless extrapolations.

8.3.1 Hypothesis Testing

Let's also consider the parts of Table 8.1 that you haven't seen before: the standard errors and those asterisks.[11] What are these things? They relate to using the model to perform statistical inference (which, by the way, is why we needed to make an assumption about the distribution of the residuals).

One common hypothesis test—and perhaps the most common hypothesis test conducted in empirical legal studies—is this one:

$$H_0 : \beta = 0$$

$$H_1 : \beta \neq 0$$

Remember: we perform a regression analysis in the first place to determine whether or not Y and X are likely related *in the population*. If $\beta = 0$ this would imply that there is no relationship. For every one unit increase in X there is a zero increase in Y. On the other hand, if we reject the null hypothesis of no relationship we can conclude that there is likely a relationship in the population. In other words, the relationship is statistically significant.

In Table 8.1, directly below the slope parameter for *Number Guilty*, we report its standard error. (We needn't provide the technical details here. Suffice to say that there is a formula that is easy to apply.) Rather than reporting a p-value or confidence interval, here we use an asterisk to indicate that the estimate is statistically significant with a p-value less than 0.05. Just as with the two-sample *t*-test, we use the *t*-distribution to compute p-values and confidence intervals for the regression slope parameter. As you might expect, statistical software usually provides p-values and confidence intervals for regression parameters.

---

[11] Again, there's also R^2, which we explain in the section below on Model Fit.

Table 8.1 also shows a standard error and result of a hypothesis test for the y-intercept. Most software packages report the results of the test:

$$H_0 : \alpha = 0$$

$$H_1 : \alpha \neq 0$$

But this test isn't so important because the y-intercept α doesn't convey information about the relationship between Y and X. It just tells us the expected value of Y when X equals zero. Sometimes we might expect this to be zero, but more often than not we don't.

In Table 8.2 we present the same results in a slightly different form. Here the table includes the standard errors and the p-values. Since p-values can be computed from the estimates and standard errors, this table doesn't contain any more information than Table 8.1 already provides. Nonetheless, some authors choose to present their models this way, though we're not sure why. For a single regression model, Table 8.1 requires one column of numbers while Table 8.2 requires three.

8.3.2 Model Fit

There is one other quantity in Tables 8.1 and 8.2 that we haven't seen before: R^2, or the *coefficient of determination*. It's a statistic that we can use to assess the fit of a regression model.

How does it work? A model that fits terribly has an R^2 of zero; that is, there is no relationship between Y and X. On the other hand, when the

Table 8.2 Linear regression of sentence length (in months) on the number of guilty counts.[12]

	Coef.	Std. Err.	p-Value
Intercept	216.92*	23.36	< 0.001
Number Guilty	14.61*	3.40	< 0.001
n			132
R^2			0.12
Resid. sd			187.64

* indicates significance at $p < 0.05$

[12] Source: ICT data.

model explains all of the variability of Y—as do the hypothetical data in Figure 8.2—the R^2 will equal 1. More generally, the coefficient of determination tells us the percentage of the variance in Y explained by the model. Because of this, you can think of R^2 as a measure of model performance. Models with larger R^2s account for more variability in Y than models with smaller R^2s. (This doesn't necessarily mean we should choose models with larger R^2s as we'll see in Chapter 9.)

We compute the coefficient of determination using the following formula:

$$R^2 = \frac{\sum_{i=1}^{n}(\hat{Y}_i - \bar{Y})^2}{\sum_{i=1}^{n}(Y_i - \bar{Y})^2}$$

The denominator of the formula looks a lot like the standard deviation, just without dividing by $(n - 1)$ and not taking the square root. It shows how much variability there is in Y. The numerator tells us how much the model explains, plugging in $\hat{Y}_i$ that comes from the model rather than the raw data. If all of the points fall exactly on the line, $\hat{Y}_i = Y_i$, $R^2 = 1$.

Figure 8.6 shows two linear regression models for data with similar slopes and intercepts. Model 1 at the top of the figure looks to be a better model because the points are, on average, much closer to the line than they are in Model 2. The R^2 statistics tell the story. Model 1 has an $R^2 = 0.85$ while Model 2 has an $R^2 = 0.41$.

For any given regression model, you might wonder whether the R^2 is big enough. This is not a question that we can use statistics to answer because it's a substantive, not a statistical question. For each dependent variable it's important to think about the amount of variability in the dependent variable for which the independent variables should account. In some applications explaining 10% or 20% might be a lot, while in others it might be trivial.[13] It just depends on the application.

The coefficient of determination isn't the only measure of model fit. The residual standard error $\hat{\sigma}$ is another. Unfortunately, there is no standard name for this statistic—it's variously called the standard error of the estimate, the root mean square error, or the conditional standard deviation. Regardless of the name, the statistic tells us about

---

[13] Imagine if we could explain as little as 4% or 5% of the variability in the price of a common stock. We could make a lot of money with a modest amount of explained variance.

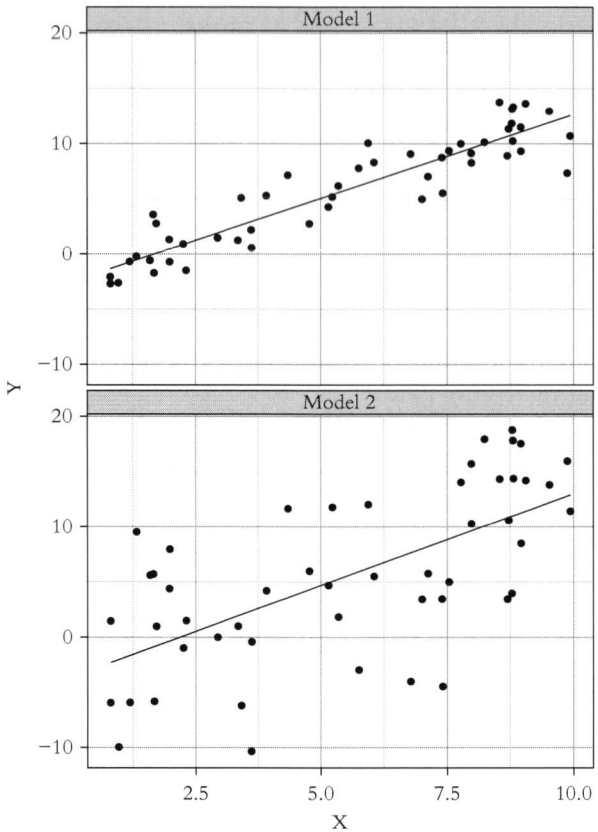

Figure 8.6 Two linear regression models with similar slopes and intercepts. For Model 1, $R^2 = 0.85$ and $\hat{\sigma} = 1.9$. For Model 2, $R^2 = 0.41$ and $\hat{\sigma} = 6.0$.

the dispersion of points around the regression line. We can interpret it like a standard deviation.

In terms of model fit, models with smaller residual standard errors are better than those with larger ones.[14] We see this pattern in Figure 8.6. Model 1 has a residual standard error of $\hat{\sigma} = 1.9$ while Model 2 has a residual standard error of $\hat{\sigma} = 6.0$. Note that our two measures of model performance work in opposite directions. Higher R^2s are better while smaller $\hat{\sigma}$s are better.

---

[14] This is true if the goal of our modeling exercise is to account for as much variability in the dependent variable as possible. For performing causal inference or making predictions, we might sometimes prefer models with larger residual standard errors.

These measures of model performance play an important role in assessing model quality. But analysts also frequently misuse them. We return to this important issue in Chapter 9, where we extend the regression model to include many independent variables. For now, we've covered everything we need to know to interpret Table 8.1.

Just one more quick point is worth making: tables aren't the only way to present the findings of the simple linear regression model. We can also use a scatterplot with the regression line and a confidence region for the expected value, that is, the average value of Y we would expect to see for a particular value of X. Figure 8.7 shows such a plot for our linear regression of sentence length on the number of guilty counts. It looks almost exactly the same as Figure 8.4 but there are two important differences. First, the figure contains a grey shaded region that shows the 95% confidence interval for the expected value of Y. This provides a visual gauge of how much uncertainty exists for our estimate of the average value of Y for each particular value of X. Note that this region gets much larger as we move toward the extreme number of guilty counts. This makes sense because there are fewer data (and therefore

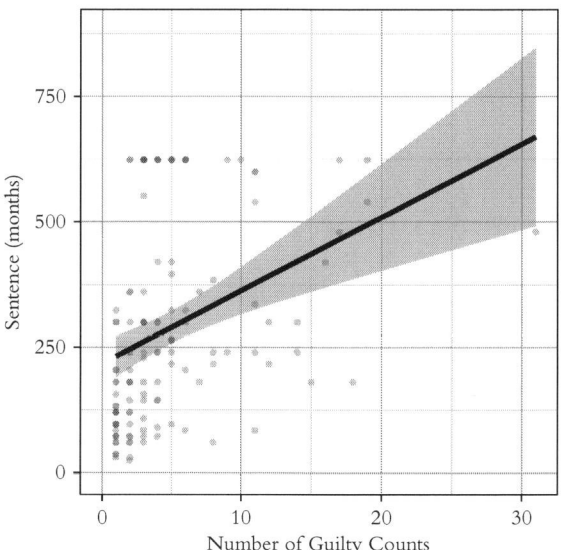

Figure 8.7 Prediction plot for linear regression of sentence length (in months) on the number of guilty counts. Grey region shows 95% confidence interval for the expected value.[15]

---

[15] Source: ICT data.

less information) at the extremes that we can use to make a prediction. Second, the scale of the y-axis of this figure is larger than in Figure 8.4. That's because we need to accommodate the wide confidence interval that goes well beyond the range of the data for 20 counts and more. As we'll see in Chapter 9 and again in Part IV, these sorts of figures are especially useful for models where the direct interpretation of coefficients isn't as easy as it is for linear regression.

* * * * * * * *

The "simple" linear regression model forms the basis for what's to come in Chapter 9—a model that allows us to control simultaneously for multiple independent variables. Linear regression and its cousins are the most commonly used models in empirical legal studies for this very reason, as we noted at the outset.

Before moving forward, though, we want to conclude with some words of caution, and one point of critique. Linear regression only works as a viable tool for understanding the relationship between two variables—and is, thus, only appropriate to use—when we think the relationship between the two variables *is approximately linear.* How would we know *ex ante* whether this is likely to hold? In simple linear regression it's easy; we can look at a scatterplot to see whether a linear relationship makes sense. If we saw a relationship between two variables that wasn't linear, it would imply that we shouldn't use linear regression. It's always important to visualize the relationship between two variables before plowing ahead with a linear regression model and making claims about statistical significance.[16]

We've also mentioned the possibility that our residuals won't follow the normal distribution. Because we cover this ground again in Chapter 9, suffice it to note here that in a comprehensive course on regression you would cover a handful of diagnostics to see whether this assumption is viable. Any regression analysis presented in print or in court should be backed up with a collection of diagnostics showing the plausibility of the model's assumptions.

These are the cautionary notes. Now to the critique. Our emphasis in this chapter has been on the linear relationship or association between a dependent variable and an independent variable. To assess

---

[16] This is more complicated to do in multiple regression models but in Chapter 9 we discuss some types of diagnostics you can use to see whether linearity holds.

this relationship some legal empirical researchers use a measure that we haven't discussed: the correlation coefficient (usually called r or R), which is a measure of linear association that runs between –1 and 1. It takes the value –1 if there is a perfect negative linear relationship, 0 if there is no relationship, and 1 if there is a perfect positive relationship. Often analysts use the term "correlation" to connote "relationship," but this isn't quite accurate. Just like the regression slope parameter β, the correlation coefficient tells us the amount of *linear* association between two variables.

So why wasn't this chapter about correlations? Because we don't think they're terribly useful. Now it's true that the correlation coefficient is related to the coefficient of determination R^2; it's just the correlation coefficient taken to the second power. The problem is that the correlation coefficient is difficult to interpret—unlike, say, the regression slope $\hat{\beta}$ (a one unit increase in our independent variable yields, on average, a $\hat{\beta}$ increase in our dependent variable). We compute a correlation coefficient by taking a regression slope $\hat{\beta}$, multiplying it by the standard deviation of Y (s_Y), and dividing it by the standard deviation of X (s_X). So it contains the same information as a regression slope, but its interpretation is on the relative scale of standard deviations. At least for us, it's a lot easier to think in terms of quantities (for example, counts, ages, months) than in standard deviations. That's why our strong preference is to report estimates from regression models rather than correlation coefficients.

9

Multiple Regression Analysis and Related Methods

The goal of most empirical projects is to draw causal inferences about how one or more independent variables affect some dependent variable of interest. As you saw in Part I of this book, research design—not statistical methods—is what empowers the researcher to perform causal inference. To put it another way, with a deficient research design no statistical method will enable the researcher to make causal claims.

For one type of study causal inference is relatively easy: experimental studies. To reiterate, experiments—which we often call the "gold standard" approach to causal inference—work in the following way. The researcher *randomly* assigns each unit of analysis to either the treatment or control group.[1] In doing so, a random process determines the value of the independent variable: either the unit of analysis is in the treatment group or the control group. The researcher then lets the process play out and observes the outcome of interest (the dependent variable).

Because the observations are randomly assigned to the treatment group or the control group, the researcher can be confident that any other factor that might influence the outcome can't be driving differences between the treatment and control group. Why? Because in both groups all potential confounding variables will balance out. A confounding variable is one that might be related to both the dependent and independent variable and could potentially mask the

---

[1] There are far more complicated experimental designs, each of which requires care when performing analysis. Nonetheless, the basic point doesn't change: what makes experimental research so powerful is that the researcher is in control of the independent variable(s). See Kinder and Palfrey (1993), Friedman and Sunder (1994), and Morton and Williams (2010) for more details.

effect of the independent variable of interest. Let's suppose that men and women react differently to a particular drug. As long as the researchers use random assignment, the number of men and women in the treatment and control groups will be roughly the same. Indeed, any factor, whether observed or unobserved, will balance out between the treatment and control groups. In a sense, an experimental design allows us to compare the factual and counterfactual by just comparing the values of the dependent variables between the two groups.[2]

As we discussed in Part I, experiments are simply impossible for many projects relating to law. Especially when studying legal institutions, we can't experimentally manipulate lots of key variables: whether a judiciary is independent, whether a judge is male or female, or whether a constitution does or does not contain a particular provision. Instead, we're left with data like those in the International Criminal Tribunal's dataset: observational data produced by the world. What makes observational data more difficult to analyze is that the researcher cannot control the independent variable of interest. The *world* controls it and so confounding factors may not balance themselves out between the treatment and control groups. As an example, men might, for some reason, disproportionally receive the treatment while women receive the control. In this case, if we observe differences between outcomes, it may be that the treatment caused them or it may be that the sex of the individual was the cause. Without conducting an experiment, it's quite difficult to know whether the independent variable of interest causes the outcome or whether some other confounding factor does the work.

What should we do with observational data? First, we need to ensure that we have a research design that gives us enough leverage to answer the research question. Second, we require a statistical approach that will allow us to control for the potential effects of other factors. There are multiple ways to do this in practice, but the most common methods of statistical control are multiple regression models and their variants. Statistical control works by using a model—and, necessarily, its assumptions—to hold all other independent variables constant to isolate the effect of the key independent variable. Because these approaches are second-best to a true experiment, any causal inferences we draw from observational data require both faith in the research design and in the assumptions of the model. There is, alas, no silver bullet.

---

[2] Quick quiz: what test would we use to compare the outcome between a treatment and control group? The two-sample *t*-test is the right answer if the dependent variable is interval.

The purpose of this chapter is to review the various methods and show how we can use them to perform causal inference. Of course, causal inference is not always the goal of empirical work. Sometimes we are developing a prediction about the future based on past data. Sometimes the descriptive task of quantifying the associations between variables is good enough. We discuss the multiple regression model in the context of causal inference, but it is useful and often even necessary for these other purposes too.

In what follows we introduce the multiple regression model, tackle a number of important issues related to model specification, describe the logistic regression model, and conclude with a discussion of other methods for causal inference with observational data.

9.1 Multiple Regression

The multiple regression model extends the simple linear regression model in one way: we can use it to include more than one independent variable. We'll continue to use Y_i to denote our dependent variable. The subscript i indicates the observation number in our dataset; it takes values $i = 1, \ldots, n$. Because we have more than one independent variable, we'll need to number each one. Let's suppose we have k independent variables. We'll call the first one $X_{1,i}$, the second one $X_{2,i}$, and so on until we get to the last one: $X_{k,i}$.

We can now write down the multiple regression model:

$$Y_i = \alpha + \beta_1 X_{1,i} + \beta_2 X_{2,i} + \cdots + \beta_k X_{k,i} + \varepsilon_i \quad \varepsilon_i \sim N(0, \sigma^2) \quad (9.1)$$

You'll note that this equation looks pretty similar to the linear regression model we considered in the last chapter—except, notably, the slope coefficients now have numbers associated with them. In fact, they're now called *partial slope coefficients*. The first is β_1 and is associated with $X_{1,i}$, the second is β_2 and is associated with $X_{2,i}$, and so on until we get to the last one, β_k, which is associated with $X_{k,i}$.

9.1.1 Interpretation

How do we interpret each of the parameters? The intercept coefficient (sometimes called the constant in the multiple regression context) α now tells us the expected value of our dependent variable when *all* of the independent variables are equal to zero. Do you see why that's the case? Think back to your high school algebra class. When all of the Xs are set to zero none of the βs come into play and so α tells us what we'd expect to see for Y.

The partial slope coefficients are the parameters of greatest interest. They show the effect of one independent variable while holding all of the rest of the independent variables constant. β_2, for example, tells us how much we expect Y to increase given a one-unit increase in X_2 *holding all of the other independent variables constant*, or, if you prefer to use the Latin, *ceteris paribus*. The same logic applies to all the other partial slope coefficients. β_1 tells us how much Y should increase for a one-unit increase in X_1 holding all the other independent variables constant. And the same thing for β_3, β_4, all the way up to β_k. This is statistical control! The linear additive form of the model in Equation 9.1 allows us to ferret out the effects of one variable by statistically holding all of the others constant. This helps to explain why the multiple regression model—and its variants for other types of dependent variables—is the most commonly used model in empirical legal studies.

Just as we were able to test hypotheses with simple linear regression, we can test hypotheses with this model as well. The most common procedure is to conduct hypothesis tests one parameter at a time, and the most common hypothesis test in a multiple regression model is the same one used for the simple linear regression model. For a multiple regression analysis we can report the results of the test:

$$H_0 : \beta_1 = 0$$
$$H_1 : \beta_1 \neq 0$$

and the test:

$$H_0 : \beta_2 = 0$$
$$H_1 : \beta_2 \neq 0$$

until we get to β_k. We report these in a table just like we would for a simple linear regression. We can also test the hypothesis of whether the intercept equals zero, but that's rarely of substantive interest.[3]

---

[3] There are general tests based on the F-distribution we can use to test linear combinations of the parameters. Although an omnibus F-test—that all of the partial slope coefficients are simultaneously equal to zero—is usually reported by statistical software, it doesn't tell us what

9.1.2 Model Fit

The residual standard error σ is the final parameter of the model. It still conveys the standard deviation of the residuals. Now, however, it doesn't tell us how far the points are from the regression line; it tells us how far the points are from the regression plane (when there are two independent variables) or from the regression hyperplane (when there are three or more independent variables). It remains a measure of model fit. Models with a smaller residual standard error fit the observed data better than models with a larger residual standard error. Because this parameter is a measure of dispersion, its values are always non-negative.

The other measure of model fit R^2 is just the same as before, although now it's called the coefficient of multiple determination. R^2 communicates the percentage of the variability of the dependent variable explained by the regression model. A model with no explanatory power whatsoever will have an $R^2 = 0.0$. A model that perfectly fits the data will have an $R^2 = 1.0$. One property of R^2 in multiple regression is that for every additional variable you add to the model, the R^2 can only get larger. Taken to the extreme, this would make it possible to obtain an $R^2 = 1.0$ by adding many independent variables.[4] As we discuss in the next section, the reason we use multiple regression is either to perform causal inference or to make sure we understand the relationships between the variables in our dataset. Trying to maximize R^2 doesn't achieve either.

Please note: most software packages report a related statistic called the adjusted R^2 which is just what it sounds: an R^2 statistic that is adjusted for the number of independent variables.[5] Although analysts often include this statistic in their tables, it can't be interpreted in the same way as the regular R^2. It's just a measure of model fit that is usually close to R^2 which, again, is the percentage of variance in the dependent variable explained by the model.

we're really interested in with a regression model—the partial effects of the independent variables and the overall quality of model fit.

[4] There are a number of automated methods called stepwise regression where the variables chosen for the model are performed automatically. We think these methods are useless for performing causal inference.

[5] Computed as follows:

$$\text{adj. } R^2 = 1 - \left[\frac{(1 - R^2)(n - 1)}{n - k - 1} \right]$$

9.1.3 An Example from the ICT Data

Let's return to the International Criminal Tribunal's (ICT's) dataset to see how multiple regression works in practice. Recall that the dependent variable is the sentence length (in months) of defendants convicted in one of the three tribunals. In Chapter 8 we used a single independent variable—the number of counts on which the court found the defendant guilty. The results from this model are presented as Model 1 in the first column of Table 9.1.

Surely, though, other factors affect the length of a defendant's sentence. In these trials there are certain aggravating factors that we'd expect to increase the length of a sentence, and a number of mitigating factors that would tend to decrease the length of a sentence. We represent them in the model as independent variables: the Number of Aggravating Factors and the Number of Mitigating Factors. There are two types of crimes that we might expect to lead to longer sentences as well: whether or not the court convicted the defendant of

Table 9.1 Multiple regression analysis of sentence length (in months).[6]

	Model 1	Model 2
Intercept	216.92*	63.34
	(23.36)	(37.62)
Number Guilty	14.61*	14.23*
	(3.40)	(2.57)
Number of Aggravating Factors		18.10*
		(7.87)
Number of Mitigating Factors		-19.04*
		(5.06)
Genocide		214.74*
		(25.33)
Crimes Against Humanity		112.21*
		(30.63)
n	132	132
R^2	0.12	0.61
adj. R^2	0.12	0.59
Resid. sd	187.64	127.83

Standard errors in parentheses. * indicates significance at $p < 0.05$

[6] Source: ICT data.

genocide or crimes against humanity. We include these as dichotomous independent variables. Genocide takes the value of 1 if the defendant is convicted of genocide and 0 otherwise; Crimes Against Humanity takes the value of 1 if the defendant is convicted of crimes against humanity and 0 otherwise.

Model 2 in Table 9.1 contains the estimates from the multiple regression analysis with the five independent variables. How did our software obtain these estimates? It used ordinary least squares, just as it did for the simple linear regression model. The computer searched over all possible parameter values to find the ones that minimized the sum of the squared residuals. For each parameter, including the intercept, the table contains the estimate, its standard error in parentheses below the estimate, and an indication of whether the coefficient is statistically significant at the 95% confidence level.

Note, first, that the multiple regression model (Model 2) fits the data far better than the simple linear regression (Model 1). Our multiple regression model accounts for 61% of the variability in sentence length; the simple linear regression model accounts for only 12% of the variability. As we would expect, the residual standard error is smaller by nearly 60 points for the multiple regression model. In addition to reporting the sample size n, the table contains the adjusted R^2 simply because some readers might be interested in it.

What do these model results tell us about the parameters of interest? All five of the partial slope coefficients are statistically significant at the conventional level of .05. We can interpret the first three. The estimate for Number Guilty is about the same between the two models. For the multiple regression model, we can claim that for each additional guilty count, the defendant can expect, on average, their sentence to increase by 14.2 months, *holding all else constant*. As we hypothesized, the Number of Aggravating Factors leads to increased sentences. On average, for every additional aggravating factor, the defendant's sentence will be 18.1 months longer, holding all other variables constant. Finally, the Number of Mitigating Factors decreases the length of the sentence. *Ceteris paribus*, for each additional mitigating factor present, the defendant's sentence decreases by 19.0 months on average. What about Genocide and Crimes Against Humanity? These are dichotomous independent variables. We can say that they are significant, but how do we go about interpreting them? Let's see.

9.1.4 Other Types of Independent Variables

So far we've discussed only interval variables as independent variables in linear regression models. But the models can also handle nominal and ordinal variables as independent variables (as long as we're careful in the way we do it). None of the statistical theory necessary to obtain estimates and standard errors relies on the assumption that the independent variables are interval.

In fact, Model 2 in Table 9.1 contains two dichotomous (or *dummy*) variables: Genocide and Crimes Against Humanity, and they too can be interpreted. Suppose we have just one independent variable X_i that takes the value of 1 or 0. (This is exactly how the Genocide and Crimes Against Humanity variables are coded. Each variable takes the value of 1 when the court found the defendant guilty of genocide or crimes against humanity respectively, and 0 otherwise.) We'll take the single variable and estimate a regression of Y on X, which produces two prediction equations. The first, when $X_i = 0$:

$$\hat{Y}_i = \hat{\alpha} + \hat{\beta} \cdot 0 = \hat{\alpha}$$

This means that the expected value of $\hat{Y}_i = \hat{\alpha}$ when $X_i = 0$. We can do the same thing for $X_i = 1$:

$$\hat{Y}_i = \hat{\alpha} + \hat{\beta} \cdot 1 = \hat{\alpha} + \hat{\beta}$$

Now the expected value of $\hat{Y}_i = \hat{\alpha} + \hat{\beta}$. The difference between these two expected values is $\hat{\beta}$. This implies that $\hat{\beta}$ can be interpreted as the difference in the average value of the dependent variable when $X_i = 1$ compared to $X_i = 0$. Does this look similar to a test you've seen before? It's very similar to the two-sample t-test to compare means; in fact, the two-sample t-test is a special case of the linear regression model.[7] Using a dichotomous independent variable allows us to compare the average value of the dependent variable across two groups. This entire process is similar to interpreting a partial slope coefficient for an interval independent variable. The only difference is that here X takes only one of two possible values (0 or 1) and in the general case X takes on a range of values. Just as it would be inappropriate to generate a prediction for the case when Number of Aggravating Factors equals 10,000

---

[7] Welch's two-sample t-test (explained in Chapter 7) doesn't require that the residual standard deviation is the same in both groups. A simple linear regression model assumes that it is. In almost every case, especially in large samples, this difference is inconsequential.

(well outside the range of our data), so, too, would it be inappropriate to generate a prediction when Genocide = 3.

Let's go back to Model 2 in Table 9.1 to see the interpretive process in action. The estimate for Genocide is 214.74. This means that sentences imposed on defendants convicted of genocide are, on average, 214.74 months longer, holding all else constant. The estimate for Crimes Against Humanity is 112.21, which means that defendants convicted of crimes against humanity receive sentences 112.21 months longer than those that do not, holding all else constant. It's interesting to note that the Genocide estimate is much larger than that for Crimes Against Humanity. Genocide occurs when a particular population is targeted for extermination. Crimes against humanity consist of a widespread and systematic attack on a population. Both are horrific, but genocide is more substantial in scope. The model confirms that defendants convicted of genocide receive longer sentences than those convicted of crimes against humanity or neither.[8]

What should we do with a nominal variable that has more than two categories or an ordinal variable? Let's start with the bad solution so that we can get to the good one. One nominal variable in our dataset is Tribunal. It can take three possible values:

1. International Criminal Tribunal for Rwanda [ICTR]
2. International Criminal Tribunal for Yugoslavia [ICTY]
3. Special Court for Sierra Leone [SCSL]

As is typical, we assign numeric values to each value (keeping in mind that our assignments are completely arbitrary). The bad solution is just to include the Tribunal variable in the dataset. If we did that, we would get three prediction equations. For the ICTR we would get:

$$\hat{Y}_i = \hat{\alpha} + \hat{\beta} \cdot 1 = \hat{\alpha} + \hat{\beta}$$

For the ICTY we get:

$$\hat{Y}_i = \hat{\alpha} + \hat{\beta} \cdot 2 = \hat{\alpha} + 2\hat{\beta}$$

---

[8] It is also possible to test the hypothesis that the coefficient on Genocide equals the coefficient on Crimes Against Humanity using an F-test. For these two coefficients we can reject the null hypothesis ($p = 0.017$), which means that the difference between the coefficients is statistically significant.

And, for the SCSL we get:

$$\hat{Y}_i = \hat{\alpha} + \hat{\beta} \cdot 3 = \hat{\alpha} + 3\hat{\beta}$$

Do you see the problem here? The difference between the ICTR and ICTY is $\hat{\beta}$. But the difference between the ICTR and the SCSL is $2\hat{\beta}$. The coding of the independent variable forces that difference to be exactly twice that of the difference between the ICTR and the ICTY. The cause is in the way we constructed the independent variable. We'd get different answers if, for example, the ICTY were coded 3 and the SCSL were coded 2.

What's the solution? Create two dichotomous variables to represent the three categories of the Tribunal variable. To see how this works, let's create a variable $X_{1,i} = 1$ that takes a value 1 if the court is the ICTR and 0 otherwise. We'll create a second variable $X_{2,i} = 1$ that takes the value 1 if the court is the ICTY and 0 otherwise. We can now go ahead and estimate our multiple regression model:

$$Y_i = \alpha + \beta_1 X_{1,i} + \beta_2 X_{2,i} + \varepsilon_i \quad \varepsilon_i \sim N(0, \sigma^2)$$

Once we fit this model and obtain our estimates, we obtain three prediction equations. For the ICTR, only the first dichotomous variable takes the value 1, so we get:

$$\hat{Y}_i = \hat{\alpha} + \hat{\beta}_1 \cdot 1 + \hat{\beta}_2 \cdot 0 = \hat{\alpha} + \hat{\beta}_1$$

For the ICTY, just the second dichotomous variable takes the value 1:

$$\hat{Y}_i = \hat{\alpha} + \hat{\beta}_1 \cdot 0 + \hat{\beta}_2 \cdot 1 = \hat{\alpha} + \hat{\beta}_2$$

For the SCSL, neither dichotomous variable takes the value 1, which is why this would be called the baseline category:

$$\hat{Y}_i = \hat{\alpha} + \hat{\beta}_1 \cdot 0 + \hat{\beta}_2 \cdot 0 = \hat{\alpha}$$

This shows that we can estimate the differences between the three courts without imposing a structure as we did by just including the Tribunal variable. $\hat{\beta}_1$ tells us the difference between the SCSL and the ICTR. $\hat{\beta}_2$ tells us the difference between the SCSL and the ICTY. We could even get the difference between the ICTR and the ICTY by comparing $\hat{\beta}_1$ and $\hat{\beta}_2$ as we did for the Genocide and Crimes Against Humanity variables. In general, for a nominal or ordinal variable with *l* categories we would just need to include (*l* - 1) dichotomous variables as independent variables.[9]

We can now include and interpret the effects of nominal or ordinal independent variables by incorporating the appropriate set of dichotomous variables. This means that our multiple regression model can handle any variable type as an independent variable! We could also include an *interaction*, when one independent variable affects the magnitude of the relationship between another independent variable and the dependent variable. So too the model can accommodate some *non-linear* relationships between the independent variables and the dependent variable.[10] (Later we'll explore how to deal with situations when our *dependent* variable is not interval.)

9.1.5 Interpreting and Presenting Results from the ICT Data

So far we have interpreted all the partial slope parameters and measures of model fit for the sentence length analysis using the ICT data. We've yet to interpret the final parameter from our analysis: the intercept. For these data the intercept doesn't make any substantive sense because it's impossible to convict someone with zero guilty counts. Nonetheless, it provides the baseline for the prediction equation that comes from the model. For some models when all the independent variables might take the value zero simultaneously, we could directly interpret the intercept as the expected value of the dependent variable when all the independent variables are zero. Just as we did with the simple linear regression, we can use the estimates in this table to develop a prediction equation:

$$\hat{Y}_i = 63.34 + 14.23 \cdot \textit{Number Guilty}_i + 18.10 \cdot \textit{Number of}$$

$$\textit{Aggravating Factors}_i - 19.04 \cdot \textit{Number of Mitigating Factors}_i$$

$$+ 214.74 \cdot \textit{Genocide}_i + 112.21 \cdot \textit{Crimes Against Humanity}_i$$

This equation will give us a predicted sentence by just subsituting the appropriate values for a defendant of interest.

What of our uncertainty about the parameter estimates? Table 9.1 provides standard errors for each. Figure 9.1 presents the estimates

---

[9] The ANOVA model is a special case of the multiple regression model. The only difference with ANOVA is that the independent variables are constructed as contrasts to make interpretation somewhat easier.

[10] Statistics textbooks cover these topics extensively; e.g. Fox (2008).

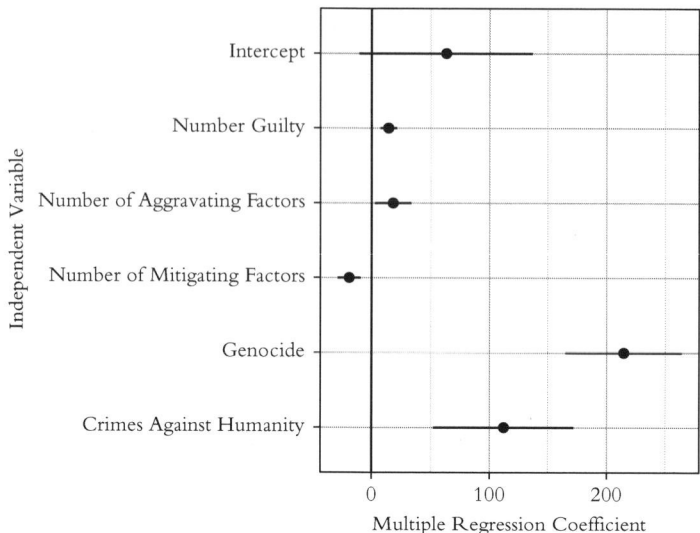

Figure 9.1 Nomogram of multiple regression parameters and 95% confidence interval for the analysis of sentence length (in months) in Table 9.1 (Model 2).[11] The dots show the regression parameter estimates and the horizontal lines show the 95% confidence intervals.

and uncertainties in a different way, using a graph called a nomogram rather than a table. Each parameter estimate is represented by a dot. The 95% confidence interval for each parameter is depicted by the horizontal line. Parameters with smaller confidence intervals are estimated more precisely than those with wider confidence intervals. Relative to comparing numbers in a table, nomograms make it easy to assess the amount of uncertainty in the coefficient estimate. We also can use the nomogram to ascertain statistical significance. When the 95% confidence interval does not cross zero, the parameter is statistically significant. All five of our independent variables are significant. The confidence interval for our estimate of the intercept contains zero. This means that the model provides us with no evidence that the intercept differs significantly from zero. (Nomograms are also useful for comparing the size of coefficients. We compare the magnitude of the Genocide and Crimes Against Humanities estimates in the next section.)

---

[11] Source: ICT data.

9.2 Model Specification

The multiple regression model is so powerful because it automatically provides statistical control. The partial slope coefficients tell us the effect of each independent variable holding all others constant. We can use the significance and magnitude of those coefficients to understand the relationships among our variables, and depending on our research design, to draw causal inferences. We also can compare models, using the residual standard deviation or the R^2 to determine which fits the data better. Yet, an important question remains. What variables should we include, and what variables needn't we include, when specifying multiple regression models?

This is a hard question to answer, as are questions about whether a linear regression model is appropriate for the data in hand. There is no set answer to either. The task of specifying the model—choosing the type of model to use and selecting the independent variables—requires a great deal of care and judgment. While statistical control is a powerful concept, it alone is not sufficient to draw causal inferences, because choices about what variables to include determine what it means to "hold everything constant." We cover only the basics here.

Before proceeding, though, we want to (re)emphasize the importance of checking our models by considering the four scatterplots in Figure 9.2, developed by Francis Anscombe in the early 1970s,[12] the so-called "Anscombe's Quartet." Each scatterplot consists of 11 data points and just one independent variable. Amazingly, the regression line has the same intercept $\hat{\alpha} = 3.0$ and slope $\hat{\beta} = 0.5$ across all four datasets; and the standard errors for the coefficients are the same, as are the residual standard deviations and the $R^2 = 0.667$. In fact, if you were to look just at the results of the regression analysis that came out of your statistical software, the results would be identical across all four panels.

But the linear regression model is appropriate only for Dataset 1. Only it contains exactly the type of data pattern amenable to modeling with a linear regression model. In Dataset 2 we clearly see a non-linear relationship. A curve would better represent these data than a straight line. In Dataset 3 there's something called an outlier. As we saw before in Chapter 6, an outlier is an observation that falls far away from the rest of the data. This single point is quite different from the others

---

[12] Anscombe (1973).

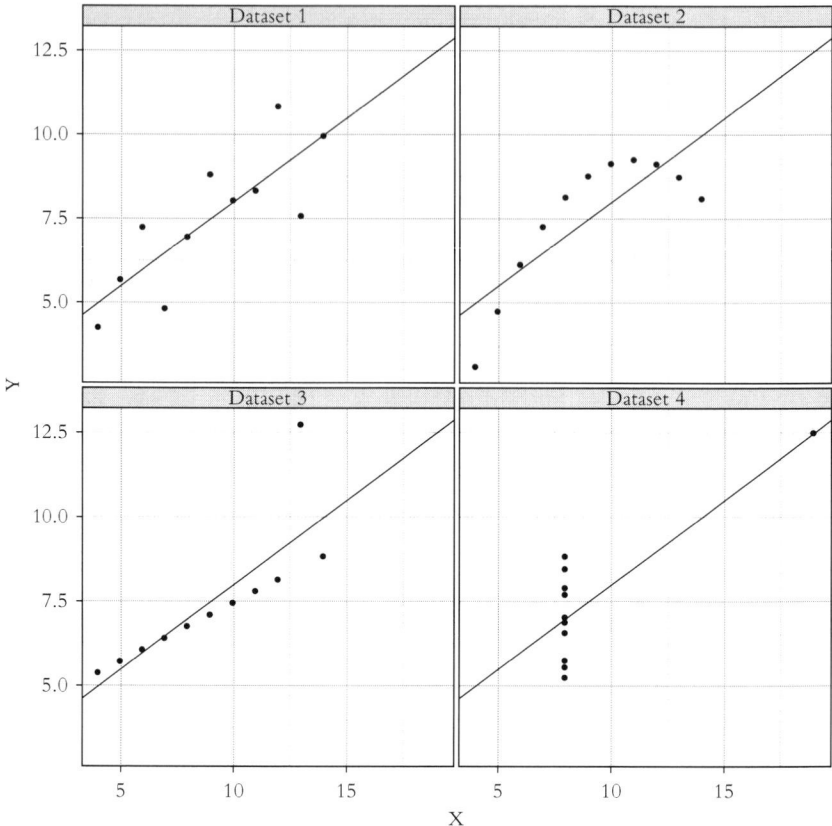

Figure 9.2 Anscombe's Quartet.[13] The lines in each panel are linear regression estimates. Each line has the same slope and intercept, and the residual standard deviation and R^2 is the same for each panel. But only for Dataset 1 would the linear regression model be appropriate.

and "pulls" the regression line away from a perfect linear relationship. To analyze these data we would need a model that could handle outliers appropriately. Dataset 4 has an independent "variable" that varies only in one instance, and that single data point drives the entire regression analysis. If we moved the point on the far right up or down, the line would move with it. The suggestion here is that Dataset 4 is sensitive to a single observation, making any conclusions non-robust.[14]

The broader implication of Anscombe's Quartet for simple linear regression is straightforward. *Always* visualize the relationship between

---

[13] Anscombe (1973).

[14] A statistic is non-robust if changing just a handful of observations dramatically changes the statistic. We saw this with the sample mean in Chapter 6.

the X and Y to ensure that the assumptions of the linear regression model are appropriate. For the situation with one independent variable, that's easy to do with a scatterplot.

For a multiple regression model with many independent variables, it's impossible to visualize all of the variables at once to see whether the assumptions of the regression model hold. The solution is to use a variety of diagnostic graphics and statistics that can accomplish the same thing as a simple (two-variable) scatterplot. These diagnostics are geared toward answering some important questions: Does the assumed linear relationship hold? Are the assumptions about the residuals reasonable? And, perhaps most importantly, are the right variables included in my model? Covering these diagnostics would require far more pages than we have and, besides, you can learn about them in many books on regression.[15] Worthy of our attention here, though, are several other important topics: the problems we could encounter when we don't include a relevant variable, models for other types of dependent variables, and the right way to think about regression analysis.

9.2.1 What Can Go Wrong

One of the nice features of the multiple regression model is that we can include many combinations of independent variables. It would be even nicer if the choice of which variables to include (and exclude!) didn't affect the inferences that we draw. But it does, and does so quite consequentially in multiple regression analysis.

Simpson discovered a paradox that illustrates how wrong things can go if the regression analysis (or any other type of statistical control) doesn't control for the right variables.[16] Consider the data plotted in Figure 9.3. The line in the figure is the linear regression line, that is, the one that best fits the data. This best-fitting line shows a negative relationship between X and Y: as X goes up, Y goes down. The slope of the line is statistically significant. If this is all we looked at, we would be comfortable with our conclusion that the relationship is negative.

More than likely, though, there's another independent variable that affects the outcome. Suppose that each data point in our hypothetical data was a person. Some of the people are men, and some are women.

---

[15] We recommend Fox (2008), Greene (2011), Gujarati and Porter (2008), Kennedy (2008), and Wooldridge (2010).

[16] Simpson (1951).

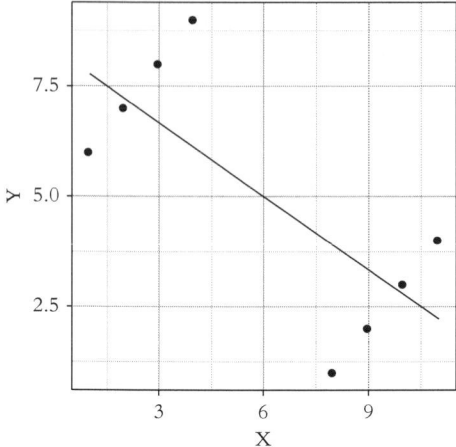

Figure 9.3 Linear regression of hypothetical Y on X, demonstrating what can go wrong if we don't include the right independent variables.

Let's suppose the men are the four data points in the upper left part of the scatterplot and the women are those in the lower right. Perhaps we should include sex as an independent variable as well. Figure 9.4 depicts what happens when we estimate a linear regression of Y on X that includes sex as another independent variable. The top panel of the figure shows that for men X and Y are *positively* related. And, paradoxically, so, too, for the women; in the lower panel, X and Y are positively related as well! The lesson here is simple: when we don't include the correct independent variables—in this case the sex of the individual—we might very well draw an incorrect conclusion about the relationship between the variables. Without controlling for sex, we would conclude that there is a negative relationship, as the regression line in Figure 9.3 shows. However, once we control for sex, as in Figure 9.4, we see that the relationship is, in fact, positive.

We do not contend that Simpson's Paradox occurs all of the time (it almost certainly does not). But it is a possibility for any observational study. Sometimes when we draw from multiple groups and combine them, we might find an effect that is completely opposite to the effect in each sub-group. One classic example comes from research on graduate school admissions at the University of California, Berkeley in 1973.[17] The study showed that if we just compared the admissions rates for male and female applicants, there was a statistically significant and large difference: 44% of men were admitted but only 35% of women.

---

[17] Freedman et al. (2007).

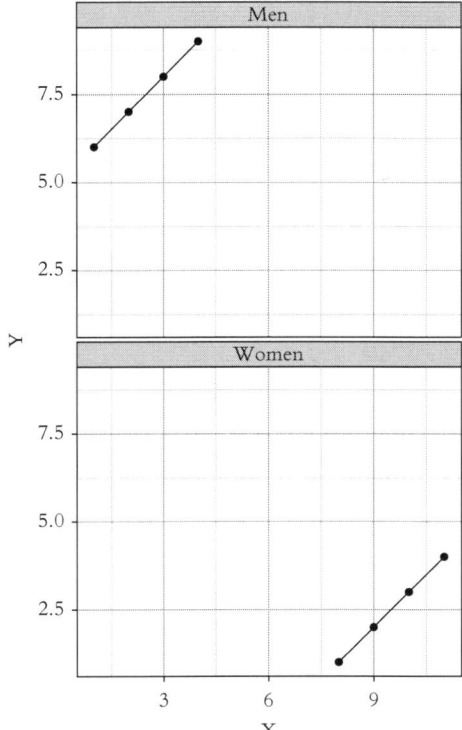

Figure 9.4 Linear regression of hypothetical Y on X controlling for sex, illustrating Simpson's paradox. The two lines represent the least squares line when simultaneously controlling for sex.

Does this mean that there was gender discrimination in graduate admissions? Freedman et al. looked at the same data at the department level. They found that *no* department was biased against women. Either the differences in admission rates were statistically insignificant, or women were *more* likely than men to get admitted. Assuming Freedman et al. were correct, without controlling for department, we'd draw an incorrect conclusion about gender bias in the university.

A related phenomenon in linear regression analysis is, as we hinted in Chapter 2, *omitted variable bias*. Simply put, in a regression analysis if we fail to include a variable that governs the relationship between the dependent variable and independent variables in the population, all the estimates of the partial slope coefficients will be biased.[18] By not including the right variables, we might be left with inferences that are wrong. The bottom line is that we need to control for the right variables in order to completely trust the answers we get.

[18] See Greene (2011).

9.2.2 *How to Choose Independent Variables*

Both Simpson's Paradox and the possibility of omitted variable bias are quite intimidating. How can we believe the estimates from any regression analysis? It turns out that there are a number of best practices we can employ when choosing what independent variables to include in our regression analysis, starting with: let theory be your guide. Theoretical considerations motivate most empirical studies, and those considerations can dictate which independent variables are causally relevant to the dependent variable and which ones are not.

Most theories in empirical legal studies allow for multiple causes. More to the point, it's implausible to believe that one and only one factor affects most legal phenomena—including the decisions judges make, the strategies litigants deploy, or the damages juries award, to name just three. It's important, then, to make sure we appropriately include variables for all of the multiple causes.

Suppose we were studying some phenomenon that had two causes: X_1 and X_2. Further suppose that X_1 was our key causal variable of interest. X_2 is another cause, and is therefore something we need to take into account. What might happen if we looked only at the relationship between X_1 and Y without including X_2? All sorts of things because X_2 would be a confounding variable, that is, a variable that when excluded affects the inferences we draw. In the last section we saw that things can go wrong if we don't include the right control variables. By leaving out X_2, we might not find a relationship between Y and X_1 that we would see if we controlled for both variables. If that's the case, we'd call X_2 a suppressor variable. Alternatively, we might find a significant relationship between Y and X_1 that went away when controlling for X_2. In this case, the first variable was spurious because X_2 was a lurking variable. We also might find that a relationship between Y and X_1 persists when controlling for X_2, but that the magnitude of the relationship changes. Whenever we have multiple causes, we might be faced with confounding factors. In the face of confounders, the best solution is to include all theoretically relevant variables.[19]

When performing causal inference, there are two other important considerations for choosing independent variables. First, suppose we

---

[19] See Agresti and Finlay (2009). When performing causal inference, we would only want to include pre-treatment variables, as we note below. Post-treatment variables would not be theoretically relevant, and so should be excluded.

have a key causal variable (a "treatment") that affects Y, called X_1. (Remember that in an experimental context a treatment is something that the researcher can control.) Perhaps we're primarily interested in how performance in law school (X_1) affects salary 15 years after graduation Y. Further suppose that we also measure some other variable X_2 that is caused by X_1 and is measured after the initial treatment (the term of art is "post-treatment"). Years in a high-paying practice would be an example of X_2.

The causal chain for these three variables is: $X_1 \to X_2 \to Y$; one's performance in law school affects years in a high-paying practice which affects salary 15 years after graduation. Should we include both X_1 and X_2 as independent variables? Not if what we care about is the causal effect of performance in law school (X_1). In this situation, if we include years in a high-paying practice (X_2) in a regression equation we wouldn't get the causal effect of X_1. That's because β_1 would tell us how much X_1 affected Y *holding years in a high-paying practice constant*. But since X_1 causes X_2 to change, we don't want to hold X_2 constant. The upshot is that when performing causal inference we should not control for post-treatment variables.

Second, we need to ensure that our independent variables are exogenous. In experimental studies, the independent variable is under the control of the researcher, so there's no way for the dependent variable Y to affect the independent variable X. In observational studies, however, while X might cause Y (that's what we're usually looking for), it also might be that Y causes X. A good example is the affect of money on elections. While money spent on campaigning (X) will likely produce more votes for a candidate (Y), donors may well choose to contribute money based on the votes a candidate will likely get. In this example Y may cause X as well.

When we have an endogenous regressor such as campaign spending, things go wrong. The estimates of the intercept α and the partial slope coefficients β_k will be *inconsistent*. This means that regardless of the size of the sample, we'll get the wrong estimate.[20] A good research design will mitigate against the inclusion of endogenous regressors.[21]

---

[20] On the other hand, a consistent estimator is one where the amount of bias disappears as the sample size gets larger.

[21] There are some solutions to deal with endogenous regressors, the most common of which is the use of instrumental variables. Econometrics texts cover these approaches in depth (e.g. Greene, 2011).

Do these various possibilities—especially of confounding variables or omitted variable bias—mean that we should toss out every variable in a regression equation? Absolutely not.[22] The research design and theory that motivate our study should dictate the independent variables in our models. Of course, we should include variables for all causes, and we should include control variables that are correlated with the key causal variable, have an independent effect on the dependent variable, and are causally prior to the key causal variable. We should never include post-treatment variables in our analyses.

But theory can take us only so far. We always start with it to specify our model but we must end with careful diagnostic work to ensure that the model fits the data reasonably well—and that it is robust to various specifications. Most empirical studies contain footnote after footnote discussing how regression estimates are affected by controlling for different factors, by including/excluding particular variables, and by substituting different measures. If the estimates for the key causal variables are stable across multiple different specifications, and if various diagnostics suggest that the assumptions of the multiple regression model are plausible, then it's reasonable to conclude that the model is capturing the correct relationship. If, however, coefficient estimates are non-robust and change with every tweak of the model, we cannot have any confidence in the estimates of the causal effect.

9.3 Logistic Regression

The regression models we've seen so far assume that we're working with an interval dependent variable. There are other types of dependent variables that we might be interested in modeling. Let's return to the study by Posner and de Figueiredo of the International Court of Justice (ICJ).[23] Recall that the authors collected the votes of ICJ judges with the goal of determining whether the judges decide cases in biased ways.[24] Their dataset covers 103 cases heard by the ICJ between 1947 and 2003, and includes information about the state-parties in

---

[22] For careful and illuminating discussions of these issues see Achen (2005), Clarke (2005), and Greenland (2003).

[23] Posner and de Figueiredo (2005); Posner (2005).

[24] We worked with their dataset in Chapters 2 and 3.

each case (such as their EU membership status, their per capita GDP, and their legal tradition) as well as information about the judge's home country, the judge's vote in the case, and the basis for the ICJ's jurisdiction.[25]

The dependent variable in their analysis is `Decision`. It takes the value 1 of the judge for the applicant country before the court, and 0 otherwise. For the sake of illustration, we'll use just one independent variable: `Judge GDP`. `Judge GDP` is the per capita gross domestic product of the judge's home country in constant 1996 dollars. To ease interpretation of the coefficients, the variable is coded in $10,000 units, so 1 represents $10,000, 2 represents $20,000, and so on. The hypothesis is that judges from countries with higher GDPs will be less likely to vote in support of countries petitioning the ICJ. The reason is that most petitions come from lower GDP states, so, on average, judges from higher GDP states would be less likely to side with the applicant state.[26] This independent variable is interval.

Figure 9.5 shows the scatterplot for these two variables, along with a linear regression line. A few things jump out. First, there is not a lot of scatter in the scatterplot! That's because the dependent variable takes on only the values of 0 or 1 (for or against the applicant country), ensuring that all the data necessarily fall along two lines. Second, the figure contains a regression line estimated by least squares, but you can see that it doesn't fit the data very well. While the line seems to show a negative relationship (as we would expect), it does not and could not possibly capture the relationship between the two variables. Third, the residuals from this regression line do not follow the normal distribution. Instead, there are a bunch of large positive residuals, a bunch of large negative residuals, and no residuals around the value 0. This means that the assumption we need to make to compute standard errors and perform inference for a regression model does not hold.

Taken collectively, the lesson of this exercise is that the linear regression model is not appropriate when we are trying to explain

[25] In their analysis of these data Posner and de Figueiredo (2005) and Posner (2005) show that judges tend to favor the countries which appointed them to the court and countries that have similar levels of wealth as the judge's home state. They also find some evidence that judges favor states that are politically and culturally similar to theirs.

[26] There are other and better ways to test this. For example, we might control for the GDP of the petitioning country. More generally, one variable can't possibly explain a phenomenon as complex as a judge's vote. We use this example for pedagical purposes only.

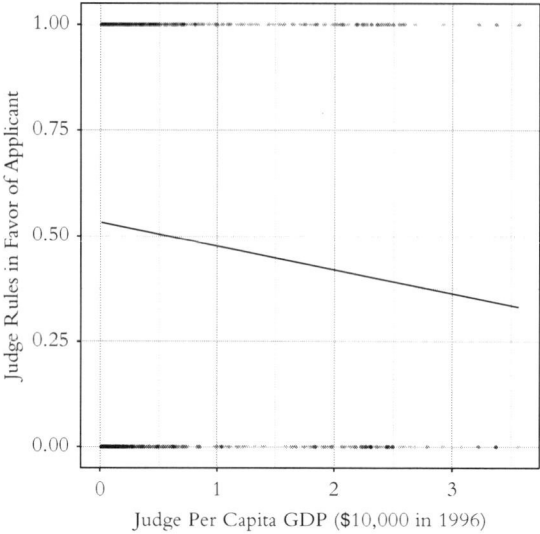

Figure 9.5 Scatterplot of the votes of ICJ judge per capita gross domestic product of the judge's country, with a regression line.[27]

a dichotomous variable. In these circumstances, a model called a *logistic regression model* (sometimes just *logit*) is far better.[28] Rather than modeling the value Y_i as we did with linear regression, we'll model the probability that Y_i takes the value 1. Since probabilities can't be smaller than 0 or greater than 1, we need to assume that the relationship between our independent variable and dependent variable is non-linear. In other words, rather than fit a line we estimate a curve. The precise curve we use for the logistic regression model is this one:[29]

$$\Pr(Y_i = 1) = \frac{\exp(\alpha + \beta X_i)}{1 + \exp(\alpha + \beta X_i)} \tag{9.2}$$

In this equation "exp" represents the transcendental number e (2.718 ...) taken to some power, so $\exp(\alpha + \beta X_i)$ is the same as $e^{\alpha + \beta X_i}$. This equation relates our independent variable X_i to our dependent variable. We still call α the intercept and β the slope, even though they are part of a non-linear relationship between our variables of interest.

---

[27] Source: ICJ data.

[28] Logistic regression is an example of a consistent estimator, that is, bias may exist in small samples but disappears as the sample size grows. Linear regression, on the other hand, is unbiased in small samples.

[29] This is the cumulative distribution function for the logistic distribution.

You might be asking, why this function? We use this function because it (like a probability) is bounded below at o and bounded above at 1. In other words, all of its values must equal or fall between o and 1. If β is positive and X_i is negative and large, the equation above will have a very small number (because the exponential of a negative number is the reciprocal of the exponential of the positive number) divided by 1 plus a very small number, which will be very close to o. If X_i is positive and large, the numerator will be a really large positive number, which, when divided by 1 plus a really large positive number, approaches 1. There are many functions that have this property, but this particular one is common in empirical legal research because it's symmetric and because it's easy to compute predicted probabilities. (The other function that appears in many studies is the cumulative normal distribution for the *probit regression model*. In most applications the choice of which function to use isn't consequential.)

Figure 9.6 shows the logit curve for the case when $\alpha = $ o and $\beta = $ 1. You'll see that the function approaches o as X goes to the left, and it approaches 1 as X goes to the right. The value of the intercept α tells us where the middle of the curve is. Moving it up or down would just shift the curve to the right or left. The slope coefficient β tells us how steep the curve should be. If β is larger than 1, the curve will be steeper than in Figure 9.6. If β is smaller than 1, it will get stretched out. For the case when $\beta = $ o, the line will be flat, which would suggest

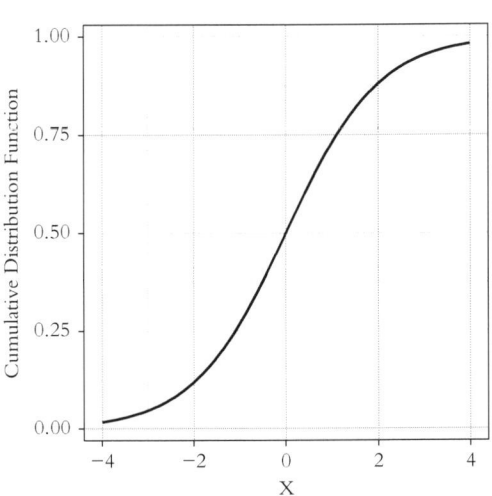

Figure 9.6 Logistic regression curve.

that our dependent variable and independent variables are not related. If β is negative, the curve gets flipped, with the line starting at 1 and dropping to 0. Just as in linear regression, the key parameter of interest is β. We want to know whether or not it is equal to 0. If we reject the null hypothesis that $\beta = 0$, we conclude that there is a statistically significant relationship between our independent and dependent variables.

Let's return to the ICJ data. Table 9.2 contains the logistic regression estimates and standard errors for an analysis of the judges' votes as a function of the GDP of their home country.[30] Focus on the estimates of the intercept $\hat{\alpha} = 0.13$ and the slope $\hat{\beta} = -0.23$.[31] Unlike linear regression where we can directly interpret a coefficient—it's how much we would expect a dependent variable to increase for a one-unit increase in the independent variable—we can't do the same for logit models because they are non-linear. All we can say from glancing at the coefficient on Judge GDP is that it is negative, as hypothesized, and it is statistically significant. This means that judges from countries

Table 9.2 Logistic regression analysis of the votes of ICJ judges on per capita gross domestic product of the judge's country.[32]

	Model 1
Intercept	0.13
	(0.08)
Judge GDP	-0.23*
	(0.07)
_n_	1146
AIC	1580.87
BIC	1621.22
$\log L$	-782.43

Standard errors in parentheses. * indicates significance at $p < 0.05$

---

[30] The way we obtain the parameter estimates is beyond the scope of this primer. Suffice it to say that statistical software can reliably estimate the intercept and slope coefficients, as well as their standard errors. Long (1997) provides a comprehensive treatment of logistic regression and the estimation method. The model is not identified and some statistical software packages will incorrectly return finite estimates of infinite parameters if there is perfect separation between the Y and X; that is, if the independent variables can perfectly predict the dependent variable. See Zorn (2005) for details.

[31] The other quantities in the table (AIC, BIC, and log L) come from the estimation method and can be used for model comparison. Our goal here is to understand how to interpret the coefficients.

[32] Source: ICJ data.

with higher GDPs are significantly less likely to side with the applicant country before the ICJ.

What we really want to know—and what most of us can't calculate in our heads as we do in linear regression—is how big the effect is. To figure this out, we can return to the prediction equation, and for this example compare the probability of voting in favor of the applicant for a judge from a country with a $10,000 per capita GDP and one from a country with a $30,000 per capita GDP. To perform the calculation we just need to plug our values $\hat{\alpha}$, $\hat{\beta}$, and X_i into Equation 9.2. Here's the predicted probability when $X_i = 1$:

$$\Pr(Y_i = 1 | X_i = 1) = \frac{\exp(0.13 - 0.23 \cdot 1.0)}{1 + \exp(0.13 + -0.23 \cdot 1.0)} = 0.48$$

We can repeat the calculation for $X_i = 3$:

$$\Pr(Y_i = 1 | X_i = 3) = \frac{\exp(0.13 - 0.23 \cdot 3.0)}{1 + \exp(0.13 + -0.23 \cdot 3.0)} = 0.37$$

We see that as we move from a per capita GDP of $10,000 to $30,000 the probability of voting for the applicant decreases by 0.11 (or 11 percentage points). We know this is statistically significant; that is, there is sufficient evidence to conclude that it is not equal to zero in the population.

Prediction equations of this sort are useful for making comparisons across a number of alternatives, but they are deficient in two ways. First, they don't convey the predicted probabilities for all values of the independent variable; we examined $10,000 and $30,000 but not values between the two (or lower or higher). Second, they don't show measures of uncertainty about the predicted probabilities; instead, they treat the parameter estimates as given.

King et al. provide a simulation-based method to overcome these deficiencies and produce figures such as Figure 9.7.[33] This shows the predicted probabilities and 95% confidence intervals for all values of our independent variable. As we saw with linear regression, we estimate the predictions more precisely in the middle of the distribution compared with the ends. Here we present only plausible values of judge GDP—ones that are in the range observed in the dataset.

---

[33] King et al. (2000). We explore these types of figures in more detail in Part IV.

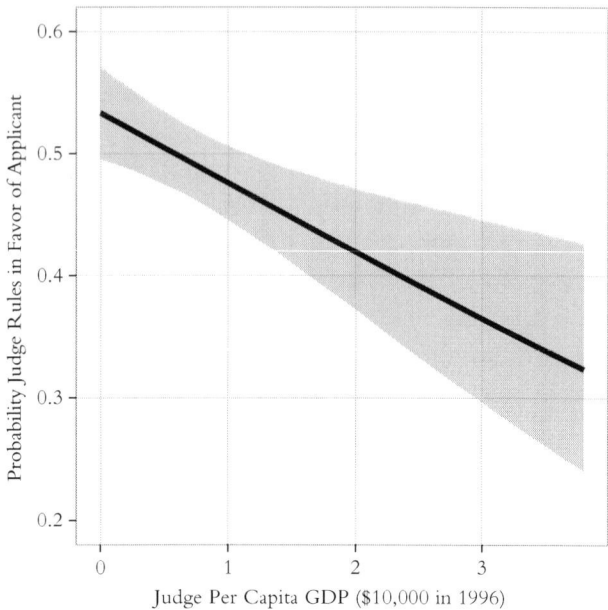

Figure 9.7 Predicted probability of an ICJ judge voting in favor of the applicant country as a function of per capita judge GDP, based on the estimates in Table 9.2. The grey region denotes 95% confidence interval.[34]

Now, we know that our hypothesis test shows that Judge GDP is statistically significant. But is it substantively significant? As we noted earlier, this is not a statistical question; it's one that only experts can address. Still, Figure 9.7 helps us out. Knowing that you might appear before a judge with around a 50% chance of siding with you compared with a judge with a 33% chance seems pretty big to us (though with just one independent variable we wouldn't want to reach any firm conclusions).[35]

This example of logistic regression is just the beginning of what we can do with these models. Chiefly, we can extend them by including more independent variables and those independent variables can be of diverse types, just as we saw with multiple regression. The only complication is that computing any predicted probability requires us to

---

[34] Source: ICJ data.

[35] Another method that we can use to interpret logistic regression coefficients is to compute something called an odds ratio or a confidential odds ratio, which is the logistic regression coefficient exponentiated. For Table 9.2 the odds ratio for Judge GDP is 0.8 with 95% confidence interval (0.70, 0.91). We strongly prefer thinking in terms of probabilities rather than odds, which is why we prefer a figure like Figure 9.7 for presenting logistic regression results.

hold the other variables at some value (perhaps their mean or mode), rather than constant as we could with multiple regression, because they're non-linear.

* * * * * * * *

We've covered a lot of ground in Chapters 8 and 9 but we've only scratched the surface. Were you in a graduate program in the social sciences, you'd probably take at least two courses on this material and cover it in far great detail.

What else would you learn? Courses in linear regression analysis discuss other types of hypotheses that can be tested within the linear framework; they also delve into regression diagnostics, including whether linearity is a good assumption, whether the residuals follow the distribution we've assumed,[36] and whether the inferences we draw are robust and not driven by outliers. If these diagnostics suggest that the model is inadequate, there are alternative models we can use. You'd also spend a great deal of time on exploratory data analysis and methods to ascertain overall model quality.[37] Finally, many non-linear relationships can be estimated using the linear regression model but it takes intuition, theory, and great care to do it properly.[38]

Other courses would cover the collection of models for dependent variables of different types. Table 9.3 contains a list. There are also courses and books on models designed for count data—variables that are defined on the non-negative integers—as well as models that deal with the timing of events where the (interval) time variable must be greater than zero. Many regression books provide the necessary know-how to estimate and interpret non-linear regression models for all types of dependent variables.[39]

---

[36] These diagnostics include testing whether or not the residuals have constant variance (i.e., are homoscedastic), whether the residuals in a time-series or spatial context are correlated with one another, and whether the residuals follow the normal distribution or something else. If these assumptions are violated, the parameter estimates will continue to be correct but the standard errors, and thus the inferences we draw, will be incorrect.

[37] E.g., specification tests like Ramsay's Regression Equation Specification Error Test (Ramsey, 1969).

[38] For excellent texts that thoroughly cover the linear regression model and related methods, we recommend Fox (2008), Greene (2011), Gujarati and Porter (2008), Kennedy (2008), and Wooldridge (2010).

[39] Long (1997) is especially good. For an introduction to event history models, we recommend Box-Steffensmeier and Jones (2004). On another subject: one problem that can plague regression analysis is missing data. Sometimes we are not able to obtain information

Table 9.3 Regression models for other dependent variables.

Dichotomous	Logit or probit
Ordinal	Ordinal logit or ordinal probit
Nominal	Multinomial (or conditional) logit or multinomial probit
Count	Poisson or negative binomial regression
Time to event	Survival model (e.g., Cox proportional hazards model)

All these regression models take the same approach to statistical control. But sometimes just including the relevant independent variables won't allow us to estimate a causal effect because the assumption of additive linear effects is insufficient. In the field of statistics and now in the social sciences scholars are beginning to apply a technique called the Rubin Causal Model.[40] Rather than using independent variables in regression equations to ensure that apples are being compared to apples, this approach uses matching of similar observations in the treatment and control groups to approximate an experimental setting with observational data. There are many ways to perform this matching exercise. But if we're able to compare a set of units matched on all observables in a treatment and control condition, we can estimate the causal effect with minimal assumptions. Performing the matching can sometimes be difficult, and, of course, it's impossible to match on variables we haven't collected. Nonetheless, the approach does facilitate comparing appropriate units. Sometimes we'll throw away data from the treatment or control group if there are no suitable matches in the other. So this is one circumstance where more data isn't necessarily better.[41]

We could go on but we're sure you get the drift. Though we've aspired to provide a reasonable primer in statistical inference, at the end of the day that's all we've provided: a primer. There's always more to learn—whether about emerging strategies (matching, for example)

for all of our units of analysis. See King et al. (2001) for a review of the relevant issues and a solution using multiple imputation.

[40] Holland (1986); Rubin (1974, 1977); Ho et al. (2007).

[41] We think matching methods will continue to grow in empirical legal studies, especially in areas where we are trying to estimate the effect of some sort of intervention. For examples of this type of analysis, see Epstein et al. (2005) which explores the effect of war on decisions of the U.S. Supreme Court, and Boyd et al. (2010) (discussed in Chapter 1), which estimates how the presence of a female judge on a three-judge panel in the U.S. circuit courts causes male judges to decide sex discrimination cases differently.

or new tricks for foundational approaches. The concluding chapter provides suggestions for those of you (and we hope you are many in number!) who are game. But before going there, we'd like you to turn the page, and learn about methods for communicating data and results. We think you'll find the material very interesting.

PART IV

Communicating Data and Results

If you've made it this far, you've learned a lot about empirical legal research, from research design to data collection to data analysis. We'd venture to say that you now know more about how to evaluate and conduct empirical studies than the vast majority of your colleagues, whether in law schools, law firms, legislative offices, or courthouses.

And therein lies the problem. Empirical legal researchers can do everything right and yet still may be unable to communicate with their audience because their audience can't even begin to decipher, much less evaluate, the results of their studies. Having read the previous nine chapters, you know what a p-value is, you understand the meaning of the term "statistically significant," and you can interpret a regression coefficient. But many consumers of empirical legal research can't.

This is one of the reasons we decided to write the next two chapters, both of which cover the communication of empirical research.[1] They reflect our belief that executing a great study is terrific—unless of course no one reads it because they can't understand it. No analyst wants to be ignored, and this goes doubly so, we think, for empirical legal researchers. Perhaps more than most, they have a strong interest in conveying their results to the statistically informed *and* uninformed. And so moving away from statements that are meaningless to most legal scholars, lawyers, policy makers, and judges—about "p-values,"

[1] The material in this part draws on two of our articles, Epstein et al. (2006) and Epstein et al. (2007).

"statistical significance," and "regression coefficients"—and toward forms of communication that "require little specialized knowledge to understand" is particularly apt for you, our readers.[2] To be even more blunt: if you want to ensure that you and your communities reap the full benefits of your study, you should aim to present your results in a way that a second-year college student could read and comprehend.[3]

There's a second motivation for including Chapters 10 and 11. Though we have no doubt that researchers want others to understand and evaluate their work, we are less certain that they know how to meet this goal. From a sample of empirical law studies we examined,[4] we spotted substantial obstacles that non-experts would confront in deciphering the results—and, frankly, obstacles that other disciplines have already hurdled. For example, many (social) scientists have "declared a war" on tables, expressing a strong preference for graphs.[5] But members of the empirical legal community continue to embrace tabular displays, especially ominous-looking ones full of regression coefficients.

And even when graphs do make their way into published work or reports, they are sometimes so "busy" or otherwise marred that they all but lose their impact.[6] In varying degrees this holds for the two figures in Figure IV.1, both of which we created based on graphs that appeared in law-related journals.[7] The top panel, for example, is too cluttered with irrelevant elements (including the depth cue, internal data labels, and legend); the data are all but obscured. The cross hatching and overabundance of tick marks don't help. The bottom panel's grid and non-circular elements interfere with, rather than show off, the data.

---

[2] King et al. (2000, 347).

[3] Paraphrased from Wright (2003, 131).

[4] For the details, see Epstein et al. (2006).

[5] See, e.g., King et al. (2000); Gelman et al. (2002); Kastellec and Leoni (2007). The preference for figures over tabular displays is hardly new. As early as 1801, William Playfair, a leading player in the development of quantitative graphs, wrote that information "obtained [in charts] in five minutes ... would require whole days to imprint on the memory, in a lasting manner, by a table ..." (quoted in Costigan-Eaves and Macdonald-Ross, 1990, 323). With new developments in the social and statistical sciences, Playfair's sentiment has become a near battle cry.

[6] For more on the concepts of "busyness" and "impact," see Chapter 10.

[7] We have altered or updated the variables and data but otherwise retain the design elements.

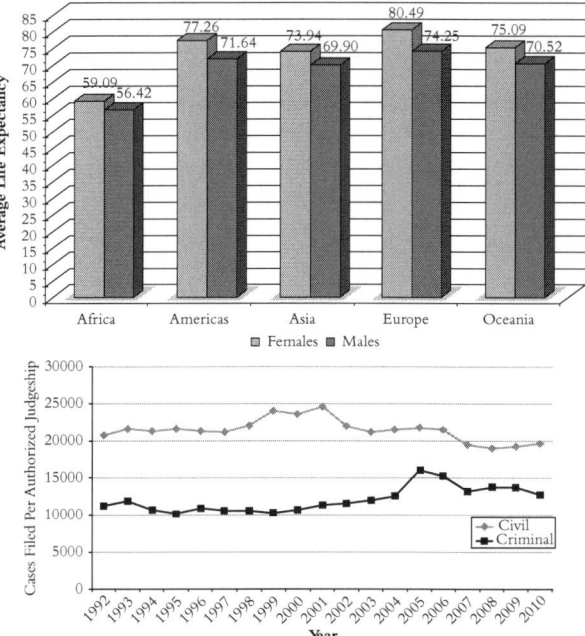

Figure IV.1 Each panel displays a figure that obscures the data and so interferes with visualization. The graph in the top panel, which shows the mean life expectancy (in years) for males and females at birth, is cluttered with irrelevant elements, including the depth cue, internal data labels, and legend. The bottom panel shows the number of criminal and civil cases filed per authorized judgeship in the U.S. Courts of Appeals, 1992–2010. The dark grid and legend obscure visualization of the data, as do the non-circular sub-elements. We offer correctives in Figures 10.4 and 10.5.[8]

These are just a few examples of the problem; the list of ills is longer, and we devote Chapters 10 and 11 to offering antidotes. But the basic point should not be missed: A very large fraction of empirical work could be improved if authors paid as much attention to how they *present* information as to how they collect and analyze it.

[8] The data in the top panel are from the World Bank, at: <http://data.worldbank. org/indicator/SP.DYN.LE00.FE.IN?display=default> and <http://data. worldbank.org/ indicator/SP.DYN.LE00.MA.IN?display=default>; regions are based on the United Nation's classification, at: <http://unstats.un.org/unsd/methods/m49/m49regin.htm>. The data in the bottom panel are from <http://www.uscourts.gov/Statistics/ FederalCourtManagementStatistics/FederalCourtManagementStatistics_Archive.aspx>.

The difficulties in conveying results arise, we suspect, because there's almost nothing in the way of guidance for legal researchers. Books and articles geared toward supplying counsel on these matters are quite rare;[9] and the various legal style guides are silent on the communication of empirical evidence. *The Bluebook*,[10] which is the primary guide for legal citation in the United States, speaks only to the question of how to cite others' figures and tables, not to matters of original presentation. The same holds for the *Canadian Guide to Uniform Legal Citation*,[11] the *Oxford Standard for Citation of Legal Authorities*,[12] and the others we consulted. Law journals, whether or not peer reviewed, provide only skeletal instructions to authors on how to convey numerical data (if they provide them at all).[13]

Happily, though, the same is not true in other disciplines. There is now a burgeoning literature in the statistical and social sciences focused on the presentation of data. Some of it amounts to little more than "armchair" guidelines for graphic design.[14] Other studies, though, make use of observational and experimental evidence to learn about how accurately and quickly people process information presented in prose versus tables versus graphs.[15] To provide but one quick example, this literature points to the poor performance of "pop charts," especially pie charts.[16] No less than William S. Cleveland, a towering figure in the field of data visualization, has demonstrated that pie charts so often mask important patterns and other properties in the data that researchers should outright reject them.[17] Based on his research on

---

[9] Exceptions include our two articles (Epstein et al., 2006, 2007) and a chapter in Lawless et al. (2010), which draws in part on our work.

[10] <https://www.legalbluebook.com/default.aspx>.

[11] <http://lawjournal.mcgill.ca/citeguide.php>.

[12] <http://www.law.ox.ac.uk/publications/oscola.php>.

[13] At the very least, they pale in comparison with, say, the science journal *Nature* (guidelines for authors available at: <http://www.nature.com/nature/authors/gta/index.html>) or even *Political Analysis*, the journal of the Political Methodology Section of the American Political Science Association, which also has detailed instructions for the preparation of tables (though not graphs), at: <http://www.oxfordjournals.org/polana/for_authors/general.html>.

[14] Fischer (2000, 151) uses the term "armchair" to describe principles for graphic design that are based on intuition rather than empirical evidence.

[15] There are many articles and books devoted to this topic. A few prominent (or interesting) examples include: Brewer et al. (2012); Cleveland (1994, 1993); Cleveland and McGill (1984); Spence and Lewandowsky (1991); Fischer (2000); Cumming and Finch (2005); Gelman (2011); Kosslyn (1994); Lewandowsky and Spence (1989); Wickham (2009).

[16] Cleveland (1994, 262–3) uses the term "pop chart" to refer to three types of graphs (pie, divided bar, and area charts) that often appear in media and business publications.

[17] Cleveland (1994, 263). Many others agree (see, e.g., Tufte, 1983; Bertin, 1981).

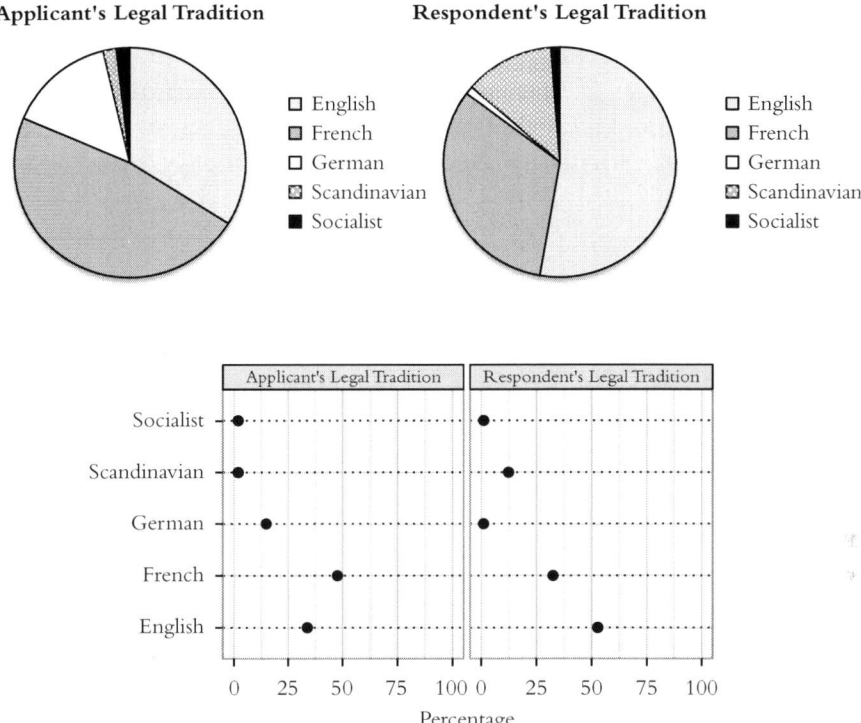

Figure IV.2 The pie charts on the top depict the type of legal tradition in applicant and respondent countries in cases before the International Court of Justice. We present the same data on the bottom with dot plots. The dot plots are superior because they facilitate lookup of the data patterns; they also ease comparisons within and between the juxtaposed panels by providing a common baseline.[18]

pattern perception, Cleveland suggests supplanting pie charts with dot plots[19]—a category of charts underdeployed in empirical legal research but prominent in many other disciplines.[20]

We wholeheartedly endorse Cleveland's recommendation, and Figure IV.2 shows why. There we provide two visual depictions of the same data, comparing pie charts (with five slices in the form of percentages) and a dot plot (with each dot representing a percentage).

The pie charts are supposed to depict the legal tradition in applicant and respondent countries involved in cases before the International

---

[18] Source: ICJ data.
[19] Cleveland and McGill (1984).
[20] For example, a LexisNexis search of all published law review articles, from 2000–2012, on "dotplot" and "dot plot" brought up eight articles, all but two of which are ours or our students'!

Court of Justice,[21] but two general problems are immediately apparent.[22] First, decoding data patterns (the so-called "lookup") becomes an unnecessarily demanding cognitive task because it requires visually estimating an angle rather than estimating a length. Second, it is hard to spot differences in the data values because the slices of the pie do not share a common baseline. Looking at the pie in the right panel of Figure IV.2, can you detect whether "Scandinavian" or "Socialist" are the bigger slices? How about the difference between "Scandinavian" and "Socialist" in the left panel? Now try comparing slices across the two panels. Owing to the lack of a common baseline, this too is no easy task. The dot plots, in contrast, have the advantage of a common baseline, which facilitates comparisons among the slices.[23]

This is just one example of the many lessons on presenting *data* that we've learned from other fields; others pertain to communicating the *results* of statistical analyses, as we shall see. Either way, without developments outside of law we would be unable to offer much in the way of guidance to researchers in law.[24] With them, we can convey strategies that, we believe, have the potential to transform empirical legal research if only by making it more accessible to all members of the law community, not to mention policy makers and citizens.

We begin in Chapter 10 with some general principles for communicating and graphing data. Chapter 11 moves to more specific strategies for effectively and accessibly presenting data and statistical results. This is fun stuff. You'll see.

---

[21] This is the dataset that Posner and de Figueiredo (2005) used in their study.

[22] We adapt this discussion from Cleveland (1994, 262) and Cleveland and McGill (1984, 545).

[23] There are several other problems with the pie charts in Figure IV.2; for example, the shading patterns are difficult to discern.

[24] Another development worth mentioning is the emergence of sophisticated statistical software. Just a decade or so ago, scholars hoping to present their results or even raw data faced a problem of no small proportion: a dearth of software able to meet their needs. The ever-popular Microsoft Excel was no more up to the task then than it is now, but neither were existing statistical packages. No longer. These days, scholars can deploy R or Stata—along with modules that they can import, including Clarify (<http://gking.harvard.edu/clarify/docs/clarify.html>) and SPost (<http://www.indiana.edu/~jslsoc/spost.htm>) for Stata and ggplot2 (Wickham, 2009) for R—to create sophisticated, yet accessible, data presentations. R and Stata enable users to customize all the fine features of a particular figure and to create (and, more importantly, re-create) figures rapidly using scripts. (The advent of fast computers on the desktop is another technological development that makes possible some of the strategies we describe in the chapters to come. Many of these methods require computationally intensive simulations that would have been prohibitively expensive in the 1990s.)

10

General Principles for Communicating and Visualizing Data and Results

In the introduction to this part, we mentioned ominous-looking tables full of regression coefficients that the vast majority of the legal community would not be able to interpret. Tables 9.1 and 9.2 provide examples of the problem (as does Table 11.7 in the next chapter). More times than we can possibly count, scholars present their results in this fashion and just as many times they lose their audience.

It's not only that these tables are forbidding and off-putting to most readers; they communicate information of little value either to the reader or author. We know that you researchers (and perhaps some of your readers) understand the *s in the tables and so will be able to spot whether the results are "statistically significant." What we rarely learn from tabular displays, however, is "how important" the results are. The logistic regression displayed in Table 9.2 tells us that judges serving on the International Court of Justice (ICJ) from countries with lower GDPs are significantly more likely to side with the applicant country (see the variable Judge GDP). But how much more likely? 0.2 times? 2 times? Or perhaps even 4 times? Certainly, as we intimated in Chapter 9, this is the quantity of interest that matters most to readers—and to us researchers too. But it is not one that we can readily discern from a tabular display of logit coefficients.[1]

Moreover, even if we could calculate a "best guess" about the likelihood of voting for or against a country based on Judge GDP, Table 9.2 communicates no useful information about the *error* surrounding that

---

[1] Some might say that the story would be different if they were ordinary least squares (OLS) coefficients. We disagree. Although OLS coefficients are easier to interpret for some people, the majority of the legal community doesn't fall into this category.

guess. Suppose we reported that the probability of a judge from a country with a very low GDP voting for the applicant is about .50, while it is only .30 for a judge from a country with a very high GDP. This would seem to be a sizable effect. But not necessarily. What if the 95% confidence interval surrounding the 0.30 was [.15, .45,], meaning that: "Our best guess about the probability of judge from a high GDP country siding with the applicant is .30, though it could be as low as .15 and as high as .45 (which is moving close to 0.50, our best guess for low GDP judges)." Such is the reality of the statistical world: we can never be certain about our best guesses (inferences) because they themselves are based on estimates. But we can report our level of uncertainty about those guesses. Most researchers understand this fact and supply the error surrounding their estimated coefficients—usually the standard error. As you can now appreciate, this is far less beneficial than conveying uncertainty about the *substantive effect* of the results.[2]

And the benefits are many. Mostly, it seems nearly incontrovertible that moving toward more appropriate and accessible presentations of data will heighten the impact of empirical legal scholarship on whatever the intended audience—academics, students, policy makers, lawyers, and judges—not to mention raise the level of intellectual discourse among scholars themselves.[3] When analysts write that "the coefficient on Judge GDP is statistically significant at the 0.05 level," they immediately turn off at least half of their readers. But if they were to translate their findings into a visual display, as we do in Figure 9.7 for the ICJ judges' votes, they would be able to supplant sterile statistical claims with the more intuitive:

Controlling for other factors, the likelihood of a judge from a country with an average per capita GDP[4] voting for the applicant is 51% (though it could be as low as 48% or as high as 55%).[5] That percentage decreases for judges from countries with a high GDP[6] to 39% (though it could be as low as 33% or as high as 45%).[7]

---

[2] As we do in Figure 9.7, which shows both the predicted probabilities and confidence intervals.

[3] This paragraph adopts and parallels sentiments expressed in King et al. (2000, 347–8).

[4] The median GDP in our sample is $3,500.

[5] The figures of 48% and 55% represent the 95% confidence interval.

[6] To calculate this, we use the figure of $24,700 (the 95th percentile in our sample).

[7] The non-linearity of the model causes the differential precision of these estimates. Worth noting too: for a model with multiple independent variables, the predictions would differ in magnitude if we were to hold the other covariates at different values.

Unlike the terms "coefficient" or "0.01 level," these sorts of statements are easy to understand even by the most statistically challenged among us.[8]

How can legal researchers develop such claims from their data and results? How might they go about visually depicting them? In the material to follow we adapt a growing literature in the social and statistical sciences to the unique needs of empirical legal researchers by delineating some general principles for (1) communicating the products of empirical legal research and (2) visualizing information. The next chapter offers more specific strategies.

10.1 General Principles for Communicating Data and Results

Emerging from the deep literature on presenting data and results are three general principles that all empirical legal research should strive to follow: (1) communicate *substance*, not statistics; (2) when communicating substantive results (that is, when performing inference) also communicate *uncertainty*; (3) regardless of whether you are communicating results or data, generally use *graphs*, not tables.

10.1.1 Communicate Substance, not Statistics

As we suggest above, in many, perhaps most data studies on law-related topics, the authors tend to emphasize statistics over substance. More often than not they claim that their result is "statistically significant at the .05 level," without ever communicating very much, if anything, about the effect of the result.[9] In other words, most authors focus on statistical significance rather than substantive significance.

Consider a study by Epstein and Landes examining the circumstances under which justices of the U.S. Supreme Court invalidate (strike down) a federal law.[10] Their chief hypothesis is this: all else equal, the justices will be more likely to strike down laws that don't comport with their ideological values—such that a liberal justice will be more

---

[8] It is important to note that confidence intervals for these two predictions could overlap (they do not here), even when there is a statistically significant difference between the predictions (see Austin and Hux, 2002).

[9] We base this claim on the mini-study reported in Epstein et al. (2006).

[10] Epstein and Landes (2012).

likely to strike down a law, say, discriminating against gays (i.e., a conservative law), and a conservative will be more likely to uphold it. To test it, Epstein and Landes estimated two logistic regression models: one for conservative laws and the other for liberal laws. The dependent variable in both is the justice's vote to uphold or invalidate the law.[11]

The primary independent variable of interest is Justice's Ideology. This variable ranges from -4.117 (the most liberal justice) to 3.835 (the most conservative justice). The expectation is that the coefficient on Justice's Ideology should be negative for conservative laws and positive for liberal laws. As for the "all else equal" part, the authors control for five factors that may lead justices to invalidate federal laws, including the Lower Court's Decision (more on this variable below). (N.B.: The researchers test their hypothesis against data drawn from the votes of 44 justices of the U.S. Supreme Court but this kind of model could be—and, in fact, has been—developed for many societies that endow their court(s) with the power to invalidate laws.[12])

The results support Epstein and Landes's expectations (standard errors are in parentheses):

- For conservative laws, the coefficient on Justice's Ideology = -0.524 (0.048)
- For liberal laws, the coefficient on Justice's Ideology = 0.409 (0.117)

The coefficients are signed in the hypothesized direction and are, Epstein and Landes tell us, "statistically significant" at $p \leq .01$.[13]

It certainly isn't wrong to note statistical significance. But neither should we be impressed with the emphasis on statistical significance inherent in statements such as this (or in tabular displays of coefficient with *s). Why? We see two sets of problems. First, no doubt some of the "statistically significant" estimates are inevitably substantively uninteresting. Take Lower Court's Decision, a control variable in Epstein and Landes's study. This variable encodes whether the court

---

[11] A vote to invalidate = 1; a vote to uphold = 0. In the next chapter, we describe their model in detail. See especially Table 11.7.

[12] Several empirical studies of courts outside the United States run along these lines. See, e.g., Carroll and Tiede (2011) (Chile), Franck (2009) (France), Garoupa et al. (2011) (Taiwan), Garoupa et al. (2013) (Spain), Weiden (2011) (Australia, Canada, and the United States).

[13] Epstein and Landes (2012, 567).

below the Supreme Court reached a liberal (= 1) or conservative (= 0) decision. The authors included it to account for the modern Supreme Court's inclination to reverse the decision of the court below; that is, even a very liberal justice tends to reverse a decision below that upholds a liberal law; and vice versa for a conservative justice. Their model shows that this hypothesis holds: a liberal (conservative) lower court decision increases the probability of a vote to invalidate a liberal (conservative) law. But the effect of Lower Court strikes us as pretty small. All other things being equal, the predicted probability of a justice voting to invalidate a liberal law when the decision below was liberal is .18;[14] it drops to .13 when the decision below was conservative.[15] A difference, yes, but one that probably isn't of much interest to Epstein and Landes's audience or, for that matter, the researchers themselves.

On the other hand, by focusing the readers' attention solely on matters of statistical significance, analysts can *understate* the importance of their results. This holds for Epstein and Landes's project,[16] and it's not alone. Take Roe's research, which developed the following theory: "Social democracies widen the natural gap between managers and . . . stockholders, and impede firms from developing the tools that would close that gap."[17] When the gap widens sufficiently, it renders "the large American-style public firm . . . unstable."[18]

According to Roe, an observable implication of this account is that the more to the left the politics of a nation, the less diffusion of ownership. To assess it, he estimated a linear regression model with the proportion of firms under diffuse ownership in the 16 richest nations as the dependent variable, and expert assessment of the nations' politics (from most left-wing to most right-wing) as the sole independent variable.

---

[14] The 95% confidence interval is [.12, .23].

[15] The 95% confidence interval is [.10, .17].

[16] For example, the coefficient on N of Cases Decided During Term is -0.006, which seems small. But its effect size is fairly large. This variable represents the number of cases the Court decided each term. The authors included it out of the belief that the more cases, the less likely the justices will be to take the dramatic step of striking down a law because they will be more pressed for time. All other things being equal, the predicted probability of a justice voting to invalidate a liberal law when the number of cases is very small (67 cases) is .24 (the 95% confidence interval is [.12, .36]); it drops to .14 when the caseload is very high (165) (the 95% confidence interval is [.10, .18]).

[17] Roe (2000, 561).

[18] Roe (2000, 543).

Table 10.1 Roe's regression of ownership on politics. * indicates $p \leq .01$. Standard errors in parentheses. The dependent variable is the proportion of firms under diffuse ownership in the 16 richest nations; the independent variable is expert assessment of the nations' politics (from most left-wing to most right-wing).[19]

	Model 1
Nation's Politics	0.329*
	(0.090)
Intercept	−0.571
	(0.289)
n	16
R^2	0.489
SEE	0.212

Roe communicates his results in two forms: Table 10.1, which we have replicated from his data, and the following statement: "the results are statistically significant."[20] This statement is true but readers should want to know "by how much," that is, what is the practical effect of politics on diffuse ownership? It turns out that the answer to this question enhances Roe's conclusion because the effect seems substantial indeed. As we move from the most liberal societies to those in the middle of the political spectrum, diffusion of ownership nearly triples, from 16%[21] to 47%.[22]

A second set of problems emerging when researchers focus on statistical significance to the neglect of effect size is that they do a disservice to their communities in both the short and long terms. In the short term, no reader can possibly make much sense of a long (or even short) list of coefficients. To provide but one example from the Epstein and Landes study,[23] all we can really say about the coefficient of .409 (on the Justice's Ideology variable for liberal laws) is that "the log odds ratio of a justice voting to invalidate a liberal law

---

[19] We produced the table from data housed in Roe (2000, 562).
[20] Roe (2000, 562).
[21] The 95% confidence interval is [-3.5, 36.0].
[22] The 95% confidence interval is [36.5, 57.2].
[23] Epstein and Landes (2012).

increases by 0.409"—a rather meaningless statement to readers *regardless of their statistical expertise*. The particular obstacle here is that the model is nonlinear, meaning that we need to know a good deal about the explanatory variables to decipher the magnitude of the coefficients. But even in the case of Roe's regression analysis, in which the coefficients are easier to interpret because the model is linear, why compel others to make the calculations, especially since many will not know how? More generally, an emphasis on coefficients and statistical significance fails to present results in a way that "requires little specialized knowledge to understand."[24] Instead of reaching the widest possible audience, researchers are limiting themselves to a very small segment of the community.

In the longer term, the emphasis on numbers and *s unaccompanied by any substantive message can work to perpetuate questionable interpretations of the results. Under present practice in empirical legal research, it is entirely conceivable—in the absence of any statements or displays about key quantities of interest—that ensuing studies will report that a variable such as Lower Court's Decision has a "statistically significant" effect on justices' votes despite its small substantive impact. Of course, we can hardly lay the blame with the consumers of data work; it is the original researchers' responsibility to provide estimates of the key quantities of interest. More importantly, they should want to communicate substantive effects because when they do, benefits accrue: it is those effects, perhaps in addition to (or even in lieu of) claims about statistical significance, that tend to get transported from study to study—thus generating more precise knowledge about the work's key findings.[25]

In short, researchers and their audience can reap substantial benefits if they move away from an emphasis on statistics and toward substance

---

[24] King et al. (2000, 347).

[25] For example, note the level of detail that Kang (2005, 1491–2) was able to offer when he described Gilliam and Iyengar (2000)—a study that communicated substance and not merely statistical significance:

[The researchers] created variations of a local newscast: a control version with no crime story, a crime story with no mugshot, a crime story with a Black-suspect mugshot, and a crime story with a White-suspect mugshot. The Black and White suspects were represented by the same morphed photograph, with the only difference being skin hue—thus controlling for facial expression and features. The suspect appeared for only five seconds in a ten-minute newscast; nonetheless, the suspect's race produced statistically significant differences in a criminal law survey completed after the viewing. Having seen the Black suspect, White participants showed 6% more support for punitive remedies than did the control group, which saw no crime story. When participants were instead exposed to the White suspect, their support for punitive remedies increased by only 1%, which was not statistically significant.

(and readers ought to demand that they do). At least conceptually, this is not difficult to do. It simply requires analysts to identify the quantity (or more likely *quantities*) most relevant to their project. Return to the example of Epstein and Landes's judicial invalidation study. They were most concerned with the extent to which the justices struck down laws that were inconsistent with their ideology and upheld laws that were—meaning that the Justice's Ideology variable was of the greatest interest to them.

Once researchers identify the key variable(s) it is just a matter of computation to estimate a quantity of interest, as well as an assessment of uncertainty about the estimate. In contemplating the 0.409 coefficient on Justice's Ideology in the liberal law model, why follow the crowd and write, "it is statistically significant at the .01 level" when it is nearly as easy to answer "how much effect does it exert?"[26] Not only do various statistical software packages enable researchers to address this question by estimating the quantity of interest; they are also capable of generating assessments of error (such as confidence intervals) through simulations (repeated sampling of the model parameters from their sampling distribution).[27]

In the next section we have more to say about the importance of conveying error (uncertainty). For now it is worth noting that while contemporary software is geared toward estimating quantities of interest and error for the results of regression and other more complicated models, the same general principle of "Communicate Substance, Not Statistics" applies with equal force to simpler statistics. Take the χ^2 statistic, which we covered in Chapter 7. Just as too many authors merely note whether a regression coefficient is "statistically significant" without providing a substantive interpretation, those reporting χ^2s sometimes do likewise. There are more informative ways to proceed.

Look at the top panel of Table 10.2, which shows the votes of judges in sex-discrimination cases by the judge's gender. Imagine if we explained the results as follows:

There is a significant difference in the win rate for the party claiming discrimination (the plaintiff) depending on the gender of the judge, which

---

[26] As it turns out, the effect of Justice's Ideology is quite dramatic. See Figure 11.9 in the next chapter.

[27] King et al. (2000, 347) describes the the Monte Carlo algorithm used for these simulations; you can implement it via the a plug-in for Stata, called Clarify, or the Zelig package in R. See also Chapter 11.

means that we can reject the null hypothesis that there is an equal chance of success regardless of whether the judge is a male or female. The judge's gender, therefore, is a statistically significant predictor of whether the plaintiff will prevail.

To us this statement is as uninformative as "the coefficient on Judge's Ideology is statistically significant at the .01 level." Far better and of more use to readers is the information conveyed in the bottom panel of Table 10.2. There we show the observed *and* expected counts—the counts we would expect in each cell if no difference existed between

Table 10.2 Votes in sex discrimination cases, by the judge's gender. The top panel shows the observed frequencies, with column percentages in parentheses; the bottom panel shows the observed frequencies, with expected frequencies in parentheses. $\chi^2_{(1)} = 11.09$, $p < .05$.[28]

	Male Judge	Female Judge	Total
Party Claiming Discrimination Wins	564 (36.2%)	140 (46.4%)	704
Party Claiming Discrimination Loses	994 (63.8%)	162 (53.6%)	1156
Total	1,558	302	1,860

	Male Judge	Female Judge	Total
Party Claiming Discrimination Wins	564 (590)	140 (114)	704
Party Claiming Discrimination Loses	994 (968)	162 (188)	1156
Total	1,558	302	1,860

[28] Data collected by the authors and available on the book's website.

male and female judges.[29] Now the contrast in the win rate just leaps out: the party alleging discrimination won (140-114 =) 26 more cases before female judges than we would have anticipated if no association existed between the judge's gender and vote. (And won 26 fewer cases before male judges.)

10.1.2 When Performing Inference, Convey Uncertainty

At the very outset of this book we stressed the importance of uncertainty. Remember the example in Chapter 1 of a poll asking people living in one of the 27 EU member countries whether they "feel safe walking alone at night in the city or area that [they] live." When we read the results of this or any other survey, we have come to expect pollsters to convey the level of uncertainty about their sample statistics. If they didn't, we would be unable to judge their results. Imagine a survey reporting that 55% of the respondents felt safe with a 95% confidence interval of ±10!—meaning it is possible that a majority *do not* feel safe.

We should expect researchers to follow suit. As we have stressed throughout, when researchers perform statistical inference—as Epstein and Landes,[30] Roe,[31] and we did in our gender example—they too have an obligation to convey their level of uncertainty. Because statistics are only estimates developed from a sample of the world (and not from the entire world) we can never be 100% certain that we've got it right.

This much you know by now, as do most empirical researchers. They take seriously the requirement to report their uncertainty. The problem is that they tend to rely on p-values and standard errors to do the work, which is unfortunate since neither conveys information of much value to many readers. All the ".090" on the estimate of .329 in Table 10.1 supplies is an estimate of the standard deviation of the estimated slope, which, standing alone, is of interest to almost no one, readers and scientists alike.[32]

That's why it's no surprise that reporting the far-more-meaningful 95% (or even 99%) confidence interval rather than (or in addition to)

---

[29] Recall from Chapter 7 that the first step in computing the χ^2 statistic is to calculate the expected count within each cell by multiplying the row marginal by the column marginal and dividing by the sample size.

[30] Epstein and Landes (2012).

[31] Roe (2000).

[32] Rather, its value lies in its role in computing 95% confidence intervals.

p-values and standard errors has become *de rigueur* in other disciplines,[33] and we recommend the same for law. In the case of Roe's project, we suggest supplanting the standard error of .090 with the 95% confidence interval [.136 (lower bound) and .522 (upper bound)].

This interval, we believe, comes far closer than the standard error to conveying what Roe wants: that his best guess about the coefficient is .328 but he is "95 percent certain" that it is in the range of .136 to .522. Because zero is not in this confidence interval, he and we can safely reject the null hypothesis of no relationship between a society's politics and ownership (without ever providing a p-value!). Likewise in Epstein and Landes' study, rather than reporting the standard error of .117 on the Justice's Ideology (liberal law), we suggest denoting the confidence interval around the coefficient of .409 [.179, .638]. (From hereinafter we use this notation [,] to indicate the lower and upper bounds of the 95% confidence interval around the estimate of the quantity of interest.)

But even then researchers would not be making the most of their analyses. This is especially true for Epstein and Landes who estimated their model using logistic regression. If they write that they are "95 percent certain" that the true logit coefficient lies between .179 and .638, they fail to speak clearly and accessibly to their audience. We recommend combining the lesson here of relating uncertainty with the general principle of conveying substantive information. For Epstein and Landes, this translates into the following claim: all else equal, the predicted probability of a very liberal justice voting to invalidate a liberal law is a very low .04 [.00, .08]; it is a much higher .51 [.33, .69] for a very conservative justice.[34] For Roe it is this: as we move from societies in the middle of the political spectrum to those on the far right, diffusion of ownership increases by nearly 60%, from 47% [36.5, 57.2] to 75% [56.7, 92.4].

---

[33] See, e.g., the authors' guidelines for the *New England Journal of Medicine*, at <http://authors.nejm.org/Misc/NewMs.asp> ("Measures of uncertainty, such as confidence intervals, should be used consistently, including in figures that present aggregated results"). *Developmental Psychology* expresses no preference for confidence intervals over standard errors ("For all study results, measures of both practical and statistical significance should be reported. The latter can involve either a standard error or an appropriate confidence interval") but it does emphasize "practical significance" or "effects" (which "can be reported using an effect size, a standardized regression coefficient, a factor loading, or an odds ratio"). Guidelines available at: <http://www.apa.org/journals/dev/submission.html>. See also the APA Publication Manual, which suggests that authors include estimates of the "effect size."

[34] See also note 26.

In both instances, readers need no specialized knowledge to under-stand either the results of the study or the researchers' assessment of their uncertainty about those results. And with this understanding they are far better positioned to evaluate the study's findings.

By offering this advice, we do not mean to suggest that all data projects must include assessments of uncertainty. Indeed, the principle is "When *Performing Inference*, Convey Uncertainty," not "When Describing Data, Convey Uncertainty." In other words, when researchers are merely displaying, describing, or summarizing their data—and not using the data they have collected to make inferences about the population that generated the data—supplying standard errors or confidence intervals is unnecessary.[35] This advice has more bearing on the creation of graphical displays, which we do not want to clutter with, say, confidence intervals, and so we consider it in some detail in the next chapter. Suffice it to note here that when we describe a basic feature of a variable in the dataset on gender and judging—that plaintiffs won 38% of the 1,806 suits and lost 62%—we see no purpose to presenting the associated uncertainty about those figures. If, on the other hand, we sought to generalize from those figures of 38% and 62% to cases we did not collect (that is, to use the sample to make an inference), then some measure of error is in order.

10.1.3 Graph Data and Results

In Chapters 2 and 3, we analyzed Elkins et al.'s research on why some constitutions endure longer than others.[36] In their study, they raise the possibility of spread or "diffusion" of practices. Because constitutions are prominent and public documents, "it seems likely that the adoption of new constitutions in other countries will increase the probability of a new constitution in a neighboring country."[37] Other studies too have noted the role of geographic diffusion, not only in the timing of constitution-making but also in the content of constitutions, legal frameworks, and doctrine.[38] Table 10.3 supplies a simple approach to considering diffusion (way too simple, we think, but useful for

---

[35] We take our cues here from Cleveland (1994, 213–15), though some scholars seem to disagree. See, e.g., Gelman et al. (2002).

[36] Elkins et al. (2009).

[37] Elkins et al. (2009, 112).

[38] See, e.g., Caldeira (1985); Glick (1992); Armour et al. (2009); Ginsburg et al. (2008). For a review of some of the literature, see Twining (2005).

pedagogical purposes). There we display each country in Europe (included in the Elkins et al.'s dataset), its geographical region,[39] and the number of words in its most recent constitution. Under a diffusion account, we might expect countries within a particular region to write constitutions of similar lengths.

To be sure, this table communicates interesting information. Were you to look long enough, you might notice that Austria has the longest constitution and Monaco the shortest. You might also spot some missing countries, most notably the United Kingdom.[40] Because it doesn't have a codified constitution, Elkins et al. excluded it from their dataset.[41]

But is Table 10.3—or tables more generally—the best way to convey the information? If our purpose is to provide readers with the *exact* figures, then the answer is yes: tables always trump graphs, as a comparison of Figure 10.1 and Table 10.3 reveals. From the table we can see that Germany's constitution contains 24,951 words; we cannot extract this information with the same degree of exactitude from the graph.

More often than not, though, the precision that only tables can relay is beside the point. Typically we want to communicate to our audience (and to ourselves) not exact values but comparisons, patterns, or trends. This is true for our mini-analysis of diffusion in constitutions. We are not especially interested in the precise ranking of the length of, say, Germany's or Andorra's constitutions; rather we hope to convey a sense of the relative lengths of constitutions so that we can eventually draw comparisons among those in different regions. Figure 10.1 better serves this purpose than Table 10.3.

More to the point, Figure 10.1 allows us to detect some potentially important patterns in the data that would be difficult, if not impossible, to spot from the tabular display. For example, it appears that the length of constitutions in Eastern Europe is far more uniform than those in Western Europe. Even if we visually eliminate Monaco and Austria (the countries with the longest and shortest constitutions in the dataset) the spread still seems greater for Western Europe.[42] The suggestion

---

[39] According to the United Nations' classification, at: <http://unstats.un.org/unsd/methods/m49/m49regin.htm>.

[40] Another is San Marino, where the constitution consists largely of statutes.

[41] Elkins et al. (2009, 49).

[42] Simple statistics confirm the visual inspection. To provide one, the standard deviation is small for Eastern Europe (3,111) relative to Western Europe (11,789). If we eliminate Monaco

Table 10.3 Length (in words) of present-day constitutions in 41 European countries, by European region. Figure 10.1 graphs the same data using dot plots.[43]

Eastern Europe		Northern Europe	
Country	Length of Constitution	Country	Length of Constitution
Belarus	13,288	Denmark	6,221
Bulgaria	10,955	Estonia	11,344
Czech Republic	14,580	Finland	12,640
Hungary	12,302	Iceland	4,089
Moldova, Republic of	12,818	Ireland	15,655
Poland	19,602	Latvia	4,977
Romania	14,663	Lithuania	12,028
Russian Federation	12,908	Norway	7,424
Slovakia	18,402	Sweden	13,635
Ukraine	19,299		

Southern Europe		Western Europe	
Country	Length of Constitution	Country	Length of Constitution
Albania	13,747	Austria	41,366
Andorra	8,740	Belgium	16,119
Bosnia and Herzegovina	5,230	France	9,452
Croatia	10,898	Germany	24,951
Greece	27,177	Liechtenstein	9,513
Italy	11,708	Luxembourg	5,601
Macedonia	9,231	Monaco	3,814
Malta	31,820	Netherlands	8,678
Montenegro	7,074	Switzerland	16,484
Portugal	35,181		
Serbia	19,891		
Slovenia	11,410		
Spain	17,608		

and Austria, the standard deviation decreases to 6,619, which is still more than twice as large as Eastern Europe's.

[43] European regions based on the UN's classification (<http://unstats.un.org/unsd/methods/m49/m49regin.htm>); number of words in constitutions is from the Comparative Constitutions Project Dataset.

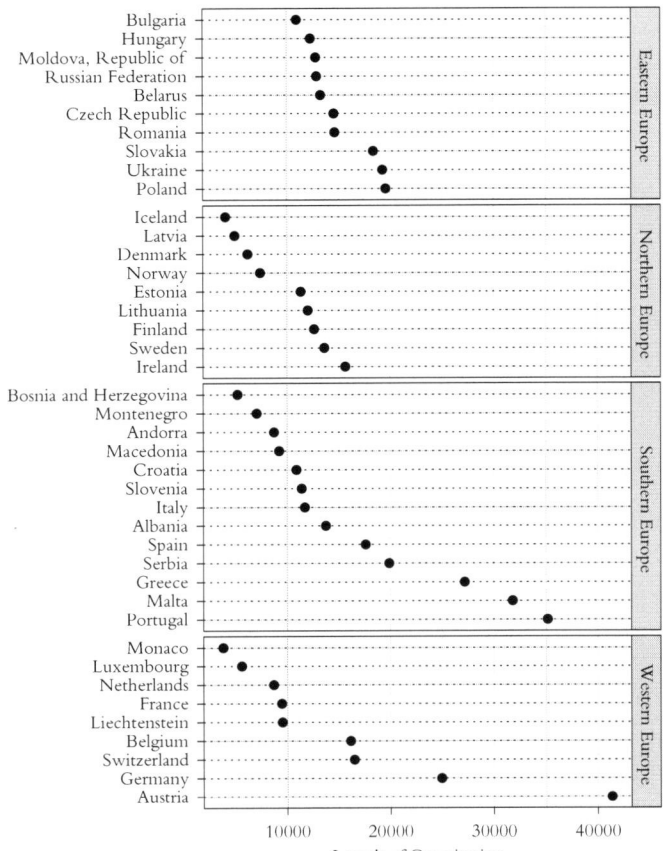

Figure 10.1 Dot plots of the length (in words) of present-day constitutions in 41 European countries, by European region. If the goal is to provide readers with exact figures, Table 10.3 is the better display. If the goal is to convey patterns or trends, as it usually is, we prefer this figure to Table 10.3.[44]

here is that diffusion appears to exist in some regions but not others. Why? This becomes an interesting question—perhaps the region is less important than the year of constitution-making—but one that did not emerge from the tabular display.[45]

[44] European regions based on UN classifications (<http://unstats.un.org/unsd/methods/m49/m49regin.htm>); number of words in constitution from the Comparative Constitutions Project Dataset.

[45] Another way to present geographic data is to shade states according to, here, the number of words. Such plots provide information about geographic contiguity, but they can obscure

More generally, if the point is to draw attention to trends or to make comparisons, as it almost always is, researchers should use graphs. This advice reflects not only our own aesthetic preference but also a growing consensus among scholars and journals in the statistical and social sciences.[46] Unless the author has a very compelling reason to provide precise information to readers, "well designed graphs are superior to tables."[47]

This recommendation applies with equal force to the presentation of *results* (see, for example, Figure 9.7 and Figure 11.8 in the next chapter) and *data* (or summaries of data) (for example, Figure 10.1).[48] It also applies to small amounts of data.[49] Prove it to yourself by comparing the left and right panels of Figure 10.2, both of which depict the length of constitutions in Southern European countries. In the left panel we reproduce the precise figures; in the right, we graphically depict the percentages (both ordered from least to most words). Surely if we stared at the numbers long enough, we could observe the patterns that emerge from the graph—for example, the closeness of Bosnia and Herzegovina, Montenegro, Andorra, and Macedonia on the short end and Malta and Portugal on the long end, not to mention the gap between Albania and Spain or the large difference between the shortest and longest constitutions. But it requires far more (unnecessary) cognitive work.

comparisons between and among states because they require readers to disentangle color gradients.

[46] See, e.g., Jacoby (1997); Gelman et al. (2002). See also *Science*, which co-sponsored a "Science and Engineering Visualization Challenge" to encourage researchers to rethink their data presentations. In its call for entries, the editors wrote "Data may be the gold standard of science, but they don't exactly glitter. A neat table of values cannot convey the significance, context, or excitement of research results to anyone besides other scientists in the same subfield. No one else quite gets the picture—including the larger community that supports the global research enterprise."

[47] Gelman et al. (2002, 121).

[48] The only meaningful distinction centers on the need to convey uncertainty. In keeping with our advice, figures depicting results should also display confidence intervals. When the goal is simply to show the data, "then show the data," without conveying uncertainty. Cleveland (1994, 215).

[49] Despite Tufte's (2001, 56) intuition that "Tables usually outperform graphics in reporting on small data sets of 20 numbers or less" and "the special power of graphics comes in the display of large data sets," some studies of perception have shown this to be questionable at best (see, e.g., Spence and Lewandowsky, 1991; Gelman et al., 2002; Gillan et al., 1998).

Country	Length of Constitution
Bosnia and Herzegovina	5,230
Montenegro	7,074
Andorra	8,740
Macedonia	9,231
Croatia	10,898
Slovenia	11,410
Italy	11,708
Albania	13,747
Spain	17,608
Serbia	19,891
Greece	27,177
Malta	31,820
Portugal	35,181

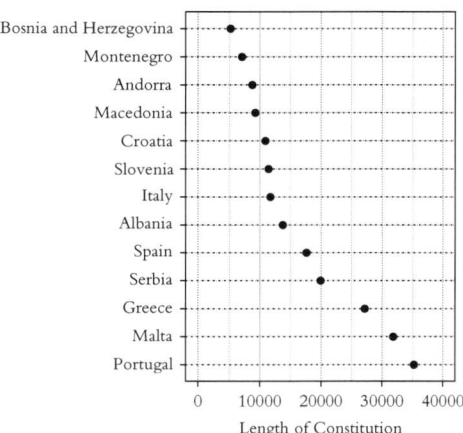

Figure 10.2 Length (in words) of present-day constitutions in countries in Southern Europe. Although it is possible from the table to observe the patterns that jump out in the graph—for example, the large difference between the shortest and longest constitutions—it requires far more (unnecessary) cognitive work.[50]

10.2 General Principles for Visualizing Data and Results

With these general principles in mind, we can begin the process of putting them into practice. In the next chapter, we outline specific strategies for presenting data and results—most of which reflect our view that tables are inferior to graphs. Here we start with three basic rules that apply to *all* graphs regardless of whether the task is to present data or results: (1) Aim for clarity *and* impact, (2) iterate, and (3) write detailed captions. These are critical to the enterprise of graphing data and results if only because "visualization is surprisingly difficult. Even the most simple matters can easily go wrong."[51] Following these three suggestions will, we believe, increase the odds of matters both simple and complex going right.

And going right for *both the audience and the researcher*. In other words, in the sections to follow we do not differentiate between graphs for

---

[50] European regions based on UN classifications (<http://unstats.un.org/unsd/methods/m49/m49regin.htm>); number of words in constitution from the Comparative Constitutions Project Dataset.

[51] Cleveland (1994, 9).

purposes of "prospecting" (that is, as part of the process of analyzing data) and "transferring" (that is, for communicating data and results). Many scholars do, reflecting their belief that "different kinds of displays are needed" depending on whether the researcher is prospecting or transferring.[52]

We take the point: just as the depiction of data and the depiction of results are distinct tasks, so too are the enterprises of analyzing a data set and presenting it. By way of example, reconsider "Anscombe's Quartet" from Chapter 9. Recall that Anscombe's point was to underscore the importance of graphing data before analyzing it. By creating the plots displayed in Figure 9.2, Anscombe was able to check the assumptions of his linear regression model, and found them wanting for three of the four datasets. At the same time, though, his demonstration illustrates a point made by proponents of the "prospecting" versus "transferring" school: No doubt researchers in Anscombe's position would not "transfer" (read: present) all the plots they made during the data-analytic phase of their work. Many, if not most, would never see life beyond their designers' computer screens.

But to us this is the *only* major distinction between graphs designed for exploratory purposes and for presentation. We agree with Cleveland, among others, who suggests that while researchers may create more pictures when they are prospecting, the same general principles of graphic design apply regardless of the researcher's purpose.[53] And so it is to those principles for careful construction and impact that we now turn.

10.2.1 *Aim for Clarity and Impact*

In 1983 the graphic designer Tufte issued his now (in)famous edict: when creating visual displays, "maximize the data-ink ratio," where "data ink" is "the non-erasable core of a graphic, the non-redundant ink ..."[54] With these words Tufte was pushing researchers to strive for clarity in their graphs—no doubt an important goal. When we construct figures, we *encode* information. What we ask of our readers is

---

[52] Wainer (1990, 345). See also Jacoby (1997, 2).

[53] Cleveland (1994). Or, as Jacoby (1997, 2) puts it, "It is my experience that carefully constructed analytic graphs also are quite effective for presentational purposes."

[54] Tufte (1983, 93).

to *visually decode* that information; if they can't do it because our display lacks clarity, our graph fails, pure and simple.[55]

It turns out, though, that following Tufte's advice to the letter can have precisely the opposite effect: inelegant, even silly, looking graphs that violate the principle of clarity. Perhaps the most important contemporary figure in scientific graphing, Tukey,[56] neatly made this point by comparing his now-famous box plot with Tufte's recommended revision (see Figure 10.3).[57] It is no wonder that to our knowledge, no researcher has adopted the Tufte revision: by maximizing the data-ink ratio—here by de-emphasizing the "central clumping" of a distribution that the box is designed to highlight—it minimizes clarity.[58] (By the way, box plots are useful and often-used graphs, and we consider them in Chapter 11.)

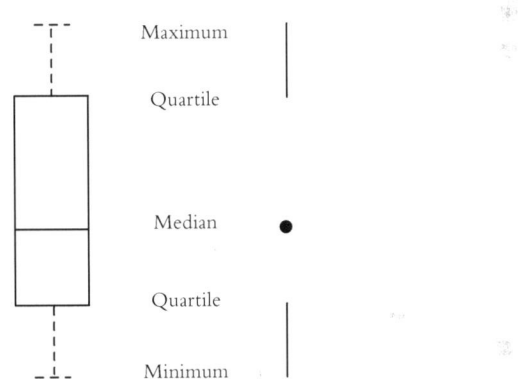

Figure 10.3 This figure shows two versions of a box plot, which Tukey created to summarize visually the distribution of a single variable. The left plot depicts Tukey's classic version; the right plot (a single line with a dot in the middle) shows Tufte's revision, which he designed to maximize "data-ink." By eliminating the box, the Tufte plot may not sufficiently emphasize the middle half of a given distribution. It also lacks the visual impact of Tukey's original design. For more on box plots, see Chapter 11.[59]

[55] We paraphrase here from Cleveland (1994, 94).

[56] See, e.g., Tukey (1977), though he may be best known for inventing the word "software."

[57] Tukey (1977, 48).

[58] For more on this point, see Tukey (1990, 329).

[59] Tukey's original box plot appears in Tukey (1977, 48). Tufte's redesign is in Tufte (2001, 125). The caption draws on Tukey's critique of Tufte. See Tukey (1990, 328–9).

The Tufte version also strips the box plot of its *impact*. This is hardly a trivial matter if we hope to grab the attention of our readers.[60] As Tukey famously put it, "The greatest possibilities of visual display lie in the vividness and inescapability of the intended message."[61]

Certainly, we do not want to encourage researchers to create the "multi-colored, three-dimensional pie charts" that fill the pages of way too many newspapers, websites, and even research reports,[62] but neither do we want them to sacrifice impact. Had William Playfair,[63] Charles Joseph Minard,[64] and E. J. Marey[65]—three of the most eminent developers of scientific graphs—failed to focus on impact, there would be little to admire.[66]

So how can researchers aim for clarity *and* impact? First, and foremost, they must eliminate what Tukey deems "busyness," what Tufte labeled "chart junk," or what Cleveland calls "visual clutter"—in other words, irrelevant or distracting elements that stand in the way of decoding. Second, they should not underestimate their readers by dumbing down graphs and thus potentially muting the impact of their displays.

Eliminate Distracting Elements.   If there is one principle of visualization on which graphic designers, statisticians, and social scientists agree, it is that researchers should eliminate irrelevant, distracting elements from their displays. And there is plenty to eliminate in many empirical legal studies. We make this point in Figures 10.4 and 10.5, which depict some of the more common problems (see also the opener to this part of the book), as well as our correctives for removing clutter and, hopefully, for making the data stand out.

Beginning with Figure 10.4, the goal is to show the mean life expectancy of males and females in five regions. Note that we transform the graph from three to two dimensions. The added dimensionality is

---

[60] Paraphrased from Tukey (1990, 328).

[61] Tukey (1990, 328).

[62] We adopt this sentiment from Wainer (1990, 341).

[63] 1759–1823.

[64] 1781–1870.

[65] 1830–1904.

[66] Visit our website and compare one of Playfair's most famous graphs (on the labor required to buy wheat in England, 1565–1820) and Friendly and Wainer's "less is more" redesign (Friendly and Wainer, 2004). No one could deny that Playfair's graph is flawed in any number of ways (see Friendly and Wainer, 2004), nor could we say that Friendly and Wainer's fails to maximize the data-ink ratio. But the result, though cleaner, seems to us far less memorable. Do you agree?

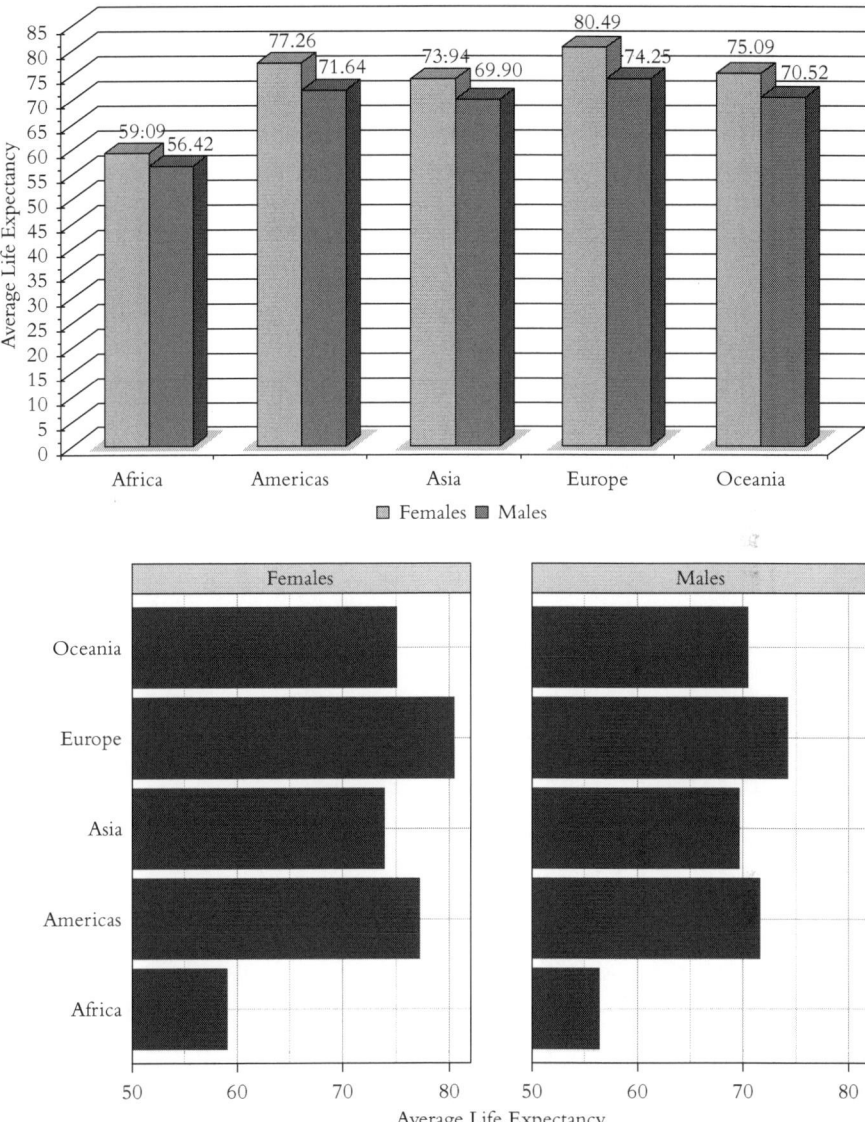

Figure 10.4 Both panels depict the mean life expectancy at birth (in years) in five regions, by gender. The bottom panel reflects our attempt to reduce clutter. Specifically, we eliminated (1) the depth cue, (2) the internal data labels, (3) tick marks on the horizontal axis, and (4) the legend. We also reduced the number of tick marks on the vertical axis and supplanted the cross hatching with a solid color. The result is a graph far easier to decode.[67]

[67] The data are from the World Bank, at: <http://data.worldbank.org/indicator/SP.DYN.LE00.FE.IN?display=default> and <http://data.worldbank.org/indicator/SP.DYN.LE00.MA.IN?display=default>. Regions are based on the UN's classification, at: http://unstats.un.org/unsd/methods/m49/m49regin.htm>.

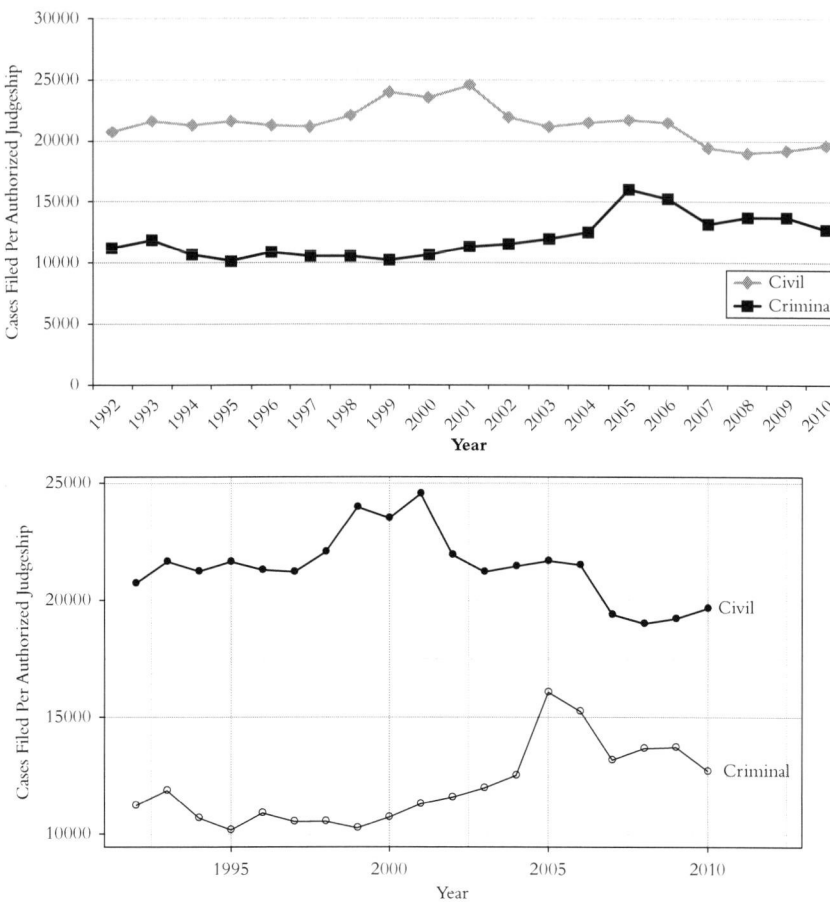

Figure 10.5 Both panels depict the number of criminal and civil cases filed per authorized judgeship in the U.S. Courts of Appeals, 1992–2010. The bottom panel reflects our attempt to improve visualization of the data. We eliminated the legend (replacing it with internal data labels) and reduced the number of tick marks and associated labels. Finally, we supplanted the non-circular sub-elements with circular connectors, though if the author's purpose is merely to show trends in new filings, the circles may be unnecessary.[68]

not only irrelevant; research has found that it can actually interfere with graph comprehension.[69] That's why most scientists, and even

[68] The data are from <http://www.uscourts.gov/Statistics/FederalCourtManagement Statistics/FederalCourtManagementStatistics_Archive.aspx>.

[69] Fischer (2000, 161).

graphic designers working for popular publications, are no longer adding superfluous dimensions, and empirical legal researchers should follow suit.

Removing the depth cue is not the only change we made to the original figure. We further reduced clutter by, first, eliminating the internal data labels (e.g., 59.09, 56.42). It seems to us that the goal is to focus readers on the *comparison* between male and female life expectancy, not on *precise values*, and so those values are unnecessary. If we are wrong, then a table would be better. Second, we altered the tick marks on both axes, eliminating those on the horizontal (verbal descriptors need not be "ticked") and reducing the number on the vertical axis, from 15 to four. According to visualization studies, three to ten marks are sufficient.[70] Third, and again in line with work on graphic perception and good design practice, we filled the bars with a solid dark color rather than cross hatches, slanted lines, or other "op-art" marks that can appear to vibrate.[71] Finally, we eliminated the legend. Splitting the original graph into two panels made it unnecessary. Which is a good thing. Because of the tendency to look back and forth between the key and the data, legends can interfere with decoding.

Note that for the graph in Figure 10.4 we moved the legend to the headings for each bar. An alternative is to describe the data keys in the caption. This is an acceptable, even standard, practice (more on captions below). Nonetheless, if it is possible to insert labels into the interior of the graph without interfering with visual assembly of the plotting symbols or lines, we recommend so doing,[72] and we've taken this step in Figure 10.5. Note that the labels neither cause too much clutter nor obscure the data. But they do improve the ability to compare criminal and civil cases because the reader need not consult a key.

Also observe that in altering the top panel of Figure 10.5 we changed the symbols connecting the lines, from non–circular to circular elements. Beware: many graphing packages offer a dazzling array of plotting symbols (squares, triangles, diamonds, and so on) but researchers should avoid almost all of them. Experimental studies

---

[70] See, e.g., Cleveland (1994, 39).

[71] See, e.g., Tufte (2001, 107, 112). He explains, "Contemporary optical art relies on moiré effects, in which the design interacts with the physiological tremor of the eye to produce the distracting appearance of vibration and movement." Tufte goes on to argue that moiré vibration, caused by cross hatching and other non-solid fill types, "has no place in data graphical design."

[72] For more on this point, see Cleveland (1994, 44–5).

show that "unless there is a serious need for more distinctions,"[73] analysts should stick to circular forms. Typically, they can gain sufficient variation in the size and fill of circles to display the data prominently. (If not, we recommend a series of smaller plots within a single figure. We'll get to this soon.)

Now observe what we did *not* change about the original Figure 10.5. First, we retained the horizontal axis as "Cases Filed Per Authorized Judgeship" and the vertical, as "Year". This conforms to standard practice of placing explanatory variables on the x- (horizontal) axis and outcomes on the y- (vertical) axis.[74] Second, we did not change the ordering of the labels on the horizontal axis, from the first (1992) to the last (2010) year in the dataset. Again, this is standard procedure for a plot that graphs data over time (sometimes called a time series plot) but not for many other data displays. More typically researchers should order the labels by decreasing frequency (or another sensible pattern), not, for example, alphabetically or even by time, as this can obscure interesting patterns.[75] Figure 10.1 (on the length of constitutions in Europe) provides an example of an ordering that we changed to facilitate comparison.

Finally, returning to Figure 10.5, note that we retained both the "Civil" and "Criminal" lines in a single picture. Because they do not clutter the display this is a reasonable decision here. In other cases, graphing too much in one rectangle can obscure the data, and should be avoided.[76] The easiest solution is to juxtapose smaller graphs within a single display.[77] We followed this strategy in plotting the length of constitutions in regions in Europe (Figure 10.1). And you'll see it again in Chapter 11 (Figure 11.8).

Trust Your Audience.   The suggested revisions to Figures 10.4 and 10.5 have the benefit of reducing clutter and so enhancing the reader's ability to decode the information they house. But the alterations do not (at least we hope not) have the effect of dumbing down the graphs. We have more faith in our readers than that and indeed, the principle we sought to follow in redesigning them is "Aim for *Clarity* and

[73] Tukey (1990, 332–3).
[74] Some exceptions do exist, most notably when a verbal descriptor accompanies each case.
[75] Gelman et al. (2002, 122).
[76] Cleveland (1994, 36).
[77] See, e.g., Cleveland (1994); Tufte (2001); Gelman et al. (2002).

Impact," not "Aim for *Simplicity* and Impact." To put it another way, to us, Strunk and White's advice for writers applies equally to graphic design: "No one can write decently who is distrustful of the reader's intelligence, or whose attitude is patronizing."[78]

Some scholars disagree, arguing that we ought to judge graphs by their simplicity— by how many words they save or by how fast viewers can comprehend them. But these criteria are far too restrictive. As Tukey pithily writes, "A picture may be worth a thousand words, but it may take a hundred words to do it."[79] And Cleveland speaks to the issue of speedy comprehension: "While there is a place for rapidly-understood graphs, it is too limiting to make speed a requirement in science and technology, where the use of graphs ranges from detailed, in-depth data analysis to quick presentation."[80]

The same, we believe, applies to work on law and legal institutions. To argue otherwise would be to eliminate graphs that may demand careful study on the reader's part but are otherwise extremely valuable, effective, and memorable. Likewise, emphasizing simplicity—a symptom, really, of a lack of faith in our audience—can lead to graphs devoid of clarity and elegance.

To provide but one example, researchers often feel compelled to start their scales with zero out of a belief that their readers will not look at tick mark labels[81] and instead will apply "the most trivial of quantitative reasoning."[82] As we show in Figure 10.6, not only does this disrespect our audience and waste space—we should aim to fill the data rectangle—but it also may interfere with decoding (see also Figure 10.4.)

Note that both panels plot the length of constitutions in Eastern Europe but the inclusion of zero obscures several potential patterns in the data—for example, the rather large gap between Bulgaria and Hungary and between the three countries with the lengthiest constitutions and all the others. Displaying the data more sensibly, as we do in the bottom panel, facilitates more effective judgment.[83]

[78] Tufte (2001, 81) makes this same point, quoting Strunk and White (1959, 50).

[79] Quoted in Wainer (1990, 341).

[80] Cleveland (1994, 117).

[81] We refer here to graphs that do not require zero. Of course, when zero is relevant, researchers must include it.

[82] See Cleveland (1994, 93) responding to Huff (1954), who claims that excluding zero is downright dishonest.

[83] We adapt this language from Cleveland (1994, 94).

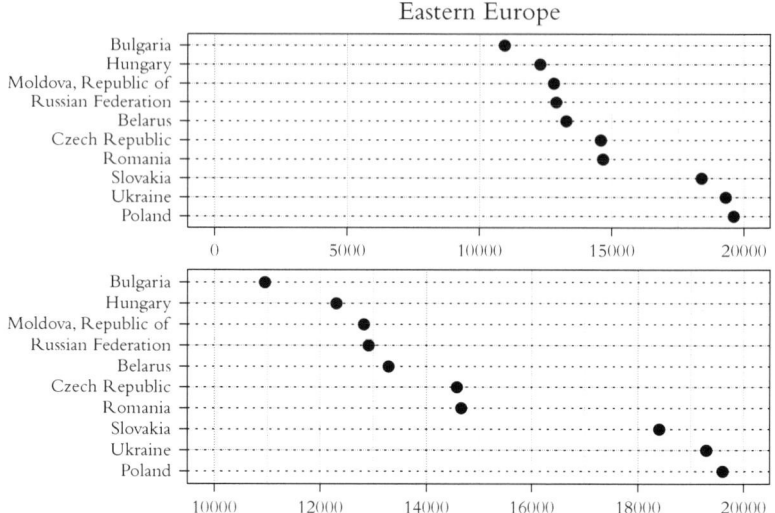

Figure 10.6 Dot plots of the length (in words) of present-day constitutions in Eastern Europe. From the top panel it is difficult to observe several potentially interesting patterns in the data, such as the gap between Bulgaria and Hungary. We excluded zero in the bottom panel to facilitate a more effective judgment about the data.[84]

This is just one example of how incorrect assumptions about the naïveté of our readers can interfere with principles of sound graphic design. The larger point is that we not only should but *must* assume that our audience will look closely at the graphs and understand them. Without this assumption, as Cleveland notes, "graphical communication would be far less useful."[85] We would go even further and ask why bother with graphs or even tabular displays if we believe our readers won't bother with them?

10.2.2 Iterate

To arrive at the bottom panel of Figure 10.6, we iterated, creating two depictions of the same data with the hope that the second provides the clearest and most effective presentation. This is usual in graph making.

---

[84] European regions based on UN classifications (<http://unstats.un.org/unsd/methods/ m49/m49regin.htm>); number of words in constitution from the Comparative Constitutions Project Dataset.

[85] Cleveland (1994, 93).

In our experience, it is nearly impossible to get it right on the first try.[86]

Consider another, perhaps more typical example of the iterative process in action. All three panels of Figure 10.7 show Americans' trust in government but the displays grow progressively clearer. Though by no means a horrid visualization of the data, the top panel contains a sufficient number of irrelevant or obscuring elements to make decoding difficult. Yet again, the inclusion of zero conceals what may be an important downward trend in the data; and the diamond symbols aren't helping much, nor are the alternate tick marks. Eliminating zero from the vertical axis and many of the tick marks from the horizontal axis, as we do in the middle panel, facilitates a more effective judgment about the data.

Still there's a problem: the use of a connected line graph suggests that data exist for each year between 1958 and 2010 when that's not the case. The American National Election survey, from where the Trust in Government Index comes, is fielded only every other year (and the Index wasn't computed at all for 1960 and 1962). By moving to a bar chart, in the bottom panel of Figure 10.7, we are better able to alert readers to the "missing" years in the dataset.

10.2.3 Write Detailed Captions

For Figure 10.7 and, in fact, for all the others throughout this book, we tried to write informative captions. This is standard operating procedure in many disciplines but not yet in empirical legal research.[87]

It should be. Detailed captions can reduce unnecessary and obstructive elements in the graph itself. Plus when the captions point out

---

[86] As a practical matter, this underscores the importance of using software that can easily reproduce graphs from scripts and provide fine control over all elements. Both Stata and R meet these criteria.

[87] Consider the following excerpt from "Figure Captions" guidelines for manuscripts submitted to the *Journal of the American Statistical Association*:

Figures must be clearly described. The combined information of the figure caption and the text of the body of the paper should provide a clear and complete description of everything that is on the figure. Detailed captions can often be of great help to the reader. First, describe completely what is graphed in the display; then draw the reader's attention to salient features of the display and briefly state the importance of these features.

Generally, it is a good idea to include the key to symbols in the caption to avoid cluttering the display. Abbreviations not already defined in the text must be defined in the caption.

At: <http://www.amstat.org/publications/index.cfm?fuseaction=style-guide>.

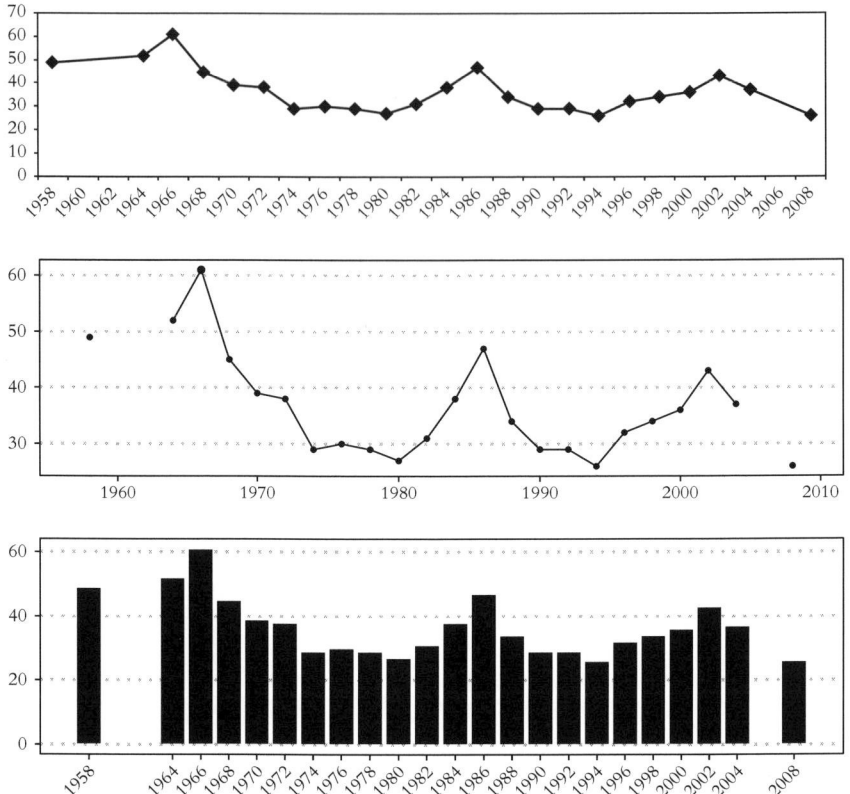

Figure 10.7 All three panels show the Trust in Government Index (developed from the American National Election Studies) on the vertical axis and year (from 1958–2008) on the horizontal axis. From the top panel it is difficult to observe the decline in trust over time. We excluded zero in the middle pattern to ease interpretation of the data, and did not connect 1958 to 1964 to accentuate data sparseness. A problem in both the top and middle panels, however, is that neither clearly delineates missing years. To fix it, we moved to a bar chart. Now readers can spot missing data; it is also easier to see that the Index is available only for even-numbered years. The sequence of charts shores up Cleveland's advice: "Don't hesitate to make two or more graphs of the same data."[88]

---

[88] Trust in Government Index is available at: <http://www.umich.edu/ nes/nesguide/ toptable/tab5a_5.htm>. The quote is from Cleveland (1994, 114).

especially interesting or crucial features of the results, they can be of great value to readers and so to authors too.

In general, we commend to you Cleveland's advice that captions should be "comprehensive and informative,"[89] ensuring that the graph is as self-contained as possible.[90] To this end, captions should include (some version of) the following information:

1. A description of everything in the display.
2. A sentence or two on particularly important features of the data or results.
3. A brief statement on why those features are important.[91]

We do not, though, want to discourage flexibility: captions will (and should) vary with the type of display and by the kinds of data and results being presented. So too it is possible to overdo a caption by providing too much extraneous information. Striving for the appropriate balance is the key.

* * * * * * * *

With this it's time to move on. Our goal in this chapter was to supply general suggestions for improving the presentation of empirical analyses. In the next chapter, we turn to more specific strategies for communicating data and results, though we stress the latter. This reflects our belief, echoed throughout, that an emphasis on sterile statistical results without an interrogation of their substantive importance does a disservice to the research, the researchers, and their readers. On the other hand, when analysts are able to communicate their findings effectively and accessibly the payoffs are considerable.

---

[89] Cleveland (1994, 55).

[90] In its instructions to authors, the *Journal of Empirical Legal Studies* makes this point as well: "Tables and figures should stand on their own. When appropriate, authors should include an explanatory note for a table or figure. The goal is to have the table or figure 'stand on its own' so that a busy reader can understand the table without reading the whole article." At: <http://onlinelibrary.wiley.com/journal/10.1111/(ISSN)1740-1461/homepage/ForAuthors.html>.

[91] We adapt this advice from the *Journal of the American Statistical Association* (<http://www.amstat.org/publications/index.cfm?fuseaction=style-guide>) and Cleveland (1993, 1994).

11

Strategies for Presenting Data and Statistical Results

In the last chapter we explored the three key principles of effective communication: (1) communicate substance, not statistics; (2) when performing inference, convey uncertainty; and (3) graph data and results. We also offered some general advice for creating visually effective displays of data, urging you to aim for clarity, to iterate, and to write detailed captions.

In other disciplines, adherence to these principles has generated benefits for the producers and consumers of empirical research, and we have no doubt that research relating to law and legal institutions will see similarly salutary effects. Most crucially, as we explained in Chapter 10, moving towards more appropriate and accessible data presentations will enhance the impact of empirical legal scholarship—regardless of whether the intended audience consists of other scholars, students, policy makers, judges, or practicing attorneys.[1] At the same time, however, we realize that legal researchers require more than general guidelines; they need on-the-ground guidance so that they can convey the results of their (carefully designed and executed!) studies to members of legal and policy communities. So here we aim to get far more specific, offering analysts advice on how to translate data and results into powerful visual presentations. (We understand that some of the material reiterates themes in Chapters 8–10. We nonetheless think that presenting research is so important that it's worth reinforcing in a chapter of its own.)

---

[1] See also King et al. (2000).

In setting out the various strategies to follow, we divide the material into two sections. In the first, we focus on communicating data; in the second, on the presentation of results. We split the material in this way because the presentation of data and results are somewhat different tasks. For example, when performing inference, authors have an obligation to convey the level of uncertainty about their results, as we stressed in Chapter 10. But when researchers are merely displaying or describing the data they have collected—and not using their sample to draw inferences about the population that may have generated the data—supplying measures of uncertainty, such as confidence intervals, may be overkill.

This is a distinction between the two sections to come. The commonality, though, may be more important. In both we adhere to the general principles laid out in Chapter 10—though none more so than the very basic idea that researchers should almost always graph their data and results. Along these lines, we agree with Gelman and his colleagues: unless the author has a very compelling reason to provide precise numbers to readers, a well-designed graph is better than a table.[2]

11.1 Communicating Data

Even though inference is the primary goal in most empirical studies (and so communicating *results* is of paramount importance), empirical legal researchers will often want to convey information about the data they have collected. And, of course, if analysts are less interested in inference than in describing the information they have collected, they will almost certainly want to display their data.

Regardless of the ultimate goal, how to go about communicating data is the subject of this section. We consider strategies for presenting (1) one variable and (2) the relationship between two variables.

11.1.1 The One-Variable Case

By now you know that the building blocks of empirical analysis are variables, or characteristics of some phenomenon that vary. We have examined many throughout; in Chapter 10 alone—Length of Constitution, Life Expectancy, and Judge's Gender among

---

[2] Gelman et al. (2002).

others. You also understand that when it comes to the task of analyzing data, it's crucial to identify whether the variables are qualitative (nominal) or quantitative (ordinal and interal). `Length of Constitution` and `Life Expectancy` are examples of quantitative variables, and in what follows we consider others such as `Judicial Independence`. To the extent that we can categorize judges—whether they are male or female—or differentiate them on the basis of this quality rather than some numerical value, `Judge's Gender` is a qualitative and not quantitative variable.

Just as the distinction between quantitative and qualitative variables is crucial for selecting appropriate statistical methods for analysis, it is also important for selecting appropriate tools for presentation. This is true to such an extent that we divide the material to follow on this basis.

Quantitative Variables: Eliminate Tables of Summary Statistics. Way back in Parts I and II, we explored research by La Porta et al. that considered whether independent judiciaries promote economic freedom.[3] Let's revisit this study, but now make use of Howard and Carey's measure of judicial independence (which we discussed extensively in Chapter 3) instead of La Porta et al.'s.[4] For our purposes, the Howard and Carey measure tells us whether or not the judiciary is fully independent.[5] To proxy economic freedom, let's go with data from the World Bank on one of La Porta et al.'s measures: the number of legal procedures necessary to register a firm so that it can begin to operate formally.[6] La Porta et al.'s working hypothesis, recall, is that the number of procedures will be longer in countries without a fully independent judiciary, all else being equal.

Before performing statistical inference to test this hypothesis, most researchers (us included!) would want to convey information about the number of legal procedures (a quantitative variable) in countries with and without a fully independent judiciary. One approach would be to create a table showing the raw data (see Table 11.1). But we don't advise it. Raw data tables are not simply unnecessary; they're

---

[3] La Porta et al. (2004).

[4] Howard and Carey (2004). See Figure 3.2.

[5] In other words, we combined their categories of partially independent and dependent.

[6] At: <http://www.doingbusiness.org/data/exploretopics/starting-a-business>. The World Bank lists 185 countries. We include only those 67 in both the World Bank and Howard and Carey datasets.

Table 11.1 Partial listing of the number of procedures to register a firm so that it can begin formally operating, by whether or not the judiciary is fully independent. We show the data for ten countries; there are 67 in the dataset.[7]

Country	Fully Independent Judiciary	Not Fully Independent Judiciary
Algeria	—	14
Argentina	—	14
Australia	2	—
Austria	8	—
Bangaladesh	—	7
Belgium	3	—
Brazil	—	13
Canada	1	—
Chile	7	—
. . .		
Zimbabwe	9	—

distracting, even frustrating. They waste space in whatever the outlet (especially now when it's so easy to post data on a website), and worse still, they almost never serve the author's purpose. Even after careful study, most readers won't be able to discern patterns in the number of procedures in countries with and without independent judiciaries, much less determine whether or not the patterns are different. Only by sorting and reordering the data, which is impossible on the printed page, could we do this. Moreover, we can't keep that many figures in our head, and the more observations in the study, the worse the problem grows.

A second approach to conveying information about a quantitative variable, such as number of procedures, is a table of descriptive statistics. The top panel in Figure 11.1 provides an example.

Tables of descriptive (or summary) statistics are more common in empirical legal research than raw data tables because analysts are usually less interested in conveying the trees of their study (the precise number of procedures for each country) than the forest (summary information about the structure of the variable Number of Procedures). By

---

[7] Data on the number of procedures are from the World Bank (<http://www.doingbusiness.org/data/exploretopics/starting-a-business>); data on the judiciaries are from Howard and Carey (2004).

Variable	Mean	Std. Dev.	Min.	Max.	n
Fully Independent Judiciary	5.42	2.47	1	11	31
Not Fully Independent Judiciary	9.42	3.56	3	17	36

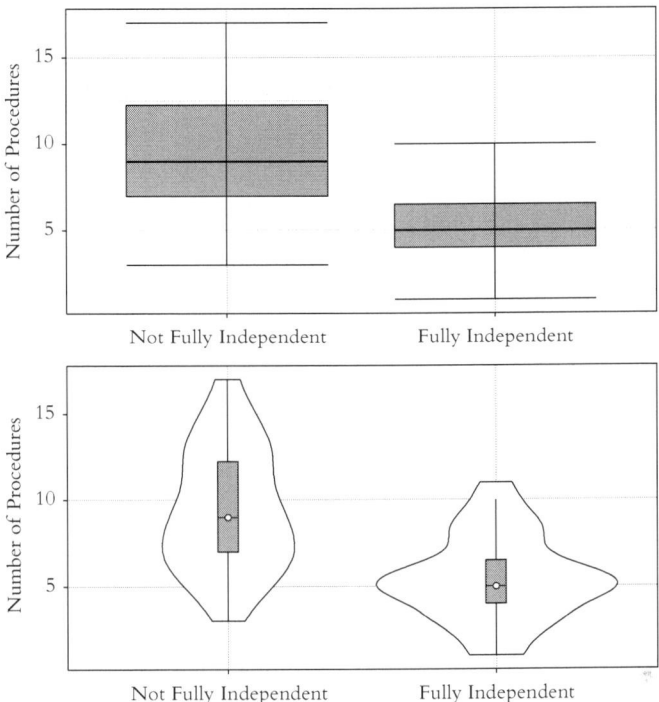

Figure 11.1 Descriptive statistics on the number of procedures to register a firm so that it can begin formally operating, by whether or not the judiciary is fully independent. If the goal is to provide summary information about the composition of the variables of interest through descriptive statistics, the precise values in the top panel do not well serve it. The box plots in the middle panel visually display the distribution of the procedures variable and do a better job of drawing attention to the median, the interquartile range, and any outliers. The violin plot provides similar information while conveying an even clearer picture of the shape of the variable's distribution.

providing the values of the mean, median, standard deviation, and minimum and maximum values, as the top panel does, this strategy comes closer to depicting the forest than raw data tables, especially when the number of observations is large. But because tables of descriptive statistics sacrifice visual clarity for the sake of artificial precision, they almost never meet this objective either. They can also obscure rather than clarify the message the authors seek to convey, especially for variables with unusually small or large observations (that is, outliers). More to the point, if the goal is to convey information about a variable's structure—including its center, spread, and shape—as it almost always is, we strongly advise replacing summary tables with appropriate graphical displays.

Let's elaborate, beginning with the center and spread of the distributions (the number of legal procedures in countries with and without an independent judiciary). The table in Figure 11.1 displays precise values for both: means and medians for the center, and standard deviations and minimum/maximum values for the spread. This is important information, to be sure, but precise values are often unnecessary. In most cases, researchers can make their point far more accessibly, powerfully, and nearly as easily with a figure. Several possibilities come to mind, though the box plot, shown in the middle panel of Figure 11.1, is an excellent and time-tested option for analysts hoping to draw attention to a comparison between two or more continuous variables, as we do here.[8]

Why box plots remain one of the most important and frequently used tools for data communication is no mystery: they are able to convey parsimoniously and clearly a lot of information about the distribution of a variable(s). As the middle panel of the figure shows, a simple box plot allows the researcher to depict not only the median but also the interquartile range (recall, another measure of dispersion[9]), the minimum and maximum values, and any outliers. As represented in the figure, the interquartile range covers the data points between the 25th and 75th percentiles; in other words, the box covers the middle 50% of the data. The minimum and maximum values are the first and last values of the data when the observations have been sorted from smallest to largest.[10]

In short, box plots can communicate the right information without losing much, if any detail. The proof, though, is in the pudding, and Figure 11.1 provides it. Now the comparison we wish to draw between

---

[8] See also Figure 10.3.

[9] See Chapter 6.

[10] Outliers typically would be represented as circles; there are none in this dataset. For more information on the box plot and its components, see Cleveland (1993); Tukey (1977).

procedures in countries with independent and non-independent judiciaries is entirely evident. The median line is lower for countries with independent judiciaries (indicating fewer procedures), and equally as noticeable, the interquartile range is smaller.

Just as box plots enhance visualization of the center and spread of a distribution relative to tables of means and medians, graphs perform far better than precise values in conveying information about the shape of the data. Think about it this way. We know from the Empirical Rule that if a variable is normally distributed (looks bell-shaped), 95% of the observations fall within two standard deviations of the mean.[11] But this rule-of-thumb is useful only when we know the variable is symmetric and bell-shaped. If it's not, knowing the precise value of the standard deviation isn't terribly valuable. And therein emerges yet another drawback of tables of descriptive statistics: they do not reveal whether the data are normally distributed. Only by inspecting the shape of a distribution can researchers and their readers know whether this condition holds. And only via a plot of the data can they conduct this inspection.

Tools for plotting distributions abound, but two excellent possibilities are *violin* and *kernel density* plots. Neither has received much attention in empirical legal studies.[12] They should.

Now widely deployed in statistics and gaining traction in the social sciences, the violin plot is a modern-day variant of the traditional box plot.[13] As the bottom panel of Figure 11.1 shows, violin plots too provide information on the center of the variables (indicated by the hollow white circles). But they also relay information that we cannot obtain from tables of descriptive statistics about the shape of the two variables. For example, while "Fully Independent" appears normally distributed, "Not Fully Independent" looks more bimodal.

The kernel density plot is a modern-day incarnation of the histogram. Recall from Chapter 6 that histograms are graphs of continuous (or nearly continuous) observations grouped into a series of vertical bars

---

[11] See Chapter 6.

[12] A Lexis search of U.S. and Canadian law reviews and journals (conducted February 15, 2013) uncovered only one result for a search of "violin" within the same sentence as "plot" or "graph": a law review article by your authors encouraging the use of violin plots (Epstein et al., 2007). Perhaps we'll have better luck with you! A search of the same journals (conducted contemporaneously) turned up 26 articles using kernel density plots.

[13] See, e.g., Hintze and Nelson (1998). Kernel density plots and violin plots require the use of computers to construct. Histograms and box plots, on the other hand, can be made with pencil and paper.

along the range of a variable's values. Although they can provide useful information, histograms have a number of disadvantages, including their arbitrarily designated "bins" and the relatively random assignment of observations to those bins.[14] By smoothing over the distribution with a continuous function, kernel density plots can ameliorate some of these problems. They work by shrinking the bin–width of a histogram and then using pieces of continuous functions to create a single, smooth curve that characterizes the distribution of the variable of interest.[15]

To provide an example, return to the variable Number of Procedures for all 67 countries in our dataset. From precise measures of central tendency (for example, the mean is 7.57) and dispersion (the standard deviation is 3.68), we learn very little about its structure. We can remedy this deficit by turning to visual displays that account for the distribution of this continuous variable. In Figure 11.2 we take this step, creating a histogram and kernel density plot for Number of Procedures.

The histogram provides some help in understanding the variable's distribution but the kernel density plot is even better. Number of Procedures appears right skewed. The mass of the distribution falls between four and ten procedures; it is more difficult to make that judgment from the histogram and impossible to do so from the table of descriptive statistics.

Having now studied the graphs in Figures 11.1 and 11.2 we hope you can understand why we so strongly recommend jettisoning tables of summary statistics. It seems to us nearly impossible to conclude that they are superior or even equal to visual depictions of a variable. If the unusual circumstance arises and more precision is needed, exact numbers are easy enough to present visually or in a caption.

Qualitative Variables: Jettison Frequency Tables. Qualitative (nominal) variables abound in the law literature. The presence (or absence) of certain constitutional provisions occasionally figures into studies of human rights;[16] research on judging often considers the race, gender, and the political party affiliation of judicial appointees (or of the

---

[14] See, e.g., Cleveland (1993); Jacoby (1997).

[15] See, e.g., Silverman (1986).

[16] E.g., Sandholtz (2012); Keith et al. (2009); Davenport and Armstrong (2004). Beck et al. (2012) is the reverse. It explores how the "global discourse of universal human rights" has affected the language of national constitutions.

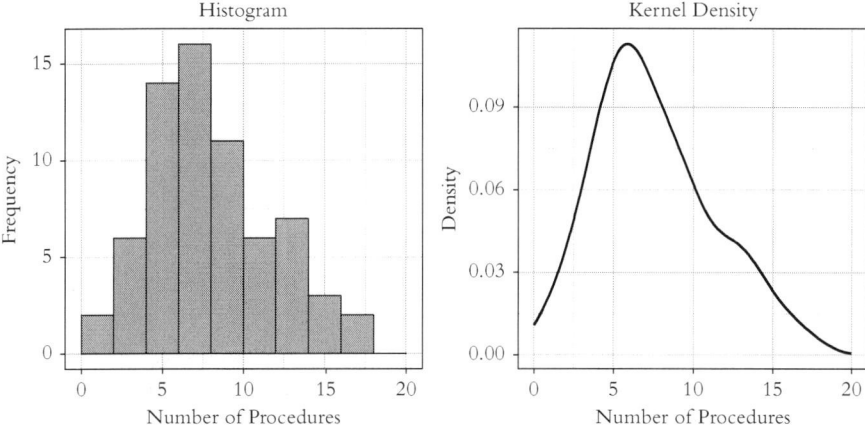

Figure 11.2 A histogram and a kernel density plot of the number of procedures to register a firm so that it can begin formally operating for 67 countries. The histogram provides the reader with a richer understanding of the variable and its distribution than a table of descriptive statistics (see the top panel of Figure 11.1). Arguably, the kernel density plot does an even better job because the existence and location of the right skew are more apparent.

political actor appointing them).[17] And the method for disposing of a case, whether by settlement, plea-bargain, non-trial adjudication, or trial, comes into play in many important empirical studies of criminal and civil litigation.[18] Throughout this book, we have seen even more examples, including region and the legal tradition of a judge's or litigant's country.

Although most researchers understand that conveying descriptive statistics for qualitative variables is uninformative,[19] they have developed equally uninformative ways to convey the variables' composition. Especially ubiquitous are frequency or one-way tables that depict the number (and, typically, the percentage) of observations falling into each category of the variable. Table 11.2 provides an example using information from Elkins et al.'s database on the contents of constitutions in 184 countries.[20]

---

[17] The literature along these lines is massive. For a recent review and an extensive bibliography, see Epstein et al. (2013).

[18] Another massive literature. For recent examples, see Boylan (2012); Huang et al. (2010); Schwab and Heise (2011).

[19] Or at least for those with more than two categories.

[20] Comparative Constitutions Project, at: <http://www.comparativeconstitutionsproject. org/>.

To be sure, this table communicates interesting information. But is Table 11.2—or, rather, frequency tables more generally—the best way to convey it? If the purpose is to provide readers with the precise figures, then the answer is yes: as we noted in Chapter 10, frequency tables always trump graphs. From Table 11.2 we know that exactly 57.61% of the countries have one-house legislatures. From the dot plots of the same data in Figure 11.3 we cannot recover this percentage with the same degree of precision. More often than not, though, as we

Table 11.2 Descriptive statistics table created from the Comparative Constitutions Project Database on provisions in 184 constitutions. Although the frequencies in the table provide details on the individual variables, it is unlikely that readers can quickly process the information; it is also unlikely that they need precise values. See Figure 11.3 for dot plots of the same data.[21]

Variable	Breakdown	Percentage
Percentage of vote needed to to approve a constitutional amendment (N = 112)	Absolute majority	7.14
	3/5s majority	8.04
	2/3s majority	75.89
	3/4s majority	8.93
How is head of state selected? (N = 174)	Heredity/royal selection	16.67
	Elected by citizens	57.47
	Elected by elite group	25.86
Number of chambers or houses in legislature (N = 184)	One	57.61
	Two	42.39
Constitution contains an explicit declaration regarding judicial independence (N = 181)	Yes	77.35
	No	22.65
Description of the state (N = 72)	Federal	27.78
	Confederal	1.39
	Unitary	70.83
Constitution specifies an official or national language (N = 183)	Official only	45.90
	National only	6.01
	Both official and national	14.21
	No except for govt. business	7.65
	No languages mentioned	26.23

[21] The Database covers 184 countries. As the n's indicate, data are missing for some variables for various reasons. For example, only if the Constitution (or parts of it) are amendable does the first variable (Percentage of the vote needed to approve a constitutional amendment) come into play.

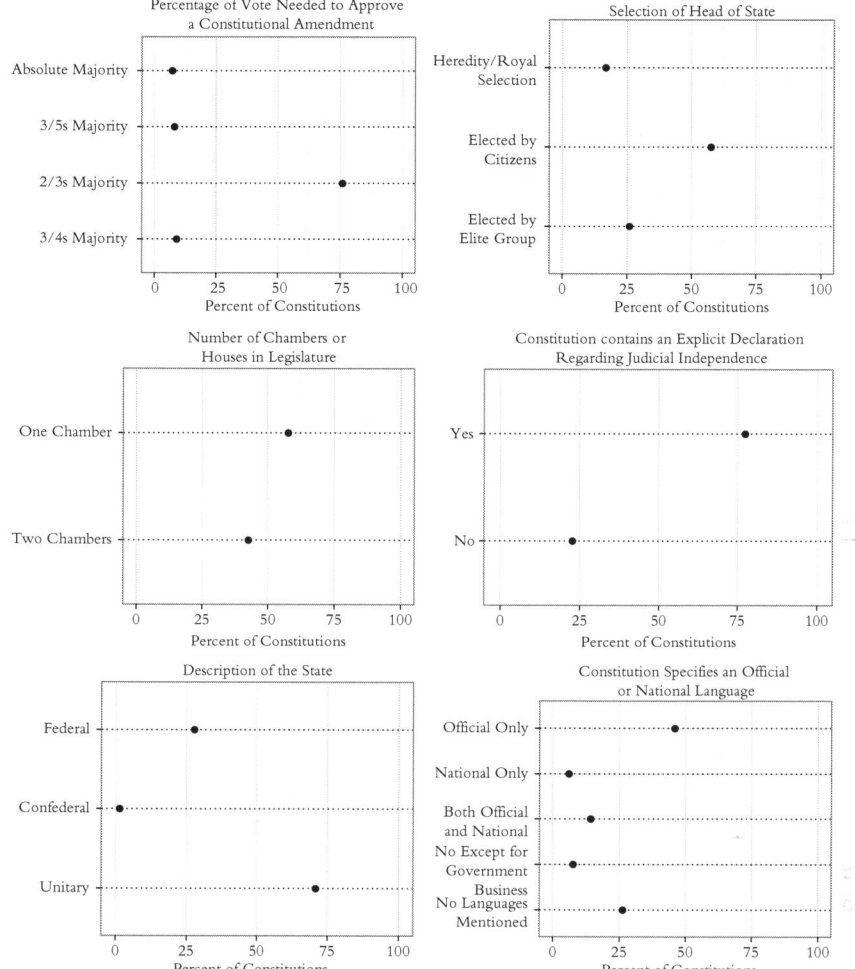

Figure 11.3 Compared to the descriptive statistics in Table 11.2, the individual dot plots provide a more visually and cognitively appealing solution to the problem of providing readers with information about the composition of individual variables in a dataset.

have stressed throughout, we are less interested in precision than with comparisons, patterns, or trends. By providing exact percentages, Table 11.2 doesn't meet this goal as well as Figure 11.3. Even for variables with fewer than three categories, the dot plots better serve this purpose than the table.

A comparison of Table 11.2's data table and Figure 11.3's dot plots clarify this point. Surely if we looked at the numbers long enough, we could observe the patterns that emerge from the graph—for example, the big gap between constitutions that specify an official language or no language and all other categories. But it requires far more (unnecessary) cognitive work.

11.1.2 The Relationship between Two (or More) Variables

Unless the authors' sole goal is to showcase particular variables in their sample, histograms, violin plots, and other univariate displays are almost always just a prelude toward the larger goal of performing inference via regression or another tool. For example, in Figure 11.1 we provided ways to summarize judicial independence and economic freedom. These are key variables in any study designed to reach an inference about whether independent judiciaries lead to greater economic liberty but they are surely not the only ones. We might use plots to summarize the others too.

When researchers want to convey information about the relationship between two variables their *goals*, *data*, and *variables* are often more variegated. In terms of their goals, sometimes they too wish to reach an inference (say, by using a χ^2 statistic) but not always. Consider Gross and Barnes's study of racial profiling in highway drug searches in the U.S. state of Maryland between 1995 and 2000.[22] As part of their investigation, Gross and Barnes present data on the percentage of automobile searches per year by the driver's race, some of which we reproduce in Table 11.3. The authors neither draw a statistical inference from the table about the effect of race on highway stops, nor do they use the data it contains in a subsequent multivariate analysis. Rather, their primary purpose, it appears, is to convey trends in searches in the state.

Table 11.3 This is a partial replication of a table in Gross and Barnes's study on racial profiling on the highways in the U.S. state of Maryland. In Figure 11.4 we use a mosaic plot to present the same data in a more concise and appealing fashion.[23]

Searches by Race	1995	1996	1997	1998	1999	2000 (Jan–Jun)
White	20.7%	22.0%	39.7%	47.3%	39.9%	39.2%
Black	74.5%	65.0%	53.5%	45.5%	54.7%	53.4%
Hispanic	3.6%	9.7%	6.9%	6.1%	5.8%	6.3%
Total Searches	564	309	116	374	607	352

[22] Gross and Barnes (2002).
[23] Table 23 in Gross and Barnes (2002).

Table 11.4 The time (in hours) it takes, on average, for a medium-size company to pay its taxes and the total number of tax payments per year for a sample of economies in 2011. The sample includes 37 economies; to conserve space we show only 10. In Figure 11.5 we use a scatterplot to summarize the relationship between the two variables—time and payments.[24]

Economy	Time to Pay Taxes	Number of Tax Payments
Afghanistan	275	20
Argentina	405	9
Australia	109	11
Bahrain	36	13
Botswana	152	32
Cameroon	654	44
Chile	291	6
Congo, Dem. Rep.	336	32
...	...	...
Vietnam	872	32
West Bank and Gaza	154	39

Turning to the data researchers use when comparing two variables, sometimes they are organized over time (as in the Gross and Barnes study) and sometimes they are cross-sectional. Table 11.4 provides an example of the latter. It shows the relationship between a dependent variable—the time (in hours) it takes, on average, for a medium-size company to pay its taxes and contributions[25]—and an independent variable—the total number of tax payments per year for a sample of economies in 2011.[26] (We'd expect time to increase as the number of payments increase.) Table 11.5, on the other hand, shows a time

[24] Data are from the World Bank (<http://www.doingbusiness.org/data/exploretopics/paying-taxes\#sub-menu-item-link>). See also note 26.

[25] More specifically, it measures "the time taken to prepare, file and pay three major types of taxes and contributions: the corporate income tax, value added or sales tax, and labor taxes, including payroll taxes and social contributions." At: <http://doingbusiness.org/methodology/paying-taxes>.

[26] Data are from the World Bank (<http://www.doingbusiness.org/data/exploretopics/paying-taxes\#sub-menu-item-link>). The World Bank collected information on 185 economies; we drew a 20% sample of their data.

Table 11.5 Life expectancy at birth (in years) for three countries. The raw data make it difficult to decipher trends over time, relative to the time series plot in Figure 11.6 of the same data.[27]

Year	China	Germany	United Kingdom
1991	69.66	75.32	76.08
1992	69.86	75.82	76.43
1993	70.05	75.87	76.39
1994	70.24	76.27	76.89
1995	70.42	76.42	76.84
1996	70.60	76.67	77.09
1997	70.77	77.07	77.21
1998	70.93	77.48	77.19
1999	71.08	77.73	77.39
...	...	...	...
2010	73.27	79.99	80.40

series (over time) data—life expectancy at birth (in years) for three countries.[28]

Finally, as you know all too well, the variables themselves can be measured at different levels. Gross and Barnes (in Table 11.3) are relating a quantitative variable (time) and a qualitative variable (race). Tables 11.4 and 11.5 also display quantitative variables, though the data are organized differently (cross-sectional versus time series).

Despite these differences in goals, data, and variables, Tables 11.3–11.5 are common in one important regard. They all miss the opportunity to convey the data in the clearest and most accessible ways, thereby depriving the authors and their audience of the ability to detect patterns.

Starting with Gross and Barnes's study,[29] the researchers seek to depict race, a qualitative variable, over time. This is something of

---

[27] Data are from the World Bank (<http://data.worldbank.org/indicator/SP.DYN.LE00.IN>).

[28] Data are from the World Bank (<http://data.worldbank.org/indicator/SP.DYN.LE00.IN>).

[29] Gross and Barnes (2002).

a challenge,[30] and researchers confronting it tend to fall back on a rough-and-ready solution: the cross-tabulation, which displays the joint distribution of two or more variables (see Chapter 7). However ubiquitous this "solution", like the table of descriptive statistics the cross-tab should be banished, and banished for a similar reason: it often obscures, rather than clarifies, the very patterns the researchers wish to highlight. Table 11.3, from Gross and Barnes's study, illustrates the problem. The researchers hope to convey information about search trends, but with three categories of race dispersed over six time periods these trends are extremely difficult to detect.

Enter the mosaic plot, which uses appropriately sized rectangles to illustrate the marginal and joint distribution of the variables. The width of each bar on the x-axis shows the marginal distribution of that variable. Within each bar, the plot shows the fraction corresponding to the variable on the y-axis.[31] Providing an example is Figure 11.4, in which we transformed Gross and Barnes's search data into a mosaic plot. Now we can visualize both the composition of the race variable in each year, as well as any trends over time. One emerges from just a quick glance at the figure: the decline in searches conducted of black drivers between 1996 and 1998. It is also clear from the width of the tiles that the fewest searches were in 1997 and the most, in 1999. Drawing the same conclusions from the authors' original table would be possible but only with concerted effort.

Mosaic plots work particularly well for the Gross and Barnes's data,[32] but they are not limited to variables organized in a time series fashion. Indeed, unless researchers need to convey raw data values—which is almost never the case—we urge them to substitute mosaic plots for cross-tabs of two categorical variables. (Tables 1.1 and 7.3 are both examples of tables that could be converted to mosaic plots.[33])

That same advice does not hold for continuous quantitative variables, as in Tables 11.4 and 11.5. The tiles on the plot would grow so small that it would make decoding impossible. In this situation,

---

[30] The challenge arises because a standard time series plot of the sort we depict in 11.6 (and discuss momentarily) is more appropriate for continuous variables and so would serve to hinder and not enhance decoding.

[31] Mosaic plots were first developed in Hartigan and Kleiner (1981) and further refined in Friendly (1994).

[32] Gross and Barnes (2002).

[33] See also Table 3.2, comparing de jure and de facto measures of judicial independence.

Searches by Race	1995	1996	1997	1998	1999	2000 (Jan–Jun)
White	20.7%	22.0%	39.7%	47.3%	39.0%	39.2%
Black	74.5%	65.0%	53.5%	45.5%	54.7%	53.4%
Hispanic	3.6%	9.7%	6.9%	6.1%	5.8%	6.3%
Total Searches	564	309	116	374	607	352

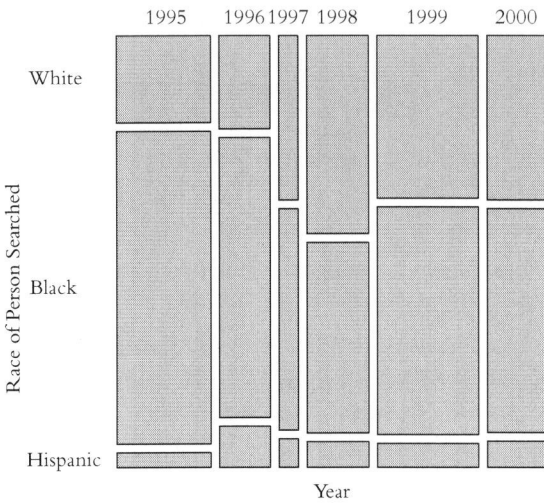

Figure 11.4 The table on the top is the same as Table 11.3, which shows data on a racial profiling. The mosaic plot on the bottom presents the same data in a more concise and appealing fashion. The width of the bars depicts the number of searches per year while the height of each tile conveys the relative number of searches that are conducted of drivers of each race during each year. With this plot, it is much easier to see, for example, the large percentage of searches in 1995 and 1996 that were of black drivers and how that percentage declines beginning in 1997.[34]

analysts should consider employing a graphic workhorse—the bivariate scatterplot.[35] As you may recall from Chapter 8, bivariate scatterplots

[34] Data are from Table 23 in Gross and Barnes (2002).

[35] In the physical, biological, and social sciences, the scatterplot predominates—at one time accounting for about 75% of the graphs in these disciplines (Spence and Garrison, 1993). As noted in Part III, analysts often use simple scatterplots before analyzing their data, and the insights gained may stimulate the production of more complicated variations or may guide the choice of a model.

display the joint distribution of the observations of two quantitative variables. When constructed with sound graphing techniques in mind,[36] they can be useful for examining the relationship between two variables.

We have taken advantage of this tool for the tax data, transforming the raw data in Table 11.4 into the scatterplot at the bottom of Figure 11.5. Note that we embellished the plot in two ways. First, we added a loess (or locally weighted regression) curve, which is a smooth plot through the middle of the distribution of plotted observations.[37] The smooth loess curve summarizes how the two plotted variables depend on one another. In Figure 11.5, it reveals a hardly unexpected trend in the data: as the number of payments increases so too does the time spent paying taxes. A second embellishment is the labeling of several outliers. Especially noticeable is Vietnam, where the number of hours is the highest in the sample but the number of payments is only slightly above the mean. This is a puzzle for the researcher to solve but one that would have been difficult to spot from a long list of raw data.

The data in Table 11.5 (partially reproduced in Figure 11.6) are also continuous but have an explicit time dimension that the researcher usually wants to convey. The problem is that meaningful trends are almost impossible to discern from exact values in a table. These data begged to be plotted but, because we collected observations about the same three countries at many points in time, scatterplots are not especially useful. Neither are mosaic plots. They can handle time series data, as we saw in Figure 11.4, but not continuous variables. Once again, the tiles would be too small.

The best solution here is a time series plot. As we hope you can see in Figure 11.6, decoding the information in the graph, as opposed to the table, is so cognitively undemanding that it takes no time at all to spot several interesting trends in the data. In all three countries, life expectancy is on the upswing (no surprise). A big gap, however, remains between China and the two European countries, though the increase appears greater for Germany than the UK.

---

[36] Like so many other visualization tools, bivariate scatterplots can go awry. To avoid problems, Cleveland (1994, 158) recommends the use of visually prominent plotting symbols, outward facing tick marks, and, where necessary, jittering, along with the avoidance of grid lines.

[37] As the smoothness parameter α increases, so too does the smoothness of the loess curve.

Economy	Time to Pay Taxes	Number of Tax Payments
Afghanistan	275	20
Argentina	405	9
Australia	109	11
Bahrain	36	13
Botswana	152	32
Cameroon	654	44
Chile	291	6
Congo, Dem. Rep.	336	32
. . .	. . .	. . .
Vietnam	872	32
West Bank and Gaza	154	39

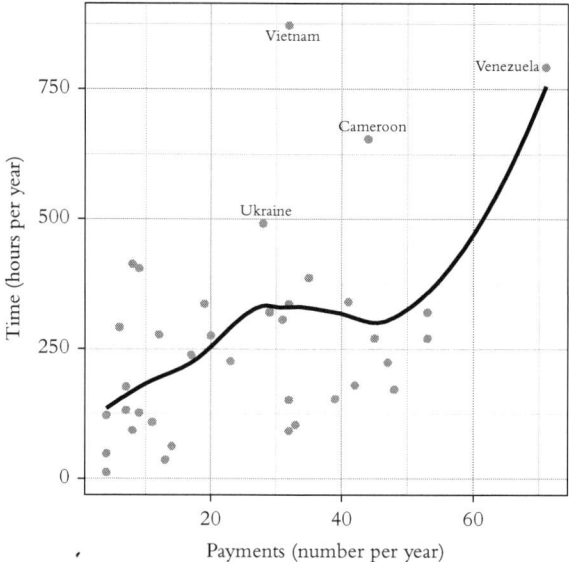

Figure 11.5 The top panel reproduces the raw data table in Table 11.4. The bottom panel is a bivariate scatterplot of the full sample. The solid line is a smooth loess curve that summarizes the relationship between the payments and hours. We've also noted several outlier economies—those where the number of payments does not provide an especially good prediction of the number of hours.[38]

---

[38] Data are from the World Bank (<http://www.doingbusiness.org/data/exploretopics/paying-taxes\#sub-menu-item-link>). See also note 26.

Year	China	Germany	United Kingdom
1991	69.66	75.32	76.08
1992	69.86	75.82	76.43
1993	70.05	75.87	76.39
1994	70.24	76.27	76.89
1995	70.42	76.42	76.84
1996	70.60	76.67	77.09
1997	70.77	77.07	77.21
1998	70.93	77.48	77.19
1999	71.08	77.73	77.39
...	...	...	...
2010	73.27	79.99	80.40

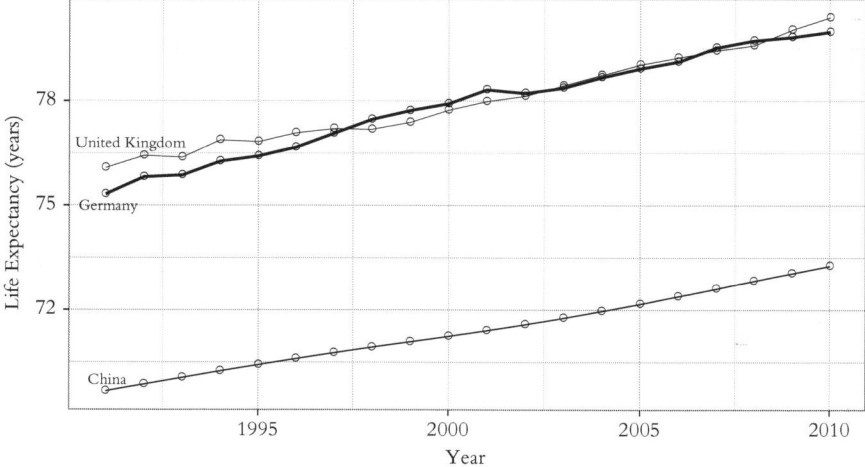

Figure 11.6 Life expectancy in years for three countries. From the raw data, partially reproduced above from Table 11.5, it is difficult to decipher trends across time. Below the table, we provide a time series plot of the same data. Data points for each year are represented by a circle. The time series plot draws attention to the upswing in life expectancy in all three countries, as well as the distance between China versus Germany and the UK.[39]

[39] Data are from the World Bank (<http://data.worldbank.org/indicator/SP.DYN.LE00.IN>).

11.2 Presenting Results

All the examples so far involve transforming tables of *data* into meaningful graphs. What about communicating *results*? More often than not researchers also use tables to convey the results of regression analysis: in this case, tables full of coefficients and measures of uncertainty that are uninformative both to laypersons and the statistically savvy alike. In what follows, we offer a step-by-step corrective.

For the sake of clarity, we rely on a single running example throughout. It's the Epstein and Landes's study of judicial invalidations of federal laws that we briefly considered in the last chapter.[40] Recall their hypothesis of interest: justices of the U.S. Supreme Court will be more likely to strike down laws that clash with their ideological values—such that a liberal justice will be more likely to strike down conservative laws (e.g., a law discriminating against homosexuals) and a conservative, more likely to uphold them. Testing this hypothesis, the authors believe, makes a contribution to debates over whether judicial activism (or, if you prefer, judicial self-restraint) is ideologically patterned or more principled.

Epstein and Landes's data consist of all votes cast by the 44 justices serving between the 1937 and 2009 terms in cases in which the Court reviewed the constitutionality of a federal law. The dependent variable is a vote to uphold (= 0) or strike (= 1) the law. The key causal variable is a scale of the justices' ideology: the higher the score, the more conservative the justice.[41] Following from the literature,[42] the researchers controlled for five other variables:

1. Direction of the lower court's decision (coded 1 for liberal; 0 if otherwise). This accounts for the justices' tendency to reverse the decision of the court below (i.e., even a very liberal justice will tend to

---

[40] Epstein and Landes (2012).

[41] The ideology scores range from -4.117 (the most liberal justice) to 3.835 (the most conservative justice). Epstein and Landes (2012) computed scores from the term-by-term Martin-Quinn scores, available at: <http://mqscores.berkeley.edu/measures.php>. They also estimated the statistical models using other measures of ideology, including the justice's party affiliation (Republican or Democrat), the appointing President's party affiliation, and the justice's Segal-Cover score (which we discussed in Chapter 4). Substituting these other measures for the Martin-Quinn scores does not produce substantively different results.

[42] For existing studies of the U.S. Supreme Court see, e.g., Lindquist and Cross (2009); Solberg and Lindquist (2007); Keith (2008). See also Chapter 10, note 12 for similar studies of courts outside the United States.

reverse a decision below that upholds a liberal law; and vice versa for a conservative justice).[43]

2. Term. This is a counter that increases by 1 with each passing term. It serves as a rough proxy for linear trends in judicial restraint, precedent, court procedures, and other factors that may influence the likelihood of invalidating federal laws.

3. Discretion. This variable controls for the means by which the case arrived at the Court. It is coded 1 if the Court had complete discretion over whether to hear a case; coded 0 if otherwise. When the Court is less constrained, the challenge to the legislative action is likely to be stronger.[44]

4. Number of (orally argued) cases. It is possible that the more cases, the more time pressured the Court is and the less likely it will be to take the dramatic step of striking down a federal law.

5. Type of law. The U.S. Supreme Court tends to subject laws restricting rights and liberties (coded 1) to more rigorous standards of review than economic laws (coded 0).

To assess the extent to which these variables help account for justices' votes to invalidate or uphold laws, Epstein and Landes employ logistic regression (logit), a common tool in legal scholarship (as discussed in Chapter 9), to estimate two models: one for conservative laws and one for liberal laws. Table 11.6 depicts the statistical estimates and, crucially, depicts them in a way that seems to follow standard operating procedure in many empirical legal studies.

As you know by now, we believe this standard approach to presenting the results of a logistic regression—or, for that matter, any multivariate regression—should be reconsidered. In particular, we suggest that researchers (1) rework tables so that they not only stand alone from the text but are themselves informative; (2) convey the substantive effects of key variables of interest; and (3) communicate uncertainty. Adhering to these rules will go some distance toward enhancing the impact of the research if only because the audience will now better understand the results.

---

[43] Between the 1946 and 2009 terms, the petitioning party won in 63% of the 4,515 cases. Computed from the U.S. Supreme Court Database (Case Centered Data Organized by Citation), using orally argued cases and the partyWinning variable.

[44] See, e.g., Clark and Whittington (2009); Colker and Scott (2002).

Table 11.6 Logistic regression analysis of the votes of 44 individual U.S. Supreme Court justices on whether to uphold or invalidate a federal law, 1937–2009. Tables of this sort are common in empirical legal research but have their share of problems. One is that the variable names are not clear. It isn't obvious, for example, that "Lowct" means the "ideological direction of the lower court's decision." We offer some correctives in Table 11.7. Another problem is that most readers won't be able to interpret the coefficients; not even the authors can, in their heads, translate them into interesting quantities. To remedy this pervasive problem, we provide suggestions on how to move from meaningless to meaningful communication. See Figure 11.8.[45]

Variable	Conservative Law	Liberal Law
Jideology	-0.524^{**}	0.409^{**}
	(0.048)	(0.117)
Lowct	-0.282^{**}	0.313^{*}
	(0.095)	(0.140)
Disc	-0.299^{**}	$-0.221^{\dagger}$
	(0.110)	(0.131)
Civlib	0.843^{**}	0.070
	(0.144)	(0.125)
Ncases	$-0.006^{\dagger}$	-0.007^{*}
	(0.003)	(0.003)
Term	0.010^{*}	0.008
	(0.005)	(0.006)
Constant	-19.997^{*}	-17.090
	(9.718)	(11.826)
n	3143	2334
Log pseudo likelihood	-1758.596	-997.721
$\chi^2_{(6)}$	156.73	40.99

11.2.1 (How to) Produce Informative Tabular Displays of Statistical Results

Throughout we have counseled against tabular depictions of data. Frankly, and for the reasons we offer below, we feel no differently about tables displaying regression estimates (e.g., Tables 11.6 and 11.7). But we understand that some readers have come to expect them; we also

---

[45] Data are from Epstein and Landes (2012).

Table 11.7 Logistic regression analysis of the votes of 44 individual U.S. Supreme Court justices on whether to uphold or invalidate a federal law, 1937–2009. The dependent variable—the justice's vote in each case—is coded 1 (a vote to invalidate) or 0 (a vote to uphold). The primary variable of interest is Justice's Ideology. This variable ranges from -4.117 (the most liberal justice) to 3.835 (the most conservative justice). Cell entries are logit coefficients and robust standard errors clustered on the justice (in parentheses). * indicates $p < 0.05$. Although this table and Table 11.6 present the same statistical results, this table better enables readers to understand the results by, e.g., eliminating multiple stars for different levels of statistical significance and providing meaningful variable names.[46]

Variable	Conservative Law	Liberal Law
Justice's Ideology	-0.524*	0.409*
	(0.048)	(0.117)
Lower Court's Decision	-0.282*	0.313*
	(0.095)	(0.140)
Discretionary Review or Not	-0.299*	-0.221
	(0.110)	(0.131)
Civil Liberties Case or Not	0.843*	0.070
	(0.144)	(0.125)
N of Cases Decided During Term	-0.006*	-0.007*
	(0.003)	(0.003)
Term of Court	0.010*	0.008
	(0.005)	(0.006)
Constant	-19.997*	-17.090
	(9.718)	(11.826)
n	3143	2334
Log pseudo likelihood	-1758.596	-997.721
Percent Reduction in Error	26.4%	8.16%

realize that, occasionally, they can convey valuable information if only to the statistically informed reader.[47] As a result, incorporating tables of

---

[46] Data are from Epstein and Landes (2012).

[47] For example, for regression models it is necessary to know the scale of the dependent and independent variable for the reader to understand what the coefficient on Justice's Ideology (-0.524 for conservative laws) actually means. Additionally, outside of the linear regression context, such substantive interpretations of coefficients are extremely difficult because they require the reader to make complex calculations that depend on the values of

estimates into presentations or papers is sometimes necessary, though surely they need not be as uninformative as Table 11.6.

One obvious problem is that the variable names are not clear; we can't expect our readers to know that "Lowct" means the direction of the lower court's decision; and the other variables are equally enigmatic. We understand how this problem comes about. When researchers enter data into a statistical package, they often shorten a variable's name (see Chapter 5); and when they estimate their regression model, they simply cut and paste the resulting table into their document. This is good practice if and only if researchers are indifferent to their audience. Hoping that no reader of our book falls into this category, we suggest using descriptive names to label the variables as we have done in Table 11.7. Note that we also clearly convey the dependent variable, a crucial piece of information, yet one surprisingly missing in many tabular displays. We use the caption for this purpose but other plausible locations include the table's title or column head.

Turning to the statistical estimates, both Tables 11.6 and 11.7 present the coefficient estimates and standard errors. As you know, this is appropriate because these numbers convey information about the direction of the effect of the coefficient (indicated by the sign on the coefficient) and the presence of statistical significance (indicated by the relationship between the standard error and the coefficient),[48] even if the coefficients themselves are difficult to interpret substantively. Troubling, however, is Table 11.6's use of three different symbols to denote statistical significance, † for $p \leq 0.10$, * for $p \leq 0.05$, and ** for $p \leq 0.01$. Because this all-too-common practice may lead readers to inappropriately compare p-values,[49] we suggest omitting the asterisks

---

the independent variables. Why ask the reader to do these calculations for a multivariate statistical analysis when conveying results in an easy-to-consume manner with figures is straightforward? We emphasize this point in the text to follow.

[48] Without the presence of a statistically significant relationship between the coefficient and the dependent variable, there is no reason to assess the substantive effect of a variable.

[49] Before performing a hypothesis test it is necessary to decide at what level of confidence (α-level) the test will be conducted. The conclusion about statistical significance rests solely on the comparison between the p-value and the confidence level. It is inappropriate to claim, for example, that one coefficient is "more significant" than another just because it has a far smaller p-value. Coefficients are either significant or they are not. It would certainly be incorrect to say that, in Table 11.6, the coefficient for Jideology is more important than Term (for conservative laws) simply because it is statistically significant at the .01 level as opposed to the .05 level.

altogether. Readers can discern whether a variable is "statistically significant" from the standard error. Alternatively, authors can choose a level (typically α = 0.05) and use just one * (see Table 11.7).

Finally, to be complete, researchers should provide summary information about their model. The n (number of cases in the sample) is essential, though it too is occasionally absent from tabular displays. ns can be placed in the caption or in a column, as we have done in Table 11.7. For models estimated by maximum likelihood, it is good practice to report the log-likelihood (or the deviance, which is -2 times the log-likelihood). This quantity is useful for a number of statistical tests. A measure of the predictive power of the model is also essential. In linear regression, R^2 or the residual standard error are among the most common; for logit models of the sort we display in the table, a reduction of error assessment works well.[50] Other alternatives are various information criteria like the Akaike information criterion (AIC) or the Bayesian information criterion (BIC) reported in Table 9.2.[51] Conversely, we advise against reporting omnibus test statistics, such as the F statistic (often used in linear regression) or likelihood ratio tests (e.g., the χ^2 test in Table 11.6). Neither conveys information that is substantively useful. If these tests are significant (and in practice, they always are), all we learn is that something in the model is related to the dependent variable.

These recommendations are designed to help authors create informative tables that do not require the reader to slog through the text in order to identify variables, for example. For those analysts more concerned with providing their audience with a feel for their estimates rather than precise values, a nomogram (see Figure 11.7) provides an ideal alternative to a table. Nomograms, recall from Chapter 9, are dot plots in which a dot represents the estimated coefficient and error bars show the confidence interval. Visually, we can determine statistical

---

[50] With the assistance of statistical software, computing the proportional reduction in error is simple. In Stata, install and use the "pre" command after you've estimated the model. The software computes the reduction in error by finding the errors when simple guessing is employed and then finding the number of errors produced by the model. The final proportional reduction in error is computed by subtracting the number of errors in the model from the number of guessing errors and dividing that number by the number of guessing errors.

[51] The Akaike information criterion (AIC) and Bayesian information criterion (BIC) are statistics than can be used to compare the relative performance of multiple statistical models. Each handles the trade-off between goodness-of-fit and model complexity differently. See Burnham and Anderson (2004) for more details.

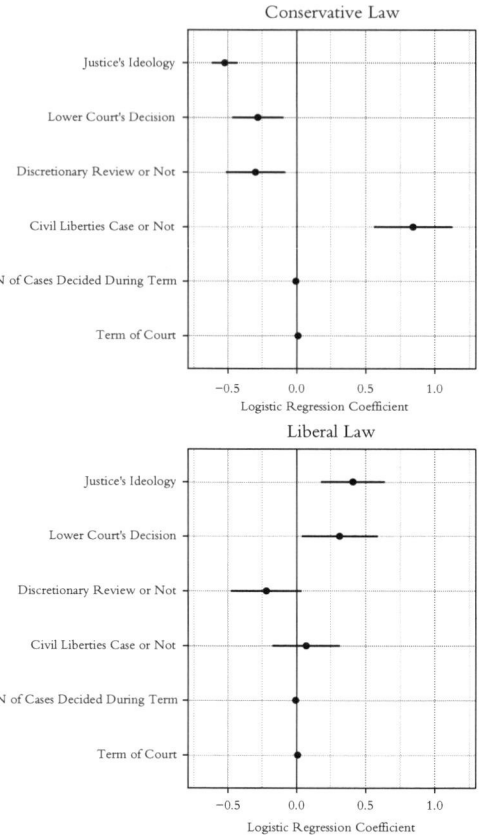

Figure 11.7 Nomograms depicting the results from Table 11.7's logistic regression analysis of whether individual justices vote to strike or uphold federal laws. Nomograms allow the reader to discern visually the estimated coefficients and the uncertainty around the estimates and to spot quickly whether the effects are statistically significant by looking at whether the confidence intervals cross zero.[52]

significance by noting whether the error bars cross zero. It is also easy to compare the relative magnitude of coefficients, if that's meaningful for the study.

11.2.2 Communicate Substantive Effects and Uncertainty about Those Effects

As researchers, we are inherently interested in whatever question we're investigating at the moment—to us, our work is exciting stuff.

---

[52] Data are from Epstein and Landes's (2012) study.

But conveying our results as we do in Table 11.7 and even in Figure 11.7 couldn't be less inviting to others. The displays of estimated coefficients that fill empirical legal articles, books, and reports aren't just ugly; they convey virtually no information of interest. Certainly, from the logistic regression analysis we could say "The estimated coefficient on Justice's Ideology of -0.524 for conservative laws means that as we move from the most conservative to the most liberal justice we move down 0.524 on a logit scale, controlling for all other variables." Because (almost) no one would understand what this means, we usually just write, "the coefficient on Justice's Ideology is statistically significant at the .05 level." But even this is not a very informative statement to our audience.[53]

In short, the way we typically present regression-based results only works to dampen enthusiasm for our research. We can do better. More to the point, we should want to do better. How? In Figure 11.8, we provide a process for moving from good to optimal communication.

As a first step, empiricists must ask themselves, "what substantively interesting features of our results do we want to convey to our readers?" In our running example of the Epstein and Landes's study, several quantities of interest come to mind, but to keep it simple we explore two: (1) the probability that a justice will invalidate a conservative law and (2) the probability that a justice will invalidate a liberal law. Communicating these probabilities is a start toward meeting Epstein and Landes's goal of engaging debates over whether left-leaning justices tend to invalidate conservative laws and right-leaning justices tend to invalidate liberal laws, as some commentators claim,[54] or whether justices embrace judicial self-restraint, leading them to uphold the constitutionality of a law even if it's at odds with their ideology, as others suggest.[55] It is also a rather straightforward way to begin the move away from a sole emphasis on statistical significance and toward a stress on substantive importance.

In Figure 11.8, under "Good Communication," we take this step by translating the inaccessible logit coefficients in Table 11.7 into substantively important quantities of interest: the odds of voting to invalidate

---

[53] See generally King et al. (2000); Gelman et al. (2002). Our inspiration for this section follows from their work, especially King et al.

[54] E.g., Weiden (2011); Solberg and Lindquist (2007); Lindquist and Cross (2009).

[55] E.g., Posner (2012), claiming that judicial self-restraint once existed but no longer does, having been supplanted first by exuberant liberal activism and later by constitutional theory.

Good Communication: Estimate A Key Quantity of Interest

Conservative Laws: Other things being equal, when a justice is extremely conservative, the likelihood of voting to invalidate a conservative law is 6%. That likelihood skyrockets to 80% when the justice is extremely liberal.

Liberal Laws: Other things being equal, when a justice is extremely conservative, the likelihood of voting to invalidate a liberal law is 41%. That likelihood plummets to 3% when the justice is extremely liberal.

Better Communication: Estimate A Key Quantity of Interest, Plus Uncertainty

Conservative Laws: Other things being equal, when a justice is extremely conservative, the likelihood of voting to invalidate a conservative law is 6% [3%–8%]. That likelihood skyrockets to 80% [73%–87%] when the justice is extremely liberal.

Liberal Laws: Other things being equal, when a justice is extremely conservative, the likelihood of voting to invalidate a liberal law is 41% [25%–58%]. That likelihood plummets to 3% [0%–6%] when the justice is extremely liberal.

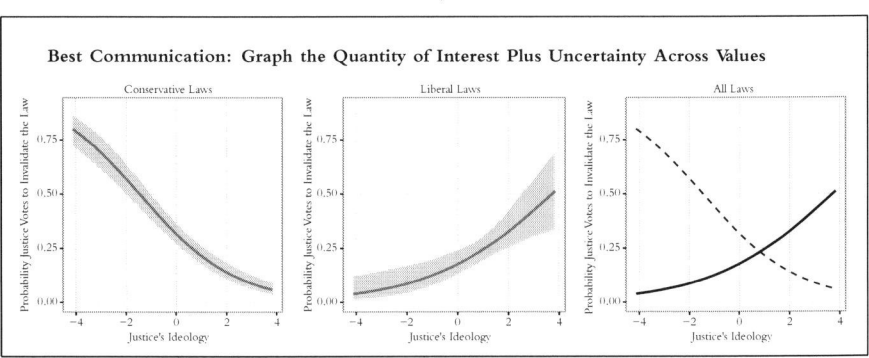

Figure 11.8 An illustration of moving from good to better communication of research results. Adapting this scheme to their own projects and needs should help researchers better relay their results. To generate the predicted probabilities and confidence intervals for varying levels of ideology, we hold all other variables at their mean or mode.

when a justice is extremely liberal (conservative) other things being equal. By this last phrase, as you know all too well by now, we mean that the other variables in the model are each set at a fixed value. For example, for the statement in Figure 11.8, we set Civil Liberties Case or Not at its mode (1 = yes, civil liberties case) and N of Cases Decided During Term at its mean. We did the same for Discretionary Review or Not (the mode is 1 = yes, discretionary review). But from our results we could just as easily have developed another counterfactual, such as the effect of Justice's Ideology for non-civil liberties cases. Alternatively, we could have shifted focus entirely and considered the effect of N of Cases Decided During Term when we hold Justice's Ideology at its mean, and said:

Other things being equal, when the number of cases is very high the likelihood of a justice invalidating a conservative law is 26%. The likelihood increases to 38% when the caseload is very low.

Estimating a quantity of interest is a good start. Even better communication entails conveying error around that estimate, as we show in Figure 11.8. Because we covered uncertainty and its importance in the last chapter, we need not go into detail here. Suffice it to note that most of us would be suspicious of a survey that failed to provide readers with the margin of error, or a table of regression estimates that omitted standard errors or confidence intervals. We should be equally skeptical of claims about substantive effects that fail to do so (via, e.g., confidence intervals).

To see why, consider two hypothetical versions of the claim above:

1. Other things being equal, when the number of cases is very high the likelihood of a justice invalidating a conservative law is 26%, though it could be as low as 22% or as high as 30%.
2. Other things being equal, when the number of cases is very high the likelihood of a justice invalidating a conservative law is 26%, though it could be as low 1% or as high as 60%.

In both examples, the (point) estimate of the impact of ideology is the same (26%) but our certainty about that estimate differs dramatically. So dramatically, in fact, that we should be highly skeptical of claim 2: because the confidence interval goes beyond 50% we cannot eliminate the real possibility of a vote to *invalidate* the law when the caseload is very high, even though the point estimate of 26% suggests the justice will uphold.

More generally, the statements above and in Figure 11.8 go some distance toward bridging the gap between researchers and their audience. Unlike the terms "statistical significance," "coefficient," or "0.05 level," "quantities of interest" and "error" are easy to understand

and, crucially, to evaluate even by our most statistically challenged readers.[56]

Even better, though, would be for researchers to take it to the next level and graph their results. The reason is this: however informative statements of the form we show in the first and second boxes of Figure 11.8 might be, they exclude a lot of information. In fact, all we learn is the probability of invalidation by *extremely conservative* or *extremely liberal* justices, and not the probability for the many justices in between. To provide these quantities, we could generate a long series of statements—what's the probability for a moderately conservative justice? A moderate justice? A moderate liberal? But why bother when graphing the range of probabilities is a far more parsimonious, and, for our readers, cognitively less demanding way to proceed.

Underscoring this point is the bottom display in Figure 11.8, reproduced in Figure 11.9. Here we show the probability of a justice voting to invalidate a conservative law (panel 1) and a liberal law (panel 2) across the range of Justice's Ideology. In both panels we use vertical lines to depict the 95% confidence intervals (our measure of uncertainty). To avoid cluttering the third panel, we eliminate the confidence intervals and simply show the two sets of probabilities.

This display, we believe, is a good example of what we mean by parsimony. It efficiently conveys a great deal of information; it would take about 200 sentences to describe each and every result depicted in the three panels.[57]

A second and perhaps even more important virtue of graphing results centers on pattern detection. From the display in Figure 11.9, several results are immediately apparent. For example, in the last panel the dashed line (liberal laws) appears far steeper than the solid line (conservative), possibly indicating that liberal justices are more strike happy than conservative justices.[58]

---

[56] King et al. (2000, 359–60) make this point, and we adopt it here.

[57] Each line shows the predicted probabilities for 100 data points, along with the lower and upper bounds for the confidence intervals for each.

[58] We say "possibly" because any comparison would need to assume an equal number of opportunities to invalidate conservative and liberal laws—an assumption that the data do not meet. Between the 1937 and 2009 terms, the Court reviewed the constitutionality of 809 more conservative laws than liberal laws. See the *n*s in Table 11.7.

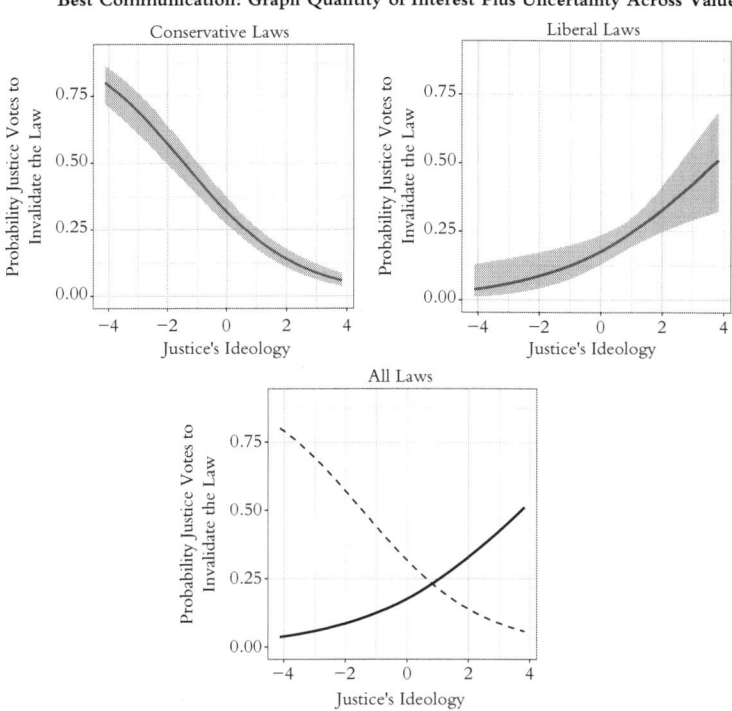

Figure 11.9 Reproduction of the final panel in Figure 11.8. Here, we use Epstein and Landes's models (in Table 11.7) to show the probability of a justice voting to invalidate a conservative law (panel 1) and a liberal law (panel 2) across the range of `Justice's Ideology`. In both panels we depict our uncertainty, in the form of 95% confidence intervals, with grey shading. To avoid cluttering the third panel, we eliminate the confidence intervals and simply show the two sets of probabilities.

11.2.3 How to Communicate Substantive Effects and Uncertainty

To us, the advantages of the kinds of statements and graphs we depict in Figure 11.8 are obvious. Readers need not struggle to make sense of regression estimates that even the analyst may have trouble understanding. Nor are critical questions left dangling, such as "are the results really important?" and "how sure is the researcher about the findings?". As we have stressed throughout, the advantages for analysts are equally obvious, ranging from the detection of patterns in their work to the ability to impart their own excitement to their audience.

If there is a downside for authors, it is that communicating quantities of interest and uncertainty requires more time and thought. To see why, think about current practice: the researcher estimates a regression model, hopefully performs some diagnostic checks, and then cuts and pastes the resulting table into a word processing file. End of story. As Figure 11.8 suggests, much more is needed—and the "more" mandates that researchers learn about procedures enabling them to estimate substantive effects and measures of uncertainty. We remain catholic about the best tools for the job, but we can say that nearly all our suggestions can be implemented using common statistical software, such at Stata and R. Three (free!) add-on packages that make calculating effects and uncertainty easy are CLARIFY[59] and SPost[60] for Stata, and Zelig[61] for the R language.

Whatever statistical package you decide to employ, it is the more general message that we hope you don't miss: estimating a model should not complete your research task. Similar thought and care should be used to communicate effectively the results of a study.

* * * * * * * *

Here and in Chapter 10 we adapted the burgeoning literature in the social and statistical sciences to the unique interests of legal scholars all in an effort to offer guidance about conveying data and results. We have been prescriptive because we believe the benefits of following our guidelines well outweigh their costs. Sure, empiricists must now familiarize themselves with a new set of tools for presenting their work, but once they do so numerous advantages will accrue. Because they will be better situated to detect patterns in their own data, their work will improve; because their audience will be better able to understand their work, its impact will be greater. If other fields are any indication, moving toward more appropriate and accessible presentations of data will heighten the impact of empirical legal scholarship regardless of the audience—no doubt a desirable goal in a discipline that rightfully prides itself on its contributions to the formation of law and public policy.

These should be sufficient incentives for change.

[59] <http://gking.harvard.edu/clarify/docs/clarify.html>.
[60] <http://www.indiana.edu/~jslsoc/spost.htm>.
[61] <http://gking.harvard.edu/zelig/>.

12

Concluding Remarks

For some of you, your journey into empirical legal research has come to an end; for others, it is just beginning.

To those in the first group, we say this: congratulations! If you have read this book all the way through, you now know enough to navigate and begin to evaluate many kinds of empirical studies, or, at the very least, to formulate questions that you can put to the studies' authors.

To provide an example, suppose you were confronted with the results of a regression model that was estimated by an expert hired by black employees suing a company for race discrimination—specifically, the employees allege that they were paid less than white workers.[1] Further suppose that the expert testifies that his regression model turned up a statistically significant difference between the salaries of black and white employees after controlling for two other independent variables: (1) job performance appraisals and (2) time in position.

What would you want to know? Here are some of the questions you should now feel confident asking:

- How did the expert define the population and how did he draw his sample?
- From where did the data come? What was the specific data collection protocol, and what steps did the expert take to minimize mistakes?
- What are the precise statistical assumptions that are needed to trust the conclusions the expert is drawing from his analysis?

---

[1] We base this example on *EEOC v. International Business Machines, Corp.*, 583 F. Supp. 875, 906 (D. Md. 1984). See also, Norris (1987).

- What is the effect size, and how certain is the expert of it? How did he determine statistical significance? At what significance level?
- How would the results change if other variables were included in the analysis, such as seniority and job level?[2]
- Are the assumptions of the linear regression model reasonable? Is the relationship linear? Do the residuals follow a normal distribution?
- Are there outliers in the dataset that might be driving the findings?

Asking these and other questions can sometimes show that a regression has "as many bloody wounds as Julius Caesar when he was stabbed 23 times by the Roman Senators led by Brutus," as Judge Richard A. Posner said of a regression analysis at issue in one of his cases.[3] Writing in the same case, Judge Posner also noted:

[N]either party's lawyers, judging from the trial transcript and . . . the briefs and oral argument in this court, understand regression analysis; or if they do understand it they are unable to communicate their understanding in plain English.[4]

Having finished this book, we hope you can do better than the lawyers (and the lower court judge[5]) in this case!

To those readers who want to continue on, we say: great! As we noted at the outset, we conceptualize *An Introduction to Empirical Legal*

---

[2] In this case, the employees' expert did not include seniority and job level. It turns out, though, that these are "significant determinants of success" at this company: when these two other factors are taken into account, the company's expert showed that the racial differences disappear (see Norris 1987, 906).

[3] *ATA Airlines v. Federal Express Corp.*, 665 F.3d 882, 895 (7th Cir. 2011).

[4] *ATA Airlines v. Federal Express Corp.*, 665 F.3d 882, 889 (7th Cir. 2011).

[5] Judge Posner also took the lower court judge to task:

Th[e] cursory, and none too clear, response to [the other side's objection to the] regression analysis did not discharge the duty of a district judge to evaluate in advance of trial a challenge to the admissibility of an expert's proposed testimony. The evaluation of such a challenge may not be easy; the "principles and methods" used by expert witnesses will often be difficult for a judge to understand. But difficult is not impossible. The judge can require the lawyer who wants to offer the expert's testimony to explain to the judge in plain English what the basis and logic of the proposed testimony are, and the judge can likewise require the opposing counsel to explain his objections in plain English.

If counsel are incapable of so doing (as apparently was the case here), Judge Posner suggested that "a judge can always appoint his own expert to assist him in understanding and evaluating the proposed testimony of a party's expert. . . . If he worries that the expert he appoints may not be truly neutral, he can ask the parties' experts to agree on a neutral expert for him to appoint": *ATA Airlines v. Federal Express Corp.*, 665 F.3d 882, 889 (7th Cir. 2011).

Research as a primer. Mastering all the topics we covered requires far more training, and we're glad you want to seek it.

What do you need to be trained in? Two areas come to mind. First, if you want to embark on an original data-collection project, you'll need to master whatever method you intend to use. Not only would it be foolish to, say, field a survey or perform an experiment without more knowledge, you'd be wasting time and resources, as Chapter 4 suggests.[6]

The other area is even more obvious—methods for analyzing data. We hope we've provided you with a solid foundation for understanding regression but you'll need to build on it if you want to estimate models with the care they deserve and require. As we noted in Chapter 9, we recommend additional training on regression diagnostics, methods to assess model fit, and the treatment of independent variables (including interactions). From there, you might consider more work on the collection of models that are tailored for non-interval level dependent variables. We mentioned some in Chapter 9—logit, probit, multino-minial logit, and survival models—but there are others. Beyond these, there are a series of topics that may be worth your time depending on the kinds of data you use. These include: ecological inference, Bayesian inference, time series, and matching methods.[7]

We recommend three approaches to obtaining additional training. First, you could "go it alone" as you did by reading this book. Our website <http://empiricallegalresearch.org> houses an up-to-date bibliography that highlights our favorite books and websites that you could consult. A second approach is to pursue additional training through workshops or formal courses. There are many options, including the workshops that we regularly co-teach.[8] And just about every social science department offers a menu of introductory and advanced methodology courses. We recommend starting with a comprehensive review of basic statistics followed by advanced courses on regression and related methods. Finally, there's collaboration. Co-authorship is the norm in the social sciences and is becoming more common in law.

---

[6] In Chapter 4 we also offer suggestions on where you can get help along these lines.

[7] See Chapter 9 for others.

[8] E.g., Conducting Empirical Legal Scholarship Workshop, at: <http://cerl.wustl.edu/training/cels14.php>. We occasionally offer an advanced workshop as well.

If you look around it shouldn't be hard to find someone, whether a consultant, faculty colleague, or even an advanced graduate student, who would be interested in working with you on an empirical project. You'd bring rich substantive knowledge and your collaborator, research design and methodological expertise, though we'd like to think that we've provided you with a sufficient background and vocabulary to contribute productively on that end too.

* * * * * * * *

If our underlying message is not clear by now let it be: we can't help but believe that more and better empirical research will lead to substantial improvements in legal scholarship, judicial opinions, and public policy. Having now come to the end of this book we only hope you agree. Thanks for reading.

Appendix A

Supplementary Materials

A.1 Additional Resources

Because supplementary material can date so quickly, we've developed a website that houses lots of resources to help you execute and evaluate empirical studies.[1] (See the Preface for the particulars.) The website also contains everything you need to replicate all the analyses in the book.

A.2 Statistics Glossary

In Part III we introduced many statistical terms that you might find unfamiliar. We've compiled a glossary for your reference when reading the book or other studies. (These are not technical definitions so please don't treat them as such.[2]) Following the glossary is a list of the statistical notation we used in Part III.

- **alternative hypothesis** – in hypothesis testing, the conclusion we draw if we reject a null hypothesis.
- **χ^2-test (chi-squared test)** – a test of statistical independence for cross-tabulations. The null hypothesis is that the variables are statistically independent.
- **coefficient** – a number that is multiplied by another number; in linear regression, we often refer to the slope coefficient.
- **confidence interval** – an interval that is computed from sample data that contains the population parameter a fixed percentage of the time (the confidence level) given repeated sampling.
- **confidence level** – when computing a confidence interval, the percentage of the time we would expect our confidence interval to contain the population parameter given repeated sampling.
- **cross-tabulation** – a table created from two categorical variables.

---

[1] <http://empiricallegalresearch.org>.
[2] For technical definitions, please consult a statistics text, such as Agresti and Finlay (2009).

- **dummy variable** – a variable that takes only values zero or one.
- **estimator** – a procedure, often a formula, for estimating (or "guessing") a parameter value.
- **graphics** – pictures of various types used to display data.
- **histogram** – a graphic that provides a visual representation of the distribution of an interval variable.
- **hypothesis testing** – a procedure used to determine whether sample data are consistent or highly inconsistent with a hypothesized parameter.
- **intercept** – a parameter estimated in a linear regression model. It captures the expected value of Y when $X = 0$. The population intercept is denoted α; it is estimated by $\hat{\alpha}$.
- **interval** – a quantitative variable that is measured on a "real" scale (e.g., income in dollars, temperature, etc.).
- **linear regression** – a statistical model that allows us to explore the linear relationship between an interval dependent variable and an independent variable. When there is just a single independent variable, we call it simple linear regression.
- **logistic regression** – a regression-type model used when the dependent variable takes the values zero or one (e.g., yes/no).
- **mean** – the average of a set of observations. The population mean is denoted μ, and the sample mean is denoted $\bar{Y}$.
- **median** – a measure of central tendency that is the 50th percentile.
- **mode** – the most frequently occurring observation in a dataset.
- **multiple regression** – a statistical model used to estimate the relationship between one dependent variable and one or more independent variables. It performs statistical control on the fly, and so is the most commonly used model in the social sciences.
- **nominal** – a qualitative variable that consists of unordered categories (e.g., region or gender).
- **null hypothesis** – in hypothesis testing, the hypothesis we typically wish to disprove.
- **one sample t-test** – a test to determine whether the sample mean differs from a hypothesized sample mean.
- **ordinal** – a quantitative variable that is not on a "real" scale (e.g., income coded as low, medium, or high).
- **ordinary least squares (OLS)** – a method used to estimate the slope and intercept parameters of a linear regression model.
- **outlier** – an unusual observation.
- **p-value** – a quantity computed from a test statistic. A p-value is the probability, assuming that the null hypothesis is true, that a random sample from the population would generate a test statistic as far away or further from the hypothesized value than the one observed. We can reject the null hypothesis when a p-value is small.

- **parameter** – a characteristic of the population. For example, μ is the population mean.
- **population** – a collection of "things" we would like to learn about; e.g., all eligible voters in Poland.
- R^2 **(R-squared)** – a measure of model fit for the linear regression model. It is the percentage of the variance in Y explained by the regression model. Sometimes called the coefficient of determination.
- **regression diagnostics** – a set of procedures undertaken after fitting a linear regression model to help assess the appropriateness of model assumptions.
- **residual** – in a regression model, the distance between each point and the regression line. It's the amount that's left over.
- **robust** – an estimator is said to be robust if it is not sensitive to changes in small numbers of observations.
- **sample** – a random subset of the population that we use to learn about a population; e.g., a random sample of $n = 1000$ eligible voters in the United States.
- **sampling distribution** – the distribution of a statistic due to chance alone under repeated sampling.
- **scatterplot** – a graphic that shows how two interval variables are related.
- **simple linear regression** – a statistical model used to model the relationship between two interval variables.
- **slope** – a parameter estimated in a linear regression model. It captures the expected increase in Y for a one unit increase in X. The population slope is denoted β; it is estimated by $\hat{\beta}$.
- **standard deviation** – a measure of dispersion of a distribution. The population standard deviation is denoted σ, and the sample standard deviation is denoted s.
- **standard error** – the standard deviation of a sampling distribution.
- **standard error of the estimate (SEE)** – the standard deviation of the residuals in a linear regression model. "Small" standard errors of the estimate imply a "good" model fit. The standard error of the estimate is often denoted $\hat{\sigma}$, and is sometimes called the root mean square error or the conditional standard deviation.
- **statistic** – a quantity computed using data from a sample. Statistics are typically used to estimate a parameter. For example, the sample mean $\bar{Y}$ is used to estimate the population mean.
- **statistical inference** – the process of learning about population parameters given a sample.
- **statistical significance** – when we reject a null hypothesis, we conclude that there is a statistically significant relationship.
- **statistically independent** – two variables that are not related are said to be statistically independent. This is the null hypothesis for the chi-squared test.

- **test statistic** – a statistic computed from a sample used to conduct a hypothesis test. Test statistics are different for every test.
- **time series data** – data collected on a single unit over time; e.g., a daily stock price for an individual stock.
- **two sample t-test** – a test to determine whether the sample mean of one group is different from the sample mean of another group.
- **variable** – a characteristic that can vary among "things" in a population or sample.

A.3 Statistical Notation

- μ (mu) – population mean
- $\bar{Y}$ (y bar) – sample mean
- n – sample size
- s – sample standard deviation
- σ (sigma) – population standard deviation
- H_0 (h naught) – null hypothesis
- H_1 (h sub one) – alternative hypothesis
- p – p-value
- χ^2 (chi-squared) – test statistic for tables
- α (alpha) – intercept parameter in a linear regression model
- β (beta) – slope parameter in a linear regression model
- R^2 (R-squared) – coefficient of determination

References

Achen, Christopher H. (2005). Let's put garbage-can regressions and garbage-can probits where they belong. *Conflict Management and Peace Science*, **22**, 237–339.

Adcock, Robert and Collier, David (2001). Measurement validity: A shared standard for qualitative and quantitative research. *American Political Science Review*, **95**, 529–46.

Agresti, Alan (2007). *An Introduction to Categorial Data Analysis* (2nd edn). Wiley-Interscience, New York.

Agresti, Alan and Finlay, Barbara (2009). *Statistical Methods for the Social Sciences* (4th edn). Prentice Hall: Upper Saddle River, NJ.

Allen, James (1994). *Natural Language Processing* (2nd edn). Addison-Wesley: Redwood City, CA.

Alm, James, McClelland, Gary H., and Schulze, William D. (1992). Why do people pay taxes? *Journal of Public Economics*, **48**, 21–38.

Alter, Karen J. (2008). Agents or trustees? International courts in their political context. *European Journal of International Relations*, **14**, 33–63.

Andrade, Flavia Cristina Drumond, Raffaelli, Marcela, Teran-Garcia, Margarita, Jerman, Jilber A., and Garcia, Celia Aradillas (2012). Weight status misperception among Mexican young adults. *Body Image*, **9**, 184–8.

Anscombe, F. J. (1973). Graphs in statistical analysis. *The American Statistician*, **27**, 17–21.

Ansolabehere, Stephen and Hersh, Eitan (2012). Validation: What big data reveal about survey misreporting and the real electorate. *Political Analysis*, **20**, 437–59.

Armour, John, Deakin, Simon, Lele, Priya, and Siems, Mathias M. (2009). How do legal rules evolve? Evidence from a cross-country comparison of shareholder, creditor and worker protection. *American Journal of Comparative Law*, **57**, 579–629.

Aspin, Larry T. and Hall, William K. (1994). Retention elections and judicial behavior. *Judicature*, **77**, 306–15.

Atkins, Burton (1990). Interventions and power in judicial hierarchies: Appellate courts in England and the United States. *Law & Society Review*, **24**, 71–104.

Austin, Peter C. and Hux, Janet E. (2002). A brief note on overlapping confidence intervals. *Journal of Vascular Surgery*, **36**, 194–5.

Axinn, William G. and Pearce, Lisa D. (2007). *Mixed Method Data Collection Strategies*. Cambridge University Press: New York, NY.

Babbie, Earl R. (2009). *The Practice of Social Research*. Wadsworth: Belmont, CA.

Baird, Vanessa A. and Javeline, Debra (2007). The persuasive power of Russian courts. *Political Research Quarterly*, **60**, 429–42.

Barro, Robert J. (1996). Democracy and growth. *Journal of Economic Growth*, **1**, 1–27.

Bates, Robert, Greif, Avner, Levi, Margaret, Laurent Rosenthal, Jean, and Weingast, Barry R. (1998). *Analytic Narratives*. Princeton University Press: Princeton, NJ.

Bayley, David H. and Garofalo, James (1989). The management of violence by police patrol officers. *Criminology*, **27**, 1–26.

Beck, Colin J., Drori, Gili S., and Meyer, John W. (2012). World influences on human rights language in constitutions: A cross-national study. *International Sociology*, **27**, 483–501.

Berdejó, Carlos and Yuchtman, Noam M. (2013). Crime, punishment, and politics: An analysis of political cycles in criminal sentencing. *Review of Economics and Statistics*, **95**, 741–56.

Bertin, Jacques (1981). *Graphics and Graphic Information*. W. de Gruyter: Berlin.

Bertrand, Marianne and Mullainathan, Sendhil (2001). Do people mean what they say? Implications for subjective survey data. *American Economic Review*, **91**, 67–72.

Bird, Steven, Klein, Ewan, and Loper, Edward (2009). *Natural Language Processing with Python*. O'Reilly Media: Cambridge, MA.

Blackstone, William (1769). *Commentaries on the laws of England*. Vol. 4. Clarendon Press: Oxford, UK.

Bornstein, Brian H. (1999). The ecological validity of jury simulations: Is the jury still out? *Law and Human Behavior*, **23**, 75–91.

Bourque, Linda B. (2007). Coding. In *Encyclopedia of Social Science Research Methods* (ed. M. S. Lewis-Beck, A. Bryman, and T. F. Liao). Sage: Thousand Oaks, CA.

Box-Steffensmeier, Janet M. and Jones, Bradford S. (2004). *Event History Modeling: A Guide for Social Scientists*. Cambridge University Press: Cambridge, MA.

Boyd, Christina L., Epstein, Lee, and Martin, Andrew D. (2010). Untangling the causal effect of sex on judging. *American Journal of Political Science*, **54**, 389–411.

Boylan, Richard T. (2012). The effect of punishment severity on plea bargaining. *Journal of Law and Economics*, **55**, 565–91.

Bradburn, Norman M., Sudman, Seymour, and Wansink, Brian (2004). *Asking Questions: The Definitive Guide to Questionnaire Design—For Market Research, Political Polls, and Social and Health Questionnaires* (revised edn). Jossey-Bass: San Francisco, CA.

Braman, Eileen (2009). *Law, Politics and Perception: How Policy Preferences Influence Legal Reasoning*. University of Virginia Press: Charlottesville, VA.

Brewer, Noel T., Gilkey, Melissa B., Lillie, Sarah E., Hesse, Bradford W., and Sheridan, Stacey L. (2012). Tables or bar graphs? Presenting test results in electronic medical records. *Medical Decision Making*, **32**, 545–53.

Breyer, Stephen (2000). Introduction. In *Reference Manual on Scientific Evidence*. Federal Judicial Center: Washington, D.C.

Brians, Craig Leonard, Willnat, Lars, Manheim, Jarol B., and Rich, Richard C. (2010). *Empirical Political Analysis*. Pearson: New Jersey.

Buccafusco, Christopher and Sprigman, Christopher (2010). Valuing intellectual property. *Cornell Law Review*, **96**, 1–45.

Burnham, Kenneth P. and Anderson, David R. (2004). Multimodel inference: Understanding the aic and bic in model selection. *Sociological Research and Methods*, **33**, 261–304.

Caldeira, Gregory A. (1985). The transmission of legal precedent: A study of state supreme courts. *American Political Science Review*, **79**, 178–94.

Caldeira, Gregory A., Wright, John R., and Zorn, Christopher J. (1999). Sophisticated voting and gate-keeping in the Supreme Court. *Journal of Law, Economics, & Organization*, **15**, 549–72.

Cameron, Charles M. and Park, Jee-Kwang (2009). How will they vote? Predicting the future behavior of Supreme Court nominees, 1937–2006. *Journal of Empirical Legal Studies*, **6**, 485–511.

Caminker, Evan H. (1994). Why must inferior courts obey superior court precedents? *Stanford Law Review*, **46**, 817–73.

Cane, Peter and Kritzer, Herbert M. (2010). Introduction. In *The Oxford Handbook of Empirical Legal Research* (eds. P. Cane and H. M. Kritzer). Oxford University Press: Oxford, UK.

Canes-Wrone, Brandice, Clark, Tom S., and Park, Jee-Kwang (2012). Judicial independence and retention elections. *Journal of Law, Economics, & Organization*, **28**, 211–34.

Canon, Bradley C. and Johnson, Charles A. (1999). *Judicial Policies: Implementation and Impact*. CQ Press: Washington, DC.

Carroll, Royce and Tiede, Lydia (2011). Judicial behavior on the Chilean constitutional tribunal. *Journal of Empirical Legal Studies*, **8**, 856–77.

Casillas, Christopher J., Enns, Peter K., and Wohlfarth, Patrick C. (2011). How public opinion constrains the U.S. Supreme Court. *American Journal of Political Science*, **55**, 74–88.

Clark, Charles E. and Shulman, Harry (1937). *A Study of Law Administration in Connecticut: A Report of an Investigation of the Activities of Certain Trial Courts of the State*. Yale University Press: New Haven, CT.

Clark, Linda L. (2008). *Women and Achievement in Nineteenth-Century Europe*. Cambridge University Press: New York, NY.

Clark, Tom S. (2006). Judicial decision making during wartime. *Journal of Empirical Legal Studies*, **3**, 397–419.

Clark, Tom S. (2011). *The Limits of Judicial Independence*. Cambridge University Press: New York, NY.

Clark, Tom S. and Whittington, Keith E. (2009). Ideology, partisanship, and judicial review of acts of Congress, 1789–2006, <http://papers.ssrn.com/sol3/papers.cfm?abstract_id=1475660>.

Clarke, Kevin A. (2005). The phantom menace: Omitted variable bias in econometric research. *Conflict Management and Peace Science*, **22**, 341–52.

Cleveland, William S. (1993). *Visualizing Data*. Hobart Press: Summit, NJ.

Cleveland, William S. (1994). *The Elements of Graphing Data*. Hobart Press: Summit, NJ.

Cleveland, William S. and McGill, Robert (1984). Graphical perception: Theory, experimentation, and application to the development of graphical methods. *Journal of the American Statistical Association*, **79**, 531–54.

Coates IV, John C. (2012). Corporate politics, governance, and value before and after *Citizens United*. *Journal of Empirical Legal Studies*, **9**, 657–95.

Cogan, Jacob Katz (2012). The 2011 judicial activity of the International Court of Justice. *American Journal of International Law*, **106**, 586–608.

Cohen, Jacob (1960). A coefficient of agreement for nominal scales. *Educational and Psychological Measurement*, **20**, 37–46.

Cole, Michael (2004). Ecological validity. In *The SAGE Encyclopedia of Social Science Research Methods* (eds. M. S. Lewis-Beck, A. Bryman, and T. F. Liao). Sage: Thousand Oaks, CA.

Colker, Ruth and Scott, Kevin M. (2002). Dissing states?: Invalidation of state action during the Rehnquist era. *Virginia Law Review*, **88**, 1301–86.

Collier, David and Adcock, David (1999). Democracy and dichotomies: A pragmatic approach to choices about concepts. *Annual Review of Political Science*, **2**, 537–65.

Corley, Pamela C., Steigerwolt, A., and Ward, A. (2013). *The Puzzle of Unanimity*. Stanford University Press: Stanford, CA.

Costigan-Eaves, Patricia and Macdonald-Ross, Michael (1990). William Playfair (1759–1823). *Statistical Science*, **5**, 318–26.

Couper, Mick P. (2011). The future of modes of data collection. *Public Opinion Quarterly*, **75**, 889–908.

Cumming, Geoff and Finch, Sue (2005). Inference by eye: Confidence intervals and how to read pictures of data. *American Psychologist*, **60**, 170–18.

Davenport, Christian and Armstrong, II, David A. (2004). Democracy and the violation of human rights: A statistical analysis from 1976 to 1996. *American Journal of Political Science*, **48**, 538–54.

de Bertodano, Sylvia (2002). Judicial independence in the International Criminal Court. *Leiden Journal of International Law*, **15**, 409–30.

DeGroot, Morris H. and Schervish, Mark J. (2012). *Probability and Statistics* (4th edn). Addison-Wesley: Boston, MA.

DeVellis, Robert F. (2011). *Scale Development: Theory and Applications* (3rd edn). Sage: Thousand Oaks, CA.

Dezhbakshs, Hashem and Rubin, Paul H. (1998). Lives saved or lives lost? The effects of concealed-handgun laws on crime. *American Economic Review*, **88**, 468–74.

Diamond, Shari Seidman (2007). Juror response to scientific and other expert testimony and how judges can help. *Journal of Law & Policy*, **16**, 46–67.

Diamond, Shari Seidman (2011). Reference guide on survey research. In *Reference Manual on Scientific Evidence* (3rd edn). National Academies Press: Washington, DC.

Diamond, Shari Seidman, Rose, Mary R., Murphy, Beth, and Meixner, John (2011). Damage anchors on real juries. *Journal of Empirical Legal Studies*, **8**, 148–78.

Diamond, Shari Seidman, Vidmar, Neil, Rose, Mary, Ellis, Leslie, and Murphy, Beth (2003). Inside the jury room: Evaluating juror discussions during trial. *Judicature*, **87**, 54–8.

Djankov, Simeon, Glaeser, Edward, La Porta, Rafael, de Silanes, Florencio López, and Shleifer, Andrei (2003). The new comparative economics. *Journal of Comparative Economics*, **31**, 595–619.

Djankov, Simeon, Porta, Rafael La, de Silanes, Florencio López, and Shleifer, Andrei (2002). The regulation of entry. *Quarterly Journal of Economics*, **117**, 1–37.

Dodge, Yadolah (2006). *The Oxford Dictionary of Statistical Terms* (6th edn). Oxford University Press: Oxford.

Dolan, Paul and Peasgood, Tessa (2008). Legal implications of the new research on happiness. *Journal of Legal Studies*, **37**, 5–31.

Dougherty, Chrys and Jorgenson, Dale W. (1996). International comparisons of the sources of economic growth. *American Economic Review*, **86**, 25–9.

Dowling, Tracy Solomon (2008). Mandating a human papillomavirus vaccine: An investigation into whether such legislation is constitutional and prudent. *American Journal of Law & Medicine*, **34**, 65–84.

Drago, Francesco, Galbiati, Roberto, and Vertova, Pietro (2009). The deterrent effects of prison: Evidence from a natural experiment. *Journal of Political Economy*, **117**, 257–80.

Driscoll, Amanda and Nelson, Michael J. (2012). The 2011 judicial elections in Bolivia. *Electoral Studies*, **31**, 628–32.

D'Souza, Dinesh (1995). *The End of Racism*. Free Press: New York, NY.

Duggan, Mark, Hjalmarsson, Randi, and Jacob, Brian A. (2011). The short-term and localized effect of gun shows: Evidence from California and Texas. *Review of Economics and Statistics*, **93**, 786–99.

Dunning, Thad (2012). *Natural Experiments in the Social Sciences: A Design-Based Approach*. Cambridge University Press: Cambridge, MA.

Eekelaar, John, Maclean, Mavis, and Beinart, Sarah (2000). *Family Lawyers: How Solicitors Deal with Divorcing Clients*. Hart Publishing: Oxford, UK.

Efron, Bradley (1981). Nonparametric estimates of the standard error: The jackknife, the bootstrap, and other methods. *Biometrika*, **68**, 589–99.

Eigen, Zev J. (2012). When and why individuals obey contracts: Experimental evidence of consent, compliance, promise, and performance. *Journal of Legal Studies*, **41**, 67–93.

Elkins, Zachary, Ginsburg, Tom, and Melton, James (2009). *The Endurance of National Constitutions*. Cambridge University Press: New York, NY.

Epstein, Cynthia Fuchs (1981). *Women in Law*. Basic Books: New York, NY.

Epstein, Lee (1995). Studying law and courts. In *Contemplating Courts* (ed. L. Epstein). CQ Press: Washington, DC.

Epstein, Lee and Clarke, Charles (2010). Academic integrity and legal scholarship in the wake of *Exxon Shipping*, Footnote 17. *Stanford Law & Policy Review*, **21**, 33–50.

Epstein, Lee and King, Gary (2002). The rules of inference. *University of Chicago Law Review*, **69**, 1–133.

Epstein, Lee and Knight, Jack (1998). *The Choices Justices Make*. CQ Press: Washington, DC.

Epstein, Lee and Landes, William M. (2012). Was there ever such a thing as judicial self-restraint? *California Law Review*, **100**, 557–78.

Epstein, Lee and Martin, Andrew D. (2005). Coding variables. In *Handbook of Social Measurement* (ed. K. Kempf-Leonard). Academic Press: Boston, MA.

Epstein, Lee and Martin, Andrew D. (2010). Quantitative approaches to empirical legal research. In *Oxford Handbook on Empirical Legal Studies* (eds. P. Cane and H. Kritzer). Oxford University Press: Oxford, UK.

Epstein, Lee, Ho, Daniel E., King, Gary, and Segal, Jeffrey A. (2005). The Supreme Court during crisis. *NYU Law Review*, **80**, 1–116.

Epstein, Lee, Landes, William M., and Posner, Richard A. (2013). *The Behavior of Federal Judges*. Harvard University Press: Cambridge, MA.

Epstein, Lee, Martin, Andrew D., and Boyd, Christina L. (2007). On the effective communication of the results of empirical studies, Part II. *Vanderbilt Law Review*, **60**, 801–46.

Epstein, Lee, Martin, Andrew D., and Schneider, Matthew M. (2006). On the effective communication of the results of empirical studies, Part I. *Vanderbilt Law Review*, **59**, 1811–71.

Epstein, Lee, Segal, Jeffrey A., Spaeth, Harold J., and Walker, Thomas G. (2012). *The Supreme Court Compendium*. Congressional Quarterly Press: Washington, DC.

Erickson, Rosemary J. and Simon, Rita J. (1998). *The Use of Social Science Data in Supreme Court Decisions*. University of Illinois Press: Urbana, IL.

Eskridge, William N. (1991). Reneging on history? Playing the Court/Congress/President civil rights game. *California Law Review*, **79**, 613–84.

Farber, Daniel A. and Frickey, Philip P. (1992). Foreword: Positive political theory in the nineties. *Georgetown Law Journal*, **80**, 457–76.

Feld, Lars P. and Voigt, Stefan (2003). Economic growth and judicial independence: Cross-country evidence using a new set of indicators. *European Journal of Political Economy*, **19**, 497–523.

Finkelstein, Michael O. (2009). *Basic Concepts of Probability and Statistics in the Law*. Springer: New York, NY.

Finkelstein, Michael O. and Levin, Bruce (2001). *Statistics for Lawyers*. Springer: New York, NY.

Fischer, Martin H. (2000). Do irrelevant depth cues affect the comprehension of bar graphs? *Applied Cognitive Psychology*, **14**, 151–62.

Flemming, Roy B. (2004). *Tournament of Appeals: Granting Judicial Review in Canada*. UBC Press: Vancouver, BC.

Fowler, Floyd Jackson (1992). How unclear terms affect survey data. *Public Opinion Quarterly*, **36**, 218–31.

Fox, John (2008). *Applied Regression Analysis and Generalized Linear Models* (2nd edn). Sage: Los Angeles, CA.

Franck, Raphaël (2009). Judicial independence under a divided polity: A study of the rulings of the French Constitutional Court, 1959–2006. *Journal of Law, Economics, & Organization*, **25**, 262–84.

Franck, Thomas (1995). *Fairness in International Law and Institutions*. Oxford University Press: New York, NY.

Frankel, Jeffrey A. and Romer, David (1999). Does trade cause growth? *American Economic Review*, **89**, 379–99.

Frankfort-Nachmias, Chava and Nachmias, David (2008). *Research Methods in the Social Sciences* (7th edn). Worth Publishers: New York, NY.

Frankfurter, Felix and Landis, James M. (1928). *The Business of the Supreme Court: A Study in the Federal Judicial System*. Macmillan: New York, NY.

Freedman, David, Pisani, Robert, and Purves, Roger (2007). *Statistics* (4th edn). Norton: New York, NY.

Friedman, Daniel and Sunder, Shyam (1994). *Experimental Methods: A Primer for Economists*. Cambridge University Press: Cambridge, UK.

Friedman, Lawrence M. (1998). Law reviews and legal scholarship: Some comments. *Denver University Law Review*, **75**, 661–8.

Friendly, Michael (1994). Mosaic displays for multi-way contingency tables. *Journal of the American Statistical Association*, **89**, 190–200.

Friendly, Michael and Wainer, Howard (2004). Nobody's perfect. *Chance*, **17**, 51–4.

Galton, Francis (1885). Presidential address, Section H, Anthropology. *Report of the British Association for the Advancement of Science*, **55**, 1206–14.

Garoupa, Nuno M., Gomez-Pomar, Fernando, and Grembi, Veronica (2013). Judging under political pressure: An empirical analysis of constitutional review voting in the Spanish Constitutional Court. *Journal of Law, Economics, & Organization*, **29**, 513–4.

Garoupa, Nuno M., Grembi, Veronica, and Lin, Shirley Ching Ping (2011). Explaining constitutional review in new democracies: The case of Taiwan. *Pacific Rim Law & Policy Journal*, **20**, 1–40.

Garrett, Geoffrey and Weingast, Barry (1993). Ideas, interests and institutions: Constructing the EC's internal market. In *Ideas and Foreign Policy: Beliefs, Institutions, and Political Change* (eds. J. Goldstein and R. O. Keohane). Cornell University Press: Ithaca, NY.

Gelman, Andrew (2011). Why tables are really much better than graphs. *Journal of Computational and Graphical Statistics*, **20**, 3–7.

Gelman, Andrew and Hill, Jennifer (2007). *Data Analysis Using Regression and Multilevel/Hierarchical Models*. Cambridge University Press: New York, NY.

Gelman, Andrew, Pasarica, Cristian, and Dodhia, Rahul (2002). Let's practice what we preach: Turning tables into graphs. *American Statistician*, **56**, 121–30.

Gennaioli, Nicola and Shleifer, Andrei (2007). Overruling and the instability of law. *Journal of Comparative Economics*, **35**, 309–28.

George, Tracey E. (2005). An empirical study of empirical legal scholarship. *Indiana Law Journal*, **81**, 141–61.

Gerber, Alan S. and Green, Donald P. (2012). *Field Experiments: Design, Analysis, and Interpretation*. W.W. Norton & Company: New York, NY.

Gibson, James L. (2008). Challenges to the impartiality of state supreme courts: Legitimacy theory and "new style" judicial campaigns. *American Political Science Review*, **102**, 59–75.

Gibson, James L. (2012). *Electing Judges: The Surprising Effects of Campaigning on Judicial Legitimacy*. University of Chicago Press: Chicago, IL.

Gibson, James L., Caldeira, Gregory A., and Baird, Vanessa (1998). On the legitimacy of national high courts. *American Political Science Review*, **92**, 343–58.

Gill, Jeff (1999). The insignificance of null hypothesis significance testing. *Political Research Quarterly*, **65**, 647–74.

Gillan, Douglas J., Wickens, Christopher D., Hollands, J. G., and Carswell, C. Melody (1998). Guidelines for presenting quantitative data in HFES publications. *Human Factors*, **40**, 28–41.

Gilliam, Franklin D. and Iyengar, Shanto (2000). Prime suspects: The influence of local television news on the viewing public. *American Journal of Political Science*, **44**, 560–73.

Ginsburg, Tom, Chernykh, Svitlana, and Elkins, Zachary (2008). Commitment and diffusion: Why constitutions incorporate international law. *University of Illinois Law Review*, **2008**, 101–37.

Glick, Henry R. (1992). *The Right to Die: Policy Innovation and its Consequences*. Columbia University Press: New York, NY.

Good, Philip I. (2001). *Applying Statistics in the Courtroom*. Chapman & Hall/CRC: Boca Raton, FL.

Gordon, Sanford C. and Huber, Gregory A. (2007). The effect of electoral competitiveness on incumbent behavior. *Quarterly Journal of Political Science*, **2**, 107–38.

Gould, Jon B. and Mastrofski, Stephen D. (2004). Suspect searches: Assessing police behavior under the U.S. Constitution. *Criminology & Public Policy*, **3**, 315–62.

Grabowski, Henry and Wang, Y. Richard (2008). Do faster Food and Drug Administration drug reviews adversely affect patient safety? An analysis of the 1992 Prescription Drug User Fee Act. *Journal of Law and Economics*, **51**, 377–406.

Gravetter, Frederick J and Forzano, Lori-Ann B. (2012). *Research Methods for the Behavioral Sciences*. Wadsworth: Belmont, CA.

Greene, William H. (2011). *Econometric Analysis* (7th edn). Prentice Hall: Boston, MA.

Greenland, Sander (2003). Quantifying Biases in Causal Models: Classical Confounding vs Collider-Stratification Bias. *Epidemiology*, **14**, 300–6.

Greiner, D. James and Pattanayak, Cassandra Wolos (2012). Evaluation in legal assistance: What difference does representation (offer and actual use) make? *Yale Law Journal*, **121**, 2118–214.

Gross, Samuel R. and Barnes, Katherine Y. (2002). Road work: Racial pro-filing and drug interdiction on the highway. *Michigan Law Review*, **101**, 651–754.

Groves, Robert M., Jr., Fowler, Floyd J., Couper, Mick P., Lepkowski, James M., Singer, Eleanor, and Tourangeau, Roger (2009). *Survey Methodology* (2nd edn). John Wiley: Hoboken, NJ.

Gujarati, Damodar and Porter, Dawn (2008). *Basic Econometrics* (5th edn). McGraw-Hill/Irwin: New York, NY.

Guthrie, Chris, Rachlinski, Jeffrey J., and Wistrich, Andrew J. (2007). Blinking on the bench: How judges decide cases. *Cornell Law Review*, **93**, 1-43.

Hall, Robert E. and Jones, Charles I. (1999). Why do some countries produce so much more output per worker than others? *Quarterly Journal of Economics*, **114**, 83–116.

Harrison, Glenn W. and List, John A. (2004). Field experiments. *Journal of Economic Literature*, **42**, 1009–55.

Hartigan, J. A. and Kleiner, Beat (1981). Mosaics for contingency tables. In *Computer Science and Statistics: Proceedings of the 13th Symposium on Interface* (ed. W. Eddy). Springer-Verlag: New York, NY.

Hayek, Frederick A. (1960). *The Constitution of Liberty*. University of Chicago Press: Chicago, IL.

Hazelton, Morgan L. W., Hinkle, Rachael K., and Martin, Andrew D. (2010). On replication and the study of the Louisiana Supreme Court. *Global Jurist*, **10**, 85–91.

Hefler, Laurence and Slaughter, Anne-Marie (1997). Toward a theory of effective supranational adjudication. *Yale Law Journal*, **107**, 273–391.

Helmke, Gretchen (2005). *Courts under Constraints: Judges, Generals, and Presidents in Argentina*. Cambridge University Press: New York, NY.

Hensley, Thomas R. (1968). National bias and the International Court of Justice. *Midwest Journal of Political Science*, **12**, 568–86.

Herrona, Erik S. and Randazzo, Kirk A. (2003). The relationship between inde-pendence and judicial review in post-communist courts. *Journal of Politics*, **65**, 422–38.

Hilbink, Lisa (2007). *Judges beyond Politics in Democracy and Dictatorship: Lessons from Chile*. Cambridge University Press: New York, NY.

Hintze, Jerry L. and Nelson, Ray D. (1998). Violin plots: A box plot-density trace synergism. *American Statistician*, **52**, 181–4.

Ho, Daniel E., Imai, Kosuke, King, Gary, and Stuart, Elizabeth A. (2007). Matching as nonparametric preprocessing for reducing model dependence in parametric causal inference. *Political Analysis*, **15**, 199–236.

Holland, Paul W. (1986). Statistics and causal inference. *Journal of the American Statistical Association*, **81**, 945–70.

Holmes Jr., Oliver Wendell (1897). The path of the law. *Harvard Law Review*, **10**, 457–78.

Howard, Robert M. and Carey, Henry F. (2004). Is an independent judiciary necessary for democracy? *Judicature*, **87**, 284–90.

Howell, William G. and Ahmed, Faisal Z. (2014). Voting for the president: The Supreme Court during war. *Journal of Law, Economics, & Organization*, **30**, 39–71.

Huang, Kuo-Chang, Chen, Kong-Pin, and Lin, Chang-Ching (2010). An empirical investigation of settlement and litigation: The case of Taiwanese labor disputes. *Journal of Empirical Legal Studies*, **7**, 786–810.

Huff, Darrell (1954). *How to Lie with Statistics*. Norton: New York, NY.

Inter-University Consortium for Political and Social Research (2012). *Guide to Social Science Data Preparation and Archiving*. ICPSR: Ann Arbor, MI.

Jackson, Howell E., Kaplow, Louis, and Shavel, Steven M. (2011). *Analytic Methods for Lawyers*. Foundation Press: New York, NY.

Jacoby, William G. (1997). *Statistical Graphics for Univariate and Bivariate Data*. Sage: Thousand Oaks, CA.

Johnson, Janet Buttolph, Reynolds, H. T., and Mycoff, Jason D. (2007a). *Political Science Research Methods*. CQ Press: Washington, DC.

Johnson, R. Burke, Onwuegbuzie, Anthony J., and Turner, Lisa A. (2007b). Toward a definition of mixed methods research. *Journal of Mixed Methods Research*, **1**, 112–33.

Jurafsky, Daniel and Martin, James H. (2008). *Speech and Language Processing* (2nd edn). Pearson Prentice Hall: Upper Saddle River, NJ.

Kagel, John H. and Roth, Alvin E. (1997). *The Handbook of Experimental Economics*. Princeton University Press: Princeton, NJ.

Kahneman, Daniel and Deaton, Angus (2010). High income improves evaluation of life but not emotional well-being. *Proceedings of the National Academy of Sciences*, **107**, 16489–93.

Kalven, Harry and Zeisel, Hans (1966). *The American Jury*. Little, Brown: Boston, MA.

Kang, Jerry (2005). Trojan horses of race. *Harvard Law Review*, **118**, 1489–593.

Kastellec, Jonathan P. and Leoni, Eduardo L. (2007). Using graphs instead of tables in political science. *Perspectives on Politics*, **5**, 755–71.

Kates, Donald B. and Mauser, Gary (2007). Would banning firearms reduce murder and suicide? A review of international and some domestic evidence. *Harvard Journal of Law & Public Policy*, **30**, 649–94.

Kay, Fiona and Gorman, Elizabeth (2008). Women in the legal profession. *Annual Review of Law and Social Science*, **4**, 299–332.

Kaye, David H. and Freedman, David A. (2000). *Reference Guide on Statistics*. Federal Judicial Center: Washington, DC.

Keith, Linda Camp (2002). Constitutional provisions for individual human rights (1977–1996): Are they more than mere 'window dressing'? *Political Research Quarterly*, **55**, 111–43.

Keith, Linda Camp (2008). *The U.S. Supreme Court and the Judicial Review of Congress*. Peter Lang: New York, NY.

Keith, Linda Camp, Tate, C. Neal, and Poe, Steven C. (2009). Is the law a mere parchment barrier to human rights abuse? *Journal of Politics*, **71**, 644–60.

Kellstedt, Paul M. and Whitten, Guy D. (2009). *The Fundamentals of Political Science Research*. Cambridge University Press: New York, NY.

Kennedy, Peter (2008). *A Guide to Econometrics* (6th edn). Wiley-Blackwell: Malden, MA.

Kinder, Donald R. and Palfrey, Thomas R. (1993). *Experimental Foundations of Political Science*. University of Michigan Press: Ann Arbor, MI.

King, Gary (1995). Replication, replication. *P.S.: Political Science and Politics*, **28**, 443–99.

King, Gary, Honaker, James, Joseph, Anne, and Scheve, Kenneth (2001). Analyzing incomplete political science data: An alternative algorithm for multiple imputation. *American Political Science Review*, **91**, 49–69.

King, Gary, Keohane, Robert O., and Verba, Sidney (1994). *Designing Social Inquiry*. Princeton University Press: Princeton, NJ.

King, Gary, Tomz, Michael, and Wittenberg, Jason (2000). Making the most of statistical analyses: Improving interpretation and presentation. *American Journal of Political Science*, **44**, 341–55.

Klerman, Daniel M and Mahoney, Paul G. (2005). The value of judicial independence: Evidence from eighteenth century England. *American Law and Economics Review*, **7**, 1–27.

Kornhauser, Lewis (1995). Adjudication by a resource-constrained team: Hierarchy and precedent in a judicial system. *Southern California Law Review*, **68**, 1605–29.

Kosslyn, Stephen M. (1994). *Elements of Graphic Design*. W. H. Freeman: New York, NY.

Kritzer, Herbert M. (2009). Empirical legal studies before 1940: A bibliographic essay. *Journal of Empirical Legal Studies*, **6**, 925–68.

La Porta, Rafael, de Silanes, Florencio López, Pop-Eleches, Cristian, and Schleifer, Andrei (2004). Judicial checks and balances. *Journal of Political Economy*, **112**, 445–70.

Landes, William M. and Posner, Richard A. (1976). Legal precedent: A theoretical and empirical analysis. *Journal of Law and Economics*, **19**, 249–307.

Landis, J. Richard and Koch, Gary G. (1977). The measurement of observer agreement for categorical data. *Biometrics*, **33**, 159–74.

Latourette, Audrey Wolfson (2005). Sex discrimination in the legal profession: Historical and contemporary perspectives. *Valparaiso University Law Review*, **39**, 859–909.

Lawless, Robert M., Robbennolt, Jennifer K., and Ulen, Thomas S. (2010). *Empirical Methods in Law*. Wolters Kluwer: New York, NY.

Le Roy, Michael K. and Corbett, Michael (2009). *Research Methods in Political Science*. Thomson Higher Education: Boston, MA.

Lewandowsky, Stephan and Spence, Ian (1989). Discriminating strata in scatterplots. *Journal of the American Statistical Association*, **84**, 682–8.

Lindquist, Stefanie A. and Cross, Frank B. (2009). *Measuring Judicial Activism*. Oxford University Press: New York, NY.

Lobao, Linda M., Hooks, Gregory, and Tickamyer, Ann R. (2007). *The Sociology of Spatial Inequality*. SUNY Press: Albany, NY.

Lofland, John, Snow, David, Anderson, Leon, and Lofland, Lyn (2006). *Analyzing Social Settings: A Guide to Qualitative Observation and Analysis*. Wadsworth: Belmont, CA.

Loftin, Colin, McDowall, David, Wiersema, Brian, and Cottey, Talbert J. (1991). Effects of restrictive licensing of handguns on homicide and suicide in the District of Columbia. *New England Journal of Medicine*, **325**, 1615–20.

Loh, Wallace D. (1984). *Social Research in the Judicial Process*. Russell Sage: New York, NY.

Lombard, Matthew, Snyder-Duch, Jennifer, and Bracken, Cheryl Campanella (2002). Content analysis in mass communication: Assessment and reporting of intercoder reliability. *Human Communication Research*, **28**, 587–604.

Long, J. Scott (1997). *Regression Models for Categorical and Limited Dependent Variables*. Sage: Thousand Oaks, CA.

Maddex, Robert L. (2005). *Constitutions of the World*. Congressional Quarterly Press: Washington, DC.

Manning, Christopher D. and Schuetze, Hinrich (1999). *Foundations of Statistical Natural Language Processing*. The MIT Press: Cambridge, MA.

Manning, Christopher D., Raghavan, Prabhakar, and Schutze, Hinrich (2008). *Introduction to Information Retrieval*. Cambridge University Press: Cambridge, UK.

Martin, Andrew D. (2008). Bayesian analysis. In *Oxford Handbook of Political Methodology* (eds. J. M. Box-Steffensmeier, H. E. Brady, and D. Collier). Oxford University Press: Oxford, UK.

Mason, David S. and Kluegel, James R. (2000). *Marketing Democracy: Changing Opinion About Inequality and Politics in East Central Europe*. Rowman & Littlefield: Lanham, MD.

McCormick, Peter (1992). The supervisory role of the Supreme Court of Canada: Analysis of appeals from provincial courts of appeal, 1949–1990. *Supreme Court Law Review*, **3**, 1–28.

Meernik, James (2011). Sentencing rationales and judicial decision making at the international criminal tribunals. *Social Science Quarterly*, **92**, 588–608.

Meernik, James and Aloisi, Rosa (2007). Is justice delayed at the international criminal tribunals? *Judicature*, **91**, 276–87.

Meernik, James, King, Kimi Lynn, and Dancy, Geoffrey (2005). Judicial decision making and international tribunals: Assessing the impact of individual, national, and international factors. *Social Science Quarterly*, **86**, 683–703.

Miron, Jeffrey A. (2001). Violence, guns, and drugs: A cross-country analysis. *Journal of Law and Economics*, **44**, 615–33.

Monahan, John and Walker, Laurens (2010). *Social Science in Law*. Foundation Press: New York, NY.

Morton, Rebecca B. and Williams, Kenneth C. (2010). *Experimental Political Science and the Study of Causality: From Nature to the Lab.* Cambridge University Press: Cambridge, UK.

Mutz, Diana C. (2011). *Population-Based Survey Experiments.* Princeton University Press: Princeton, NJ.

Nadler, Janice and Diamond, Shari Seidman (2008). Eminent domain and the psychology of property rights: Proposed use, subjective attachment, and taker identity. *Journal of Empirical Legal Studies*, **5**, 713–49.

Nisbett, Richard and Wilson, Tim (1977). Telling more than we know: Verbal reports of mental processes. *Psychological Review*, **84**, 231–59.

Norris, Barbara A. (1987). Multiple regression analysis in Title VII cases: A structural approach to attacks of "missing factors" and "pre-act discrimination". *Law and Contemporary Problems*, **49**, 63–96.

O'Connor, Sandra Day (1991). Portia's progress. *NYU Law Review*, **66**, 1546–58.

Ostberg, C. L. and Wetstein, Matthew E. (2007). *Attitudinal Decision Making in the Supreme Court of Canada.* UBC Press: Vancouver, Canada.

Owens, Ryan J. (2010). The separation of powers and Supreme Court agenda setting. *American Journal of Political Science*, **54**, 412–27.

Payne-Pikus, Monique R., Hagan, John, and Nelson, Robert L. (2010). Experiencing discrimination: Race and retention in America's largest law firms. *Law & Society Review*, **44**, 553–84.

Pearson, Karl (1900). On the criterion that a given system of deviations from the probable in the case of a correlated system of variables is such that it can be reasonably supposed to have arisen from random sampling. *Philosophical Magazine Series 5*, **50**, 157–75.

Peresie, Jennifer L. (2005). Female judges matter: Gender and collegial decision-making in the federal appellate courts. *Yale Law Journal*, **114**, 1759–90.

Pérez-Liñán, Aníbal and Castagnola, Andrea (2009). Presidential control of high courts in Latin America: A long-term view (1904–2006). *Journal of Politics in Latin America*, **1**, 87–114.

Posner, Eric A. (2005). The International Court of Justice: Voting and usage statistics. In *Proceedings of the Annual Meeting (American Society of International Law)*, **99**, 130–2.

Posner, Eric A. and de Figueiredo, Miguel F. P. (2005). Is the International Court of Justice biased? *Journal of Legal Studies*, **34**, 599–630.

Posner, Eric A. and Sunstein, Cass R. (2008). Introduction to the conference on law and happiness. *Journal of Legal Studies*, **37**, 51–4.

Posner, Richard A. (2012). The rise and fall of judicial self-restraint. *California Law Review*, **100**, 519–56.

Quinn, Kevin M., Monroe, Burt L., Colaresi, Michael, Crespin, Michael H., and Radev, Dragomir R. (2010). How to analyze political attention with minimal assumptions and costs. *American Journal of Political Science*, **54**, 209–28.

Rachlinski, Jeffrey J., Guthrie, Chris, and Wistrich, Andrew J. (2006). Inside the bankruptcy judge's mind. *Boston University Law Review*, **86**, 1227–65.

Rachlinski, Jeffrey J., Johnson, Sheri Lynn, Wistrich, Andrew J., and Guthrie, Chris (2008). Does unconscious racial bias affect trial judges? *Notre Dame Law Review*, **84**, 1195–246.

Rahn, Wendy M., Krosnick, Jon A., and Breuning, Marijke (1994). Rationalization and derivation processes in survey studies of political candidate evaluation. *American Journal of Political Science*, **38**, 582–600.

Rakove, Jack N. (1985). James Madison and the Bill of Rights. <http://www.apsanet.org/content_8300.cfm>.

Ramsey, James B. (1969). Tests for specific errors in classical linear least-squares regression analysis. *Journal of the Royal Statistical Society. Series B (Methodological)*, **31**, 350–71.

Ramseyer, J. Mark and Rasmussen, Eric B. (2001). Why are Japanese judges so conservative in politically charged cases? *American Political Science Review*, **95**, 331–44.

Rea, Louis M. and Parker, Richard A. (2005). *Designing and Conducting Survey Research: A Comprehensive Guide* (3rd edn). Jossey-Bass: San Francisco, CA.

Retting, Richard A., Williams, Allan F., Farmer, Charles M., and Feldman, Amy F. (1999). Evaluation of red light camera enforcement in Oxnard, California. *Accident Analysis and Prevention*, **31**, 169–74.

Roberts, Alasdair (2001). Structural pluralism and the right to information. *University of Toronto Law Journal*, **51**, 243–71.

Roe, Mark J. (2000). Political preconditions to separating ownership from corporate control. *Stanford Law Review*, **53**, 539–606.

Ros-Figueroa, Julio and Staton, Jeffrey K. (2014). An evaluation of cross-national measures of judicial independence. *Journal of Law, Economics, & Organization*, **30**, 104–37.

Rosenbaum, Paul R. (2010). *Observational studies* (2nd edn). Springer-Verlag: New York, NY.

Rosenberg, Gerald N. (2008). *The Hollow Hope: Can Courts Bring About Social Change?* (2nd edn). University of Chicago Press: Chicago, IL.

Rubin, Allen and Babbie, Earl (2011). *Research Methods for Social Work*. Brooks/Cole: Belmont, CA.

Rubin, Donald B. (1974). Estimating causal effects of treatments in randomized and nonrandomized studies. *Journal of Educational Psychology*, **6**, 688–701.

Rubin, Donald B. (1977). Assignment to treatment group on the basis of a covariate. *Journal of Educational Statistics*, **2**, 1–26.

Rubin, Herbert J. and Rubin, Irene S. (2004). *Qualitative Interviewing: The Art of Hearing Data* (2nd edn). Sage: Thousand Oaks, CA.

Salzberger, Eli and Fenn, Paul (1999). Judicial independence: Some evidence from the English Court of Appeal. *Journal of Law and Economics*, **42**, 831–47.

Sandholtz, Wayne (2012). Treaties, constitutions, courts, and human rights. *Journal of Human Rights*, **11**, 17–32.

Satterthwaite, F. E. (1946). An approximate distribution of estimates of variance components. *Biometrics Bulletin*, **2**, 110–14.

Schkade, David, Sunstein, Cass R., and Kahneman, Daniel (2000). Deliberating about dollars: The severity shift. *Columbia Law Review*, **100**, 1139–75.

Schlegel, John Henry (1995). *American Legal Realism & Empirical Social Science.* University of North Carolina Press: Chapel Hill, NC.

Schneider, Martin R. (2005). Judicial career incentives and court performance: An empirical study of the German labour courts of appeal. *European Journal of Law and Economics*, **20**, 127–44.

Schwab, Stewart J. and Heise, Michael (2011). Splitting logs: An empirical perspective on employment discrimination settlements. *Cornell Law Review*, **96**, 931–56.

Scott, Kevin M. (2006). Understanding judicial hierarchy: Reversals and the behavior of intermediate appellate judges. *Law & Society Review*, **40**, 163–92.

Segal, Jeffrey A. and Cover, Albert D. (1989). Ideological values and the votes of U.S. Supreme Court justices. *American Political Science Review*, **83**, 557–65.

Segal, Jeffrey A. and Spaeth, Harold J. (2002). *The Supreme Court and the Attitudinal Model Revisited.* Cambridge University Press: New York, NY.

Segal, Jeffrey A., Westerland, Chad, and Lindquist, Stefanie A. (2011). Congress, the Supreme Court, and judicial review: Testing a constitutional separation of powers model. *American Journal of Political Science*, **55**, 89–104.

Sekhon, Jasjeet and Titiunik, Rocio (2012). When natural experiments are neither natural nor experiments. *American Political Science Review*, **106**, 35–57.

Shi, Leiya (1997). *Health Services Research Methods.* Delmar: Albany, NY.

Shugerman, Jed Handelsman (2010). The twist of long terms: Judicial elections, role fidelity, and American tort law. *Georgetown Law Journal*, **98**, 1349–413.

Shulman, Kate (2012). The case concerning the temple of Preah Vihear (Cambodia v. Thailand): The ICJ orders sweeping provisional measures to prevent armed conflict at the expense of sovereignty. *Tulane Journal of International and Comparative Law*, **20**, 555–70.

Silver, Nate (2012). *The Signal and the Noise: Why So Many Predictions Fail—but Some Don't.* Penguin Press: New York, NY.

Silverman, Bernard W. (1986). *Density Estimation for Statistics and Data Analysis.* Chapman & Hall: Boca Raton, FL.

Simon, Dan (2012). *In Doubt: The Psychology of the Criminal Justice Process.* Harvard University Press: Cambridge, MA.

Simpson, Edward H. (1951). The interpretation of interaction in contingency tables. *Journal of the Royal Statistical Society. Series B (Methodological)*, **13**, 238–41.

Solberg, Rorie Spill and Lindquist, Stefanie A. (2007). Activism, ideology, and federalism: Judicial behavior in constitutional challenges before the Rehnquist court, 1986–2000. *Journal of Empirical Legal Studies*, **3**, 237–61.

Songer, Donald R., Segal, Jeffrey A., and Cameron, Charles M. (1994). The hierarchy of justice: Testing a principal-agent model of Supreme Court-circuit court interactions. *American Journal of Political Science*, **38**, 673–96.

Sorenson, H. W. (1970). Least-squares estimation: From Gauss to Kalman. *IEEE Spectrum*, **7**, 63–8.

Spence, Ian and Garrison, Robert F. (1993). A remarkable scatterplot. *American Statistician*, **47**, 12–19.

Spence, Ian and Lewandowsky, Stephan (1991). Displaying proportions and percentages. *Applied Cognitive Psychology*, **5**, 61–77.

Spriggs, II, James F. (1996). The Supreme Court and federal administrative agencies: A resource-based theory and analysis of judicial impact. *American Journal of Political Science*, **40**, 1122–51.

Staton, Jeffrey K. (2010). *Judicial Power and Strategic Communication in Mexico*. Cambridge University Press: New York, NY.

Staton, Jeffrey K. and Vanberg, Georg (2008). The value of vagueness: Delegation, defiance, and judicial opinions. *American Journal of Political Science*, **58**, 504–19.

Staudt, Nancy (2011). *The Judicial Power of the Purse: How Courts Fund National Defense in Times of Crisis*. University of Chicago Press: Chicago, IL.

Stigler, Stephen M. (1986). *The History of Statistics: The Measurement of Uncertainty before 1900*. Harvard University Press: Cambridge, MA.

Stone, Alec (1992). *The Birth of Judicial Politics in France: The Constitutional Council in Comparative Perspective*. Oxford University Press: New York, NY.

Strunk, Jr., William and White, E. B. (1959). *The Elements of Style*. Macmillan: New York, NY.

Student (1908). The probable error of a mean. *Biometrika*, **6**, 1–25.

Sullivan, Kathleen M. (2002). Constitutionalizing women's equality. *California Law Review*, **90**, 735–64.

Sunstein, Cass R., Hastie, Reid, Payne, John W., Schkade, David A., and Viscusi, W. Kip (2002). *Punitive Damages: How Juries Decide*. University of Chicago Press: Chicago, IL.

Sunstein, Cass R., Schkade, David, and Ellman, Lisa (2006). Ideological voting on federal courts of appeals: A preliminary investigation. *Virginia Law Review*, **90**, 301–54.

Tabarrok, Alexander and Helland, Eric (1999). Court politics: The political economy of tort awards. *Journal of Law and Economics*, **42**, 157–88.

Thernstrom, Stephan and Thernstrom, Abigail (1999). *America in Black and White*. Simon & Schuster: New York, NY.

Tourangeau, Roger, Rips, Lance J., and Rasinski, Kenneth (2000). *The Psychology of Survey Response*. Cambridge University Press: Cambridge, UK.

Traut, Carol Ann and Emmert, Craig F. (1998). Expanding the integrated model of judicial decision making: The California justices and capital punishment. *Journal of Politics*, **60**, 1166–80.

Tufte, Edward R. (1983). *The Visual Display of Quantitative Information*. Graphics Press: Cheshire, CT.

Tufte, Edward R. (2001). *The Visual Display of Quantitative Information* (2nd edn). Graphics Press: Cheshire, CT.

Tukey, John W. (1977). *Exploratory Data Analysis*. Addison-Wesley: Reading, MA.

Tukey, John W. (1990). Data-based graphics: Visual display in the decades to come. *Statistical Science*, **5**, 327–39.

Twining, William (2005). Social science and diffusion of law. *Journal of Law and Society*, **32**, 203–40.

Tyler, Tom R. (2006). *Why People Obey the Law*. Princeton University Press: Princeton, NJ.

Vanberg, Georg (1998). Abstract judicial review, legislative bargaining, and policy compromise. *Journal of Theoretical Politics*, **10**, 299–326.

Viscusi, W. Kip (2006). Monetizing the benefits of risk and environmental regulation. *Fordham Urban Law Journal*, **33**, 1003–42.

Wainer, Howard (1990). Graphical visions from William Playfair to John Tukey. *Statistical Science*, **5**, 340–6.

Walker, Thomas, Epstein, Lee, and Dixon, William J. (1988). On the mysterious demise of consensual norms in the United States Supreme Court. *Journal of Politics*, **50**, 361–89.

Weiden, David L. (2011). Judicial politicization, ideology, and activism at the high courts of the United States, Canada, and Australia. *Political Research Quarterly*, **64**, 335–47.

Weiss, Robert S. (1995). *Learning from Strangers: The Art and Method of Qualitative Interview Studies*. Free Press: New York, NY.

Welch, B. L. (1947). The generalization of "Student's" problem when several different population variances is involved. *Biometrika*, **34**, 28–35.

Wickham, Hadley (2009). *ggplot2: Elegant Graphics for Data Analysis*. Springer: New York, NY.

Wilson, Betha (1990). Will women judges really make a difference? *Osgoode Hall Law Journal*, **28**, 507–22.

Wooldridge, Jeffrey M. (2010). *Econometric Analysis of Cross Section and Panel Data*. The MIT Press: Cambridge, MA.

Wright, Daniel B. (2003). Making friends with your data. *British Journal of Educational Psychology*, **73**, 123–36.

Zikopoulos, Paul C., deRoos, Dirk, Parasuraman, Krishnan, Deutsch, Thomas, Corrigan, David, and Giles, James (2013). *Harness the Power of Big Data: The IBM Big Data Platform*. McGraw-Hill: New York, NY.

Zink, James R., II, Spriggs, James F., and Scott, John T. (2009). Courting the public: The influence of decision attributes on individuals' views of court opinions. *Journal of Politics*, **71**, 909–25.

Zorn, Christopher (2005). A solution to separation in binary response models. *Political Analysis*, **13**, 157–70.

Index

Printed and bound by CPI Group (UK) Ltd, Croydon, CR0 4YY